Building Business Models with Machine Learning

Ambika N.
St. Francis College, India

Vishal Jain
Sharda University, Greater Noida, India

Cristian González García
University of Oviedo, Spain

Dac–Nhuong Le
Vietnam National University, Vietnam

IGI Global
Scientific Publishing
Publishing Tomorrow's Research Today

Vice President of Editorial	Melissa Wagner
Managing Editor of Acquisitions	Mikaela Felty
Managing Editor of Book Development	Jocelynn Hessler
Production Manager	Mike Brehm
Cover Design	Phillip Shickler

Published in the United States of America by
IGI Global Scientific Publishing
701 East Chocolate Avenue
Hershey, PA, 17033, USA
Tel: 717-533-8845
Fax: 717-533-8661
E-mail: cust@igi-global.com
Website: https://www.igi-global.com

Library of Congress Cataloging-in-Publication Data

Names: N, Ambika, 1976- editor. | Jain, Vishal, 1983- editor. | Gonzalez Garcia, Cristian, 1985- editor. | Le, Dac-Nhuong, 1983- editor.
Title: Building business models with machine learning / edited by Ambika N, Vishal Jain, Cristian González García, Dac-Nhuong Le.
Description: Hershey, PA : IGI Global, [2025] | Includes bibliographical references and index. | Summary: "The book aims to give data scientists, business experts, and decision-makers a thorough and constructive manual for incorporating learning into organizational plans. To fully utilize learning to provide flexible, data-driven business models, it aims to act as a vital road map, offering readers the knowledge and resources they need"-- Provided by publisher.
Identifiers: LCCN 2024047063 (print) | LCCN 2024047064 (ebook) | ISBN 9798369338841 (hardcover) | ISBN 9798369350973 (paperback) | ISBN 9798369338858 (ebook)
Subjects: LCSH: Organizational learning. | Machine learning. | Business--Data processing.
Classification: LCC HD58.82 .B83 2025 (print) | LCC HD58.82 (ebook) | DDC 658.3/124--dc23/eng/20241120
LC record available at https://lccn.loc.gov/2024047063
LC ebook record available at https://lccn.loc.gov/2024047064

British Cataloguing in Publication Data
A Cataloguing in Publication record for this book is available from the British Library.

Table of Contents

Detailed Table of Contents

Chapter 1

Siji A. Thomas, Independent Researcher, UAE
Sini Kurien Thomas, Independent Researcher, USA

Financial fraud remains a persistent threat to various sectors including the public sector, government and finance industry, with fraudsters continuously adapting their strategies to exploit weaknesses in existing preventive measures, particularly with the increasing reliance on new technologies. This chapter delves into the potential of Machine Learning (ML) applications to support fraud detection capabilities within the financial sector. A comprehensive review of literature is conducted to investigate the effectiveness of various ML algorithms, including Support Vector Machine (SVM), Logistic Regression (LR), Random Forest (RF) and Convolutional Neural Networks (CNN), in identifying the fraudulent activities. The research categorizes existing literature based on several criteria, such as the type of fraud analyzed, ML algorithms utilized and efficiency of various detection strategies of financial fraud. Additionally, the authors in this chapter identifies the key challenges in current methodologies, alongside with potential future research directions.

Chapter 2

Ashwini S. Diwakar, Surana College, Bangalore, India
B. Shravani, Surana College, Bangalore, India
H. Asha, Surana College, Bangalore, India

Communication and information sharing between individuals have changed dramatically as a result of the internet and social media platforms combined with explosive growth. Due to the development and expansion of online technology, a vast amount of data is generated as well as being available on the web for internet users. There has been a noticeable rise in the usage of foul language in user comments. Furthermore, Twitter is a well-known medium where users are allowed to voice any opinion. The proliferation of antisocial activities, including hate speech, cyberbullying, and the use of harsh language, is a direct result of overuse of social media. The prevalence of hostile comments on social media platforms calls for the development of practical and efficient solutions. Consequently, numerous intriguing algorithms have been developed to identify these kinds of languages. The objective of this chapter is to introduce strategies, equations, and techniques that could be used to evaluate Twitter tweets to identify instances of abusive language.

Chapter 3

The relationship between artificial intelligence (AI) and the incorporation of environmental, social, and governance (ESG) aspects in modern business and technology is explored in this chapter. The paper investigates how AI could provide workable solutions to the pressing societal sustainability concerns of today. The chapter focuses on the moral implications of environmentally conscious technology, AI-powered predictions for ESG metrics, moral supply chains, and upcoming laws. As AI and ESG become more integrated, there are chances for companies who prioritize sustainability to increase their market share by implementing eco-friendly practices. This confluence makes it possible to integrate cutting-edge technology with sustainability objectives, creating a relationship that has the potential to be really revolutionary.

Chapter 4

Digital transformation (DX) is reshaping businesses across all industries. However, many DX initiatives fail to achieve their desired outcomes. Business analysis (BA) plays a critical role in bridging the gap between strategic vision and successful execution in these initiatives. This article explores the value proposition of BA for DX projects, focusing on key areas of contribution. It outlines a framework for integrating BA practices throughout the DX lifecycle, from strategy definition to solution implementation. The article concludes by discussing the evolving skillset required for business analysts to navigate the complexities of DX initiatives.

Chapter 5

The word "business model" has been around for years, yet companies naturally conceive, establish, and execute their models from the start. Business models and their key approaches must be studied. Leaders base company decisions on their own expertise and preference. Decision-making in business data analytics is based on data, removing cognitive and personal biases. Effective corporate data analysis can boost a company's competitiveness. Business data analytics quantifies internal and external aspects, helping stakeholders and IT understand organizational success and customer responsibility. This chapter discussed Business Data Analytics methodologies and their importance.

Chapter 6

Satya Shree, APS College of Arts and Science, India
C. Manjunath, APS College of Arts and Science, India

In today's dynamic business landscape, organizations are increasingly recognizing the pivotal role of business analytics in refining and optimizing their business models. This study explores the integration of business analytics into various aspects of the business model, including value proposition, customer segments, revenue streams, and operational efficiency. Through a comprehensive review of existing literature and case studies, this research elucidates the significance of leveraging data-driven insights for strategic decision-making and sustainable competitive advantage. Key themes investigated include predictive analytics for market forecasting, customer behavior analysis for targeted marketing strategies, optimization of supply chain management through data-driven logistics, and the role of business intelligence in enhancing operational agility. The study also delves into challenges such as data privacy concerns, skill gaps, and organizational resistance, offering insights into effective implementation strategies.

Chapter 7

NV Suresh, ASET College of Science and Technology, India
Ananth Selvakumar, ASET College of Science and Technology, India
Gajalaksmi Sridhar, ASET College of Science and Technology, India
Vishal Jain, Sharda University, India

This assessment paper jumps into the space of dynamics with respect to systems in electronic business, taking a gander at the joining of PC-based information computations to smooth out studying decisions. Affiliations are searching for novel techniques for Figuring out how to stay serious while additionally expanding pay considering the always-developing robotized industry. The survey turns around grasping the execution of electronic thinking models for dynamic with respect to and their impact on the web business district. The assessment looks at the significant guidelines of dynamic with respect to its standard procedures, highlighting the impediments that arise in a rapidly making business region. Using PC-based information computations offers a promising response for addressing these challenges by attracting steady assessment of monster datasets, expecting market floats, and changing studying systems in like manner. The turn of events and plan of re-enacted knowledge calculations for surveying redesign, taking into account factors like competitor appraisal are key areas of assessment.

Chapter 8

Pooja Soni, Maharana Pratap University of Agriculture and Technology, India
Vikramaditya Dave, Maharana Pratap University of Agriculture and Technology, India

Renewable energy technologies play a crucial role in addressing the global energy transition to-wards sustainability. Solar photovoltaic (PV) systems and fuel cells are two prominent sources of clean energy; however, they exhibit intermittent and variable power generation patterns, hindering their widespread adoption. This paper proposes a novel approach to enhance the performance of Solar PV-Fuel Cell Hybrids (SPV-FCH) through the integration of Artificial Intelligence (AI) techniques. The synergy between solar PV and fuel cells aims to create a more reliable and continuous power generation system by combining the intermittent nature of solar energy with the consistent output of fuel cells. This paper discusses the design and implementation of the AI-enabled control system for SPV-FCH hybrids, highlighting its effectiveness in achieving improved energy yield, grid stability, and cost-effectiveness.

Chapter 9

Metasebia Adula, Bule Hora University, Ethiopia
Shashi Kant, Bule Hora University, Ethiopia
Mando Genale, Bule Hora University, Ethiopia

This chapter examines the Green financing effect on Sustenance finance models with mediation of corporate social responsibility in Ethiopia. CSR principles guide financial institutions in prioritizing investments aligned with sustainable development goals, engaging stakeholders in decision-making processes, and integrating environmental and social factors into risk assessment. Sustainable business practices are adopted, enhancing reputation and attracting stakeholders valuing social responsibility. Regulatory compliance is ensured, aligning finance models with legal requirements and societal expectations. Future directions involve strengthening transparency, fostering collaboration and innovation, building capacity and awareness, incentivizing sustainability, developing impact measurement methodologies, and aligning with the SDGs. Ethiopian finance models may satisfy social requirements, promote sustainable development, and build trust by incorporating CSR practices.

Chapter 10

Kartikey Raghuvanshi, Delhi Technical Campus, Guru Gobind Singh Indraprastha University, India

Ayasha Malik, IIMT College of Engineering, Greater Noida, India.

Veena Parihar, Symbiosis Institute of Geo-informatics, Symbiosis International, Pune, India

In the rapidly evolving landscape of business intelligence, the integration of Machine Learning (ML) and pattern recognition techniques has emerged as a transformative force, revolutionizing decision-making processes across various industries. This paper explores the crucial role played by ML and pattern recognition in enhancing the capabilities of business intelligence models, with a focus on their practical applications and impact on real-world scenarios. The importance of accurate and timely decision-making in today's dynamic business environment cannot be overstated. Traditional business intelligence systems have limitations in handling the complexity and volume of data generated daily. ML algorithms, with their ability to analyze vast datasets and identify intricate patterns, offer a solution to this challenge. Through the application of supervised and unsupervised learning techniques, businesses can extract valuable insights from data, enabling informed and strategic decision-making.

Chapter 11

Allampalli Harini, Pragati Engineering College, India

Manjula Devarakonda Venkata, Pragati Engineering College, India

Doodala Kondababu, Pragati Engineering College, India

This chapter proposes a novel Machine Learning-based Framework for Human Activity Recognition tailored to address the complexities and challenges inherent in accurately identifying and categorizing human activities from sensor data. ML-HARF integrates advanced machine learning algorithms with a comprehensive data preprocessing pipeline to extract meaningful features from raw sensor data. Leveraging a diverse array of sensor modalities, including accelerometers, gyroscopes, and magnetometers-HARF captures rich spatiotemporal patterns characteristic of human activities. The framework employs a hierarchical classification approach, wherein low-level features are initially extracted and subsequently aggregated to infer higher-level activity labels.ML-HARF outperforms other methods in extensive experiments on benchmark datasets, attaining state-of-the-art accuracy rates in a variety of activity recognition tasks In real-world applications like sports analytics, healthcare monitoring and human-computer interaction systems, the framework's efficiency and scalability are also demonstrated.

Chapter 12

Giulia Rita Sala, ESADE, Spain
Saverio Barabuffi, Scuola Superiore Sant'Anna, Italy
Giulio Ferrigno, Scuola Superiore Sant'Anna, Italy
Enrico Marcazzan, Scuola Superiore Sant'Anna, Italy

This book chapter explores the shifting contours of big data monetization in the digital transformation era, focusing on the Human Data Income (Hudi) model. Based on the literature on big data and innovation management, as well as on the so-called Data-Driven Innovation framework, this chapter explores the challenges that are inherent in the process of turning personal information into an asset. To better understand these challenges, it carries a deep case study analysis for Hudi and assesses what the business model does to individuals, businesses, and society as a whole and gives valued insights into the monetization of data and value creation. Drawing on these results, the chapter helps in contributing to a more grounded understanding of the opportunities, challenges, and consequences that come innately with the evolving landscape of data economy, shaping future discussions and research engagements in this field.

Chapter 13

Amit Kakkar, Lovely Professional University, India
Manoj Goyal, Lovely Professional University, India
Dhrupad Mathur, S.P. Jain School of Global Management, Saudi Arabia

Machine learning recommendation systems are one of the best and most far-reaching utilisation of AI advances in business. These are the product instruments used to give ideas to clients based on their needs. Expansion in the number of choices, be it several online sites or several items, has made it hard for the client to look over many items. Today, there is no framework for banks to help relate to clients' monetary decisions and proposition them with applicable items according to their inclination before approaching the bank. Like some other businesses, monetary assistance seldom has any like, input, and perusing history to record evaluations of administrations. So, it becomes a test for constructing recommended systems for monetary administrations. The advantage of these recommended systems is that they give the customer better recommendations based on their savings, spending, and investment needs.

Preface

In today's rapidly evolving business landscape, organizations are increasingly recognizing the transformative potential of machine learning (ML) in enhancing decision-making processes, optimizing operations, and gaining a competitive edge. As the pace of change accelerates, the integration of machine learning into business strategies has become not only a necessity but a crucial factor in staying ahead.

This book, *Building Business Models with Machine Learning*, is designed to serve as a comprehensive guide for decision-makers, business executives, data scientists, and entrepreneurs who are eager to understand and leverage machine learning to create resilient, data-driven business models. Our objective is to offer constructive insights into the intersection of machine learning and business strategy, providing practical knowledge for the successful incorporation of ML techniques into organizational frameworks.

We take you through the foundational principles of machine learning, showing you how to apply its methodologies to real-world business challenges. By exploring topics such as sustainability, finance, governance, and data analysis, we aim to demonstrate how ML can fuel innovation, sustainability, and long-term growth in business. Through in-depth case studies and practical examples, this book illustrates the broad range of applications of machine learning, from business analytics and socially responsible investing to fraud detection and healthcare.

CHAPTER OVERVIEWS

Chapter 1

Financial fraud remains a significant concern across various industries, particularly in sectors reliant on financial transactions. This chapter delves into the application of machine learning (ML) for improving fraud detection capabilities within the financial sector. A thorough review of existing literature is presented, examining various ML algorithms, including Support Vector Machine (SVM), Logistic Regression (LR), Random Forest (RF), and Convolutional Neural Networks (CNN), and their effectiveness in detecting fraudulent activities. The chapter also explores the challenges faced by current methodologies and offers insights into potential areas for future research to enhance fraud detection systems.

Chapter 2

With the rise of social media platforms like Twitter, the proliferation of hostile content, including hate speech and cyberbullying, has become a pressing issue. This chapter focuses on identifying and combating abusive language on social media through machine learning techniques. It presents a range of strategies, equations, and methods for evaluating Twitter tweets to detect abusive language. The chapter highlights various algorithms designed to filter out harmful content, offering practical solutions for managing online toxicity and promoting healthier digital communication environments.

Chapter 3

As sustainability continues to gain importance, artificial intelligence (AI) is increasingly seen as a tool for addressing environmental, social, and governance (ESG) challenges. This chapter explores how AI can help businesses achieve their sustainability goals by providing solutions to environmental concerns, improving supply chain practices, and predicting ESG metrics. It emphasizes the moral implications of integrating eco-conscious technologies and highlights the potential for AI-driven innovations to enhance business models that prioritize sustainability, creating opportunities for companies to boost their market presence while addressing pressing societal issues.

Chapter 4

Digital transformation (DX) is reshaping industries, yet many DX initiatives fail to reach their full potential. This chapter discusses the critical role that business analysis (BA) plays in bridging the gap between strategy and execution in DX projects. It presents a framework for integrating BA practices throughout the digital transformation lifecycle, from strategy formulation to solution implementation. The chapter also examines the evolving skill set required for business analysts to navigate the complexities of digital transformation and ensure the success of these initiatives.

Chapter 5

Business models are influenced by the way organizations leverage data to make decisions. This chapter explores the importance of business data analytics in driving effective decision-making and enhancing competitiveness. It discusses various methodologies for analyzing both internal and external data, helping organizations understand their performance and improve customer engagement. By removing cognitive biases and relying on data-driven insights, businesses can gain a strategic advantage, making this chapter essential for anyone seeking to understand the role of data analytics in modern business practices.

Chapter 6

Business analytics plays a pivotal role in optimizing business models, driving decision-making, and maintaining a competitive edge. This chapter explores how organizations can integrate business analytics into key areas of their business model, such as value proposition, customer segmentation, and operational efficiency. It discusses the importance of predictive analytics, customer behavior analysis, and data-driven logistics in refining business strategies. Additionally, the chapter addresses the challenges of data privacy, skill gaps, and organizational resistance to analytics, providing practical insights into overcoming these barriers.

Chapter 7

As electronic businesses continue to evolve, understanding the role of computerized decision-making systems becomes crucial. This chapter examines the integration of computer-based information algorithms to streamline decision-making processes in the fast-paced world of online business. It highlights the challenges posed by rapid market changes and the need for adaptive decision-making strategies. By using advanced computational models, businesses can anticipate market shifts and refine their strategies, thereby improving decision-making accuracy and efficiency.

Chapter 8

Renewable energy technologies, particularly solar photovoltaic (PV) systems and fuel cells, are essential to the global transition toward sustainability. However, their intermittent power generation can hinder widespread adoption. This chapter proposes a novel solution to enhance the performance of Solar PV-Fuel Cell Hybrids (SPV-FCH) through the integration of Artificial Intelligence (AI). By combining solar energy's variability with the consistent output of fuel cells, this approach aims to create a more reliable energy system. The chapter discusses the AI-enabled control systems that improve energy yield, grid stability, and cost-effectiveness, contributing to the growing field of sustainable energy technologies.

Chapter 9

This chapter explores the role of green financing in shaping sustainable finance models, particularly in Ethiopia. It examines how corporate social responsibility (CSR) principles guide financial institutions to prioritize investments that align with sustainable development goals (SDGs). By integrating environmental and social factors into financial decision-making, businesses can enhance their reputations, attract stakeholders, and comply with regulations. The chapter outlines future directions for strengthening green financing, fostering innovation, and aligning financial practices with the SDGs to promote sustainable development and build trust.

Chapter 10

In today's data-driven business environment, traditional business intelligence systems struggle to handle the complexity of large datasets. This chapter explores how machine learning (ML) and pattern recognition techniques are transforming business intelligence models. By leveraging supervised and unsupervised learning algorithms, businesses can analyze vast datasets, uncover intricate patterns, and make more informed decisions. This chapter highlights the practical applications of ML in improving decision-making processes and offers insights into the impact of these technologies on the future of business intelligence.

Chapter 11

Building upon the previous chapter, this section proposes an advanced machine learning-based framework for human activity recognition (ML-HARF) that addresses challenges related to sensor data processing. By integrating multiple sensor modalities, such as accelerometers and gyroscopes, the framework captures complex spatiotemporal patterns. It uses a hierarchical classification approach to extract and categorize features from raw data, achieving state-of-the-art accuracy in various activity recognition tasks. The chapter discusses the framework's scalability and efficiency, emphasizing its real-world applications in sectors like healthcare and sports.

Chapter 12

This chapter examines the growing trend of big data monetization in the digital transformation era, focusing on the Human Data Income (Hudi) model. It explores the challenges of turning personal data into valuable assets and offers a case study analysis of the Hudi model, which aims to provide individuals with the opportunity to monetize their personal data. The chapter discusses the implications of data-driven innovation and the ethical concerns surrounding data privacy and ownership, offering insights into the future of the data economy.

Chapter 13

Recommendation systems are transforming various industries, and the financial sector is no exception. This chapter discusses how machine learning-powered recommendation systems can enhance the customer experience by offering personalized financial products and services. These systems analyze customer data, including spending habits and investment preferences, to recommend relevant products. The chapter explores the challenges of building effective recommender systems for the financial sector and highlights their potential to provide better, data-driven recommendations to customers.

The scope of this book is broad, targeting both seasoned professionals and those new to the field. Whether you are a business executive looking to adopt AI-driven solutions, a data scientist seeking to refine your technical expertise, or a student interested in exploring the synergy between technology and business, you will find invaluable insights here. The topics covered include:

- Sustainability in business models and financing
- Artificial intelligence applications in business
- Climate and green financing, impact investing, and carbon financing
- Data analysis using deep learning, including traffic series and financial sectors
- Healthcare innovations through reinforcement learning and federated models
- Fraud detection in the online ecosystem using machine learning
- Socially responsible investing and governance frameworks

Each chapter provides a vital roadmap for understanding and utilizing machine learning to develop adaptable, future-ready business strategies. It is our hope that this book will inspire readers to think creatively, strategically, and sustainably in leveraging the power of machine learning to shape the businesses of tomorrow.

We invite you to embark on this journey of discovery, armed with the knowledge and tools to apply machine learning to create business models that not only succeed but thrive in a constantly changing world.

Ambika N
St. Francis College, India

Vishal Jain

Sharda University, India

Cristian González García

University of Oviedo, Spain

Dac-Nhuong Le

Vietnam National University, Vietnam

Chapter 1
A Detailed Investigation on Online Financial Fraud Detection Using Machine Learning Algorithms

Siji A. Thomas
Independent Researcher, UAE

Sini Kurien Thomas
Independent Researcher, USA

ABSTRACT

Financial fraud remains a persistent threat to various sectors including the public sector, government and finance industry, with fraudsters continuously adapting their strategies to exploit weaknesses in existing preventive measures, particularly with the increasing reliance on new technologies. This chapter delves into the potential of Machine Learning (ML) applications to support fraud detection capabilities within the financial sector. A comprehensive review of literature is conducted to investigate the effectiveness of various ML algorithms, including Support Vector Machine (SVM), Logistic Regression (LR), Random Forest (RF) and Convolutional Neural Networks (CNN), in identifying the fraudulent activities. The research categorizes existing literature based on several criteria, such as the type of fraud analyzed, ML algorithms utilized and efficiency of various detection strategies of financial fraud. Additionally, the authors in this chapter identifies the key challenges in current methodologies, alongside with potential future research directions.

I. INTRODUCTION

Online financial fraud detection is a critical component in securing digital transactions and protecting financial systems. The reliance on e-commerce, online banking and the growth of other digital platforms enhances the risk of fraudulent activities. These encompass a wide range, including fraudulent Credit Card (CC) transactions, data theft and cyber-attacks, as mentioned in Almazroi *et al* (2023). Detecting and preventing such fraud is essential to safeguard users and institutions. The proliferation

DOI: 10.4018/979-8-3693-3884-1.ch001

of ecommerce and extensive uptake of online payment techniques has controlled a marked growth in fraudulent actions. The various sectors, such as healthcare, are transformed the online transaction which makes a more convenient and available for the consumers. Nevertheless, this availability reaches with a significant challenge such as financial losses in each year due to the result of fraudulent transactions and an inclination to be raised as a technological advance. To address these issues, the fraud detection system is implemented by the organizations which combine the algorithms and annual processes that are designed to identify fraudulent activities automatically. These automated components typically utilize historical data to identify patterns linked to previous fraud, allowing them to flag real time suspicious transactions. By continuous analysis of transactional data, these algorithms can adapt to emerging fraud tactics, thereby improving their effectiveness over time. As industries increasingly depend on credit cards for daily transactions, enhancing the sophistication of these fraud detection systems will be vital to reducing losses and safeguarding both businesses and consumers from financial risks. According to Wang *et al* (2020), the notable surge in CC transactions handled via electronic payment systems presents valuable data pool that are efficiently leveraged for development of a data-driven fraud detection system. The datasets pertaining to CC transactions encompass a range of features suitable for integration into ML models, such as transaction specifics, cardholder information, and transaction chronicles. These datasets utilized for fraud detection showcase distinct attributes, including the absence of publicly available data sets (Taha *et al,* 2020). Despite the abundance of CC transaction data, there exists notable scarcity of available datasets for researchers to employ in investigations (Mehbodniya *et al,* 2021). Recent research reveals that the unfair practice of manipulating online reviews significantly undermines consumer trust. Hasan *et al* (2022) argued that, even when respondents are aware that reviews have been manipulated, their trust remains affected. Meanwhile, the manual aspect involves fraud investigators examining individual transactions and providing binary feedback (Singh *et al,* 2022). Fraudulent transactions pose a major obstacle to e-commerce growth and contribute to substantial economic losses. The shift of business operations to internet and rise of electronic monetary transactions in ever-expanding cashless economy underscore the importance of accurately detecting fraud to safeguard such transactions. The authors in Alghamdi *et al* (2024) mentioned that, the CC fraud occurs when an unauthorized individual utilizes CC details to make purchases without the consent of the cardholder. For detecting the CC fraud through the techniques like SMOTE and AdaBoost which is employed by ML techniques, leveraging SMOTE to solve the issues in datasets of the real-world. It access various algorithms like Logistics Regression (LR), Support Vector Machine (SVM), Decision Tree (DT), Extra Tree (ET) and Random Forest (RF). Through integration of Adaptive Boosting (AdaBoost) with these methods, the study attains noteworthy outcomes. The ET-AdaBoost and XGB-AdaBoost models notably reach a Matthews Correlation Coefficient (MCC) of 0.99. However, the researchers intend to expand their investigation by verifying the suggested framework on supplementary CC fraud datasets obtained from financial institutions (Ileberi *et al,* 2021). Preventing wallet-based transaction fraud with LightGBM, particularly by minimizing false alarms, provides substantial benefits. This advanced technique achieves an impressive 97% accuracy rate in detecting fraudulent activities, which is essential for fostering user trust in digital payment systems. Such high accuracy significantly reduces false positives, ensuring that legitimate transactions are not incorrectly flagged as fraudulent, thereby enhancing user experience and satisfaction. Moreover, LightGBM excels in efficiency and speed when processing large datasets, enabling real-time fraud detection without sacrificing system performance. To effectively identify the complex patterns and to manage the varied data types which makes it particularly for the future environment of transaction through online. Moreover, it allows the model to change it to a new processed data, where it ensures the fraud detection system remnants against the threats in ever-changing numerical scene. Additionally, the reduction of the false alarm has been decreased to 6,249. However, future research should persist in exploring the effectiveness of both Machine Learning (ML) technologies and classical methods to enhance fraud detection in electronic wallets and digital payments. While ML offers advanced pattern recognition capabilities, it may require extensive labelled data for training, which can be difficult to obtain. Additionally, ML models can suffer from overfitting which in turn makes difficulty in understanding their decision-making process. Classical methods, while more interpretable, may not adapt well to evolving fraud tactics (Iscan *et al,* 2023). Figure 1 illustrates the different types of fraud detection techniques.

Figure 1. Different types of fraud detection method

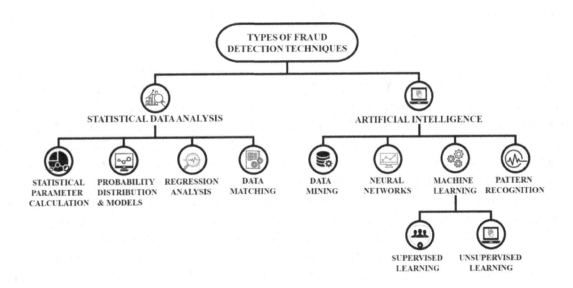

The combination of minority oversampling through Generative Adversarial Networks (GANs) and RF algorithm in ensemble form significantly boosts detection accuracy in CC fraud detection, concurrently slashing the need for labor intensive manual analysis. Results demonstrate 1.9% improvement in overall performance and 3.2% increase in detection rate and achieving 0% false alarm rate. However, exploration into other domains featuring rare events such as variance detection and medical analysis, remains unexplored (Glaleb *et al,* 2023). An ensemble of neural networks, coupled with feature engineering, enhances CC fraud detection. The classifiers demonstrate superior performance when trained with resampled data. Notably, proposed Long Short-Term Memory (LSTM) collective surpasses other algorithms attaining specificity and sensitivity of 0.998 and 0.996. However, further advancements in resampling and feature selection techniques are required to optimize classification performance. Online payment fraud encompasses everything from outlier detection to risk management employs several elements to address these challenges: ML for economic optimization, fraud detection of ML outcomes and risk model that predicts fraud risk while factoring in countermeasures. By optimizing the ML model, the expected losses are further reduced to 52%. These outcomes are achieved with small False Positive Rate (FPR) of 0.4%. However, the final aggregation depends on a monitoring step that uses information of existing fraud cases to assign varying weights to each pair of model-feature. While this method can improve detection accuracy, it also has several drawbacks. First, reliance on historical fraud data may introduce biases, as it can fail to account for emerging fraud tactics that have not yet been documented. Additionally, basing weights on past fraud patterns can result in a static model that struggles to adapt to new and evolving threats, limiting the system's responsiveness and allowing some fraudulent activities to go undetected. The complexity involved in determining appropriate weights may also lead to computational inefficiencies, making real-time detection difficult. Lastly, if the selected models or features are inadequate, the entire aggregation process may produce suboptimal outcomes, ultimately undermining the effectuality of fraud detection efforts in dynamic and rapidly changing digital environments (Esenogho et al, 2022; Vanini et al, 2023). A comparative analysis of CC fraud detection using Simulated Annealing trained Artificial Neural Networks (SA-ANN) and Hierarchical Temporal Memory (HTM) reveals those simulations on two benchmark datasets German and Australian Combined Control Facility (CCF) data. Moreover, Hierarchical Temporal Memory Cortical Learning Algorithms (HTM-CLA) significantly outperformed LSTM-ANN on these datasets by a factor of 2:1. Nonetheless, the highest accuracy was achieved using SA-ANN technique, suggesting that HTM-CLA are not superior to other established neural network methods (Osegi et al, 2021). The usage of ML and data mining for intelligent fraud detection in financial statements highlights the benefits of semi-supervised methods for Financial Statement Fraud Detection (FSFD). These techniques need only a minor number of labelled samples to attain robust learning and identify patterns within a larger pool of unlabeled data. The review found half of semi-supervised learning algorithms examined surpassed performance of supervised methods. However, it notes that more focus on unstructured data within financial fraud detection field is necessary for significant advancements (Ashtiani et al, 2022). As per Chaudhan et al, 2020, the representation of fine-grained co-occurrences related to behavior in fraud detection for e-commerce payment system serves as a robust model for analysing transactional characteristics. This approach improves the accuracy and effectiveness of behavioural models used to identify the fraudulent activities. By closely examining the intricate relationships among various transaction attributes, these models can more accurately flag suspicious behaviours and patterns indicative of fraud. However, the application of this advanced data enhancement technique to other types of behavioural models remains largely uncharted territory, indicating a gap in the current research landscape. In this chapter, the authors conduct a thorough exploration of online financial fraud detection utilizing Machine Learning (ML) algorithms. They aim to assess the efficacy of various algorithms by conducting a comparative analysis among several prominent ML techniques, including SVM, LR, RF and CNN. This comparative analysis is crucial for determining which algorithm demonstrates the strongest performance in detecting fraudulent transactions, ultimately contributing to more secure online payment systems. By evaluating these different approaches, the authors not only shed light on their respective strengths and weaknesses but also lay a path for future advancements in fraud detection.

II. CONTRIBUTIONS OF THIS SURVVEY

Online financial encompasses a type of business funding that provides upfront credit to businesses that are predominantly operating online. Mismanagement of fraud can result in significant repercussions, including a sharp decline in public trust towards governmental bodies and industries. When fraud is poorly handled, it can foster skepticism and uncertainty among citizens, leading to diminished confidence in institutions that are expected to safeguard their interests. This erosion of trust can have broader implications, potentially damaging a country's international standing and economic reputation. Investors may hesitate to engage with entities perceived as corrupt or ineffective, which can deter foreign investment and hinder economic growth. Ultimately, the fallout from fraud mismanagement can create a pervasive sense of insecurity, impacting societal stability and economic resilience. This chapter significantly examines the hybridized approach of ML algorithm, the main subscriptions of this review are as below,

- To analyze the role of ML algorithm
- To detect the online fraud detection in digital transactions
- Technical properties of various methods are considered
- To analyze the comparison various techniques such as SVM, LR, RF and CNN

III. REVIEW OF CONVENTIONAL TECHNIQUES FOR FRAUD DETECTION

Although there are several conventional techniques, this section describes only some of the techniques along with their methods.

A. Group Search Firefly Algorithm (GSFA) for Online Fraud Detection

The FA is swarm intelligence simulation inspired by the behaviour of fireflies has been proposed in this technique. This paper outlined here introduces a hybrid approach that combines swarm metaheuristic to attack the CC fraud detection issues. A novel variation of the Firefly Algorithm (FA), called the Generalized Firefly Algorithm (GSFA), was developed to optimize both SVM and an extreme machine learning technique. Datasets typically include a multitude of attributes, many of which may be irrelevant or redundant. These unnecessary attributes can significantly hinder classification accuracy by expanding the search space and complicating the optimization process. The GSFA metaheuristic addresses this challenge effectively by incorporating three control factors that can be customized for each specific NP-hard problem. This tailored approach significantly enhances the algorithm's ability to navigate the search space efficiently, which is critical for tackling complex problems. By optimizing these parameters, GSFA can better adapt to the unique characteristics of various datasets, leading to improved convergence rates and the identification of optimal solutions. Moreover, this flexibility allows further exploration of possible solutions, reducing the chances of becoming trapped in local optima. As a result, the overall classification performance is markedly improved, enabling accurate predictions. Additionally, the algorithm's adaptability can make it suitable for an extensive range of applications, from fraud detection to resource allocation, thereby expanding its utility across different fields. Ultimately, this versatility and efficiency make GSFA a valuable tool in addressing complex computational challenges. Additionally, it is essential to conduct further assessments of the algorithm's performance across various NP hard challenges (Jovanovic *et al*, 2022). Figure 2 shows the flowchart of GSFA for detecting the financial fraud.

Figure 2. Flowchart of group search Firefly algorithm

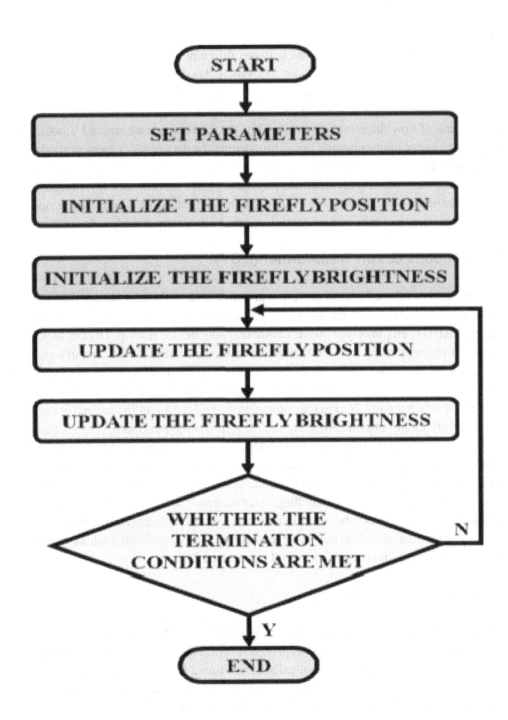

(Liu et al, 2017)

B. Fine Grained Co-occurrences for Behaviour Based Fraud Detection

The authors in Wang *et al*, 2022 presented an enhancement data for behavioural modelling is the primary focus in utilizing fine grained co-occurrences for behaviour-based fraud detection in digital payment facilities. The system identifies complex correlations among transactional attributes by utilizing a data graph that maps the connections between different variables in an organized manner. This graphical representation facilitates a deeper analysis of how various attributes interact, uncovering intricate patterns that may signal fraudulent activity. Additionally, the model employs heterogeneous network embedding techniques to enhance the representation of these relationships, thereby improving the understanding of how different elements within the data are interconnected. Looking forward, an exciting opportunity for future research lies in broadening the data enhancement methods to encompass a wider array of behavioural models. This could include generalized agent-based models and group-level models, alongside the current individual and population-level frameworks. By expanding in this way, the model would be able to capture more nuanced behavioural dynamics, providing a richer context for analysing fraud patterns and enhancing detection accuracy across diverse scenarios and user interactions.

C. Heterogeneous Graph Transformer (HGT)

Tang *et al*, 2021 developed a fraud detection in online review systems through HGT. This approach tackles issues of camouflage and inconsistency comprehensively. Fraud Aware Heterogeneous Graph Transformer (FAHGT) employs type aware feature mapping device manage HGT data, followed by implementation of several scoring methods to mitigate contradiction and detect camouflage. A label-aware counting technique has been developed to clear out noisy neighbours in order to identify camouflage behaviours. This system uses a combined method called the score head mechanism to integrate two neural modules, both of which are involved in the computation of edge weight in the final feature aggregation. Neighbouring features are subsequently combined to form a more informative representation, providing deeper insights into the underlying data. The FAHGT has demonstrated significant performance enhancements compared to several baseline methods across various datasets, highlighting its effectiveness in capturing complex relationships within the data. Looking ahead, there are plans to further develop the model's capabilities, especially in handling dynamic graph data, which is essential for applications where relationships evolve over time. Additionally, there is an aim to extend the model's fraud detection capabilities to other domains, allowing for its application in diverse fields such as finance, healthcare, and cybersecurity, thereby increasing its overall impact and utility.

D. Neutral Factorization Method

An online telephony fraud detection method utilizing Neural Factorization Autoencoder (NFA) is proposed in this method. This innovative approach leverages NFA to scrutinize customer calling patterns, enabling the detection of fraudulent calls in real time. The model integrates NF Machines and Auto encoder effectively capture and model calling patterns enhanced by a memory module for dynamic adaptation to evolving customer behavior. Figure 3 shows the flow chart of NF method. The empirical findings indicate superior performance compared to baseline methods achieving AUC 91.06%, 91.89% True Positive Rate (TPR), FPR 14.76% and F1 score 95.45%. Moving forward, that aims to extend this methodology to address other forms of telecommunication fraud. Additionally, it aspires to enhance efficiency by exploring optimized solutions, leveraging cutting-edge ML techniques within transformer architecture to minimize execution time of detection system (Wahid *et al* 2024).

Figure 3. Flow diagram of neutral factorization method

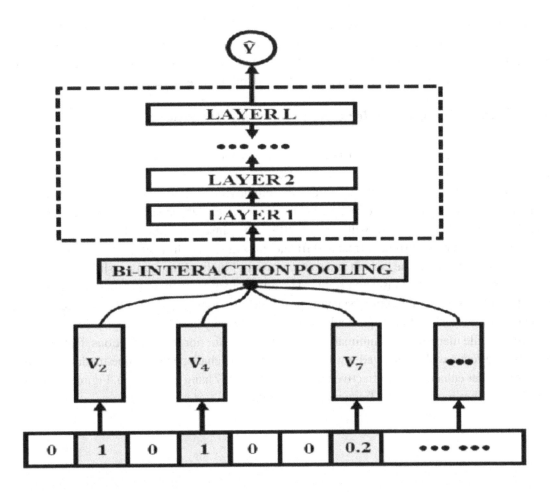

E. CC Fraud Detection Using Neural Factorization Autoencoder Method

CC fraud detection using improved deep learning models offers numerous advantages. These advanced algorithms can figure out various numbers of transaction data with remarkable speed, identifying intricate patterns and anomalies which shows fraudulent activities. The efficiency of deep learning algorithms to learn from large datasets enables continuous enhancement in detection accuracy, making them particularly effective in adapting to evolving fraud tactics. Moreover, improved architectures, such as CNNs and Recurrent Neural Networks (RNNs), can capture both spatial and temporal relationships in the data, further enhancing detection capabilities. The automated nature of these models also reduces the need for extensive manual oversight, streamlining the fraud detection process. However, there are significant drawbacks to consider. The accuracy of deep learning simulations largely depends on the quality and quantity of training data; inadequate or biased datasets can lead to inaccurate predictions. High false positive rates, weakening sincere transactions and potentially trusting customers are some of the factors which leads to suffering the models. The computational complication of Deep Learning (DL) algorithms faces different issues such as interpretability which makes it difficult to understand the decision-making process. At last, the maintenance and implementation of the models are expertise specialized, intensive resource making and stabled updates to apprise new fraud approaches. Balancing these advantages and disadvantages is essential for effective fraud detection (Sulaiman *et al*, 2024).

F. Fraud Detection Method for Low-Frequency Transaction

Introducing novel approach to construct individual behavior, aimed at enhancing accuracy of low frequency users' behavior by integrating present transaction group behavior and transaction status. Initially, leverage of user's historical transactions exclusively, employing an optimal risk determination algorithm to establish users personalized transaction behavior baseline. Subsequently, applying Density Based Spatial Clustering of Applications with Noise (DBSCAN) clustering algorithm, it extracts behavioural characteristics from both current normal and fraudulent samples, culminating in the formulation of the collective behavior within the current transaction group. Finally, leveraging a sliding window mechanism that extracts current transaction status. The amalgamation of these three components results in the creation of a refined transaction behavior profile for the user. The method presented in this paper demonstrates significant efficacy, particularly for low-frequency users, as it adeptly discerns fraudulent transactions while maintaining a minimal misjudgement rate for normal transactions. However, moving forward to the focus will be directed towards addressing the challenge of online model updating, with the aim of further enhancing the effectiveness of the method (Zhang *et al*, 2020). Figure 4 demonstrates the fraud detection model for low frequency transaction.

Figure 4. Flowchart of fraud detection method for low frequency transaction

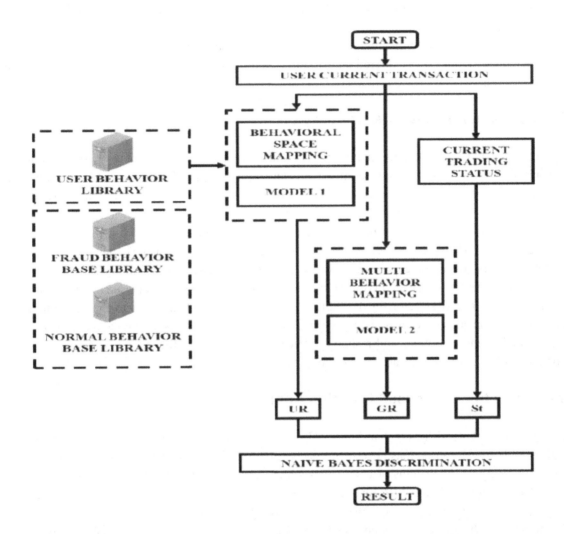

(Zhang et al, 2020)

G. CatBoost and XGBoost to Enhance the LightGBM Method

Fraud detection in financial data using various ML methodologies has been mentioned in Hashemi *et al*, 2022. This includes weight-tuning as a pre-process for unbalanced data, alongside the incorporation of CatBoost and XGBoost to enhance the accuracy of the LightGBM method. These techniques are crafted to ensure precise detection of fraudulent activities while improving the system's adaptability and scalability for diverse transaction environments. By utilizing advanced algorithms, the model can swiftly respond to emerging fraud patterns, enhancing its effectiveness in dynamic contexts. The main goal of this technique is to reduce the high rate of false positives in which the online CC transactions are digitally mistaken which is identified as fraudulent. Lowering the existences is an important factor for customer satisfaction which produce a fraudulent alerts that infuriate the customers and reduce the trust of the customer in the system. Furthermore, a decrease in false positives leads to operational cost savings by reducing the need for manual reviews of flagged transactions. Nevertheless, implementation of these techniques requires a facilitated algorithms which produce a challenge that are related to the quality of the data.

H. Online Fraud Detection Using Fuzzy LR

Charizanos et al. (2024) have introduced an online fuzzy fraud detection framework for CC transactions that leverages fuzzy logic to manage uncertainty and imprecision in transaction data. This approach allows for more nuanced assessments of fraud risk, which is essential given the significant variation in transaction patterns among legitimate users. The framework integrates expert knowledge through fuzzy rules, facilitating informed decision-making based on contextual factors. However, there are notable disadvantages. The ability of the system is to avoid the developing fraud patterns without an manual usage where it depends on the expert defined rules of fuzzy based system which has the capability to improve the effectiveness of the quality of the input data. This leads to the main issue to be established. Additionally, there is a risk factor for the high rate false positives which leads to the non-important transaction rejection and users non-satisfactory ability. At last, the system is integrated into the previous structure which is more complex and resource-intensive that requires a fine-tuning which ensures the transparent performance in a unstable fraud site.

I. Analysis of the Supervised Learning Approach

The utilization of algorithms such as SVM, DT, RF and LR are employed to prevent and identify the fraudulent with online transactions. These approaches that offer an valuation of stable fraud detection in the region using the algorithms or approaches which is mentioned early. The model achieves high accuracy by leveraging labelled historical data, which serves as a crucial resource for training and refining its predictive capabilities. From the analysis of the given data, the detection outcomes resulted as dependable and the patterns that identifies the model which is linked to the fraudulent parameters. It promotes the visible main features that influence the fraud detection which enable the stakeholders to provide a particular element which affects the conclusion of the model. Nonetheless, the complexity of the model that addresses the issues for clarification and for making the system difficult for the users to fully comprehend its operation. This complexity necessitates continuous retraining to adapt fraud patterns, ensuring the model remains effective in a constantly changing threat landscape (Reddy *et al*, 2022).

J. Fraud Detection in Credit Risk Assessment
Through Supervised Learning Techniques

Detection of CC in risk assessment with supervised learning algorithms provides an investigation of extensive historical data to identify the patterns that the fraud detection characteristics resulted in more accurate risk factors. As per the data required and resulted, the algorithms are improved continuously, and the accuracy of the detection process is also improved due to the trained datasets. DT, SVM

AND NN are some examples of methods that provide stakeholders with a stable understanding with a decision-making process and the factors that influence risk assessments. Nevertheless, the dependence on the labelled information that presents a risk factor which is expensive and time-consuming and to obtain the datasets with high quality. Additionally, the high rates of false negatives have resulted from supervised learning models which are unable to identify the supervised and unknown fraud patterns that are not present in the training sets. Moreover, these models rises a risk of overfitting which occurs when it functions well on the datasets which are trained but not the new data Lastly, implementing supervised learning algorithms demands considerable computational resources and expertise, making them less accessible to smaller organizations (Xu et al, 2024)

K. Machine Learning-Based Fraud Detection System Utilizing a Risk Management Strategy

The integration of ML-driven fraud detection techniques into a risk management framework in which the large volume of transaction information is detected in real time. The main methodology of this system involves data collection and pre-processing, development and feature selection of various ML models within the risk management framework. This system allows a development for the intermittent patterns and strategies with traditional methods. This improves the fraud detection precision and accuracy of the method. Additionally, the model of ML algorithm takes a new data that keeps well that enables them to adjust the fraud strategies. The field of industry prioritises the fraud detection according to their potential impact whenever the risk management framework is implemented. This enables more sophisticated resources allocation. Nonetheless, the complexity of the ML simulations are difficult to understand which leads to the risk factor in decision making process (Guo *et al*, 2024).

L. Utilizing Machine Learning Algorithms for Real-Time Fraud Detection Method

The analysis of the detection of the fraud in real-time using ML algorithms that also uses the digital payment systems in which the huge volume of data for transaction and patterns that point out the fraudulent actions of the systems. The main methodology is of performance evaluation using relevant metrics and of continuous updating and monitoring of the model to detect the fraudulent activities. These features reduces the financial losses and also increases the overall security and improves the accuracy of the fraud detection. Moreover, the model of ML algorithms absorbs new information and they constantly change the methods and strategies which lowers the possibilities of false negatives. Real-time detection provides an easier action of fraudulent transaction and protecting the financial factors as well as customers. However, the complexity of the ML algorithms leads to the interpretation and impeding the decision-making processes. Moreover, the quality of the training data is more effective which leads to the insufficient predictions of the fraudulent activities. The high rates of false positives has the potential to results in cancelled transactions and rejections of the data transactions. It also requires an intensive method for the detection purpose for the system (Nakra *et al* 2024).

L. Effective Credit Card Fraud Detection Using Meta-Heuristic Techniques and Machine Learning Algorithms

Efficient CC fraud detection through the use of meta-heuristic techniques and machine learning algorithms presents several advantages. These ML algorithms are suddenly access the huge volumes of data transaction that efficiently evaluate the complexity of the patterns and that indicate the fraudulent behaviour. Some methods such as Particle Swarm Optimization (PSO) and GA are used to improve the ML models optimization and also increase in their efficacy and accuracy in fraud detection. By integrating these approaches, organizations can create a more resilient detection system that adapts to changing fraud tactics over time. Moreover, these techniques often reduce the need for manual intervention, streamlining the detection process and allowing teams to concentrate on critical investigations. However, customers lose their faith and the satisfaction, if they mistakenly identify the genuine transaction of the fraudulent data due to high false positives rates. The complexity of merging meta-heuristic techniques with machine learning algorithms can also lead to implementation challenges, necessitating substantial resources and expertise. Furthermore, continuous maintenance and tuning are vital to adapt to new fraud strategies, which can be both resource-intensive and costly for organizations (Mosa *et al*, 2024).

Advanced techniques for detecting online fraud are reviewed in this section. The GSFA is the first intervention to deploy swarm intelligence to detect credit card fraud. The next subdivision discusses a fine-grained co-occurrence technique that uses behavior-based detection to describe intricate transactional interactions. Next, the HGT approach is discussed, which improves detection by taking into account online review inconsistencies and camouflage. Fraudulent calls are identified by the NFA using pattern analysis. This section also presents a novel approach for low-frequency transactions that accurately profiles behaviour by fusing historical and current data. Lastly, it looks at ways to enhance fraud detection in banking by utilising CatBoost and XGBoost enhancements to the LightGBM technique, pointing out issues with data quality. The efficacy of several ML algorithms in fraud detection which are examined in the next section.

IV. REVIEW OF MACHINE LEARNING TECHNIQUES

A. ML and Blockchain

The authors in Ashfaq *et al*, 2022 introduced a secure fraud detection model that seamlessly integrates ML and blockchain technologies. This innovative approach leverages two powerful ML algorithms, XGBoost and RF, for transaction classification. By training on datasets containing both fraudulent and legitimate transaction patterns, these techniques accurately predict new incoming transactions. Figure 5 shows the flowchart of ML algorithm using SMOTE. The integration of blockchain technology fortifies the model's fraud detection capabilities within the Bitcoin network. While generating synthetic malicious data points using SMOTE enhances performance and yields superior results, several notable disadvantages must be considered. A major limitation is the model's susceptibility to adversarial attacks, where malicious actors craft inputs specifically designed to mislead the algorithm. This vulnerability can undermine the benefits gained from synthetic data generation. Additionally, relying on SMOTE may lead to over-fitting, as the model could become overly specialized in the artificially created data, hindering its ability to generalize to real-world scenarios. This may reduce its effectiveness in identifying novel fraudulent activities. Furthermore, the computational demands of generating synthetic data can increase processing times, particularly in real-time applications, potentially impacting system efficiency. Finally, the quality of the synthetic data is paramount; if the generated points fail to accurately represent genuine fraudulent patterns, the model's overall accuracy and reliability may suffer, posing significant risks to its effectiveness in practical implementations.

Figure 5. Flowchart of ML algorithm using SMOTE

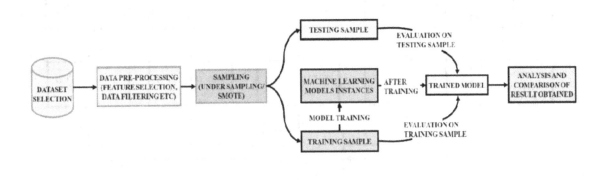

(Khalid et al, 2024)

B. Fraud Detection Empowered With Fussed ML

Real time shill order fraud detection system permitted by Fused ML is proposed in this method. This model is structured into two phases such as training and validation, with data split into 70% for training and 30% for validation. It comprises three sub modules such as first module employs two ML algorithms such as SVM and ANN, simultaneously trained on same dataset to find bidding fraud. The predictions generated by SVM and ANN are fed into a fuzzy-based fused module. Within this module, a fuzzy logic mechanism processes these inputs to generate a final output, effectively leveraging the strengths of both algorithms. This novel fused machine learning approach achieves an impressive prediction accuracy of 99.63%, demonstrating its effectiveness in accurately identifying outcomes. Moreover, simulation results indicate that this fused method outperforms existing techniques, underscoring its superior performance. This integration of SVM and ANN through fuzzy logic not only enhances predictive capabilities but also provides a robust solution for tackling complex decision-making challenges. However, there remains area for improvement in accuracy and thus, enhancing accuracy will be a key focus for future iterations (Abidi *et al*, 2021). Figure 6 illustrates the flowchart of fused ML online financial fraud detection.

Figure 6. Flowchart of Fussed ML online financial fraud detection

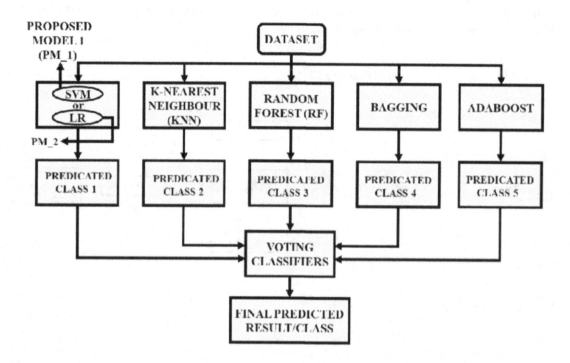

C. K-NN Under Sampling Technique Along With CatBoost

An enhanced CC fraud detection model utilizing ML is presented in this paper. Given the pressing need to combat fraudulent CC transactions, this study explores sixty six ML models through a two-stage evaluation process. Leveraging real world dataset of European cardholders and employing K-fold validation, each model is rigorously assessed. Among these models, All KNN undersampling method combined with CatBoost (AllKNN-CatBoost) emerges as top performing model. The AllKNN-CatBoost approach is meticulously compared with existing approaches, demonstrating superior performance with 97.94%, AUC value, 95.91% Recall value and 87.40% F1 score value. However, future efforts to explore alternative datasets and optimization algorithms come with their own set of disadvantages. First, the availability and quality of alternative datasets can be inconsistent, potentially leading to unreliable insights. Additionally, different datasets may not adequately represent the specific patterns of credit card fraud, making it challenging to achieve effective model training. Furthermore, the complexity of optimization algorithms may introduce increased computational demands, which can hinder real-time processing capabilities. Lastly, relying on new datasets and algorithms may necessitate extensive re-training of existing models, resulting in time and resource constraints that could delay the deployment of improved fraud detection systems (Alfaiz *et al*, 2022).

D. CC Fraud Detection Using FPMA Technique and Apriori Growth

The Apriori approach was published by the authors in Vipin *et al*, 2017, and the two steps of the FP tree methodology are listed here. The first stage builds the FP Split Tree, which is a more effective method of producing candidate sets than the FP Tree because it only requires one full database scan as opposed to the latter's two. The efficiency is about twice as high as before Mining the FP Split tree produced by the Apriori growth algorithm marks the second phase of the process. This approach is significantly more time-efficient than the traditional FP-Growth algorithm, primarily because it eliminates the need for continuous recursive construction of FP-Split trees. In FP-Growth, this recursive generation can create substantial computational overhead, especially with larger datasets. By leveraging the FP Split tree, the algorithm effectively reduces the search space, enabling faster access to relevant frequent itemset. This increased efficiency not only speeds up the mining process but also improves overall performance, making it especially beneficial for managing complex data scenarios. By eliminating the need for recursive searches, the FP Split Tree significantly simplifies the complexity of the FP Tree. Additionally, it only requires a single database scan, unlike the FP Tree, which demands two scans, and the Apriori algorithm, which typically necessitates multiple scans. However, the effectiveness of this method can be impacted by long-pattern formations, complicating the detection process. The entire workflow for detecting fraudulent card activity is depicted in Figure 7, offering a clear visual representation of the method's efficiency and structure.

Figure 7. Complete process of fraudulent card usage detection

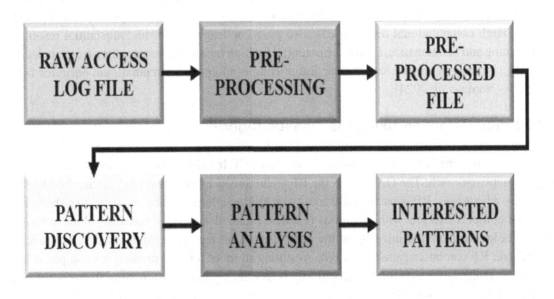

(Vipin et al, 2017)

E. Improved Incremental and Interactive FPMA for Fraud Detection

The authors in Sherly *et al*, 2015 developed a distributed FPM technique using parallel approaches for both count distribution and compressed distribution of data. This method creates frequent item sets without creating local frequent sets that use little memory by using a prefix-based equivalency class partitioning strategy. This method updates the frequent patterns with less time complexity by using a variety of support values. Additionally, by maintaining the almost frequent items established with the aid of two minimum support thresholds, it allows the user to interactively modify minimum support value according to their own conveniences. Thus, in a short amount of time, the method is able to quickly and accurately construct a user spending profile with minimal help. The challenge lies in interactively and gradually identifying all noteworthy recurring trends in order to stop online financial fraud.

F. Financial Fraud Identification Using Advanced Machine Learning Techniques

Analysing the financial fraud detection using the deep learning algorithms for a massive amount of the complex data and patterns that are not noticed by the standard methods which improves the precision of detecting the fraudulent data transactions thereby lowers the financial losses that are developed by organizations. Additionally, deep learning algorithms improve continuously as they process new data, enabling them to adapt swiftly to evolving fraud tactics and minimize false negatives. Their automated nature boosts efficiency, facilitating real-time detection and response to potential fraud, which is essential in fast-paced financial environments. Nevertheless, the deep learning models are quite challenging due to the complexity of the system which leads to problems in visibility of the fraudulent transactions. Moreover, the quantity and quality of the data that is used for training that are crucial factors for evaluating the crucial factors for determining the strategies that are not sufficient for the predictions of fraudulent activities. High computational demands can also pose challenges, requiring substantial resources for model training and maintenance. Lastly, the potential for high false positive rates may frustrate legitimate customers, resulting in unnecessary transaction rejections and possible reputational harm for financial institutions (Nama *et al*, 2024).

G. CC Fraud Detection Using the Genetic Algorithm

The authors in Ileberi *et al*, 2022 presented a ML based CC fraud detection engine that chooses features using a genetic approach. The GA utilizes the RF technique as its fitness evaluation method because of several key advantages. RF is particularly adept at handling a large number of input variables, making it ideal for complex datasets with numerous features. It can also manage missing values independently, which helps maintain the integrity of the analysis without requiring extensive data pre-processing. Furthermore, RF is robust against noisy data, resulting in more reliable predictions compared to other methods. A significant reason for RF's popularity is its effectiveness in addressing the over-fitting issue that often plagues traditional DTs, which can result in models that excel on training data but fail with new data. Furthermore, the RF manages the some classes which are not performing the datasets with imbalance of class data. Due to the adaptability, it is used with both the continuous and categorical data which leads to the useful tool for a variety of application in a variety of domain.

H. Financial Fraud Detection with Quantum Graph Neural Network (QGNN)

The fraud detection of financial cases is utilized by some special qualities of graph structures and quantum computing which improves the detection of accuracy by the complex modelling of relationship within the transaction of data. Their capability to process large datasets simultaneously enables faster analysis than traditional methods, making them ideal for real-time fraud detection. Furthermore, QGNNs are quite better for finding the complex patterns and corrections in the data that are conventional algorithms that leads to the system resistant to new types of fraud detection. Nevertheless, the implementation of the quantum algorithm that are specialised for a technological call and with the knowledge which is costly and strictly restrict the access of many institutions. Moreover, the technology is still in its previous stages of development, system and scalability where the integration issues are raised in real-world applications. Additionally, QGNNs are challenging for understand and this could lead to the affect of transparency of the decision making processes. Furthermore, the reliance on quantum principles introduces uncertainties, as the field is still developing (Innan *et al*, 2024).

I. Fraud Detection with Machine Learning

Fraud detection using ML allows rapid analysis of large quantity of data, which identifies the patterns effectively that may signal the fraudulent activity. This ability enhances the accuracy in identification. ML improves the predication ability by continuously learning from new data. However, the quantity and the quality of the training data are crucial for the detection efficacy of the fraudulent activities which are incomplete that leads to predictions that are not accurate of the system (Olushola *et al*, 2024).

J. Predicting Money Laundering with Machine Learning and ANN methods

For the prediction of fraudulent activities for the transaction of the data that enables the quick processing by utilizing the ML algorithms and ANN. This method that successfully transact the huge amount of the data which be like as the complexity od the data and the anomalies that leads to the illegal activity. The ability of the system is to revise the previous data that makes it possible to continuously improve the accuracy and are skilled at identifying the exchanging strategies. Furthermore, ANNs are identified with the non-linear relationship in data where the conventional techniques that improves the detection skills. Additionally, the manual views are required in this system which productively boosts the resources for more enquiries inside the organisation. However, the both quantity and quality of the training datasets that are crucial to these models where the efficacy of the system is affected. Furthermore, the ML algorithms to generate high rates of false negatives are generated which would leads to the affect of customer confidence and useless investigation. Due to its complexity, ANNs provide the interpretability issues that makes it challenging for stakeholders to understand the process of decision made. At last, the systems are intensive which regularly upgrades and specialised knowledge to adjust the new strategies (Lokanan *et al*, 2024).

K. Decision Tree Algorithm Enhanced with Regression Analysis for Fraud Detection in CC Transactions

Bagchi and his co-authors (2021) added regression analysis to a decision tree algorithm to create an enhanced credit card fraud detection system. Regression analysis and decision trees were integrated in order to improve the system's capacity to detect fraudulent transactions with greater accuracy and to efficiently track and report suspicious activity. The resulting system demonstrated a high level of effectiveness, achieving an accuracy rate of 81.6%, indicating its strong performance in correctly classifying transactions. Additionally, the system successfully detected all test intrusions, showcasing its reliability in identifying known fraudulent activities. However, the study also highlights several notable drawbacks. The regression analysis and DT are together which increases the system complexity, which leads to the management and execution is more difficult. The risk of over-fitting is more challenging which is faced by the system. The untested datasets are poorly developed that again leads to the over-fitting issues. The complexity has been increased due to the inapplicable of the real-world applications. Huge datasets processing are also cause scalability problems which handle the various volumes of the data effectively. This inefficiency leads to the complicated infrastructure that decrease the accuracy and slower processing times. This meets the issues such as raises of cost and complexity of the system. Ultimately, while combining decision trees and regression can yield powerful insights, the associated difficulties necessitate careful consideration and robust solutions to ensure effective deployment and maintenance.

Advanced machine learning methods for online fraud detection are reviewed in this area. For credit card fraud, RF and XGBoost are used first, and for behavior-based detection, SVM and ANN are used. In order to effectively detect fraudulent calls, Apriori Growth, FPMA, and decision trees are presented. KNN is discussed for addressing camouflage and inconsistent reviews. Lastly, this study examines the integration of GA with RF to enhance fraud detection in banking, focusing on the challenges related to data quality. By employing GA, the model can optimize feature selection and strengthen the RF's ability to identify fraudulent patterns, thus improving detection accuracy. The next section will present a comparative analysis of traditional fraud detection methods, such as rule-based systems, alongside modern machine learning techniques, highlighting their respective strengths and weaknesses. This comparison aims to demonstrate how advanced methods can achieve superior performance in combating fraud, ultimately enhancing security measures within the banking sector.

V. COMPARATIVE ANALYSIS

The performance of the some conventional techniques is analyzed through a comparative analysis. This comparative analysis is shown for various techniques in Table 1.

Table 1. Comparative analysis of conventional techniques

Sl. No	Author (Publication Year)	Methodology Used	Advantages	Disadvantages
1.	D Zhang et al (2020)	Sampling techniques and SVM	The results indicate that the implementation of new criteria and an innovative weighting scheme able to significantly enhance effectiveness of CC fraud detection. Crucially, this approach reduces the financial losses banks incur from CC fraud.	Material improvement is evident from linear case, which compensates for decrease in accuracy.
2.	Hangjun Zhou et al (2021)	Intelligent and distributed Big Data approach to implement graph embedding algorithm Node2Vec.	• The system has the capability to handle transactions instantly, swiftly identifying any fraudulent activities and thereby minimizing potential losses. • As the volume of financial transactions expands, this scalability becomes essential for effective real-time fraud detection.	Implementing a distributed big data approach demands proficiency in managing extensive data sets, configuring distributed systems, and overseeing computational resources effectively.
3.	Amit Gupta et al (2021)	Utilizing Naive Bayes, C4.5 DT and bagging ensemble ML algorithms.	• Naïve Bayes demonstrates remarkable computational efficiency and speed. • Its effectiveness persists even when dealing with extensive datasets, rendering it highly applicable in real-world scenarios where prompt fraud detection is imperative.	Naive Bayes often exhibits subpar performance when handling continuous variables or non-normally distributed data.
4.	Poongodi et al (2021)	Support Vector Machine with Information Gain (SVMIG)	SVMIG has demonstrated high accuracy in identifying fraudulent transactions.	• However, implementing combination of multiple algorithms such as SVM, information gain, and Apriori pose complexities. • Moreover, training an SVM would be computationally demanding, particularly after dealing with a large number of features.
5.	Mohamad Khedmati et al (2020)	Support Vector Data Description (SVDD) in conjunction with Density-Based Spatial Clustering of Applications with Noise.	This method provides result indicated that employing this method enhances fraud detection process compared to two class classifiers, demonstrating improvements in both speed and performance.	However, development approach for fine-tuning the parameters of SVDD were not reached the expected accuracy.
6.	Hilal et al (2022)	SVM and ANN	Detection techniques provides its ability to enhance the accuracy of identifying fraudulent activities, a critical aspect in preventing financial losses.	Nevertheless, the demand more meticulous design and tuning in comparison to simpler models. Additionally, these models typically necessitate a higher quality and quantity of data.
7.	Udayakumar et al (2023)	Deep Fraud Net method	Deep fraud Net method provides an enhanced detection and classification of cyber security and financial fraud risks.	However, this detection technique faces the issues of lack of accessibility and imbalanced datasets.
8.	Warghade et al (2020)	Isolation Forest Method-SMOTE	• It has enhanced accuracy. • The method identifies a reduced fraud outlier.	Nonetheless, the method faces a class imbalance issues and also provides high false positive rates.

The performance of various ML algorithms are compared its performance are discussed in Table 2.

Table 2. Comparative analysis of different machine learning algorithms

Sl. No.	Author (Publication Year)	Methodology	Advantages	Disadvantages
1.	Riany *et al* (2021)	ANN method is used as the data analysis method.	ANN possess the capability to learn difficult patterns and relations within data, resulting in high prediction accuracy.	However, they necessitate a substantial amount of data to train effectively, and their performance heavily relies on the quality of this data.
2.	Seera *et al* (2024)	ML techniques such as SVMs and ANNs.	Intelligent systems able to achieve extensive coverage of fraudulent transactions with a minimal false alarm rate, thereby enhancing detection effectiveness.	Erroneously flagging legitimate transactions as fraudulent or overlooking actual instances of fraud result in inconvenience and financial repercussions.
3.	Karthika *et al* (2023)	One-dimensional Dilated Convolutional Neural Network (DCNN)	• Dilated CNNs demonstrate efficiency in handling successive data and capturing complex patterns, thus enhancing the accuracy of fraud detection. • The system autonomously identifies suspicious transactions, minimizing the need for manual intervention.	The complexity of CNNs poses challenges in interpreting their decision-making processes.
4.	Rout *et al* (2021), Aburbeian *et al* (2023).	SVM, DT and RF	• ML algorithm in complex patterns from transaction data, resulting in precise fraud detection. • ML techniques efficiently manage large volumes of transaction data.	• Certain ML models may be complex and pose challenges in interpretation. • The models are more complex, which made it difficult to interpret.
5.	Asha *et al* (2021)	SVM, ANN and k-nearest neighbour (KNN)	Achieving an accuracy of approximately 96%, this method proves highly effective for CC fraud detection.	• ANNs able to indeed be intricate and demand expertise for development and interpretation. • There's a risk of overfitting if the model becomes excessively complex, leading it to fit noise in the data.
6.	Alharbi *et al* (2022)	CNN technique	Utilizes a deep features extracted from the proposed CNN achieved an impressive accuracy of 99.81%.	However, the text2img-based classification method was not extended to address similar challenges in CC fraud detection.
7.	Megdad *et al* (2022)	SVM and ANN technique	The classifier with balanced dataset provides a better performance in Accuracy, precession Recall and the F1 score.	However, identification of online transaction fraud poses growing challenges as illicit payments become increasingly similar to appropriate ones.
8.	Vengatesan et al (2020)	KNN method for CC fraud detection	• Enhanced better scalability. • Capable of recognising the complex patterns. • Reduced false positive rates.	However, the method faces some data quality issues which affects the effectiveness of the detection system.
9.	Sorour *et al* (2024)	SVM technique	• It leads to better fraud detection accuracy. • This method is less sensitive to noisy data.	However, the dataset size is large which leads to the longer to processing times compared to simpler algorithm.

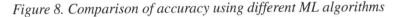

Figure 8. Comparison of accuracy using different ML algorithms

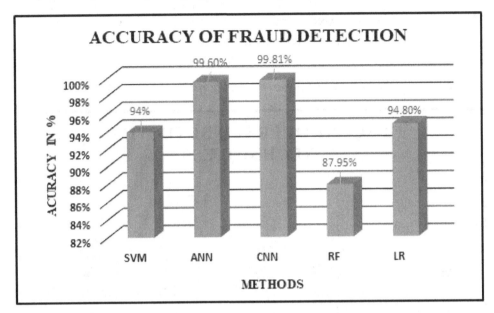

Figure 8 illustrates a comparison of accuracy achieved by different machine learning algorithms, including SVM (Triveni *et al*, 2020), ANN (Abidi *et al*, 2021), RF (Ilebari *et al*, 2022), LR (Mehbodniya *et al*, 2021) and CNN (Balawi *et al*, 2023). Notably, the CNN algorithm achieves an enhanced accuracy rate of 99.81%, demonstrating superior performance in terms of accuracy.

Figure 9. Comparison of specificity using different ML algorithms

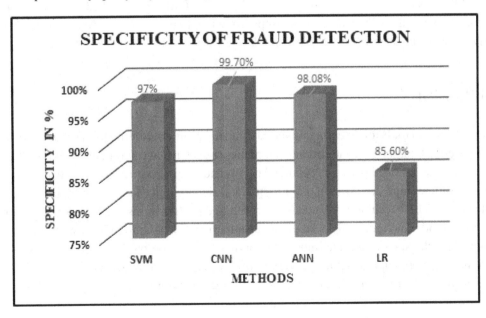

In Figure 9, a comparison of specificity among various machine learning techniques for online financial fraud detection. Specifically, the comparison includes SVM (Esenogho *et al*, 2022), CNN (Safari *et al*, 2022), LR (Hussein *et al*, 2021) and ANN (Abidi *et al*, 2021). Notably, the CNN achieves an impressive specificity of 99.70%, outperforming the other techniques.

Figure 10. Comparison of F1-score using different ML algorithms

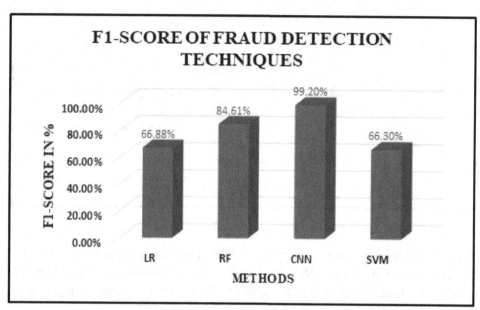

In Figure 10, a comparison of F1 score for online financial fraud detection using various techniques such as LR (Alfaiiz *et al*, 2022), RF (Ilebari *et al*, 2022), SVM (Almazroi *et al*, 2023) and CNN (Alshingiti *et al*, 2023) reveals that CNN achieves an impressive F1-score of 99.2%. This suggests that CNN is particularly effective in detecting credit card fraud.

VI. CONCLUSION

ML provides potent tools for detecting financial fraud in online environments. Through the analysis of extensive datasets, ML algorithm patterns and anomalies suggestive of fraudulent behaviour. The authors in Arjun et al, 2024 mentioned that strict financial norms and standards are followed by machine learning approaches for online fraud detection in order to guarantee compliance and dependability in identifying fraudulent activity. These techniques make use of cutting-edge algorithms to evaluate transactional data, spot suspicious trends, and reduce risks all the while adhering to legal obligations on accountability and transparency. The chapter summarize important contributions made by different scholars in the field, shedding light on various approaches and methods employed in combating financial fraud. SVM, FPMA, LR, RF, ANN and CNN are among the commonly employed algorithms for this purpose. ML substantially decreases time and resources required for fraud detection compared to traditional manual verification methods. Nevertheless, it is crucial to continually update and terrain models with fresh data to uphold efficacy. This chapter primarily focused on the financial fraud detection using ML algorithm such as SVM, RF, LR, CNN; their performance of accuracy is analyzed and compared with each other. From the comparative analysis, it is concluded that CNN can achieve a higher accuracy of 99.81% (Balawai *et al*, 2023) that is superior to other ML algorithms. Moreover, the comparative analysis of specificity and F1-score of various ML techniques are presented. Both the comparisons shows that the CNN achieves a better specificity of 99.7% (Safari *et al*, 2022) and enhanced F1-score of 99.2% (Alshingiti *et al*, 2023). There are many datasets that are used for the detection of online financial fraud such as IEEE-CIS fraud detection dataset, CC fraud detection dataset, elliptic CC fraud detection dataset and eBay datasets. In the future, an improved technique can be employed to enhance the performance across various applications. The application of Recurrent Neural Networks with Long Short-Term Memory (RNN-LSTM) is used for the purpose of detecting the fraudulent activities which is the primary goal. It is a successful method to address the issues suited with the datasets imbalance which leads to the correct detection accuracy. RNN-LSTM is able capture the temporal patterns of the transaction of the data. Moreover, plans include combining additional neural network algorithms to further strengthen online fraud detection capabilities, resulting in a more robust and effective system for safeguarding financial transactions.

REFERENCES

Abidi, W. U. H., Daoud, M. S., Ihnaini, B., Khan, M. A., Alyas, T., Fatima, A., & Ahmad, M. (2021). Real-Time Shill Bidding Fraud Detection Empowered with Fussed ML. *IEEE Access : Practical Innovations, Open Solutions*, 9, 612–621. DOI: 10.1109/ACCESS.2021.3098628

Aburbeian, A. H. M., & Ashqar, H. I. (2023). Credit Card Fraud Detection Using Enhanced Random Forest Classifier for Imbalanced Data. *International Conference on Advances in Computing Research*, 605-616. DOI: 10.1007/978-3-031-33743-7_48

Al Balawi, S., & Aljohani, N. (2023). Credit Card Fraud Detection System Using Neural Networks. *The International Arab Journal of Information Technology*, 20(2), 234–241. DOI: 10.34028/iajit/20/2/10

Alfaiz, N.S, Fati, S.M (2022). Enhanced Credit Card Fraud Detection Model Using ML. *MDPI Journal - Electronics*, 11.

S. Alghamdi, T. Daim, S. Alzahrani (2024). Technology Assessment for Cybersecurity Organizational Readiness: Case of Airlines Sector and Electronic PaymenT. *IEEE Transactions on Engineering Management*, 71, 01-18.

Almazroi, A. A., & Ayub, N. (2023). Online Payment Fraud Detection Model Using ML Techniques. *IEEE Access : Practical Innovations, Open Solutions*, 11, 188–203. DOI: 10.1109/ACCESS.2023.3339226

Alshingiti, Z., Rabeah A., Jalal Al-Muhtadi, Qazi Emad Ul Haq, Kashif Saleem and Muhammad H. F (2023). A Deep Learning-based Phishing Detection System Using CNN, LSTM, and LSTM-CNN. *MDPI- Electronics*, 12.

Arjun, S., & Moparthi, N. R. (2024). Fraud Detection in Banking Data by Machine Learning Techniques. *Journal of Electrical Systems*, 20(2), 2773–2784. DOI: 10.52783/jes.2056

Asha, R. B., & Suresh Kumar, K. R. (2021). Credit Card Fraud Detection Using Artificial Neural Network. *Global Transitions Proceedings*, 2(1), 35–41. DOI: 10.1016/j.gltp.2021.01.006

Ashfaq, T. Khalid, R, Yahaya, A.S, Aslam, S, Azar, A.T, Alsafari, S. Hameed (2022). A Machine Learning and Blockchain Based Efficient Fraud Detection Mechanism. *MDPI Journal- Sensors*, 22.

M. N. Ashtiani and B. Raahemi (2022). Intelligent Fraud Detection in Financial Statements Using ML and Data Mining: A Systematic Literature Review. *IEEE Access*, 10, 04-25.

Bagchi, D., Mukerjee, A., & Pal, S. (2021). A One Step Further Approach to Fraud Detection. *Journal of Computing Science and Engineering : JCSE*, 2, 112–119.

Charizanos, G., Demirhan, H., & İçen, D. (2024). An Online Fuzzy Fraud Detection Framework for Credit Card Transactions. *Expert Systems with Applications*, 252, 124–127. DOI: 10.1016/j.eswa.2024.124127

Chauhan, N., & Tekta, P. (2020). Fraud Detection and Verification System for Online Transactions: A Brief Overview. *International Journal of Electronic Banking*, 2(4), 267–274. DOI: 10.1504/IJEBANK.2020.114762

Esenogho, E., Mienye, I. D., Swart, T. G., Aruleba, K., & Obaido, G. (2022). A Neural Network Ensemble with Feature Engineering for Improved Credit Card Fraud Detection. *IEEE Access : Practical Innovations, Open Solutions*, 10, 400–407. DOI: 10.1109/ACCESS.2022.3148298

Ghaleb, F. A., Saeed, F., Al-Sarem, M., Qasem, S. N., & Al-Hadhrami, T. (2023). Ensemble Synthesized Minority Oversampling Based Generative Adversarial Networks and Random Forest Algorithm for Credit Card Fraud Detection. *IEEE Access : Practical Innovations, Open Solutions*, 11, 694–710. DOI: 10.1109/ACCESS.2023.3306621

Guo, Lingfeng, Runze Song, Jiang Wu, Zeqiu Xu, and Fanyi Zhao (2024). Integrating a Machine Learning-Driven Fraud Detection System Based on a Risk Management Framework, 1.

Gupta, A., Lohani, M. C., & Manchanda, M. (2021). Financial Fraud Detection Using Naive Bayes Algorithm in Highly Imbalance Data Set. *Journal of Discrete Mathematical Sciences and Cryptography*, 24(5), 1559–1572. DOI: 10.1080/09720529.2021.1969733

Hasan, Iqbal, and S. A. Rizvi (2022). AI-driven fraud detection and mitigation in e-commerce transactions. *Proceedings of Data Analytics and Management: ICDAM*, 1.

Hashemi, S. K., Mirtaheri, S. L., & Greco, S. (2023). Fraud Detection in Banking Data by Machine Learning Techniques. *IEEE Access : Practical Innovations, Open Solutions*, 11, 3034–3043. DOI: 10.1109/ACCESS.2022.3232287

Hilal, W., Gadsden, S. A., & Yawney, J. (2022). Financial Fraud: A Review of Anomaly Detection Techniques and Recent Advances. *Expert Systems with Applications*, 193, 193. DOI: 10.1016/j.eswa.2021.116429

Hussein, Ameer S., Rihab S. K., Shaima M. Mohamed N., and Haider Salim A. (2021). Credit Card Fraud Detection Using Fuzzy Rough Nearest Neighbor and Sequential Minimal Optimization with Logistic Regression. *International Journal of Interactive Mobile Technologies*, 15.

Ileberi, E., Sun, Y., & Wang, Z. (2021). Performance Evaluation of ML Methods for CC Fraud Detection Using SMOTE and AdaBoost. *IEEE Access : Practical Innovations, Open Solutions*, 9, 86–94. DOI: 10.1109/ACCESS.2021.3134330

Ileberi, E., Sun, Y., & Wang, Z. (2022). A Machine Learning based Credit Card Fraud Detection using the GA algorithm for feature selection. *Journal of Big Data*, 9(1), 24. DOI: 10.1186/s40537-022-00573-8

Innan, N., Sawaika, A., Dhor, A., Dutta, S., Thota, S., Gokal, H., Patel, N., Khan, M. A.-Z., Theodonis, I., & Bennai, M. (2024). Financial Fraud Detection Using Quantum Graph Neural Networks. *Quantum Machine Intelligence*, 6(1), 7. DOI: 10.1007/s42484-024-00143-6

Iscan, C., Kumas, O., Akbulut, F. P., & Akbulut, A. (2023). Wallet-Based Transaction Fraud Prevention through LightGBM with the Focus on Minimizing False Alarms. *IEEE Access : Practical Innovations, Open Solutions*, 11, 65–74. DOI: 10.1109/ACCESS.2023.3321666

Jovanovic, S. Milos, Zivkovic, M, Tanaskovic, Bacanin (2022). Tuning ML Models Using a Group Search Firefly Algorithm for Credit Card Fraud Detection. *MDPI Journal- Mathematics*, 10.

Karthika, Jegadeesan, Senthilselvi, Ayothi (2023). Smart Credit Card Fraud Detection System based on Dilated Convolutional Neural Network with Sampling Technique. *Multimedia Tools Applications*, 82, 01-18.

Khalid, A. Rehman, N. Owoh, Omair U., Moses A., Jude O., John A. (2024). Enhancing Credit Card Fraud Detection: An Ensemble Machine Learning Approach. *Big Data and Cognitive Computing*, 8.

Khedmati, Mohamad, Masoud Erfani, Mohammad GhasemiGol (2020). Applying Support Vector Data Description for Fraud Detection. *ArXiv Journal*, 618.

Liu, Aiming, Kun Chen, Quan Liu, Qingsong Ai, Yi Xie, Anqi Chen (2017). Feature Selection for Motor Imagery EEG Classification based on Firefly Algorithm and Learning Automata. *MDPI Journal: Sensors*, 17.

Lokanan, M. E. (2024). Predicting Money Laundering Using Machine Learning and Artificial Neural Networks Algorithms in Banks. *Journal of Applied Security Research*, 19(1), 20–44. DOI: 10.1080/19361610.2022.2114744

Manjeevan, S., & Chee Peng, C. P. (2024). An intelligent payment card fraud detection system. *Annals of Operations Research*, 334(1-3), 445–467. DOI: 10.1007/s10479-021-04149-2

Megdad, Mosa MM, Samy S. Abu-Naser and Bassem S. Abu-Nasser (2022). Fraudulent Financial Transactions Detection Using ML. *International Journal of Academic Information Systems Research*, 6.

Mehbodniya, A., Alam, I., Pande, S., Neware, R., Rane, K. P., Shabaz, M., & Madhavan, M. V. (2021). Financial fraud detection in healthcare using ML and deep learning techniques. *Security and Communication Networks*, 2021, 1–8. DOI: 10.1155/2021/9293877

Mosa, D. T., Sorour, S. E., Abohany, A. A., & Maghraby, F. A. (2024). CCFD: Efficient Credit Card Fraud Detection Using Meta-Heuristic Techniques and Machine Learning Algorithms. *Mathematics*, 12(14), 2250. DOI: 10.3390/math12142250

Nakra, V., Pandi, K. G. P., Paripati, L., Choppadandi, A., & Chanchela, P. (2024). Leveraging Machine Learning Algorithms for Real-Time Fraud Detection in Digital Payment Systems. *International Journal of Multidisciplinary Innovation and Research Methodology*, 3, 165–175.

Nama, F. A., & Obaid, A. J. (2024). Financial Fraud Identification Using Deep Learning Techniques. *Al-Salam Journal for Engineering and Technology*, 3(1), 141–147. DOI: 10.55145/ajest.2024.03.01.012

Olushola, A., & Mart, J. (2024). Fraud Detection Using Machine Learning. *ScienceOpenPreprints*.

Osegi, E. N, E. F. Jumbo (2021). Comparative Analysis of Credit Card Fraud Detection in Simulated Annealing Trained Artificial Neural Network and Hierarchical Temporal Memory. *ML with Applications*, 6.

Poongodi, K., & Kumar, D. (2021). Support Vector Machine with Information Gain Based Classification for Credit Card Fraud Detection System. *The International Arab Journal of Information Technology*, 18, 199–207.

Reddy, Dhoma H, and N. Sirisha (2022). An Analysis of the Supervised Learning Approach for Online Fraud Detection. *Computational Intelligence and Machine Learning*, 3.

Riany, M., Sukmadilaga, C., & Yunita, D. (2021). Detecting Fraudulent Financial Reporting Using Artificial Neural Network. *Journal of Accounting Auditing and Business*, 4(2), 60–69. DOI: 10.24198/jaab.v4i2.34914

Rout and Minakhi (2021). Analysis and Comparison of Credit Card Fraud Detection Using ML. *Artificial Intelligence and ML in Business Management*, 81-93.

Safari, E., & Peykari, M. (2022). Improving the Multilayer Perceptron Neural Network using Teaching-Learning Optimization Algorithm in Detecting Credit Card Fraud. *Journal of Industrial and Systems Engineering*, 2, 159–171.

Sherly, K. K., & Nedunchezhian, R. (2015). A Improved Incremental and Interactive Frequent Pattern Mining Techniques for Market Based Analysis And Fraud Detection in Distributed And Parallel Systems. *Indian Journal of Science and Technology*, ●●●, 8.

Singh, A., Anurag, J., & Biable, S. E. (2022). Financial Fraud Detection Approach based on Firefly Optimization Algorithm and Support Vector Machine. *Applied Computational Intelligence and Soft Computing*, 2022, 1–10. DOI: 10.1155/2022/1468015

Sorour, S. E., AlBarrak, K. M., Abohany, A. A., & Amr, A. (2024). Abd El-Mageed. Credit Card Fraud Detection Using the Brown Bear Optimization Algorithm. *Alexandria Engineering Journal*, 104, 171–192. DOI: 10.1016/j.aej.2024.06.040

Sulaiman, S. S., Nadher, I., & Hameed, S. M. (2024). Credit Card Fraud Detection Using Improved Deep Learning Models. *Computers, Materials & Continua*, 78(1), 1049–1069. DOI: 10.32604/cmc.2023.046051

Taha, A. A., & Malebary, S. J. (2020). An Intelligent Approach to CC Fraud Detection Using an Optimized Light Gradient Boosting Machine. *IEEE Access : Practical Innovations, Open Solutions*, 8, 25579–25587. DOI: 10.1109/ACCESS.2020.2971354

Tang, S., Jin, L., & Cheng, F. (2021). Fraud Detection in Online Product Review Systems via Heterogeneous Graph Transformer. *IEEE Access : Practical Innovations, Open Solutions*, 9, 64–73. DOI: 10.1109/ACCESS.2021.3084924

Trivedi, N. K., Simaiya, S., Lilhore, U. K., & Sharma, S. K. (2020). An efficient credit card fraud detection model based on machine learning methods. *International Journal of Advanced Science and Technology*, 29, 14–24.

Udayakumar, R., Joshi, A., Boomiga, S. S., & Sugumar, R. (2023). Deep Fraud Net: A Deep Learning Approach for Cyber Security and Financial Fraud Detection and Classification. *Journal of Internet Services and Information Security*, 13, 138–157. DOI: 10.58346/JISIS.2023.I4.010

Vanini, P., & Sebastiano, R. (2023). Online Payment Fraud: From Anomaly Detection to Risk Management. *Financial Innovation*, 9(1), 9. DOI: 10.1186/s40854-023-00470-w

Vengatesan, K., Kumar, A., Yuvraj, S., Kumar, V., & Sabnis, S. (2020). Credit Card Fraud Detection Using Data Analytic Techniques. *Advances in Mathematics: Scientific Journal*, 9, 1185–1196.

Vipin Kumar Choudhary, Divya. (2017). Credit Card Fraud detection using Frequent pattern mining using FP-Modified Tree and Apriori Growth. *International Journal of Advanced Technology and Innovative Research*, 9, 2370–2373.

Wahid, A., Msahli, M., Bifet, A., & Memmi, G.Wahid & Abdul. (2024). NFA: A Neural Factorization Autoencoder based Online Telephony Fraud Detection. *Digital Communications and Networks*, 10(1), 158–167. DOI: 10.1016/j.dcan.2023.03.002

Wang, C., & Changqi, W. (2020). LAW: Learning Automatic Windows for Online Payment Fraud Detection. *IEEE Transactions on Dependable and Secure Computing*, 18, 22–35. DOI: 10.1109/TDSC.2020.3037784

Wang, D., & Zhu, H. (2022). Representing Fine-Grained Co-Occurrences for Behavior-Based Fraud Detection in Online Payment Services. *IEEE Transactions on Dependable and Secure Computing*, 19(1), 301–315. DOI: 10.1109/TDSC.2020.2991872

Warghade, S., Desai, S., & Patil, V. (2020). Credit card fraud detection from imbalanced dataset using machine learning algorithm. *International Journal of Computer Trends and Technology*, 68(3), 22–28. DOI: 10.14445/22312803/IJCTT-V68I3P105

Xu, T. (2024). Fraud Detection in Credit Risk Assessment Using Supervised Learning Algorithms. *Computer Life*, 12(2), 30–36. DOI: 10.54097/qw9j1892

Zhang, D., Bhandari, B., & Black, D. (2020). Credit Card Fraud Detection Using Weighted Support Vector Machine. *Applied Mathematics*, 11(12), 1275–1291. DOI: 10.4236/am.2020.1112087

Zhang, Z., Chen, L., Liu, Q., & Wang, P. (2020). A Fraud Detection Method for Low-Frequency Transaction. *IEEE Access : Practical Innovations, Open Solutions*, 8, 210–220. DOI: 10.1109/ACCESS.2020.2970614

Zhou, H., Sun, G., Fu, S., Wang, L., Hu, J., & Gao, Y. (2021). Internet Financial Fraud Detection Based on a Distributed Big Data Approach With Node2ve. *IEEE Access : Practical Innovations, Open Solutions*, 9, 78–86.

Chapter 2
Abusive Language in Twitter's Tweets by Sentimental Analysis

Ashwini S. Diwakar
Surana College, Bangalore, India

B. Shravani
Surana College, Bangalore, India

H. Asha
Surana College, Bangalore, India

ABSTRACT

Communication and information sharing between individuals have changed dramatically as a result of the internet and social media platforms combined with explosive growth. Due to the development and expansion of online technology, a vast amount of data is generated as well as being available on the web for internet users. There has been a noticeable rise in the usage of foul language in user comments. Furthermore, Twitter is a well-known medium where users are allowed to voice any opinion. The proliferation of antisocial activities, including hate speech, cyberbullying, and the use of harsh language, is a direct result of overuse of social media. The prevalence of hostile comments on social media platforms calls for the development of practical and efficient solutions. Consequently, numerous intriguing algorithms have been developed to identify these kinds of languages. The objective of this chapter is to introduce strategies, equations, and techniques that could be used to evaluate Twitter tweets to identify instances of abusive language.

DOI: 10.4018/979-8-3693-3884-1.ch002

1. INTRODUCTION

People may now connect more than ever before, thanks to the internet, which has become a need in our everyday lives. The widespread availability of the internet has significantly transformed our way of life. We have instant access to the Internet, social media conversations and information exchange.

On social networking platforms, people may easily express their opinions, sentiments, and criticism in the form of sentimental feelings. Through postings and tweets on social media sites like Facebook, Twitter, Instagram, Snapchat, and so forth, they can express their thoughts. Depending on their level of mental stability, they voice their opinions and verbally abuse others in an attempt to cause mental harm.

Tweets and messages that are offensive are meant to irritate or offend someone, whether on purpose or accidentally. Insensitive material incites people to participate in wicked deeds against the law, hurts religious feelings, and incites aggression against others without justification. One well-known platform is social media, where everyone may freely share their opinions via text, voice messages, videos, emojis, pictures, and other media. In a split second, comments or tweets expressed on one social media site can quickly travel across others, going viral.

Swearing is the act of using language that is prohibited to communicate one's feelings to an audience. These terms are also occasionally referred to as foul language, dirty language, profanity, or vulgar vocabulary. (Jay, 1992, 1999). Cursing is not limited to face-to-face contacts; it also occurs in multilingual online discussions on social media and in online forums such as Twitter, where users frequently write spontaneously and in colloquial language. One of the most intriguing data sources for studies on swearing is regarded to be Twitter. When someone swears, they are expressing their emotions to the people who are listening to them through taboo language, also known as dirty language, swear words, offensive language, curse words, or vulgar language. (Pamungkas et al., 2023).

The problem of people posting inappropriate content online has become more delicate in recent years. But when the content is shared on public platforms, the sheer force of digital media and its potential to reach people of all ages will surely bring these problems to the notice of researchers and aid in their search for solutions. As evidenced by several well-known research tasks, the volume of user-generated content on public media platforms is growing, underscoring the significance of invective speech identification. Identifying and removing abusive content from social media is still a tedious and time-consuming task, therefore developing automatic detection techniques would be excellent. Machine learning can be used to automatically classify posts on social media that are harmful. When employing a machine learning strategy, hate speech can be detected in user comments from two domains that perform better than a cutting-edge deep learning method. Twitter uses large-scale machine learning and artificial intelligence (AI) for sentiment analysis, image classification, fake account detection, and other purposes. Human sentiment can be analysed by utilizing a variety of approaches, instruments, and strategies based on reviews, postings, tweets, and comments.

2. ROLE OF AI AND ML IN SENTIMENT ANALYSIS

Significant progress has been achieved by artificial intelligence and machine learning in both personal and professional domains of daily life. These days, almost anything can be found and verified online, including feelings and emotions of all types. Rapid digitization has demonstrated its extraordinary influence and worldwide presence. The modern era means of expressing thoughts are social media posts, tweets, blogs, online forums, review portals, and many others. All of them add to the billions of user-generated contents that currently drives actual commerce and other parts of the situation.

Every social media platform maintains a certain level of transparency, increasing the likelihood of persuading other users. However, millions of different viewpoints on the same topic can exist on the same site. Because the tweets that are expressed may contain precise information or even a general perspective, the research community is more interested in undertaking additional research. This marked the inception of the sentiment analysis (or opinion mining) principle. Sentiment analysis allows sentimental patterns to be classified in diverse instances, sentimental tweets to be accessed, and sentimental web data to be analysed.

The basic ideas needed to comprehend the significance and use of invective language in the sentimental analysis paradigm are presented in this chapter.

It adopts a methodical approach and offers a comprehensive discussion of different sentiment analysis levels, strategies, instruments, machine learning algorithms, and other aspects linked to creating an effective method of limiting and controlling the use of abusive language on public platforms like Twitter and other online community forums. This is as opposed to focusing on a certain area or listing the particular method in an unorganised manner.

The technique of determining the positive, neutral, or negative feeling of a piece of content or data is known as sentiment analysis, as was covered in the lines above. Opinion mining is a subset of data mining that involves the extraction and analysis of language to provide actionable information for business intelligence. The news, blogs, and internet groups provide a large portion of the data.

The practice of gleaning important information from random, unstructured language seen on a range of websites and online groups is known as sentiment analysis. Examples of this include social media chats and live blogging on sites like Instagram, Facebook, Twitter, and WhatsApp.

However, the benefits of AI sentiment analysis cannot be restricted to count 10. Added to these benefits, just considering an example where AI uses Facial Sentiment analysis that includes the state of art. Although Facial Expression Recognition (FER) is a laborious and complicated process, it is useful in many fields, including human-computer interaction, emotionally charged robots, and healthcare. Even with FER's advancements increasing its effectiveness, obtaining high precision remains difficult. The six most universal human emotions are fear, surprise, disgust, happiness, and sadness. (Keyur Patel, et al.,2020).

The Goal of Sentiment Analysis With ML

Social media platforms interact with users, provide a range of services, and gather data about their ideas and opinions. Sentiment analysis is a machine learning method that may distinguish between ideas that are successful or unsuccessful in text, complete texts, paragraphs, lines, or subsections.

On social networking sites like Facebook, Instagram, WhatsApp, and Twitter, the communication settings can occasionally be perplexing. It's important to express sensitive information about people's thoughts about any idea, concept, or policy.

Consider the following scenario: Customers usually check evaluations from previous customers before making any form of online purchase. Based on client sentiment, the company can determine the benefits and drawbacks of its product. In this case, the customer's review or rating of the product is what both buyers and sellers rely on. These opinions are beneficial to both parties. For the user, managing all these perspective on textual data is challenging.

Sentiment Classification

An automatic method for determining if a sentence conveys a popular, favourable, or negative attitude on an item is sentiment analysis. Various Sentiment Classification Levels:

A. **Document Level:** The entire deed is utilised to categorise simple information at the document level, separating it into classes based on productivity and inefficiency.
B. **Sentence Level:** Sentences are further classified into positive, negative, and common classes by the sentiment classification, which further classifies them as instinctive or objective at the sentence level.
C. **Aspect or Feature Level:** This kind of emotion classification addresses the issue of item feature extraction and identification from source data. Numerous machine learning techniques, such as Naive Bayes, Support-Vector Machine, and Maximum Entropy Classifier techniques, are utilised for sentimental analysis of large amounts of data. These techniques make it possible to use a lot of data strategically and effectively to aid in decision-making.

Methods of Machine Learning Based Sentiment Analysis

There are several methods for calculating the conflict analysis data. Machine learning is the most widely used and effective sentiment analysis technique is basic one.

Data Collection

Regardless of word count, data sets can be used for any kind of text categorization assignment. Word removal and case folding were the only treatment these data sets went through before being used for sentiment analysis.

Data Preprocessing

Preparing text data for feature vector construction and feature selection processing is the objective of this pre-processing step. A fundamental issue with computers is that they cannot process text data instantly. Numbers must also be understood in relation to textual data. Typically, term serve as the text's defining qualities. This gives the text representation a high dimension. To magnify the performance of categorization and processing efficiency, features must be filtered to eliminate noise and minimize dimensions.

Classification Algorithms for Sentiment Analysis

The Multinomial Naïve Bayes method and the K-Nearest Neighbour algorithm are two prominent and widely used classification algorithms that are very often used to direct the sentiment polarity of users' opinion based on provided opinion data like classification Algorithm for Support Vector Machines.

Evaluation Metrics

Evaluating the results of each algorithm using metrics such the confusion matrix, recall, efficiency, and F-Score measurement.

Figure 1. The sensitization analysis framework for awareness prediction.

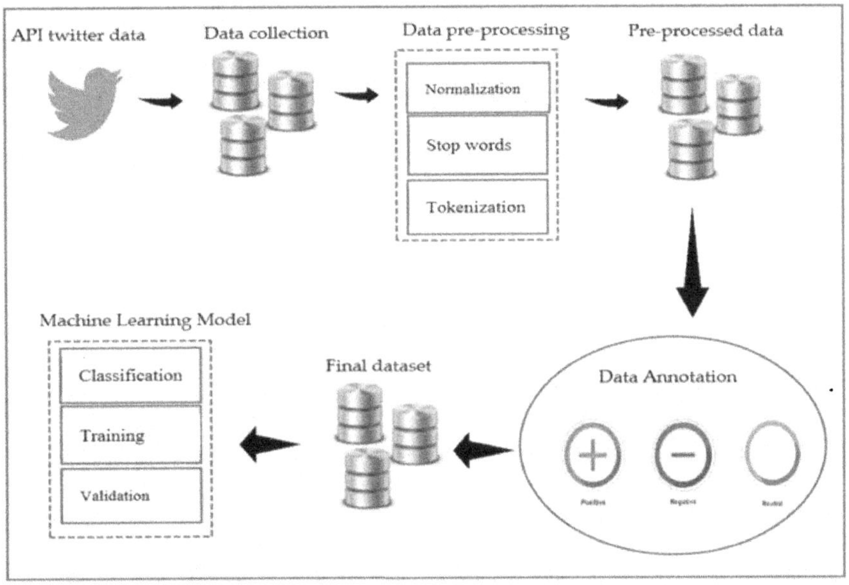

(Sumayh S. Aljameel et al.,2021)

Role of Sentiment Analysis Using AI

Artificial Intelligence is the buzzword of the modern world, permeating every aspect of human existence. Artificial intelligence (AI) is becoming a hot topic as more and more systems, particularly in the health care sector, are being automated. Public engagement with research and media representations can greatly influence future inventions due to their adaptability.

Scenario: In this context, we investigate the concept that public fear of artificial intelligence (AI) stems from bad news media coverage of AI, particularly the purported use of Terminator movie graphics. This idea is brought up as a possible roadblock to the public and media interactions that AI researchers and developers could have with the public. This feeling of peril is what we call the **"Terminator Syndrome"**. It can be interpreted as blind beliefs that could put a stop to the public conversation about artificial intelligence before it even begins.

This study used both quantitative and qualitative methodologies to evaluate the notion that news outlets and social media platforms like Facebook and Twitter have negative coverage of artificial intelligence. However, contrary to what some have asserted, it was found that the evidence does not reflect the purportedly negative sentiment on AI in the mainstream media. We conclude with a conversation about the current understanding of AI risk and what the critical social sciences can contribute to the development of ethical AI innovations in the domains of society, life science, and digital health. This relates to policies pertaining to innovation.

Figure 2. Benefits and AI sentimental analysis

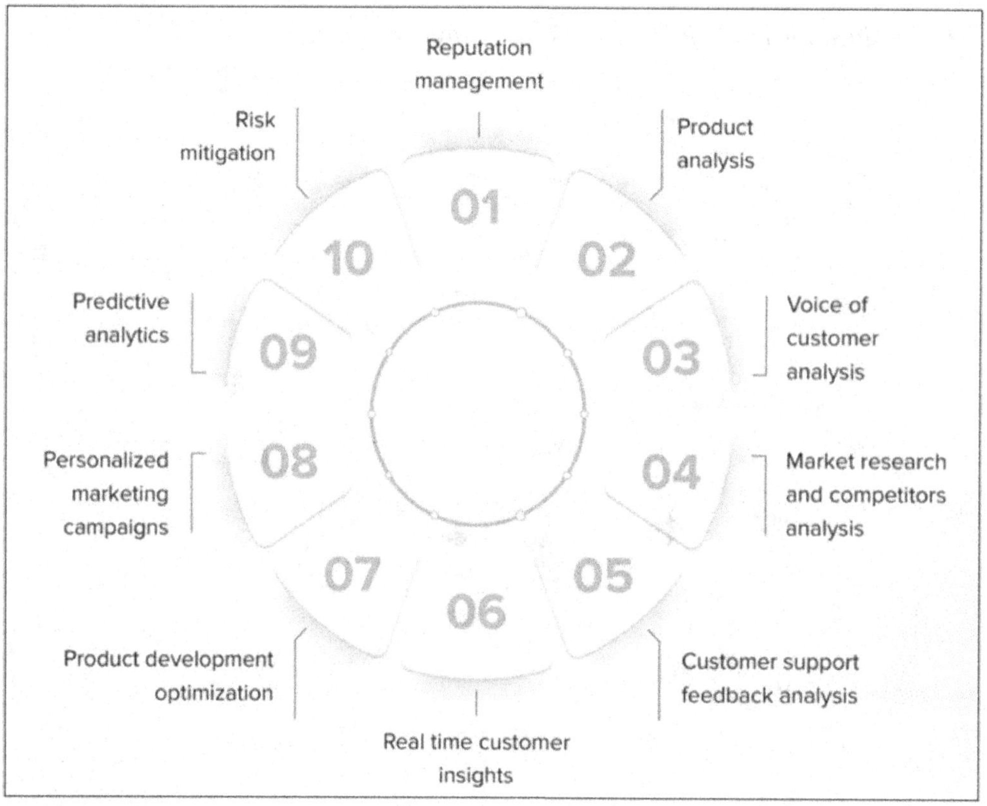

(Sudeep Srivastava,2023)

3. METHODOLOGY USED FOR SENTIMENTAL ANALYSIS

A text document can be converted into numerical data that a computer system can use using a natural language processing approach called Bag of Words (BOW). The most fundamental and popular approach uses a bag of words to first numerically represent a document, and then machine learning methods are used to process the data. We must first convert text format into numerical representation before carrying out any additional processing for any Natural Language Processing operation. Using machine learning algorithms on unprocessed text requires first converting text format into numerical representation. We call this process "text embedding."

To incorporate a text format, two methods are available: Word vectors and Document vectors. Individual words in the text can be represented as vectors using word vectors. The document is transformed into a series of word vectors throughout. Conversely, the entire document is in Document Vector.

The field of text categorization appeared a long time ago (Salton G. & McGill M G., 1983), however categorization based on sentiment perhaps first appeared in [(Das . S and Chen .M, 2001);(Morinaga S, Yamanishi .K, Tateishi. K, and Fukushima.,2012; (Pang.B, Lee.L, and Vaithyanathan.S, 2002); (Tong. R, 2001); (Turney.P.D, 2002); (Wiebe.J,2000.)] The standard approach to text categorization (Salton. G & McGill M G., 1983) has been the bag-of-words method (BOW). **This assortment of single words is sometimes referred to as a collection of unigrams.** Because unigrams are independent of one another, the occurrence of one in a text does not affect the appearance of any other unigram. Over the past three decades, other sophisticated algorithms have been created; yet the bag of words method remains the most often used due to its ease of use, readability, and excellent performance.

The three main methods that are frequently used in sentiment analysis are hybrid, machine learning, and lexicon-based approaches. Both the lexicon-based method and the machine learning-based approach use the bag-of-words in sentiment analysis. The classifiers in the machine learning supervised technique employ unigrams as features. The lexicon-based method gives a polarity score to each unigram that occurs in the lexicon; the total polarity score of the text is then determined by adding the polarities of all the unigrams. Recently, more advanced algorithms for sentiment analysis have been developed, considering not only the content of the message but also its origin, the writer's friends, the publication environment, and network structure. For example, how simultaneously classifying tweets, users, and attributes can improve the sentiment clustering quality for Twitter (Hu X., Tang L., Tang J., and Liu H., 2013) Presented a sociological method for sentiment analysis in noisy, short texts by utilising social connections

A. Data Pre-Processing

We only address the message's textual content in this chapter. We provide a methodical approach to both machine learning and lexicon-based classification. The next part discusses the data preparation step, or pre-processing, that is necessary for all three approaches i.e. lexicon-based, machine learning and hybrid-based approaches. We carry out the pre-processing stages prior to utilising sentiment analysis techniques. The following steps are often included in a pre-processing procedure.

Creation of Bag-of-Words or Tokenization

The input string from the raw data is broken down into tokens: comprising words and other elements for example URL links. **Tokenization is the process of breaking up a written document into smaller pieces known as tokens.** Tokens in this context can be words, characters, or sub words. Thus, there are three main categories of tokenization: word, character, and sub word (n-gram characters) tokenization.

Example: Consider the input string as **All the Best**

The most popular method for creating tokens is based on space. The tokenization of the text yields three tokens: **All-The-Best, assuming space as a delimiter.** Since every token is a word, word tokenization is exemplified by it.

Extraction on N-Grams

This method groups corresponding words into what are known as n-grams, which are sentences. The N-grams approach can reduce bias, but it may also make statistics more sparse. The quality of text classification has been demonstrated to increase with the inclusion of n-grams ([24]; [25]; [26]); nevertheless, there is no one-size-fits-all method for selecting n-gram sizes. Trigrams are groupings of three nearby words, and bigrams are collections of two nearby words in a text.

Lemmatization and Stemming

The process of stemming involves substituting words with their stems, or roots. When several words, such speak, speaker, and speaking, are mapped into one word, speak, and are counted collectively, the BOW's dimensionality is decreased. Applying stemming, however, requires caution since it can amplify bias.

Removal of Stop Words

Prepositions, articles and other words with a connecting role in a phrase are examples of stop words. Although there isn't a set list of stop words, some search engines use some of the most often used short function words, like "which", "on", "the", "is", and "at". Despite their frequent recurrence in the text, they can be eliminated because they don't change the sentence's overall meaning.

B. The Following are the Three Fundamental Approaches That are Commonly Applied in Sentiment Analysis

Figure 3. Sentimental analysis approaches

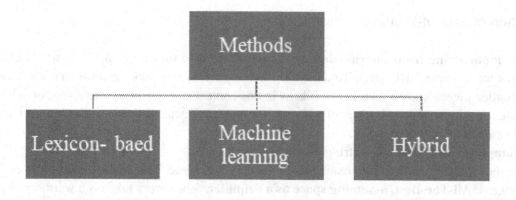

Lexicon-based -Lexicon is the most straightforward way to classify sentiment. Lexicons are collections of tokens, and each token represents a text's neutral, offensive, or non-offensive nature with a predefined score. This classifier uses a lexicon to match words in a sentence and decide which category to assign it to. There are two approaches used under the lexicon-based methods: **the Dictionary-Based** Approach and **the Corpus-Based Approach.**

Machine Learning- Sentiment classification could be done with approach available in machine learning. Sentiment analysis is the practice of determining and measuring the unseen sentiment of text or speech through the usage of text analysis, natural language processing, computational linguistics, and other techniques. In machine learning method labelled dataset is used where the polarity of a sentence is already mentioned. We extract the feature from that dataset, and that feature aids in the classification of the input sentence's unknown polarity. **Supervised and un-supervised learning are the two classification of machine learning techniques.**

Hybrid -The methods employed in rule-based and automatic sentiment analysis models are combined in a hybrid sentiment algorithm. This approach builds a more sophisticated and precise sentiment analysis model by fusing NLP and machine learning approaches.

Algorithms Used for Analysis

It is nearly hard to manually identify and filter offensive remarks from large online comment streams. For this, deep learning (DL) and conventional machine learning (ML) techniques incorporating natural language processing (NLP) have been extensively employed.

The three most popular machine learning techniques for identifying abusive language are ensemble learning (Pelle et al., 2018), word and character n-grams (Ptaszynski. et al. 2019; Park J.H. & Fung P., 2017) and vocabulary-based algorithms (Gitari et al., 2015; Chen. Y.et al.2012). A few research have used and compared deep learning (DL) models with machine learning (ML) models, such as bidirectional long short-term memory (BLSTM) (Ingi Sigurbergsson, G., Derczynski, L., 2019), recurrent neural networks (RNN), convolutional neural networks (CNN) (Park J.H. & Fung P., 2017; Lee et al., 2018), and long short-term memory (LSTM) (Badjatiya et al., 2019), in order to detect offensive language.

The sentiment underlying the comments and tweets can be found, examined, and predicted using a variety of algorithms. Naive Bayes, Logistic Regression, Support Vector Machines, Linear Regression, and Deep Learning are a few of the algorithms. These algorithms are trained using pre-labelled data and are utilised as a classification model. The following subsections briefly describe the ML algorithms used in this study.

Decision Tree Algorithm: The DT algorithm creates smaller subsets of a dataset in order to construct tree-structured classification or regression models. There are leaf nodes and decision nodes in this arrangement. A categorization or decision is represented by a leaf node, but a decision node has two or more branches (Wang & Witten, 1997).

Logistic Regression: The logistic function is used by the logistic regression algorithm (LR algorithm), a machine learning model, to determine the correlation between one dependent variable (the output variable) and one or more independent variables (input variables). LR uses probability to group observations into a specific set of classes. In order to establish the discriminatory value at which an instance will belong to one class or another, it defines a threshold value. Moreover, binary classification and binary output certainty prediction are two additional uses for the LR method (Dreiseitl & Ohno-Machado, 2002; Peng et al., 2002).

K-Nearest Neighbours Algorithm: KNN is a supervised instance-based classification technique that addresses regression and classification issues. The primary concept is that similar instances are presumed to be members of the same class. As a result, in order to classify a new test point, the KNN method finds its K closest neighbours and then classifies the test point according to the neighbour's most frequent class (Aha et al., 1991).

Naïve Bayes Algorithm: Based on the Bayes Theorem, Naive Bayes (NB) is a statistical supervised machine learning classification technique that identifies the class to which an instance is most likely to belong. Because it doesn't rely on the usage of rules or any other explicit description of the classifier, it is a simple and quick approach. NB makes the assumption that the existence of one feature in a class has no bearing on the existence of any other feature. As a result, it functions well with separate features (Domingos.P and M. Pazzani.M, 1997).

Random Forest Algorithm: The RF algorithm is made up of several decision trees that categorise data according to predetermined principles. Each decision tree in the RF represents a distinct feature subset that was chosen via replacement from the training data. The prevention of overfitting is a key benefit of the RF algorithm's unique structure (Safavian.S.R and Landgrebe.D,1991).

Support Vector Machine Algorithm: A supervised machine learning algorithm is the SVM algorithm. In order to more accurately identify the classes, SVM converts the input into higher dimensional spaces. To map the dataset into the higher spaces, it incorporates a kernel function (Boser.B.E, Guyon.I.M, and Vapnik.V.N.1992).

XGBoost Algorithm: A gradient boosting framework is used by the scalable decision-tree-based ensemble machine learning method XGBoost. It yields good outcomes in a variety of machine learning competitions. Apart from its scalability, XGBoost has several other benefits that set it apart from the other classifiers. Its capacity to handle sparse data, cope with missing values, and harness the power of parallel and distributed processing are just a few to highlight. Its usage of several CPU cores to run the model makes it faster than many other methods (Chen.T and Guestrin.C, 2016).

Tools Used for Analysis

There are several tools available to predict the emotions behind the words posted on social media. With the support of these tools, reviews, comments, and tweets that contain pre-defined keywords will be gathered, monitored, and examined in public. The emotions conveyed in the messages will also be examined. Several of the widely used analytical instruments Talkwalker, MeaningCloud, **Social searcher, Rosette**, Enginuity Analytics, Free Sentiment Analyzer, & many more.

MeaningCloud: Use MeaningCloud's Sentiment Analysis API to do multilingual sentiment analysis. This web application performs sentiment analysis based on aspects to determine if a given topic is discussed in a good, negative, or neutral light. We can also define a dictionary to contain any specialised terms you may need in your line of work. Identifying opinion from fact, detecting sentiment inside a text's sentences, and detecting global sentiment—a broad assessment of the customer's expressions in a given text-are some of MeaningCloud's strongest features.

Talkwalker: Talkwalker offers a social media search engine called Quick Search. With this application, you can automatically analyse social media interactions to gather insights from all of your brand mentions. It's helpful for determining new trends, obtaining content ideas, and assessing marketing results. In 25 languages, Quick Search can analyse the emotion of your social media mentions! By keeping an eye on every issue as it arises, real-time social listening enables you to gain insight into customer sentiment towards your product or brand.

Social Searcher: Social searcher keeps track of usernames, hashtags, and keywords on all social media networks. Numerous social data, such as audience insights, trending hashtags, and social influencers, will be sent to you. A sentiment analysis tool that offers the general sentiment of social media data on all platforms as well as a breakdown of well-liked posts that have been classified as positive or negative is included in the free edition.

Rosette: The sentiment analysis tool provided by Rosette is easy to use. The API allows you to do more in-depth analysis as well as sentiment analysis on social media data. For instance, the attitude that consumers convey when they bring up a particular brand, business, or individual. By using morphological analysis and lemmatization—the grouping of inflected word forms so they are not examined separately—Rosette is able to identify components of speech. You may teach Rosette's sentiment analysis engine to recognise up to 30 languages if your business is international.

4. TWITTER USING SENTIMENT ANALYSIS

There are various techniques where twitter deals with different sentiment analysis techniques such as Twitter sentiment analysis using NLP, Multinomial Naive Bayes and Logistic Regression.

a) **Twitter Sentiment Analysis Using Natural Language Processing Techniques:**

For Opinion mining, Suryawanshi et al., (2020) [21] says that a large quantity of data is needed from people thoughts on Twitter. In natural language processing, several approaches help retrieve tweets from Twitter directly (Krishna. Prasad.K.2020).

The tweets are unstructured. To produce structured data for opinion mining, tweets must be processed and cleaned. Prior to the analysis, any links, hashtags, capitalized terms, repeated phrases, short-form terms, spelling mistakes, special symbols, Twitter characters, and any leftover material are removed from the data. Extracting and converting text to a data frame, eliminating text URLs, getting rid of stop words like (the, a,), usernames, profiles, deleting numbers, unneeded spaces, erasing dots, and translating Latin to ASCII Emojis are all examples of data cleaning.

Text from tweets is removed as part of the data removal procedure. The resultant part contains only the text of tweets after processing and cleaning. A tool called **Vader lexicon tool** makes the word for tweets is one by one and provides the word meaning from WordNet. This growing value of words is measured and marked as a tweet sentiment score. This helps in classifying every tweet as positive, normal, and negative by using a machine learning classification.

SOME INTERSTING FACTS WITH RESPECT TO NATURAL LANGUAGE PROCESSING TECHINQUES:

Twitter Tweets With NLP Techniques- With Arabic Language

This is one of the interesting facts where the sentiment analysis of Arabic tweets was conducted by applying Naïve Bayes algorithm of Machine leaning technique, to run Arabic sentiment analysis of tweets. This was tried through a Python library, i.e., Natural Language Toolkit (NLTK). They avoided laborious work by using a labelled dataset of Arabic tweets in which its sentiment labels are based on emoji dictionaries. The dataset was split into 50% positive and 50% negative. The applied preprocessing techniques were stemming, normalization, tokenization, and stop words removal.

Behdenna et al. [21] used Arabic sentiment analysis to identify an opinion expressed in Arabic tweets. They collected 500 tweets and manually tagged them. First, tweets were extracted and tokenized into words and converted from text into Attribute-Relation File Format (ARFF) to be used by Weka tool 3. Second, 10-fold cross-validation method was used to train SVM and NB classifiers. The achieved results scored 82.1% for precision, and 81.4% for recall with the NB classifier. SVM scored the highest precision and recall at 86%.

Thus, sentiment analysis is proven to be a valuable source of information mining, especially for situations related to the need of analysing a large amount of data related to the public, such as studying public behaviour towards the COVID-19 pandemic, and its effect on public life. Moreover, it can be concluded that the three machine learning classifiers: SVM, NB, and KNN, are widely used in this field due to their high accuracy. (Sumayh S. Aljameel et al.,2021)

b) Twitter sentiment analysis using Multinomial Naive Bayes and Logistic Regression:

Some of the challenges of Sentiment analyses on Twitter are mentioned below:

(i) Some tweets are easily recognizable in informal languages, and some brief words barely hint at emotion.

(ii) A lot of hashtags, URLs, acronyms, emoticons, and hashtags are utilized on Twitter.

Some of the ideas like "tweets before delivery," "extraction techniques," and "table design" make use of the accuracy of different machine learning algorithms. Using the train data on the test results, machine learning techniques are used to exercise the algorithms, which include the logistic regression algorithm and Multinomial Naive Bay.

Real Time Scenario: The airline sentiment data set and IMDB analysis datasets are the data sets considered by the author. All types attain the good results in machine learning when practicing the Count Vectorizer functionality. The author observes that the test set results from the Logistic Regression with Count Vectorizer features (Krishna . Prasad .K.2020)

Twitter Sentiment Classification Using Machine Learning Techniques

There are various Machine learning methods applied to Tweet classification such as the Multilayer Propon (MLP), Naïve Bayes, Fuzzy Classification, Decision Tree, and Support Vector Machines (SVM.). These methods aid in the examination of different component vectors with a doled-out class, allowing the connection dependence between each part and the assessment to be identified. In the Twitter dataset, performance metrics like alertness, duration, accuracy, and F calculation are examined where these methods are assessed.

Till now, we clarified regarding the various techniques and ML methods that plays an important role in sentimental analysis especially in TWITTER TWEETS.

Considering a Specific Topic in Twitter Tweets

Let's take an example of COVID-19 tweets from twitter where the vast amounts of data with great potential was used to analyse and extract information that give companies a competitive advantage for this business. In this case, Twitter served as a good source which obtained.

unstructured data from the tweets. Given the volume of feelings and variety of data variables accessible in this dataset, sentiment analysis will be useful in understanding insights into improving business intelligence and operations.

Considering Another Real Time Scenario

"Sentiment Analysis of COVID-19 Epidemic Using Machine Learning Algorithms on Twitter": Sudheer Kumar Singh, Dr. Prabhat Verma Dr. Pankaj Kumar (2020) analysed the tweets to know the sentiments of people during the pandemic. The tweets involve the Challenges faced by people and the sentiments and are predicted as positive, negative and neutral. These sentimental analysis helps us to protect the people from the disease(Saai Mahesh Srinivasan, Preksha Shah and Snehitha Sai Surendra,2021).

The tweets, which can be classified as positive, negative, or neutral, talk about the difficulties and emotions that people are facing. These poignant analyses help keep individuals healthy.

Optimizing Machine Learning Programming Algorithms for Sentiment Analysis in Social Media

As social networking sites like Facebook, Instagram, WhatsApp, and Twitter are taking the world of communication by storm, it is becoming increasingly important for the records that reside on these platforms to share pertinent information about people's opinions, attitudes, and convictions regarding any kind of product, advice, or even plans.

During Twitter data assessment, Numerous preprocessing approaches to text messages have been tested and compared and the preprocessing of tweets has an outstanding responsibility to play. The use of Twitter has sparked even more research work to understand the emotions using Twitter records. that the components of Twitter records provide helpful knowledge about any subject under discussion and impart people's opinion over those subject matters.

Clustering, sorting, regression, and rule extraction are a few common groups of artificial intelligence problems. [36] [REF 5]

5. USAGE OF MACHINE LEARNING IN TWITTER

Machine learning is mainly used to find the relevant topics and hashtags in twitter with the usage of various algorithms that helps in the study of user behaviour and determine what topics and hashtags are popular among certain people. As we have discussed in earlier topics, Machine learning and AI also helps in detection of fake accounts, image classification and more.

Classifying of Twitter Users - Using Machine Learning

User classification: The task is to gather the values of user attributes such as political orientation, ethnicity etc automatically by leveraging observable information from the user's Twitter feed which is classified into 3 classes like:

- The user behaviour
- The network structure
- The linguistic content

Purpose of the User Classification Model

1. To offer a broad evaluation of the relative importance, resilience, and capacity for generalization of features for the purpose of user classification.
2. To investigate the usefulness of linguistic data in user classification.

ML framework for user classification. The set of features we explore below is used in conjunction with a supervised machine learning framework providing models for specific user classification tasks. As a learning algorithm, we use Gradient Boosted Decision Trees - GBDT (Fried- man 2001) (any other algorithm could be adopted), which consists of an ensemble of decision trees, fitted in a forward stepwise manner to current residuals. Friedman (2001) shows that GDBT competes with state-of-the-art machine learning algorithms such as SVM (Friedman 2006) with much smaller resulting models and faster decoding time. In the following, we describe our feature classes in more detail. [REF 6]

A General Model for User Profiling

- Profile Features: "Who you are":

Most of the social media sites including Twitter will have the public access to some default profile information such as the username, the location, and a short introduction of any user account holder. Twitter also provides access to other basic user information, such as the number of a user's friends, followers and tweets, also the user's gender and ethnicity. There will be restrictions for some attributes like age and for documents, photos and other display which comes under the visibility choice of the user.

Around 15,000 random users were asked a pool of editors to identify the ethnicity and gender of the user based on only the avatar picture: less than 50% of the pictures were correlated with a clear ethnicity while 57% were correlated with a specific gender. We found that pictures can often be misleading: in 20% of the cases, the editors verified that the picture was not of the account owner, but of a celebrity or of another person (Pennacchiotti, M., & Popescu, A.-M. 2021).

Thus, the profile fields can be a useful tool for bootstrapping training data, the statistics provided above indicate that there is insufficient high-quality data in them to be directly applied to user classification.

- Tweeting Behaviour: "How you tweet":

Tweeting behaviour is characterized by a set of statistics capturing the way the user interacts with the micro-blogging services. It gives the information such as the average number of messages per day, number of tweets posted, number of replies, number of chats, replies through images and if images, checking for the censored images, sarcasm in the image or insulting images or sometimes might be the positive images. Adding to this, emojis or emoticons also plays a major role in finding out the Tweeting behaviour – "how you tweet".

- Linguistic Content: "What you tweet":

The user's lexical usage and the primary subjects of interest are summarized in linguistic content information. Basic language data can be used to categorize individuals across a variety of platforms, including formal documents, blogs, spoken conversation transcripts, and search sessions.

Prototypical words (LING - WORD) – here, the classes can be described by prototypical words or 'proto words' which means the phrases that indicate the general interests of members of that class as well as typical lexical expressions for members of that class.

Prototypical hashtags (LING - HASH) - Twitter users generally use hashtags i.e. sequences of characters prefixed by '#' to denote the topic of their tweet. hashtags are also used to facilitate the retrieval and surfacing of information on a particular topic. We propose that, if students in a class share interests, statistics on hashtag usage can be utilized to identify the most popular subjects among them.

- Social Network: "Who you tweet":

SOC – FRIE - "Friend" accounts: Automatically, Democrats are more likely to follow the accounts of Democratic politicians. Here the twitter searches for the highlighting words like 'FRIENDS' where a basic mechanism employed to bootstrap proto words. In order to establish a collection of class-specific archetypal "friend" accounts F, one might examine the social network of the training set's users. Percentage of all Twitter accounts followed by users which are part of F for each prototypical "friend" account, a Boolean feature is set to 1 if the user follows the account and set to 0 otherwise.

Twitter Spam Account Detection Using Machine Learning

When developing a model for detecting spam accounts, the idea of machine learning is modified. The training and testing phases make up the two fundamental components of a machine learning system. The framework of Machine Learning based Spam Account Detection is given in the below diagram:

Figure 4. A spam account detection framework based on machine learning

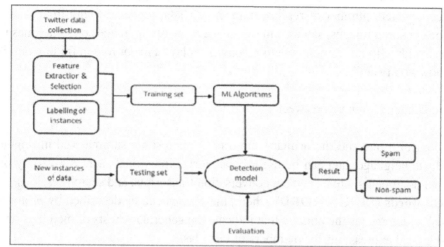

(Shivangi Gheewala and Rakesh Patel.2018)

- The very first step is gathering Twitter data. To gather data, either use publicly available sources or crawl the Twitter streaming API.
- The next step is extraction of features from dataset. Various type of features such as account/user-based feature, content-based feature that falls under a similar type, graph-based feature which is grouped uniquely and embedding URL based feature under separate group, can be used in spam account detection. Features that show more effectiveness in yielding correct result are selected for spam account detection.
- At this point, the small collection of samples is classified as spam or non-spam for training purposes. Spam filtering services or manual labelling are also used. Spam filtering systems identify as spam those instances that are labelled as non-spam and enable those that are labelled as spam that are blocked as effective spam.
- Finally, Machine Learning based detection models are trained with labelled samples and then tested to identify class of particular data instance. Finally, detection models are evaluated with evaluation parameters like accuracy, detection rate, true positive, false negative, recall, precision, etc.

6. QUICK LOOK INTERNAL VIEW OF MACHINE LEARNING METHODS OF TWITTER

In the Twitter Social Network, if we consider the **TRENDS**, then we must consider the Predicting Trends in the Twitter world.

Twitter tries to assist users in learning about what is trending right now because it is natural for members of a social network to be curious about what is being discussed currently. For this, Twitter periodically declares a set of Trending Topics by identifying the most used keywords or phrases that are being most discussed by users in Twitter at a certain point of time.

CONSIDER A SCENARIO: For the recent IPL Matches, the keyword (hashtag) #RCB was a trending topic on the days whenever the match will be between RCB vs any of the IPL teams.

Twitter uses its own algorithm to determine which subjects' trend, and this formula isn't made public to thwart spammers and other intruders. However, it is understood that, to decide whether a topic is trending, Twitter considers variables such as the topic's "freshness" in addition to its overall popularity. The ability to make this prediction accurately will have important impact on several aspects of how social systems are used nowadays.

The Challenges of Predicting Popularity of Information in Twitter

One of the main Challenges if **Supremely dynamic and unstructured nature of the data** posted in social media. For example, in a very short period, a new keyword can become popular on Twitter. Due to these difficulties, the research community on social media analysis has focused a great deal of emphasis on the difficulty of predicting what topic will trend or become popular shortly.

Recollecting Important Terminologies in Twitter Media

Tweet: A tweet can also be called as microblog. It is a message or status update posted by a user. Tweets can contain specific keywords, hashtags, URLs, and other content, but they are limited to 140 characters.

Hashtags: You can use a hashtag to draw attention to specific terms in a tweet. To indicate that a term is a hashtag, it needs to be preceded with a # symbol. Hashtags are ideally used to indicate topics that are important now.

Trends: A term or hashtag that is trending on Twitter at a specific period may show up in the list of Trending Topics, which are the subjects that people are talking about the most at that moment. Twitter declares a set of trending topics periodically – may be every day which allows users an easy way to follow tweets on these popular topics.

Dataset: Twitter is an online social network that offers an API5 for gathering various types of data, including as user profiles, tweet streams that are broadcast on the platform, and more.

With the Reference of the paper REF – 12, Twitter provides a 1% random sample of all tweets posted in the Twitter website world-wide. The team designed a Web-based crawler to collect the 1% Twitter random sample, and collected the sample during a particular day, and the first six hours of the next day.

That is referred to as 2 days – Day 1 and Day 2 respectively. Table 1 summarizes the statistics of the dataset collected over the two days.

1% of the Twitter stream is equal to the millions of tweets per day.

Table 1. Statistics of the data set, i.e., the 1% random sample of tweets provided by Twitter, crawled over a particular day (Day 1) and the first six hours of the next day (Day 2).

DAY	#Tweets	#Users	#Hashtags	#Trends
Day 1	40,51,506	31,45,957	2,37,100	67
Day 2 (first 6 hours)	10,87,149	9,36,169	74,203	67

Table 1 displays the quantity of tweets gathered daily as well as the number of unique users who posted the tweets gathered daily and the quantity of hashtags used in these tweets. Additionally, the team has used the Twitter API to collect the set of trending topics (hashtags) on those two days, i.e., the set of keywords which Twitter (Anubrata Das.et al.2015).

Thus, Social network services have become a viable source of information for users. In Twitter, information deemed important by the community propagates through retweets. Studying the characteristics of such popular messages is important for several tasks, such as breaking news detection, personalized message recommendation, viral marketing, and others. (Liangjie Hong, Ovidiu Dan and Brian D. Davison.2011).

7. TWITTER(X) ALGORITHM

The open-sourced recommendation algorithm on Twitter (X) is a synthesis of several algorithms that is always changing to improve the platform's user experience and engagement.

Through clicks, likes, replies, and other activities, it gathers user data and uses it to provide customized recommendations.

Twitter (X) just unveiled a redesigned home screen with two separate parts: "**Following**" mode and "**FOR YOU**" mode. Users who have voluntarily decided to follow accounts are shown content in the "Following" section whereas, Personalized recommendations are provided in the "For You" section based on the algorithm's observations.

Users can easily alternate between various modes, giving them the freedom to customize their feeds to suit their tastes. With this change, users have more control over their experience by being able to determine if the "For You" feed matches their interests and preferences.

Choosing of Tweets by the Algorithm

There are four main phases in the content recommendation pipeline that the Twitter (X) algorithm uses to function. candidate sourcing, ranking, combining, serving, and making use of filters, heuristics, and product attributes. These phases are essential for customizing content recommendations to users' tastes and actions.

Ranking Signals of Twitter (X) Algorithm

Twitter (X) uses an algorithm to make decisions based on a few signals that cover different facets of user interaction and engagement with content. It is crucial for users and creators to comprehend the subtleties of these signals to maximize their visibility and use Twitter (X)'s platform efficiently.

A Brief Analysis of Every Ranking:

- **Relevance:** The algorithm used by Twitter (X) ranks tweets according to how relevant they are to specific users, considering engagement history, topic alignment with user interests, and content similarity.

- **Recency:** Users may stay up to current with the newest material and conversations as they happen in real time thanks to this signal, which makes sure that recent tweets are prioritized higher in the timeline.

- **Variety:** The algorithm uses a variety of signals to maintain a varied and interesting timeline experience, making sure that users' varied interests and preferences are catered to with a variety of material types, subjects, and sources.

- **Engagement:** High-engagement tweets—likes, retweets, and replies—are elevated in the timeline to highlight content that is probably going to appeal to a larger audience.

- **Images and videos:** The algorithm gives more weight to tweets that include multimedia, including images and videos, because this type of material typically draws in more attention from users and generates higher levels of interaction than text-only tweets.

- **Replies and comments:** Each comment and reply plays a unique part in increasing a tweet's prominence and exposure on Twitter (X), adding to the platform's overall engagement and social interaction. Direct answers to a tweet are represented by comments, which show a high level of involvement and increase the message's exposure and relevancy. Retweets provide direct answers as well as more extensive discussions based on the tweet, demonstrating user engagement and involvement. The algorithm on Twitter (X) states that a reply is worth 27 times more than a like. Moreover, you can increase the engagement of your primary tweet by 150 times simply responding to a comment on it. While both metrics are important for assessing the impact of a tweet, replies are seen to be more significant for assessing the performance of a tweet.

- **Likes:** Likes are a sign of a tweet's popularity and favorable response. They affect your content's exposure on other people's timelines by acting as a signal of user interest and happiness. Higher like counts on tweets are frequently regarded as indicators of greater engagement, and the algorithm may give them priority.

- **Retweets**: Retweets show that people think the content is important or relevant enough to spread to their own followers, which increases the content's visibility. Because these indicators are worth twice as much as a like, the algorithm values them higher and considers them to be more influential. More retweets increase a tweet's visibility in users' timelines and search results, increasing its overall impact and influence on the site.

- **Quote Tweets**: Quote retweets function similarly to retweets in that users share your tweet along with their own content or remark. Quote retweets, on the other hand, indicate a user's wish to add their viewpoint or elaborate on the original tweet, which fosters a deeper degree of interaction. Compared to retweets, this extra layer of detail improves the discourse surrounding the tweet and increases its value in the eyes of Twitter (X)'s algorithm.

Added to this Twitter(X) Algorithm, Choosing of Tweets by The Algorithm can also be applied for the Emoji Tweets. Emoji tweets also defines the abusive language that can be classified by using the Naïve Bayes Algorithm. Emojis are visual symbols that take the form of images to express ideas. Because the images convey information, they allow text to be read and comprehended in accordance with its intended meaning. Each tweet on the Twitter timeline, which combines text and emojis, will be categorized into multiple groups. The recommended algorithm is Naïve Bayes. It calculates the probability of Emoji tweet to obtain the text classification with Emojis(Siti Sendari, et al .2020).

8. TWITTER'S RECOMMENDATION ALGORITHM

Twitter wants to provide you with the most up-to-date information about global events. To reduce the large volume of Tweets posted every day to a select few topmost Recommendation algorithm is required to get Tweets that eventually appears on individual device's timeline.

REFERENCES

Aha, D. W., Kibler, D., & Albert, M. K. (1991). Instance-based learning algorithms. *Machine Learning*, 6(1), 37–66. DOI: 10.1023/A:1022689900470

Badjatiya, P., Gupta, S., Gupta, M., & Varma, V. (2019). Deep learning for hate speech detection in tweets. *International World Wide Web Conference Committee*, 759–760.

Boser, B. E., Guyon, I. M., & Vapnik, V. N. (1992). A training algorithm for optimal margin classifiers. Proc. 5th Annu. Workshop Comput. Learn. Theory (COLT), 144–152. https://www.scirp.org/reference/ReferencesPapers?ReferenceID=1409252

Chen, T., & Guestrin, C. (2016). XGBoost: A scalable tree boosting system. Proc. 22nd ACM SIGKDD Int. Conf. Knowl. Discovery Data Mining, 785–794. https://arxiv.org/abs/1603.02754 DOI: 10.1145/2939672.2939785

Chen, Y., Zhou, Y., Zhu, S., & Xu, H. (2012). Detecting ofensive language in social media to protect adolescent online safety. *Proc. - 2012 ASE/IEEE Int. Conf. Privacy, Secur. Risk Trust 2012 ASE/IEEE Int.Conf. Soc. Comput. Soc.*, 71–80.

Das, A., Roy, M., Dutta, S., Ghosh, S., & Das, A. K. (2015). Predicting Trends in the Twitter Social Network: A Machine Learning Approach. https://www.researchgate.net/publication/294482813_Predicting_Trends_in_the_Twitter_Social_Network_A_Machine_Learning_Approach

Das, S., & Chen, M. (2001). Yahoo! for amazon: Extracting market sentiment from stock message boards. International Journal of Engineering Development and Research. http://www.ijedr.org

Domingos, P., & Pazzani, M. (1997). On the optimality of the simple Bayesian classifier under zero-one loss. *Machine Learning*, 29(2–3), 103–130. https://www.researchgate.net/publication/245220694_On_the_Optimality_of_the_Simple_Bayesian_Classifier_under_Zero-OneLoss

Dreiseitl, S., & Ohno-Machado. (2002). Logistic regression and artificial neural network classification models: A methodology review. *Journal of Biomedical Informatics*, 35(5–6), 352–359. https://www.sciencedirect.com/science/article/pii/S1532046403000340 PMID: 12968784

Gitari, N.D., Zuping, Z., Damien, H., & Long, J. (2015). A lexicon-based approach for hate speech detection. Int. J. Multimed. Ubiquitous Eng., 10, 215–230. https://doi.org/.10.4.21DOI: 10.14257/ijmue.2015

Hong, L. (2011). Predicting Popular Messages in Twitter. https://citeseerx.ist.psu.edu/document?repid=rep1&type=pdf&doi=a772b2d623e90159021d093333c55dbeeac7bd2c

Hu, Tang, Tang, & Liu. (2013). Exploiting social relations for sentiment analysis in microblogging. Proceedings of the Sixth ACM International Conference on Web Search and Data Mining, WSDM '13, 537–546. https://dl.acm.org/doi/10.1145/2488388.2488442

Ingi Sigurbergsson, G., & Derczynski, L. (2019). Offensive Language and Hate Speech Detection for Danish. arXiv e-prints. arXiv:1908.04531.

Krishna. Prasad, K. (2020). A Literature Review on Application of Sentiment Analysis Using Machine Learning Techniques. *International Journal of Applied Engineering and Management Letters*, 4(2), 41–77. https://papers.ssrn.com/sol3/papers.cfm?abstract_id=3674982

Lee, Y., Yoon, S., & Jung, K. (2018). Comparative Studies of Detecting Abusive Language on Twitter. CoRR. abs/1808.1.

Morinaga, S. (2012). Survey on mining subjective data on the web. *Data Mining and Knowledge Discovery*, 24(3), 478–514. DOI: 10.1007/s10618-011-0238-6

Pang, B., Lee, L., & Vaithyanathan, S. (2002). Thumbs up? Sentiment classification using machine learning techniques. Proceedings of the ACL-02 Conference on Empirical Methods in Natural Language Processing, 10, 79–86. https://aclanthology.org/W02-1011

Park, J. H., & Fung, P. (2017). One-step and Two-step Classification for Abusive Language Detection on Twitter. DOI: 10.18653/v1/W17-3006

Pelle, R., Alcântara, C., & Moreira, V. P. (2018). A classifier ensemble for offensive text detection. https://www.researchgate.net/publication/330300271_A_Classifier_Ensemble_for_Offensive_Text _DetectionDOI: 10.5753/webmedia.2018.4582

Peng, C. Y. J., Lee, K. L., & Ingersoll, G. M. (2002). An introduction to logistic regression analysis and reporting. *The Journal of Educational Research*, 96(1), 3–14. DOI: 10.1080/00220670209598786

Pennacchiotti, M., & Popescu, A.-M. (2021). A Machine Learning Approach to Twitter User Classification. *Proceedings of the International AAAI Conference on Web and Social Media*, 5(1), 281-288. DOI: 10.1609/icwsm.v5i1.14139

Ptaszynski, M., Lempa, P., Masui, F., Kimura, Y., Rzepka, R., Araki, K., Wroczynski, M., & Leliwa, G. (2019). Brute-Force Sentence Pattern Extortion from Harmful Messages for Cyberbullying Detection. *Journal of the Association for Information Systems*, 20(8), 1075–1128. DOI: 10.17705/1jais.00562

Safavian, S. R., & Landgrebe, D. (1991, May/June). A survey of decision tree classifier methodology. *IEEE Transactions on Systems, Man, and Cybernetics*, 21(3), 660–674. DOI: 10.1109/21.97458

Sendari, S., Ilham, A. E. Z., Lestari, D. C., & Hariyadi, H. P. (2020). Opinion Analysis for Emotional Classification on Emoji Tweets using the Naïve Bayes Algorithm. Knowledge Engineering and Data Science, 3(1), 50–59. https://core.ac.uk/download/pdf/354311294.pdf

Srinivasan, S. M., Shah, P., & Surendra, S. S. (2021). An Approach to Enhance Business Intelligence and Operations by Sentimental Analysis. Journal of System and Management Sciences, 11(3), 27-40. https://www.researchgate.net/publication/355859167DOI: 10.33168/JSMS.2021.0302

Srivastava, S. (2023). Harnessing the Power of AI Sentiment Analysis-10 Benefits and Use Cases for Business. https://appinventiv.com/blog/ai-sentiment-analysis-in-business

Sumayh, S. (2021). A Sentiment Analysis Approach to Predict an Individual's Awareness of the Precautionary Procedures to Prevent COVID-19 Outbreaks in Saudi Arabia. *International Journal of Environmental Research and Public Health*, 18(1), 218. DOI: 10.3390/ijerph18010218 PMID: 35010479

Tong, R. (2001). *An operational system for detecting and tracking opinions in on-line discussions. In Working Notes of the SIGIR Workshop on Operational Text Classification.* https://dl.acm.org/doi/10.1007/s10579-020-09515-3

Turney, P. D. (2002). Thumbs up or thumbs down? Semantic orientation applied to unsupervised classification of reviews. Proceedings of the 40th Annual Meeting on Association for Computational Linguistics, ACL '02, 417–424. https://aclanthology.org/P02-1053.pdf

Wang, Y., & Witten, I. (1997). Inducing model trees for continuous classes. Proc. 9th Eur. Conf. Mach. Learn._https://www.researchgate.net/publication/33051395_Induction_of_model_trees_for_predicting_continuous_classes

Wiebe, J. (2000). *Learning subjective adjectives from corpora. In Proceedings of the Seventeenth National Conference on Artificial Intelligence and Twelfth Conference on Innovative Applications of Artificial Intelligence.* AAAI Press. https://cdn.aaai.org/AAAI/2000/AAAI00-113.pdf

Chapter 3
An Investigation on the Barriers Preventing Artificial Intelligence From Being Widely Used in Social, Governance, and Environmental Activities

Sabyasachi Pramanik

https://orcid.org/0000-0002-9431-8751

Haldia Institute of Technology, India

ABSTRACT

The relationship between artificial intelligence (AI) and the incorporation of environmental, social, and governance (ESG) aspects in modern business and technology is explored in this chapter. The paper investigates how AI could provide workable solutions to the pressing societal sustainability concerns of today. The chapter focuses on the moral implications of environmentally conscious technology, AI-powered predictions for ESG metrics, moral supply chains, and upcoming laws. As AI and ESG become more integrated, there are chances for companies who prioritize sustainability to increase their market share by implementing eco-friendly practices. This confluence makes it possible to integrate cutting-edge technology with sustainability objectives, creating a relationship that has the potential to be really revolutionary.

INTRODUCTION

A summary of the ways in which the promotion of sustainability is aided by the amalgamation of environmental, social, and governance (ESG) concepts with artificial intelligence (AI).

Environmental, social, and governance (ESG) and artificial intelligence (AI) are closely related fields that play a significant part in contemporary business and technology (Makridakis, 2017; Saetra, 2021). The term artificial intelligence (AI) describes a wide range of technological developments that allow computers to mimic human thought processes. It is frequently referred to as "intelligence of machines" (Trujillo, 2021). Natural language processing, robotics, computer vision, and machine learning are some

DOI: 10.4018/979-8-3693-3884-1.ch003

of these technologies. Artificial intelligence is transforming several industries and commercial processes. It has the potential to tackle important societal issues including the pressing need for long-term solutions to current problems (Nishant et al., 2020; Sestino & De Mauro, 2022).

ESG is a comprehensive taxonomy that takes into account an organization's non-financial needs in relation to the environment, society, and governance, according to Johnson Jr. et al. (2020). There are two main variables that contribute to ESG. Businesses all across the globe must abide by laws and regulations that place a strong emphasis on meeting requirements and proving knowledge in subjects unrelated to finance (Krishnamoorthy, 2021). Climate change, carbon emissions, and the wise use of finite resources like trash, water, and air are all examples of environmental concerns. In the continuous struggle, societal issues including employment, racial and social justice, child labor, health and safety, inclusion and diversity, human trafficking, data privacy, and the general well-being of workers and humanity are taken into account. The following are listed as governance factors by Johnson Jr. et al. (2020): organizational goal; legislative and societal impact; issues with compensation and corruption; and the board's and management's independence, control, and evaluation. Technological solutions that aim to address or ameliorate the fundamental problems at the core of the ecological crisis have emerged as a result of the increased global awareness and urgency surrounding it (Falk & van Wynsberghe, 2023).

According to the UN (1987), sustainable development is the process of meeting present-day needs without endangering the ability of future generations to meet their own needs. Together with the 17 sustainable development goals, the UN created Agenda 2030 (Schrijver, 2008). It takes a strong commitment to corporate social responsibility, or CSR, to achieve sustainable development. According to Zhao and Fariñas (2023), corporate social responsibility (CSR) includes socially conscious investing, protecting stakeholders' interests, advancing sustainable development, and improving company governance. Artificial intelligence (AI) has the potential to improve corporate social responsibility (CSR) programs by increasing their effectiveness and efficiency (Naqvi, 2021). As the value of social and environmental responsibility has grown, sustainability has emerged as a top priority for businesses. As a company that understood the importance of sustainability, Unilivers made a concerted effort to get other businesses to follow suit. A good example of an ESG case study is Unilever's Sustainable Living Plan, which was launched in 2010. One innovative approach called a "virtual circle of growth" is the Unilever Sustainability Living Plan (Lawrence et al., 2018). Three fundamental tenets of sustainability served as the foundation for the strategy: raising the quality of living for people inside the company's value chain, reducing the negative environmental consequences of Unilever products, and improving the health and well-being of one billion people. Unilever's broad sustainability project demonstrates the company's commitment to incorporating social, governance, and environmental considerations into its basic business strategy. In order to make sure that board membership and leadership matched the company's commitment to sustainability as stated by its governance principles, Unilever encouraged openness and appropriate hiring practices. This project shows how a large international consumer products company may successfully strike a balance between profitability and a steadfast dedication to environmental preservation, social responsibility, and open governance practices. According to Carney (2021), Unilever is the top company for exemplifying ESG initiatives.

Artificially intelligent (AI) robots can learn from experience, adapt to new information, and carry out tasks that are similar to those of humans (Duan et al., 2019, p. 63). As a result, AI seems to be an extremely fortunate area. Artificial intelligence (AI) is now widely acknowledged as a key element in the ongoing digital transformation of several sectors. Even in homes and businesses, AI is becoming more and more common (Chawla & Goyal, 2022; Singh & Chouhan, 2023). It helps businesses make data-driven choices, automate processes, and extract useful information from large datasets. However, the evaluation of an organization's effect on environmental, social, and governance (ESG) problems using the ESG framework becomes more important as an increasing number of firms globally realize the benefits of implementing sustainable practices (Nishant et al., 2020; Kar et al., 2022). In the modern, fast-paced world, corporate sustainability is essential as businesses are facing a decline in their average lifespan, which makes long-term survival a critical concern (Dhanda & Shrotryia, 2021).

Notable is the growing attention that AI is receiving in the domains of finance and sustainability, as well as the relationship that it has with ESG concerns. As environmental, social, and governance (ESG) issues become more prevalent in businesses and the financial sector, new financial instruments and technologies are being developed. These tools seek to achieve a balanced approach by providing financial benefits while also taking social and environmental concerns into account. Furthermore, AI fosters an atmosphere that supports the application of moral values and environmental conservation while concurrently reducing poverty, air pollution, and resource depletion throughout the integration process.

According to Nishant et al. (2020), artificial intelligence is very valuable in mitigating poverty, pollution, depletion of resources, and in promoting environmental and social governance. ESG principles help companies make strategic decisions that will increase their profits while promoting an equitable and healthy global community. These guidelines spell out what is required of businesses in terms of morality and responsibility. Dandha and Shrotrya (2021) investigate why businesses decide to put sustainability first in order to get a competitive advantage as opposed to only donating to charities or totally swapping out traditional business methods with sustainable ones.

the time frame for addressing urgent managerial, social, and environmental concerns via the use of advanced approaches. Artificial intelligence (AI) helps businesses quickly evaluate and improve their performance by gathering and analyzing large volumes of data on environmental, social, and governance (ESG) concerns (Hoa and Demir, 2023). According to studies, businesses all over the globe are using sustainability reports more and more to effectively communicate information on social and environmental issues. This trend is mostly due to stakeholder demand.

The quest of sustainability will benefit immensely from artificial intelligence. This has a number of advantages, including enhancing corporate governance, lessening the effect on the environment, and encouraging moral conduct at work. The potential exists for artificial intelligence (AI) to improve the openness and accountability of environmental, social, and governance (ESG) systems. Consequently, this would raise stakeholders' trust in businesses' dedication to environmentally and socially responsible goals (Chong et al., 2022). Intelligent technology (AI) and ecological social responsibility (ESG) have the power to transform company operations and usher in a time when morality, social responsibility, and sustainable development are essential.

Organizations monitoring various facets of the long-term sustainability of human efforts have multiplied inside government agencies, big businesses, and the public sector (Walker et al., 2019). Incorporating environmentally friendly ideas into business strategy planning has come a long way in the last few years. Nowadays, big businesses need to explain and record important decisions while also being aware of how they affect the environment and society (Saetra, 2021). The approach entails gradually replacing the antiquated term "corporate social responsibility" with a variety of ESG (environmental, social, and governance) initiatives, frameworks, and metrics (Verbin, 2020).

This chapter's main goal is to discuss social, governance, and environmental challenges and investigate how artificial intelligence (AI) may be used to solve them. Businesses now need to evaluate their administrative, social, and environmental achievements since environmentally conscious business practices are becoming more and more important in the global marketplace. This topic has been the subject of several research studies, such as those by Yoon et al. (2018), Lam et al. (2016), and Tammuruji et al. (2016). The "environmental" component comes in first place, with the idea of "governance" coming in second, according to a study done in 2023 by Sood et al. It seems that the third component, "social," has the least impact on the way an investigator makes decisions. Ellili (2022) found that, for a sample of thirty publicly listed companies in the United Arab Emirates, the inclusion of ESG data enhanced financial statement reporting and investment efficiency between 2010 and 2019.

Lourenço et al. (2012) assert that modern businesses need to adopt sustainable business methods. Companies may reduce their carbon emissions and get a competitive edge over other businesses in their industry by employing ecologically friendly practices. Additionally, Albuquerque et al. (2019) asserts that integrating environmental, social, and governance (ESG) factors is a praiseworthy tactic that helps businesses raise returns, lower systemic risk, and enhance overall operational efficiency and effectiveness. The methods have shown promise. Lee and Zhang (2019) suggest that the discovery of anomalies and catastrophic interruptions might be facilitated by the use of artificial intelligence-generated data and ESG standards. This basically means projecting or projecting what will happen in the future, which is particularly important in the current global setting when social, political, and environmental concerns have a significant influence on markets and business financial results. Lee and Zhang (2019) found a number of parallels between data generated by intelligent devices and sustainability measures in their research. The findings suggest that using certain ESG metrics is necessary to achieve long-term success.

Nevertheless, because of the many issues that crop up throughout the process, fully integrating AI into ESG is not an easy undertaking. As noted by Hao and Demir (2023), it is essential to overcome a few issues before using AI into ESG operations. The ethical and responsible use of AI, correct evaluation of morality and performance, data security and privacy issues, technological difficulties, unresolved legal issues, and the maintenance of negative preconceptions about certain groups are a few of the hurdles to take into account. Creating a distinct communication channel between AI systems for autonomous robots and human supervisors presents another set of difficulties.

The concept of artificial intelligence (AI) and how it relates to environmental, social, and governance (ESG) ideas will be discussed in this chapter. This means looking at the challenges of integrating AI into ESG (environment, social, and governance) processes and the unique roles that AI plays in fostering positive social and environmental outcomes. The purpose of this book is to provide leaders and business managers clear guidance on how to use AI's creative powers to advance various ESG objectives. It does this by outlining the possible advantages and risks of fusing AI with ESG.

1.2 Integrating Social, Governance, and Environmental Aspects via the Use of Artificial Intelligence

The use of artificial intelligence on environmental, social, and governance (ESG) issues is examined in this chapter. A noteworthy accomplishment is the incorporation of AI with environmental, social, and governance elements inside the framework of expanding commerce (EY, 2023). The complex relationships that impede the quick use of AI in sustainable businesses must be understood. According to Jaber (2022), artificial intelligence systems are made to examine large amounts of data, identify certain patterns, and then generate theories or even predictions. This chapter offers a variety of instruments and strategies that businesses and institutions may use to face and overcome challenges head-on. By working together, firms may provide the foundation for an AI-driven society in the future, which would greatly improve the community's present situation.

Hao and Demir (2023) conducted a comprehensive analysis of the elements that support or hinder the incorporation of artificial intelligence in ESG sectors. But their research goes beyond a cursory examination and explores more nuanced topics like stimuli and technological difficulties. Their work is examined in this chapter because it is creative in identifying triggers that are strongly associated with issues relating to the environment, society, or government. According to them, these technological constraints and triggers provide insightful information that forms the basis of our investigation into the many obstacles preventing AI inside the ESG. Companies that follow environmental, social, and governance (ESG) guidelines and are sustainable perform financially better than those that don't (Moro–Visconti, 2022).

However, this study intends to add to the body of knowledge by analyzing the many barriers that prevent artificial intelligence from being fully integrated into the environmental, social, and governance (ESG) context, building on the research done by Hao and Demir (2023). Through a thorough examination of the complex interactions between technological, regulatory, ethical, and data-related concerns, our goal is to significantly add to the growing body of knowledge. This will enable businesses to confidently go ahead and handle this challenging environment. The primary aim is to facilitate organizations' efficient use of artificial intelligence (AI), transforming it from an intriguing technical instrument into a potent facilitator of sustainable practices. This will set the stage for a time in the future when ESG considerations are not just embraced but also essential to operational success.

According to Hirsch's (2021) research, companies don't really understand how much carbon their IT system contributes to. People and organizations may both lessen their environmental effect by implementing energy-efficient practices, greener technology, and sustainable habits. To do this, one must educate themselves about carbon footprints and make a concerted effort to minimize them. However, a few companies have a clear method for calculating their carbon impact. According to Zhao and Fariñas (2023), governments and businesses must work together to solve the environmental issues and health risks related to artificial intelligence.

This chapter's aims are to provide an overview of the study's objectives and research methods.

This chapter examines how to address social, governance, and environmental challenges using artificial intelligence (AI) and sustainable projects. This chapter's goal is to list the major roadblocks that businesses face throughout the integration process and provide several suggestions on how to get over them. Review case studies that illustrate best practices, moral conundrums, legal issues, and possible ramifications for operations in the future. This chapter reviews the material that is currently available on the difficulties associated with AI-ESG and offers suggestions for those who want to ensure sustainability and equity in the outcomes generated by AI. As a result, this chapter makes reference to the relevant body of existing literature on the fusion of AI and ESG. It's critical to recognize that practical solutions might be put in place to remove the obstacles preventing artificial intelligence from being widely used for governance, social, and environmental goals.

2. THE INTEGRATION OF ENVIRONMENTAL, SOCIAL, AND GOVERNANCE CONCERNS WITH ARTIFICIAL INTELLIGENCE PRESENTS A VARIETY OF INTRICATE CHALLENGES

There are several obstacles in the way of integrating AI with ESG, and each one brings to light a different nuance of this subject. We will look closely at these barriers to have a better understanding of the difficulties that businesses face (as shown in Figure 1).

2.1. Data Availability and Quality

In order to support artificial intelligence-driven ESG (Environmental, Social, and Governance) activities, the modern era of oil production necessitates the highly efficient collection and processing of varied and multi-user data. Still, it's a difficult undertaking. The complex terrain of data reliability, quality, and availability is examined in this chapter. It highlights the difficulties businesses have in acquiring accurate and trustworthy data. The technological revolution has led to organizations going through a digital transformation, especially in the fields of cloud computing, automation, artificial intelligence, and data analytics (Jedynak et al., 2021). This process highlights the need of objective, high-quality data since it is essential to producing positive outcomes that endure. Data is more than just a resource; it is the lifeblood of AI-powered ESG projects, and the quality of the data directly affects the efficiency and accuracy of these efforts. Investigative journalism group ProPublica discovered that the COMPAS system performed more accurately in classifying black defendants as high-risk in a contentious case involving algorithmic decision-making in the US for predicting recidivism (the likelihood of a convicted person committing another crime). Moreover, it was incorrect to assume that white criminals would interpret the incidents differently (Angwin et al., 2016). According to Macpherson et al. (2021), fintech and AI-powered ESG screening and analysis solutions are now recognized as "strategic facilitators" that may reduce biases in ESG data and mitigate inequalities in ESG ratings.

2.2. Ethical and Privacy Considerations

When using AI for sustainable decision-making, issues of fairness, lucidity, and possible unintentional harm to people come to light as major ethical considerations. This section offers a thorough examination of these moral dilemmas, with a focus on AI-driven sustainability projects that adhere to morally sound standards and sound logic. ESG includes privacy-related issues as well as those pertaining to data gathering, storage, and utilization. Maintaining confidentiality and security is essential when working with sensitive ESG-specific data. Ethics and data privacy are essential for achieving long-term goals. This becomes clear when talking about the privacy and ethical issues that come up when AI is successfully integrated into the environmental social governance (ESG) framework. The capacity of an AI to have positive social and environmental effects is what makes it excellent. This entails actively advancing corporate social responsibility via formal and informal channels, participating in campaigns that uphold these principles, and abiding by laws and regulations. Adopting an ethical framework and efficiently governing the field of AI will ensure its sustained growth. Employing truthful, ethical, and legal data may provide businesses the information and options they need to make decisions, giving them a distinct "data advantage" over competitors (Stuck & Grunes, 2016).

3. BUDGETARY CONSTRAINTS AND RESOURCE AVAILABILITY

As a result, it's critical for businesses to carefully examine all of the many cost-related challenges they face. These fees include not only the initial installation of the AI but also the continuing expenditures of system maintenance and personnel training. For businesses, finding solutions to problems involving resource sharing is essential. As a result, it is essential to ensure that all resources be used as efficiently as possible. As such, it is essential that AI programs be in line with broader goals. Reaching a balanced balance between aspirations, cost-focused tactics, and environmental aims may be very difficult for a business. It would certainly be advantageous to use a methodical approach and a fair distribution of the available resources.

2.4. Inadequate Knowledge and Awareness

A certain set of skills is required for the creation and use of AI-enabled ESG integration solutions. The basic components of successfully negotiating difficult, rocky terrain are covered in this section. This indicates how crucial it is to put in place initiatives that teach, prepare, and include stakeholders in comprehending the benefits and drawbacks of artificial intelligence. The desire of potential responders to actively participate in public education and information sharing programs is a barrier to closing this knowledge gap. According to Enholm et al. (2022), there are misunderstandings about the integration of AI into a corporate plan as well as discrepancies regarding the main activities that generate value. Therefore, it is crucial to look into the claim that autonomous learning always results in unintentional prejudice against certain groups of people (Larsson et al., 2019). Furthermore, there were reservations about this approach's possible formality.

2.5. Regulatory and Legal Complexities

To successfully integrate AI and ESG practices into enterprises, a thorough legal and regulatory framework must be established. A thorough analysis of the legal frameworks governing artificial intelligence operations in connection to EGS will be part of the project. Therefore, in order to guarantee the long-term sustainability of AI systems, adherence to both current and new legislation is essential. Firms need to proactively develop steps to minimize these complex conditions and conduct a full analysis and resolution of existing compliance-related difficulties and concerns in order to traverse these challenging environments. Rigid compliance procedures must be put in place due to artificial intelligence's dynamic nature and potential legal repercussions. The argument for developing sustainable and controlled AI systems is strong, especially considering the unexpected nature of AI. However, a number of significant challenges need to be deliberately and properly resolved before AI can be effectively integrated into ESG. To guarantee that AI achieves a thorough degree of disruption and that enterprises do not become immoral or unethical, these issues must be addressed first and foremost.

Figure 1. Barriers to AI adoption in ESG integration

Figure 1: Barriers to AI Adoption in ESG Integration

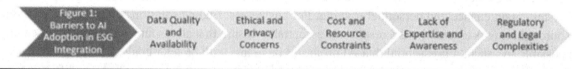

3. BREAKING THROUGH BARRIERS: ENCOURAGING AI INTEGRATION IN ESG

When attempting to penetrate the environmental, social, and governance spheres, AI faces several challenges. However, creative solutions may be able to get over these barriers and make it easier to use AI into green initiatives. Larsson et al. (2019) carried out further research with the objective of augmenting trust in the use of artificial intelligence and machine learning. Transparency and accountability go hand in hand. The lack of transparency or "black boxes" that result from algorithmic decision-making is one of the accountability challenges (Pasquale, 2015). Establishing interdisciplinary collaboration, encouraging trust in AI applications, and always keeping an eye on legal and governance issues are all essential components of sustainable AI. In Section Two, we look at some solutions (see Figure 2) that aim to remove an obstacle and make it possible for AI to utilize ESG.

Figure 2. Strategies for overcoming barriers

Figure 2: Strategies for Overcoming Barriers

Figure 2: Strategies for Overcoming Barriers

- Data Solutions
- Ethical AI Frameworks
- Cost-Effective Approaches
- Capacity Building
- Advocacy and Regulation

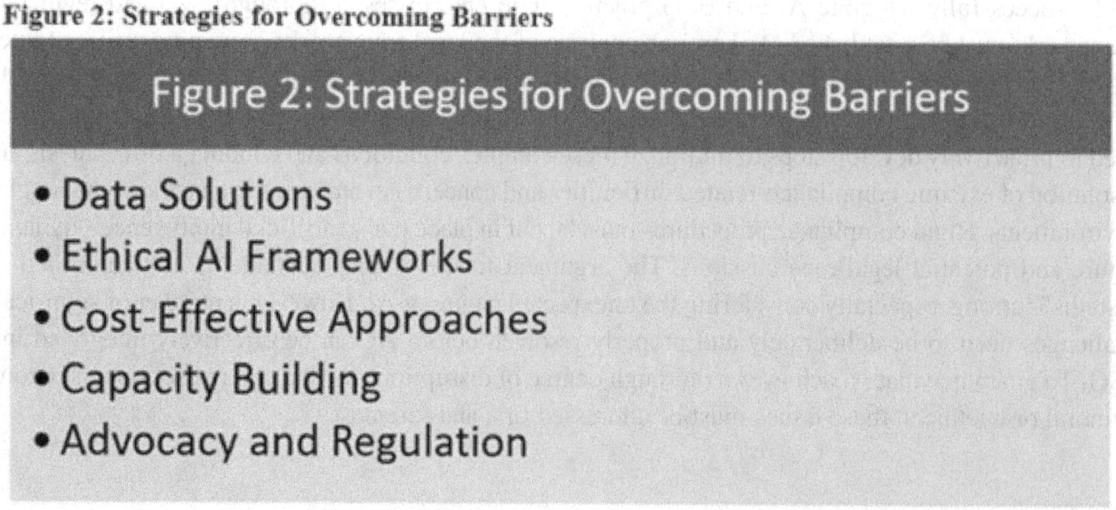

3.1. Data Solutions

Data is the core element at the heart of AI-driven ESG integration. Many approaches to data management are covered in this section, such as data standards, data cleaning, and open data initiatives. By putting these strategies into practice, you can be sure that the data is easily accessible and of the highest quality needed for the smooth integration of AI with ESG regulations. The many examples of successful partnerships or collaborations between businesses, governments, and data providers in this chapter highlight the need of teamwork in data research. According to Smith et al. (2020), real-world examples show how people may work together to solve data problems and guarantee the long-term viability of AI systems.

3.2. Ethical AI Frameworks

This section addresses the creation of AI systems grounded in the values of accountability, transparency, and justice, with a particular emphasis on the integration of environmental, social, and governance (ESG) factors. As a result, businesses will have to establish moral guidelines and standards for AI that satisfy environmental, social, and governance (ESG) requirements. The presentation ought to show how following these guidelines might direct the creation of ethically conscious AI systems. Genuine case studies on the use of AI in social responsibility and environmental conservation will be provided to readers. Knowledge-based and principled methodologies are part of an approach that structures the deployment of AI for ESG goals using examples of such applications.

3.3. Economical Methods

The integration of artificial intelligence into environmental, social, and governance (ESG) activities might sometimes be hampered by monetary restrictions and limitations. The methods for cutting expenses are explicitly examined in this section, with a focus on calculating ROI and assessing expense-benefit ratios. As such, it provides decision-makers with an organized method for integrating AI, potentially leading to cost savings and enabling astute financial judgment. With an emphasis on scalability and cloud integration, this section of the book offers a thorough description of how to apply resource constraints and economies for AI deployment in an effective and efficient manner. The research shows how integrating AI into companies might improve their financial sustainability by allowing for the low-cost and scalable use of AI across the board (Kamble et al., 2020).

3.4. Improving the Development of Organizations

However, there are a number of ways that people and organizations may use current technology to boost their performance in the future. Therefore, it is imperative that enterprises place a high priority on lifelong learning, offering advice on developing artificial intelligence and environmental, social, and governance (ESG) management capabilities. One may successfully overcome knowledge gaps and develop a specialized mindset in sustainable AI by using ESG-focused training and education. Because of this, this area is essential for creating a workforce that is trained to deal with the implications of environmental, social, and governance aspects on artificial intelligence in the future. According to Brauer et al. (2019), this section gives individuals and organizations the tools they need to implement sustainable AI successfully.

3.5. Governance and Promotion

The importance of lobbying techniques in influencing laws and regulations related to the combination of AI and ESG. Lawmakers are always working to enact significant reforms. Examples of cooperatives that have successfully progressed ethically acceptable AI and adjusted to changing legal constraints are given in this chapter. These discussions show many viewpoints on how interested groups and regulators collaborate to promote sustainability. In order to facilitate legislative changes that might aid in the implementation of AI-based ESG (Environmental, Social, and Governance) practices, this chapter's provisions encourage moral and legal reform (Bietti et al., 2021). After accounting for each of these components, we provide a thorough strategy for any company looking to get beyond the barriers and challenges associated with integrating AI into ESG. In order to improve readers' comprehension and skill in AI-driven sustainability and so contribute to a more just and ecologically sustainable future, the book offers useful solutions and real-world examples.

4. CASE STUDIES: EFFECTIVE EXAMPLES OF OVERCOMING BARRIERS TO ARTIFICIAL INTELLIGENCE ADOPTION IN ESG INTEGRATION

This chapter includes real-world examples of how businesses have successfully addressed the use of artificial intelligence (AI) in connection to environmental, social, and governance (ESG) aspects. The articles are noteworthy because they address the issues that came up during the use of AI for sustainability and provide solutions and insightful analysis.

4.1 Watson for Sustainability from IBM

IBM's Watson for Sustainability is one example of a solution to environmental, social, and governance (ESG) concerns. Watson, an IBM cognitive technology, conducted a thorough analysis of a sizable quantity of ESG-related data. The summary above shows how IBM overcame issues with data quality by combining and cleaning damaged data using creative methods. Consequently, via the use of data-driven decision making and the integration of verified data from several sources, IBM's ESG performance was enhanced. This emphasizes how important it is to keep data consistent and accurate in AI-powered ESG projects.

4.2 Microsoft's Framework for Ethical AI

A case study that highlights Microsoft's ethical commitment to environmental, social, and governance (ESG) by using ethical AI ideas is presented to illustrate this commitment. The tech giant created an AI framework based on ethics—a concept that is based on transparency, responsibility, and justice—in order to achieve this goal. Microsoft assured us that their AI-powered sustainability program met these standards. This case shows how ethics must be taken into account while using AI in ESG and provides guidance on how to use AI within businesses in a responsible manner.

4.3 Amazon's Cloud-Based AI Solutions

The integration of EGS via Amazon's cloud-based AI capabilities demonstrates the company's adoption of cost-effective strategies. Amazon used scalable cloud services like QPoint to reduce the initial cost of artificial intelligence. This shows how an artificial intelligence system based on the cloud may be both flexible and affordable over an extended length of time.

4.4 Google's Educational and Capacity Building Programs

As an example, Google took action to increase public awareness of how companies might close perception and knowledge gaps and enhance their capabilities. Financial support has been given via projects that aim to close the knowledge gaps in the public on AI, as well as training courses and educational materials. The goal of this assistance is to cultivate an environment that supports technology's long-term viability. This situation also highlights the need of hiring stakeholders—people with the necessary education and training to fully assess the benefits and drawbacks of artificial intelligence in the context of social, political, and environmental considerations.

5. THE EUROPEAN UNION'S ARTIFICIAL INTELLIGENCE REGULATION FRAMEWORK

An interesting case study on regulation and lobbying may be found in the European Union's attempts to create a legislative framework for the fusion of artificial intelligence (AI) with environmental, social, and governance (ESG) activities. Through its interaction with stakeholders and the execution of various legislations, the European Union has built an environment that is favorable to the ethical and sustainable use of AI. This case study serves as an excellent example of how proactive legislation and business-government collaboration may promote sustainable behavior.

This chapter analyzes real-world settings to look at the important lessons and standards of excellence that may be learned from these case studies. Readers may get insightful knowledge on a variety of subjects, such as overcoming data issues, coming up with affordable solutions, maintaining AI ethics, enhancing AI capabilities, and promoting legislative reforms. These case studies serve as motivating models for other businesses who encounter comparable obstacles in their business models yet use AI to meet their long-term objectives. These illustrations provide as a source of motivation for other businesses with comparable challenges to use AI to address long-term goals. These represent the revolutionary potential of artificial intelligence (AI) to revolutionize the integration of environmental, social, and governance (ESG) concerns, given that obstacles are met with strategic thought, steadfast commitment to sustainability, and suitable technological application.

5. FUTURE PROSPECTS AND CONCLUDING REMARKS

This chapter offers key takeaways that should be considered and supported by a high quality benchmark drawn from actual circumstances. The topics include using appropriate techniques to economically tackle data concerns, promoting moral AI models, augmenting AI capabilities, and supporting regulatory framework enforcement.

The anticipated difficulties and changes in this sector that are probably going to affect the future are examined in this chapter. The supply chain presents ethical managers with workable options, and artificial intelligence is becoming more and more of an influence on society. To accelerate adoption, artificial intelligence forecasting for ESG indicators is a technology that is being used more and more. Moreover, these concerns would include challenges related to data securitization, legal framework creation, and ethical standards for AI design.

5.1. Forecasting Future Trends and Difficulties

As artificial intelligence becomes more and more prevalent in the integration of environmental, social, and governance (ESG) concerns, sustainability-focused businesses must adapt. Future issues in this field include expected challenges and developments. Creating moral supply chain management plans and quantifying social effect using AI-powered solutions. For the futures market, artificial intelligence-based forecasting of ESG indicators is a popular technique. Companies need to be ready for new issues including data security, changing laws and regulations, and the need for moral AI frameworks.

5.2. Prospects for the Future

Businesses that use artificial intelligence and sustainable development methods stand to gain a great deal. Comprehensive analysis of possible uses of AI to further sustainability initiatives, including the creation of environmentally friendly products, improving stakeholder participation in ESG programs, and creating new revenue streams through AI-driven ESG services, is provided in the section that follows. The emerging green artificial intelligence ecosystem presents a chance for companies to improve their market standing by using an eco-friendly approach.

5.3. A Synopsis of the Emerging Field

AI and ESG bring cutting-edge technology and the urgent problem of sustainability together. Data-driven, open, and transparent strategies have the power to completely change how businesses utilize ESG. This improves the environment and social well-being while empowering artificial intelligence to solve pressing issues.

CONCLUSION: OVERCOMING OBSTACLES TO REACH LONG-TERM OBJECTIVES

The most important lesson to be learned from this chapter is the need of removing barriers to artificial intelligence applications. To reach a sustainable future, organizations and stakeholders need to address data issues, implement ethical AI efforts, encourage affordability, boost capacity development, and advocate for better regulation. They will be able to take the lead in the sustainability space and understand the disruptive potential of AI as a result. Significant progress is being made at the nexus of sustainability and technology. Businesses that use AI and solve social and environmental issues may continue to hold the top spot when it comes to ethics, teamwork, and innovation. As a combination of technologies, AI and ESG provide a set of concepts meant to promote a more equitable and environmentally conscious future. We may work toward a day where AI and ESG work together to create a global community that benefits from their combined efforts.

REFERENCES

Albuquerque, R., Koskinen, Y., & Zhang, C. (2019). Corporate social responsibility and firm risk: Theory and empirical evidence. *Management Science*, 65(10), 4451–4469. DOI: 10.1287/mnsc.2018.3043

Angwin, J., Larson, J., Mattu, S., & Kirchner, L. (2016). Machine Bias. ProPublica. https://www.propublica.org/article/machine-bias-risk-assessments-in-criminal-sentencing

Buallay, A., Fadel, S. M., Al-Ajmi, J. Y., & Saudagaran, S. (2020). Sustainability reporting and performance of MENA banks: Is there a trade-off? *Measuring Business Excellence*, 24(2), 197–221. DOI: 10.1108/MBE-09-2018-0078

Carney, M. (2021). *Value(s): Building a Better World for All*. Public Affairs.

Chawla, R. N., & Goyal, P. (2022). Emerging trends in digital transformation: A bibliometric analysis. *Benchmarking*, 29(4), 1069–1112. DOI: 10.1108/BIJ-01-2021-0009

Chong, S., Rahman, A., & Narayan, A. K. (2022). Guest editorial: Accounting in transition: influence of technology, sustainability and diversity. *Pacific Accounting Review*, 34(4), 517–525. DOI: 10.1108/PAR-07-2022-210

Datta, A., Tschantz, M. C., & Datta, A. (2015). Automated Experiments on Ad Privacy Settings – A Tale of Opacity, Choice, and Discrimination. *Proceedings on Privacy Enhancing Technologies. Privacy Enhancing Technologies Symposium*, 1(1), 92–112. DOI: 10.1515/popets-2015-0007

Dhanda, U., & Shrotryia, V. K. (2021). Corporate sustainability: The new organizational reality. *Qualitative Research in Organizations and Management*, 16(3/4), 464–487. DOI: 10.1108/QROM-01-2020-1886

Duan, Y., Edwards, J. S., & Dwivedi, Y. K. (2019). Artificial Intelligence for Decision Making in the Era of Big Data–Evolution, Challenges, and Research Agenda. *International Journal of Information Management*, 48, 63–71. DOI: 10.1016/j.ijinfomgt.2019.01.021

Ellili, N. O. D. (2022). Impact of ESG disclosure and financial reporting quality on investment efficiency. Corporate Governance: An International Journal of Business in Society.

Enholm, I. M., Papagiannidis, E., Mikalef, P., & Krogstie, J. (2022). Artificial Intelligence and business value: A literature review. *Information Systems Frontiers*, 24(8), 1709–1734. DOI: 10.1007/s10796-021-10186-w

EY. (2023). Artificial intelligence ESG stakes, Discussion paper. Retrieved from https://assets.ey.com/content/dam/ey-sites/ey-com/en_ca/topics/ai/ey-artificial-intelligence-esg-stakes-discussion-paper.pdf

Falk, S., & van Wynsberghe, A. (2023). Challenging AI for Sustainability: What ought it mean? *AI and Ethics*. Advance online publication. DOI: 10.1007/s43681-023-00323-3

Hao, X., & Demir, E. (2023). Artificial intelligence in supply chain decision-making: an environmental, social, and governance triggering and technological inhibiting protocol. Journal of Modelling in Management, ahead-of-print. DOI: 10.1108/JM2-01-2023-0009

Hirsch, P. B. (2021). Footprints in the cloud: The hidden cost of IT infrastructure. *The Journal of Business Strategy*, 43(1), 65–68. DOI: 10.1108/JBS-11-2021-0175

Jaber, T. A. (2022). Artificial intelligence in computer networks. *Periodicals of Engineering and Natural Sciences*, 10(1), 309–322. DOI: 10.21533/pen.v10i1.2616

Jedynak, M., Czakon, W., Kuźniarska, A., & Mania, K. (2021). Digital transformation of organizations: What do we know and where to go next? [DOI]. *Journal of Organizational Change Management*, 34(3), 629–652. DOI: 10.1108/JOCM-10-2020-0336

Johnson, C. E.Jr, Stout, J. H., & Walter, A. C. (2020). Profound Change: The Evolution of ESG. *Business Lawyer*, 75, 2567–2608.

Kar, A. K., Choudhary, S. K., & Singh, V. K. (2022). How can artificial intelligence impact sustainability: A systematic literature review. *Journal of Cleaner Production*, 376, 134120. Advance online publication. DOI: 10.1016/j.jclepro.2022.134120

Kitsios, F., & Kamariotou, M. (2021). Artificial Intelligence and Business Strategy towards Digital Transformation: A Research Agenda. *Sustainability (Basel)*, 13(4), 2025. DOI: 10.3390/su13042025

Krishnamoorthy, R. (2021). Environmental, Social, and Governance (ESG) Investing: Doing Good to Do Well. *Open Journal of Social Sciences*, 9(7), 189–197. DOI: 10.4236/jss.2021.97013

La Torre, M., Sabelfeld, S., Blomkvist, M., Tarquinio, L., & Dumay, J. (2018). Harmonising non-financial reporting regulation in Europe: Practical forces and projections for future research. Meditari Accountancy Research, 26(4), 598-621.

Larsson, S. (2019). Artificial Intelligence as a Normative Societal Challenge: Bias, Responsibility, and Transparency. In Festschrift for Håkan Hydén. Lund: Juristförlaget.

Lawrence, J., Rasche, A., & Kenny, K. (2018). Sustainability as Opportunity: Unilever's Sustainable Living Plan. In Lenssen, G., & Smith, N. (Eds.), *Managing Sustainable Business* (pp. 435–455). Springer. DOI: 10.1007/978-94-024-1144-7_21

Lee, Y.-J., & Zhang, X. T. (2019). AI-Generated Corporate Environmental Data: An Event Study with Predictive Power. In J. J. Choi & B. Ozkan (Eds.), Disruptive Innovation in Business and Finance in the Digital World (Vol. 20, pp. 65-83). Emerald Publishing Limited. DOI: 10.1108/S1569-376720190000020009

Lourenço, I., Branco, M., Curto, J., & Eugénio, T. (2012). How does the market value corporate sustainability performance? *Journal of Business Ethics*, 108(4), 417–428. DOI: 10.1007/s10551-011-1102-8

Macpherson, M., Gasperini, A., & Bosco, M. (2021). Artificial Intelligence and FinTech Technologies for ESG Data and Analysis. DOI: 10.2139/ssrn.3790774

Makridakis, S. (2017). The forthcoming Artificial Intelligence (AI) revolution: Its impact on society and firms. *Futures*, 90, 46–60. DOI: 10.1016/j.futures.2017.03.006

McDonnell, M.-H., & Cobb, J. (2020). Take a Stand or Keep Your Seat: Board Turnover after Social Movement Boycotts. *Academy of Management Journal*, 63(4), 1028–1053. DOI: 10.5465/amj.2017.0890

Miller, T. (2019). Explanation in artificial intelligence: Insights from the social sciences. *Artificial Intelligence*, 267, 1–38. DOI: 10.1016/j.artint.2018.07.007

Moro-Visconti, R. (2022). *Augmented Corporate Valuation: From Digital Networking to ESG Compliance*. Palgrave Macmillan. DOI: 10.1007/978-3-030-97117-5

Musleh Al-Sartawi, A. M., Hussainey, K., & Razzaque, A. (2022). The role of artificial intelligence in sustainable finance. *Journal of Sustainable Finance & Investment*, 1–6. DOI: 10.1080/20430795.2022.2057405

Musleh Al-Sartawi, A. M., Razzaque, A., & Kamal, M. M. (Eds.). (2021). *Artificial Intelligence Systems and the Internet of Things in the Digital Era. EAMMIS 2021. Lecture Notes in Networks and Systems* (Vol. 239). Springer.

Naqvi, A. (Ed.). (2021). *Artificial intelligence for asset management and investment: a strategic perspective*. Wiley. DOI: 10.1002/9781119601838

Nishant, R., Kennedy, M., & Corbett, J. (2020). Artificial Intelligence for Sustainability: Challenges, Opportunities, and a Research Agenda. *International Journal of Information Management*, 53, 102104. DOI: 10.1016/j.ijinfomgt.2020.102104

Pasquale, F. (2015). *The Black Box Society. The Secret Algorithms That Control Money and Information*. Harvard University Press. DOI: 10.4159/harvard.9780674736061

Sætra, H. S. (2021). A Framework for Evaluating and Disclosing the ESG Related Impacts of AI with the SDGs. *Sustainability (Basel)*, 13(15), 8503. DOI: 10.3390/su13158503

Sestino, A., & De Mauro, A. (2022). Leveraging artificial intelligence in business: Implications, applications, and methods. *Technology Analysis and Strategic Management*, 34(1), 16–29. DOI: 10.1080/09537325.2021.1883583

Singh, A., & Chouhan, T. (2023). Artificial Intelligence in HRM: Role of Emotional–Social Intelligence and Future Work Skill. In Tyagi, P., Chilamkurti, N., Grima, S., Sood, K., & Balusamy, B. (Eds.), *The Adoption and Effect of Artificial Intelligence on Human Resources Management, Part A* (pp. 175–196). Emerald Studies in Finance, Insurance, and Risk Management. DOI: 10.1108/978-1-80382-027-920231009

Sood, K., Pathak, P., Jain, J., & Gupta, S. (2023). How does an investor prioritize ESG factors in India? An assessment based on fuzzy AHP. *Managerial Finance*, 49(1), 66–87. DOI: 10.1108/MF-04-2022-0162

Stuck, M., & Grunes, A. (2016). *Big data and competition policy*. Oxford University Press. DOI: 10.1093/law:ocl/9780198788133.001.0001

Tarmuji, I., Maelah, R., & Tarmuji, N. H. (2016). The impact of environmental, social and governance practices (ESG) on economic performance: Evidence from ESG score. International Journal of Trade. *Economics and Finance*, 7(3), 67–74.

Trujillo, J. (2021). The Intelligence of Machines. Filosofija. Sociologija. 2021, 32(1), 84–92. DOI: 10.6001/fil-soc.v32i1.4383

United Nations. (1987). *Report of the World Commission on Environment and Development: Our Common Future ('Brundtland Report')*. Oxford University Press.

Verbin, I. (2020). *Corporate Responsibility in the Digital Age: A Practitioner's Roadmap for Corporate Responsibility in the Digital Age*. Routledge. DOI: 10.4324/9781003054795

Vinuesa, R., Azizpour, H., Leite, I., Balaam, M., Dignum, V., Domisch, S., Felländer, A., Daniela Langhans, S., Tegmark, M., & Fuso Nerini, F. (2020). The role of artificial intelligence in achieving the Sustainable Development Goals. *Nature Communications*, 11(1), 1–10. DOI: 10.1038/s41467-019-14108-y PMID: 31932590

Walker, J., Pekmezovic, A., & Walker, G. (2019). *Sustainable Development Goals: Harnessing Business to Achieve the SDGs through Finance, Technology and Law Reform*. John Wiley & Sons. DOI: 10.1002/9781119541851

Xie, J., Nozawa, W., Yagi, M., Fujii, H., & Managi, S. (2019). Do environmental, social, and governance activities improve corporate financial performance? *Business Strategy and the Environment*, 28(2), 286–300. DOI: 10.1002/bse.2224

Yoon, B., Lee, J. H., & Byun, R. (2018). Does ESG performance enhance firm value? Evidence from Korea. *Sustainability (Basel)*, 10(10), 3635. DOI: 10.3390/su10103635

Zhao, J., & Fariñas, B. G. (2023). Artificial Intelligence and Sustainable Decisions. *European Business Organization Law Review*, 24(1), 1–39. DOI: 10.1007/s40804-022-00262-2

KEY TERMS AND DEFINITIONS

Analytics that Predict: When it comes to Artificial Intelligence (AI) and Environmental, Social, and Governance (ESG) aspects, the capacity to predict future results is critical. To improve their sustainability and overall performance, organizations will employ AI-driven data to detect and mitigate hazards related to the environment, society, and governance. Dealing with much complexity is part of navigating the complicated legal and regulatory environment. As such, it is essential to comply with both current and emerging requirements. By taking early steps and developing strong compliance plans, legal and regulatory issues may be overcome. When incorporating AI into environmental, social and governance (ESG) activities, accountability and transparency are essential. The ethical and responsible use of this AI technology to evaluate and improve ESG performance will reassure stakeholders that companies are making an effort to achieve their goals.

Artificial Intelligence Solutions Hosted in Amazon's cloud: Scalability might lower the upfront expenses associated with putting AI into practice, improving the sustainability goals' financial sustainability. Amazon's usage of cloud-based solutions demonstrated this.

Cooperation: Cooperation between regulators and industry players is necessary to promote moral AI and uphold legal requirements. Encouraging moral and legal reforms creates an atmosphere that is conducive to AI inclusion in ESG.

Data Accessibility and Quality: The optimal use of AI in ESG integrations requires easily accessible qualitative and quantitative data that is readily available. Data standards, data cleaning, and open data initiatives all help to improve the quality and accessibility of data.

Data Solutions: Businesses, governments, and data repositories may work together to tackle data difficulties via collaborative efforts on data projects. Successful collaborations may improve the data's dependability and accuracy.

Incorporating Environmental, Social, and Governance (ESG) Considerations With Artificial Intelligence (AI): It combines innovations with steady technical advancement. Stakeholders are guaranteed objectivity, traceability, and dependability when artificial intelligence is included into ESG. Giving organizations a transformative perspective on their environmental, social, and governance (ESG) concerns, this is an innovative method to solving environmental and social issues. The term "environmental, social, and governance" (ESG) is a methodical process for assessing the possible harm that an organization might do to issues related to the environment, society, or government. The word "sustainability" is still widely used in many fields. Businesses have realized that they must coordinate their operations with environmental guidelines. ESG principles steer companies towards ethical behavior, which in turn promotes environmental sustainability and fosters a more equitable modern society. Because AI must abide by ethical norms for the integration of environmental, social, and governance (ESG) principles, ethical and privacy considerations emerge while employing AI. Therefore, it's critical to carefully consider decisions pertaining to equity, openness, and the possibility of unanticipated outcomes. To further protect critical ESD data, strong security mechanisms and privacy restrictions must be put in place. Sustainability and social responsibility should be included into AI frameworks via the application of ethical norms and guidelines. Through case studies derived from real-world situations, the use of ethical AI in combination with an Environmental, Social, and Governance (ESG) framework is shown. Data integrity is essential for AI-driven ESG projects, as shown by IBM's Watson for Sustainability, which addressed data quality challenges using sophisticated data cleaning and integration techniques. Inadequate comprehension and knowledge Success in an AI-driven ESG strategy requires certain skills and expertise. It is essential to close the knowledge gaps among pertinent parties and carry out critical programs including public awareness, education, and training to illustrate the possible advantages and constraints of integrating AI into ESG processes. Microsoft's Ethical AI Framework highlights the ethical issues associated with using AI for environmental, social, and governance (ESG) objectives, demonstrating the company's commitment to moral principles. With the use of AI-powered ESG services, AAI has the potential to increase stakeholder engagement in ESG initiatives like the creation of sustainable products and create new revenue streams. investigating new paths for the growth and impact of sustainability-oriented companies in an AI environment that is becoming more and more prevalent.

Obstacles and Challenges: Combining artificial intelligence (AI) with environmental, social, and governance (ESG) principles presents a number of obstacles. Entities must overcome several main constraints, including as technological difficulties, legal frameworks, privacy and data security concerns, ethical considerations, biases, and data quality problems, in order to reap significant benefits from AI in their ESD operations.

Predicting Future Patterns and Expecting Difficulties: The adoption of moral supply chain management systems, the use of artificial intelligence to social impact assessments, and the application of predictive analytics to environmental, social, and governance (ESG) aspects assessment are among the anticipated advancements. Concerns about data protection and the constantly changing regulatory landscape provide challenges.

Restrictions on Costs and Resources Available: Financial use based on AI with ESG integration faces several obstacles. It is also crucial to distribute resources and costs for both initial and continuing maintenance in an efficient manner. The approach is a meticulous and deliberate planning procedure aimed at saving expenses while fulfilling sustainability objectives. Data from artificial intelligence (AI) systems and environmental, social, and governance (ESG) sources are combined and analyzed as part of the data integration process. The data must be thoroughly examined and combined for this procedure. These include a wide range of data, such as governance indicators, environmental statistics, and other development outcome metrics. Using high-quality data is essential to improving the forecast and assessment accuracy of AI-powered ESG operations.

Chapter 4
Business Analysis for Digital Transformation Initiatives:
A Bridge Between Strategy and Execution

Minh Tung Tran
https://orcid.org/0000-0002-4238-882X
FPT University, Vietnam

ABSTRACT

Digital transformation (DX) is reshaping businesses across all industries. However, many DX initiatives fail to achieve their desired outcomes. Business analysis (BA) plays a critical role in bridging the gap between strategic vision and successful execution in these initiatives. This article explores the value proposition of BA for DX projects, focusing on key areas of contribution. It outlines a framework for integrating BA practices throughout the DX lifecycle, from strategy definition to solution implementation. The article concludes by discussing the evolving skillset required for business analysts to navigate the complexities of DX initiatives.

INTRODUCTION

Digital transformation is the profound and accelerating transformation of business activities, processes, competencies, and models to fully leverage the changes and opportunities of digital technologies and their impact in a strategic and prioritized way. A digital initiative is the process of macro-level strategic impact of digital transformation on the organization or industries. Initiatives are designed to create different goals that the institutions want to reach in the short and long term. The initiatives are divided into many sub-projects and programs, which can make it easier to manage and monitor. Digital initiatives can also bring negative impacts to the organization. This happens because digital initiatives will change the working pattern from manual to digital. Negative impacts that can happen include an increase in the unemployment level because the organization feels the new system can perform better than humans, changing business processes causing chaos, and the worst is when the initiative fails. There are many factors that can cause digital initiatives to fail. One of the most common factors is the failure to design the business process properly because the business process is a bridge of how the system or

DOI: 10.4018/979-8-3693-3884-1.ch004

the application will work, so it will affect the next step of the business. (de Lucas Ancillo & Gavrila, 2023; Zoltners et al., 2021).

THEORACTICAL FRAMEWORK

1. Key Concepts in Digital Transformation

An initiative centered on digital transformation will span five or more years and consume a significant amount of an organization's IT effort. Digital transformation initiatives are proving ground for CIOs' IT leadership while the jury is out on what IT will mean to the business in the digital age; successful transformation is a chance to show the value that IT can provide. But IT has its work cut out. Digital transformation often involves hard decisions about whether to build the digital capabilities needed to compete more effectively with new entrants and incumbents or fundamentally reinvent the business. (Dąbrowska et al., 2022)

Digital transformation can refer to anything from IT modernization to the wholesale changes of an organization. It's often used to reference the latter, as ours does. That said, digital transformation is often used more specifically as a means to an end, rather than a set of disruptive and groundbreaking technologies. In this way, digital transformation can be thought of as the integration of digital technology into all areas of a business, resulting in a fundamental change in how businesses operate and deliver value to customers. A digital transformation initiative may be motivated by many goals, but avoiding being outflanked by new, more nimble competitors is a common impetus. Integrate AMA, more specifics here. (Van Veldhoven & Vanthienen, 2022)

The topics of digitalization and technology-based company transformation are not new, but have grown so rapidly and have unleashed so many changes that nearly every business is now affected. There are many interpretations of what digital transformation is, but for me it's the process of using technology to radically change and empower business and the interactions with customers, and it's a very important concept to the changing landscape of a modern business. (Ritter & Pedersen, 2020)

2. Role of Business Analysis in Digital Transformation

A massive part of the role of business analysis includes obtaining stakeholder requirements and constructing a business case to gain approval for the answer(s). This might involve the development of a comprehensive marketing strategy which describes the modifications involved and expected benefits and costs. These may be summarized using business approach models, which are an IT artifact used to represent the plan for a particular undertaking or activity. This is crucial within the context of a digital transformation task as many modified approaches can also involve implementation of recent IT platforms and/or structures and the purpose of the assignment can be to enhance present IT systems and assist, an area frequently left exposed using techniques such as business procedure reengineering. This all presents a clear direction for a business analyst. (Giorgi et al., 2022)

With that established, it's significant to think of the area in question. Business enterprise analysis is defining business desires, understanding the current state, and making sure that offered answer(s) are in line with the enterprise desires. Business analysts do not try to define the technological solutions, they try to define the best answers for the commercial enterprise using data technology. In the scope of digital transformation, this provides an answer to the pervasive problem "what should I be seeking to do", this is a common problem for groups considering to use technologies except a clear concept of what they are making an attempt to achieve. The answer typically includes a combination of new system and/or technology improvement, in the scope of business analysis this might involve scoping projects and breaking challenge into phases within the task. (Zamani et al., 2024)

3. Business Analysis Techniques for Digital Transformation

Business analysis techniques are used to identify the business needs, understand the structure and dynamics of the organization, and to recommend solutions that will enable the organization to achieve its goals. Digital is the use of technology to radically improve performance or reach of enterprises. Digital transformation, in the context of this paper, is both about iterative exploitation of digital technologies and capabilities to significantly improve and change the business, and about radically changing the way business is done. It will involve new principles, new processes, new business models, and new public and private services; it will have a profound effect on society. So, the question is, how well do traditional business analysis techniques apply to digital transformation initiatives? In recent years, there has been a push to identify and define new analytical techniques to better understand the feasibility, the costs, and the business cases for transformation. This section suggests that the BA community should not be so quick to discard existing techniques, and that a mix of old and new can provide the bridge between strategy and execution that is so often missing. (Chawla & Goyal, 2022; Peng & Tao, 2022; Van Veldhoven & Vanthienen, 2022).

4. Identifying Business Needs and Objectives

It is important to understand the current state of the business organization in order to determine the steps to get the digital transformation initiative underway. This can be achieved through a comprehensive review that clearly defines where the business is versus where it needs to be. Many frameworks exist that can help determine a business' maturity level in its use of IT. The next step is to identify the areas that require improvement. This may involve a specific business process or a strategic initiative such as better utilizing mobile or cloud-based technologies. In some cases, there might be a need to define completely new capabilities. Enterprise architecture can be extremely useful in mapping which business needs and objectives that the digital initiative needs to target. This will involve creating models of the current and future state, and then conducting a gap analysis to determine the changes required in an IT context. (Van Veldhoven & Vanthienen, 2022)

5. Stakeholder Analysis and Engagement

Stakeholders are groups of people who have a vested interest in an organization or an initiative. Effective engagement with these stakeholders can have an extremely positive impact on the execution of an initiative and its eventual outcome. An extensive body of literature exists which advocates for stakeholder engagement in projects, linking such engagement to project success and improved performance. However, stakeholder engagement is not always appropriate. There are instances where stakeholder analysis will determine that certain stakeholders should be monitored, but not engaged. Such an approach is clearly less resource intensive. (Shaukat et al., 2022). This chapter aims to provide a clear guide to conducting stakeholder analysis and engagement, with the purpose of improving the chances of initiative success. This is achieved by providing a logical process for stakeholder mapping and categorization, discussing the development of understanding about stakeholders that is vital in the identification of their differing requirements and the subsequent engagement approach. Finally, the discussion is set in a project context, and potential impacts of effective stakeholder engagement are described. (Ebekozien et al., 2024)

6. Requirements, Elicitation, and Documentation

The requirements documentation produced should be used as a tool for communication between the system builder and the stakeholders to have clear objectives in building the system. It can also be used as a legal agreement if the system builder is a separate organization or person from the stakeholders. The requirements may also serve as the basis for a contract between the developer and the customer. If the documented requirements are included in a legal agreement between the two, then any dispute regarding whether the completed system does or does not meet the customer's expectations can be referred back to the requirements. (Laux et al., 2024)

Requirements elicitation is the process of identifying the requirements for a system. The system should deliver the facilities that meet the customer's required function, and the goal is to find the best solution for the customers and the system itself. It is also defined as a set of activities used to discover the requirements of the system from stakeholders and other sources. The goal of this activity is to produce a stable set of requirements that have been agreed upon by stakeholders and can be used as the basis for any further development of the system. This process is the first step in building a system. Many failures in information systems are caused by a too quick jump to system building or by skipping this part, and some team members do not understand the concept of the system to be built. In this case, this step is the most crucial step in system development. If the requirements of the system are unclear and partial, then the resulting system will not satisfy the customer and will not meet their expectations. (Li et al., 2021)

7. Business Process Analysis and Improvement

The first is a flowchart. This is a diagram defined as a formalized graphic representation of a logical sequence, work or manufacturing process, organization chart, or similar formalized structure. The second is activity-based costing. This is a method of accounting in which all costs incurred in carrying out an activity or group of activities are collected, classified, and recorded. These costs are then expressed in terms of the activity output. The third model is functional analysis. This is a structured technique derived from role and task analysis for defining and understanding a sequence of activities and their relationships. The last model is value stream mapping. This is a lean-management method for analyzing the current state and designing a future state for the series of events that take a product or service from its beginning through to the customer. Model construction is commonly taught in universities as IS students usually become business analysts who specialize in business process analysis. (Asudani et al., 2023)

Business process analysis is a disciplined approach for identifying and then improving a business process, in order to achieve better business results. This work is motivated by the need to support the initiatives of digital transformation. Typically, organizations go into digital transformation without proper understanding of how things are being done currently. Improvement should be done to the business process because a later stage of the business process is used as the basis to develop information systems that support the business. Redesign might lead to extra cost in system development. The step of analyzing and identifying the business process commonly consists of constructing a set of representational models. There are four types of models. (Beerepoot et al., 2023)

8. Data Analysis and Management

Usually, at the beginning, we do not have a clear picture of what an analysis will produce, so it needs an iterative process with the business owner. The result is a clear understanding of what data or information can support the business process. In this case, sometimes we need to purchase additional data or just change a little bit of the business process because of considerations from the analysis. The effect can happen on the business process reengineering, and we should go back to the business process analysis. But it is not a problem because iteration is common in everything related to this automation and data. The change is the positive side, now you have a clear reason why you must change. Now your data is 'telling' you. (Yang et al., 2022)

An important step for making data effective is conducting data analysis. It can be defined as the process of inspecting, cleaning, transforming, and modeling data with the objective of discovering useful information, informing conclusions, and supporting decision-making. Data analysis has an important role in increasing the efficiency and effectiveness of using the data. At this stage, we know clearly what the information requirements are to support business processes. We already have data in the warehouse, but we need to sort and analyze the data to ensure we get the useful information to support our business process. (Wang et al., 2022)

9. Technology Evaluation and Selection

In order to facilitate the evaluation and selection of systems, it can be wise to seek advice from someone who has a strong understanding of the available technologies. This may involve the hiring of a consultant or the use of a recruitment firm with expertise in a given area. In some cases, the recruitment of extra IT staff will be necessary to address gaps in IT knowledge identified throughout the course of a project. (Mukhuty et al., 2022)

Once an understanding of the potential changes has been developed, the onus is on the initiative team to evaluate and select technologies. The objective during this phase is to identify and evaluate potential systems solutions that will address the business needs and to select the best solution for the business. This requires a clear understanding of the technology that is being evaluated. In most cases, the high-level characteristics of a system can be ascertained through interaction with system vendors and through product literature. However, when assessing whether a given product is suitable for the business, it is necessary to understand the inner workings of the system and to ascertain its flexibility. (Gyamfi et al., 2022)

EVALUATION OF AVAILABLE TECHNOLOGIES

1. Change Management and Adoption Strategies

The purpose of change management is to provide academic activity aimed at understanding the students' perspective and to facilitate voluntary changes of individuals, teams, or organizations to effectively achieve the strategic objectives. With adequate change management, students will understand the needs for change, how it will affect them, and how they can best involve themselves in the change process. This is particularly important because Information Systems initiatives often bring about automation of tasks or even replacement of certain job roles with others. It is important to give these future users a reason to support the change and to show them how they may best fit into the new system. This might mean bettering their skills in order to take advantage of new system functionalities, or in some cases, it might mean escalating training efforts for employees whose jobs will change radically. These duties are all a part of preparing the environment for change. The next steps are then to install the change and make sure it does not get disposed of. This will involve a variety of efforts, but a key ingredient will be to make sure that the new system is adopted and is perceived as the current way of doing things. Measures of system disposal often led to user rejection of the new system and reverting back to the old process. This can be prevented by showing the value of the new system and making it the automatic choice. Finally, a post-implementation reinforcement will confirm the change and help smooth the transition for any users who may still be struggling. (Jöhnk et al.2021), (Latifah et al.2024)

2. Project Management and Execution

The first step toward success is having a clear plan on the steps that need to be achieved. This will require breaking the transformation down into a number of work packages that can be completed by a team of people within a realistic time frame. Each work package will need to be completed to achieve a certain objective, which works as a measure of success for that task. This will be a lengthy process; however, it is crucial in ensuring that everyone is on the same page and working towards a common goal. (Baiyere et al.2020)

The project management stage is a critical, yet frequently overlooked, step that will determine the overall success of the digital transformation. At a high level, the project management phase involves taking the output from the strategy phase and putting it into action. This requires a clear understanding of what needs to be done, when it needs to be completed, who will be doing the work, and how much it will cost. All of this needs to be achieved within the constraints of time, scope, cost, and quality of the organization. (Nadkarni & Prügl, 2021)

3. Monitoring and Evaluation of Digital Transformation Initiatives

An example from SKF shows how they identified 40 projects that up to date had no overall quantified target. They created a matrix to define the value and the confidence of success of each project and from this selected the ones with the highest value and confidence. These were then given specific targets. If at any point through implementation or upon review the confidence of success was low, they would drop the initiative. This method was successful in driving out projects that were not fully aligned with the strategy with no risk or loss. (Sollberger et al., 2023)

Developing an evaluation strategy should overlap with the initiatives it is assessing. Where data is being collected that has enabled decisions and actions, suggest the creation of an evaluation plan to follow the work through to completion. This is a good method for assessing individual projects or initiatives and can be cheaply and effectively done through a simple ROI analysis to compare the amount invested with the value created. More complex initiatives will require a more thoroughly comprehensive evaluation plan. (Nieminen, 2024)

The accomplishment of a digital transformation will be thrilling. Having changed how you operate, how you deliver worth to consumers, and how you take knowledgeable choices, the improvement will symbolize the creation of a modernized company. The journey has established a newly discovered competitive edge that can enhance profitability. Bringing about change of this depth represents a serious endeavor. As we have discussed, it may envelop time periods and several initiatives and will easily be jeopardized by reverting to outmoded habits and fail to realize the full potential. Periodic evaluation can monitor the track of progression and assess the value of the change. It may sound pedantic, however, reverting a misguided initiative early can often save wasting resources that will later become a larger investment to correct the mistake. At a more complex level, it is critical to preserving the continuity of new processes and preventing a backslide into the old ways. Finally, the ability to illustrate the value gained will give confidence to stakeholders and secure continued investment. All of these will become factors in deciding how successful the transformation has been. (Kraus et al., 2021)

4. Risk Management in Digital Transformation

Digital transformation is associated with high dependency on technology. Implementing new technology and automation will bring uncertainty in reducing efficiency and the chances of increasing costs. Also, it involves the risk of losing critical mass and potential failure, as there will be continuous change in process and technology. Thus, while considering digital transformation initiatives, importance has to be given in managing the risk effectively. This often means the difference between a successful project and a failure. It is less about preventing problems from occurring, and more about the ability to mitigate any impacts and to continue with the initiative effectively. The main objective of risk management is not to eliminate all uncertainties, but to help ensure that the initiatives meet their objectives in full with minimum disruption. (Nadkarni & Prügl, 2021)

5. Governance and Compliance in Digital Transformation

Knowing how to effectively govern a digital transformation project is crucial. The primary objectives of governance should be: providing proper management of the project, assuring the project adds continual value to the organization, and making sure the project is on the right track towards successful completion. Having powerful governance can easily be the difference between a successful project and a failed one. If the governance is ineffective, it is unlikely the project will be completed on time or on budget. This is highlighted by information system professionals stating "a project's success can be directly linked to the methods used to manage it". This shows that without strong governance, the chances of success are slim. (Marion and Fixson, 2021)

Governance requires a solid structure to be effective. The key factors to successful governance are leadership, decision-making authority, and establishing processes to support the endeavor. Once these have been determined, there must be constant oversight from the governing body to make sure the project stays on the right track. Regular checks should be made to compare the project's current status with the original plan, highlight any discrepancies, and adjust the plan accordingly. In the case of any changes to the business requirements, the governance team must directly analyze the impact on the project and fully understand what changes may need to be implemented. (Konopik et al., 2022)

CONCLUSION

The research has presented a number of case study examples and has been informed by ongoing action research in collaboration with industry. The outcome is a holistic and integrated set of tools, techniques and insights for practice.

The research has outlined a range of problems and challenges faced by modern organizations and a corresponding set of tools and techniques provided by the discipline of business analysis. These tools and techniques have been integrated into a conceptual 'intervention framework' aligning high-level strategy with detailed implementation. (Sestino and De, 2022)

This research has examined how business analysis can enable and support digital transformation initiatives, by bridging the often cited strategy-implementation gap. A systems-thinking approach was taken, considering the enterprise as a system and aiming to understand the inter-relationships between strategy, business model, process, IT systems and organizational change. (Butt et al., 2024)

With the digitization of the global economy, organizations face increased levels of innovation, technological disruption, and disintermediation in their markets. Enterprises are using digital technology not only to produce new types of digital goods and services, but also to create new business models and new ways of differentiating themselves in the market. (Bresciani et al., 2021)

REFERENCES

Asudani, D. S., Nagwani, N. K., & Singh, P. (2023). Impact of word embedding models on text analytics in deep learning environment: A review. *Artificial Intelligence Review*, 56(9), 10345–10425. Advance online publication. DOI: 10.1007/s10462-023-10419-1 PMID: 36844886

Baiyere, A., Salmela, H., & Tapanainen, T. (2020). Digital transformation and the new logics of business process management. *European Journal of Information Systems*, 29(3), 238–259. DOI: 10.1080/0960085X.2020.1718007

Beerepoot, I., Di Ciccio, C., Reijers, H. A., Rinderle-Ma, S., Bandara, W., Burattin, A., Calvanese, D., Chen, T., Cohen, I., Depaire, B., Di Federico, G., Dumas, M., van Dun, C., Fehrer, T., Fischer, D. A., Gal, A., Indulska, M., Isahagian, V., Klinkmüller, C., & Zerbato, F. (2023). The biggest business process management problems to solve before we die. *Computers in Industry*, 146, 103837. DOI: 10.1016/j.compind.2022.103837

Bresciani, S., Huarng, K. H., Malhotra, A., & Ferraris, A. (2021). Digital transformation as a springboard for product, process and business model innovation. *Journal of Business Research*, 128, 204–210. DOI: 10.1016/j.jbusres.2021.02.003

Butt, A., Imran, F., Helo, P., & Kantola, J. (2024). Strategic design of culture for digital transformation. *Long Range Planning*, 57(2), 102415. Advance online publication. DOI: 10.1016/j.lrp.2024.102415

Chawla, R. N., & Goyal, P. (2022). Emerging trends in digital transformation: A bibliometric analysis. *Benchmarking*, 29(4), 1069–1112. Advance online publication. DOI: 10.1108/BIJ-01-2021-0009

Dąbrowska, J., Almpanopoulou, A., Brem, A., Chesbrough, H., Cucino, V., Di Minin, A., Giones, F., Hakala, H., Marullo, C., Mention, A.-L., Mortara, L., Nørskov, S., Nylund, P. A., Oddo, C. M., Radziwon, A., & Ritala, P. (2022). Digital transformation, for better or worse: A critical multi-level research agenda. *R & D Management*, 52(5), 930–954. DOI: 10.1111/radm.12531

de Lucas Ancillo, A., & Gavrila, S. G. (2023). The impact of research and development on entrepreneurship, innovation, digitization and digital transformation. *Journal of Business Research*, 157, 113566. Advance online publication. DOI: 10.1016/j.jbusres.2022.113566

Ebekozien, A., Aigbavboa, C. O., & Ramotshela, M. (2024). A qualitative approach to investigate stakeholders' engagement in construction projects. *Benchmarking*, 31(3), 866–883. DOI: 10.1108/BIJ-11-2021-0663

Giorgi, S., Lavagna, M., Wang, K., Osmani, M., Liu, G., & Campioli, A. (2022). Drivers and barriers towards circular economy in the building sector: Stakeholder interviews and analysis of five European countries policies and practices. *Journal of Cleaner Production*, 336, 130395. DOI: 10.1016/j.jclepro.2022.130395

Gyamfi, B. A., Agozie, D. Q., & Bekun, F. V. (2022). Can technological innovation, foreign direct investment and natural resources ease some burden for the BRICS economies within current industrial era? *Technology in Society*, 70, 102037. Advance online publication. DOI: 10.1016/j.techsoc.2022.102037

Jöhnk, J., Weißert, M., & Wyrtki, K. (2021). Ready or not, AI comes—An interview study of organizational AI readiness factors. *Business & Information Systems Engineering*, 63(1), 5–20. DOI: 10.1007/s12599-020-00676-7

Konopik, J., Jahn, C., Schuster, T., Hoßbach, N., & Pflaum, A. (2022). *Mastering the digital transformation through organizational capabilities: A conceptual framework*. Digital Business., DOI: 10.1016/j.digbus.2021.100019

Kraus, S., Jones, P., Kailer, N., Weinmann, A., Chaparro-Banegas, N., & Roig-Tierno, N. (2021). Digital transformation: An overview of the current state of the art of research. *SAGE Open*, 11(3), 21582440211047576. DOI: 10.1177/21582440211047576

Latifah, I. N., Suhendra, A. A., & Mufidah, I. (2024). Factors affecting job satisfaction and employee performance: A case study in an Indonesian sharia property companies. *International Journal of Productivity and Performance Management*, 73(3), 719–748. DOI: 10.1108/IJPPM-03-2021-0132

Laux, J., Wachter, S., & Mittelstadt, B. (2024). Three pathways for standardisation and ethical disclosure by default under the European Union Artificial Intelligence Act. *Computer Law & Security Report*, 53, 105957. Advance online publication. DOI: 10.1016/j.clsr.2024.105957

Li, X., Wang, Z., Chen, C. H., & Zheng, P. (2021). A data-driven reversible framework for achieving Sustainable Smart product-service systems. *Journal of Cleaner Production*, 279, 123618. Advance online publication. DOI: 10.1016/j.jclepro.2020.123618

Marion, T. J., & Fixson, S. K. (2021). The transformation of the innovation process: How digital tools are changing work, collaboration, and organizations in new product development. *Journal of Product Innovation Management*, 38(1), 192–215. DOI: 10.1111/jpim.12547

Mukhuty, S., Upadhyay, A., & Rothwell, H. (2022). Strategic sustainable development of Industry 4.0 through the lens of social responsibility: The role of human resource practices. *Business Strategy and the Environment*, 31(5), 2068–2081. DOI: 10.1002/bse.3008

Nadkarni, S., & Prügl, R. (2021). *Digital transformation: a review, synthesis and opportunities for future research*. Management Review Quarterly., DOI: 10.1007/s11301-020-00185-7

Nieminen, J. H. (2024). Assessment for Inclusion: Rethinking inclusive assessment in higher education. *Teaching in Higher Education*, 29(4), 841–859. Advance online publication. DOI: 10.1080/13562517.2021.2021395

Peng, Y. & Tao, C. (2022). Can digital transformation promote enterprise performance?—From the perspective of public policy and innovation. Journal of Innovation & Knowledge. https://doi.org/DOI: 10.1016/j.jik.2022.100198

Ritter, T., & Pedersen, C. L. (2020). Digitization capability and the digitalization of business models in business-to-business firms: Past, present, and future. *Industrial Marketing Management*, 86, 180–190. Advance online publication. DOI: 10.1016/j.indmarman.2019.11.019

Sestino, A., & De Mauro, A. (2022). Leveraging artificial intelligence in business: Implications, applications and methods. *Technology Analysis and Strategic Management*, 34(1), 16–29. DOI: 10.1080/09537325.2021.1883583

Shaukat, M. B., Latif, K. F., Sajjad, A., & Eweje, G. (2022). Revisiting the relationship between sustainable project management and project success: The moderating role of stakeholder engagement and team building. *Sustainable Development (Bradford)*, 30(1), 58–75. DOI: 10.1002/sd.2228

Sollberger, V. D., Korthaus, A., Barg, A., & Pagenstert, G. (2023). Long-term results after anterior cruciate ligament reconstruction using patellar tendon versus hamstring tendon autograft with a minimum follow-up of 10 years—A systematic review. *Archives of Orthopaedic and Trauma Surgery*, 143(7), 4277–4289. DOI: 10.1007/s00402-022-04687-9 PMID: 36441213

Van Veldhoven, Z., & Vanthienen, J. (2022). Digital transformation as an interaction-driven perspective between business, society, and technology. *Electronic Markets*, 32(2), 629–644. Advance online publication. DOI: 10.1007/s12525-021-00464-5 PMID: 35602117

Wang, J., Xu, C., Zhang, J., & Zhong, R. (2022). Big data analytics for intelligent manufacturing systems: A review. *Journal of Manufacturing Systems*, 62, 738–752. Advance online publication. DOI: 10.1016/j.jmsy.2021.03.005

Yang, J., Xiu, P., Sun, L., Ying, L., & Muthu, B. (2022). Social media data analytics for business decision making system to competitive analysis. *Information Processing & Management*, 59(1), 102751. DOI: 10.1016/j.ipm.2021.102751

Zamani, E. D., Griva, A., Spanaki, K., O'Raghallaigh, P., & Sammon, D. (2024). Making sense of business analytics in project selection and prioritisation: Insights from the start-up trenches. *Information Technology & People*, 37(2), 895–918. DOI: 10.1108/ITP-09-2020-0633

Zoltners, A. A., Sinha, P., Sahay, D., Shastri, A., & Lorimer, S. E. (2021). Practical insights for sales force digitalization success. *Journal of Personal Selling & Sales Management*, 41(2), 87–102. DOI: 10.1080/08853134.2021.1908144

Chapter 5
Business Analytics in Business Models

Dina Darwish
Ahram Canadian University, Egypt

ABSTRACT

The word "business model" has been around for years, yet companies naturally conceive, establish, and execute their models from the start. Business models and their key approaches must be studied. Leaders base company decisions on their own expertise and preference. Decision-making in business data analytics is based on data, removing cognitive and personal biases. Effective corporate data analysis can boost a company's competitiveness. Business data analytics quantifies internal and external aspects, helping stakeholders and IT understand organizational success and customer responsibility. This chapter discussed Business Data Analytics methodologies and their importance.

INTRODUCTION

Regarding the utilization of Business Processes and Information, once the strategy and the overall strategic key performance indicators (KPIs) have been developed, a framework, a focus, and objectives can be established for the operational business processes and initiatives. The information and analysis that are generated must be directed towards the management and modification of business processes in order to achieve the strategic goals that are made evident by the key performance indicators (KPIs). The purpose of business analysis initiatives is to facilitate the modification of business procedures and activities in such a way that they are geared towards the accomplishment of the organization's strategic outcomes. For instance, those in charge of making operational decisions in areas such as sales, marketing, manufacturing, general management, human resources (HR), and finance can make use of information and knowledge to improve the efficiency of their actions on a regular basis.

What (the offered value), who (the target consumers), how (the mechanism for creating and selling value to the customer), and why (the process for extracting and assigning income from the sale of value to the consumer) are the four components that form the foundation of contemporary views regarding the business model. Within the framework of the first, aspects such as the value proposition, customer segments, key resources, and key activities are derived. Within the framework of the second, an operational model is created, which includes logistics, marketing support for activities, and sources of commercial

DOI: 10.4018/979-8-3693-3884-1.ch005

effect. In this context, the simplest model scheme, which consists of four elements, is combined with an inclusive approach to social entrepreneurship, which reflects the role that target groups play in the model. The authors pointed out that the theory of social impact serves as the foundation for any model, which is a uniqueness that is associated with the process of creating business models in the context of social entrepreneurship. According to this theory, the production of a social effect should be the primary focus of any organization, and it should be regarded as a value that is equivalent to the value that is constructed economically.

Since the 1990s, the term "business model" has been steadily present in scientific research on the corporate sector of the economy. This segment of the economy has not been filled with a single empirical content for a considerable amount of time, but rather has the quality of generalizing the company's primary market idea and its strategy. It is common practice to refer to innovations that are associated with a technology, product, or business process when discussing the business model. This is due to the fact that the inventive potential of a firm has been expressed exactly in a product, technology, or process for a long time, and these aspects of a business idea were the center of attention. To a certain extent, this is the situation at the moment. There is a logical connection between the category of a business model and other ideas, such as corporate strategy, business process, and value chain. When we combine these ideas into a single line of reasoning, we can argue that a company strategy is what determines its empirical projection or business model, which is a business process for developing a value chain.

Following the year 1995, the phrase "business model" became frequently utilized. The first stage is considered to be the stage that comes along with a significant shift in the culture of business towards the digital economy being implemented. Relationships between the ideas of "business model" and "strategy," "business model" and "productivity," and "business model" and "innovation, opportunities, and resources" are developed during the second stage of the process. In conclusion, the third stage is distinguished by a significant increase in the level of competition that exists between businesses. As a result of the expansion of the Internet, the business model has gained popularity. People are aware that the business climate is more uncertain in the context of globalization and the acceleration of technological advances, and that the most important aspect in determining success for a firm is the business models that it employs.

BACKGROUND

A business model that is innovative has the potential to bring about a strategic competitive advantage; an organization ought to be able to develop in the course of the new economic environment. The organization is able to remain competitive because to the presence of numerous useful novel technologies that are incorporated into an innovative business model, which is considered to be a new management template. The word swiftly acquired popularity not only among practitioners but also among business scientists as a result of the development of information and communication technologies (ICT) and the introduction of enterprises that operate on the Internet. Over the course of this time period, language has extended over a variety of communities, including marketing, management, banking, and information and communication technology (ICT). Furthermore, this vocabulary is utilized in a variety of situations, including a business plan, business strategy, value creation, globalization, and design organization.

In his presentation and analysis of a business model, David Watson (Watson, 2005) examines and evaluates the following six components: competitors, customers, economics, management, products, and suppliers. According to Chesbrough (Chesbrough, 2006), it provides a fresh and unique perspective on each particular component. Barriers to market entry, the danger of substitute products, competition within the sector, and the advantage of being the first on the market are the factors that influence the level of competition in a given market context. Customers are rated based on the traits they possess, the sorts of contracts they have, and the payment rates they pay. When evaluating management, morality, checking for conflicts, accounting standards, previous successes, and connections with partners are all taken into consideration. When conducting product analysis, the primary areas of focus are brand loyalty, competitive advantage, new product development, differentiation, sales points, and innovations in value chain development. The bargaining power of suppliers and their ability to make opportunistic purchases establish their status. This model has a lot of steps. The fact that the model analyses industry characteristics, such as competition, which are related to the environment of the business model but are not part of the components of the business model is what gives it its distinctive advantage. There are five different types of markets that are used to identify consumer categories. These markets are mass, segmented, niche, diversified, and multilateral. The term "mass market" refers to a big gathering of consumers who have similar requirements and issues. One type of customer is segmented, which means that they are divided into groups based on the same qualities. Products and services that are specifically designed for the consumer can be found in niche markets. Diversified markets cover two or more separate industries, each of which has its own unique set of requirements and difficulties. Multilateral transactions involve the utilization and interconnection of segments. For example, the VISA credit card provider establishes ties between three distinct groups, namely banks, cardholders, and retailers. The development of primary value, which is outlined in the mission statement of the firm and specifies the principal product or service that the company offers to the customer, serves as the foundation of the business. The corporation adds "additional value" (or a combination of other values) to the primary cost, which is referred to as value added. This is done in order to improve the way a customer perceives a product or service.

MAIN FOCUS OF THE CHAPTER

Business Model

In practice, the word "business model" has been used for a number of years; yet, businesses construct, define, and implement their models in a subconscious manner from the very beginning of their operations. The idea of a business model, as well as the primary methods that can be utilized to comprehend it must be studied. A comprehensive presentation and study of the business model of the corporation, as well as an examination of the impact that classifiers have on the way the company operates in its day-to-day operations. Through the examination of the connections that exist between the primary components of the business model, it has been demonstrated that it is possible to recognize issues that arise with regard to the compliance and sustainability of the business model. The depiction of a business model through system elements is one of the most general schemes that can be used to provide a systematic description of a business model. Additionally, the features of each component of the business model, including customers, distribution, cost, resources, activities, and revenues, have to be determined.

The concept of the value chain, which was initially introduced, is considered to be one of the most important aspects of strategic management. Also, the value that the company provides to the customer is the outcome of two different kinds of activities: the primary activities and the auxiliary activities. A number of different methodologies for data collection can be utilized. In general, these methods consist of specific text mining techniques that have been utilized in the past for the purpose of processing the primary textual characteristics of research documents that are associated with business models.

Data Collection

The first phase consisted of gathering the necessary information from the database. For the purpose of this procedure, the type of document, or the subject category, in order to incorporate all pertinent information from the published documents that were available. In addition to the journal article, the proceedings paper, the book chapter, and other sorts of papers, these documents also include other types. Furthermore, these documents are classified as belonging to the many subject groups, which include aspects such as business, management, computer science, and information systems.

Data Preparation

In the step of data preparation, the raw dataset that was obtained in the stage before this one has a variety of textual attributes. For the sake of this investigation, just certain instances of them have been utilized in each strategy. Zhang and his colleagues (Zhang et al., 2016) conducted a research study in which they were able to compare the utilization of author keywords with Keywords Plus in the World Wide Web. As a general conclusion, they suggested that the Keywords Plus should also be taken into consideration in bibliographic analyses. This is due to the fact that the tremendous quantity of these terms and the extensive variety of their meanings might lead to a number of benefits.

One of the various text mining algorithms just analyses keywords, while the other one analyses the abstract, and the other two analyze the title, the abstract, and the keywords. The presence of a wide variety of these attributes inside the input corpus has made it possible to generate findings that are based on a variety of attributes, which in turn has enabled the presentation of multidimensional analyses on the documents that were gathered. Additionally, it is anticipated that these studies will, in general, have a greater level of depth and accuracy in comparison to the situation in which only one characteristic is utilized.

The authors pre-processed the constructed corpus after selecting the textual qualities based on the planned study purposes. This was done in order to make the text ready for applying the primary analyses and to increase the quality of the results. The tokenization of the text, the removal of words that do not provide any information, the compounding of phrases that are similar, and the consideration of n-grams are all components of the pre-processing step. Therefore, once this stage is completed, a text that is fully prepared and free of any errors serves as the foundation for analysis in each of the text mining processes.

Data Processing

Co-word Analysis Callon, Courtial, Turner, and Bauin (Callon et al., 1983) were the ones who initially presented the idea of using co-word analysis as one of the methodologies for text mining (Yan et al., 2015) . According to Callon, Courtial, and Laville (Callon et al., 1991), this method is predicated on the fundamental concept that the co-occurrence of significant terms is a means of describing the relations that exist between the contents of a certain collection of documents. Words that are used in an article are good representatives that reflect the content of the article, and the co-occurrence of two words in different articles is an indication of their relationship with each other. The more frequently two words appear together, the closer their relationship will be (Feng et al., 2017). The principal assumptions that underpin the co-word analysis are as follows: Words within an article are good representatives that reflect the content of the article. This method has been utilized by researchers in recent years to accomplish a variety of objectives, including the evaluation of research and development impacts, the assessment of technological development trends, the analysis of research trends and hotspots, and the summarization of the evolution of research subjects (Wang et al., 2015).

Within the scope of this investigation, the utilization of co-word analysis made it feasible to accomplish two primary categories of macro- and micro-purposes. This involves identifying significant keywords and illustrating the connections between them, which are considered to be among the micro-goals, whilst the macro-goals consist of the identification of significant issues in the field of business model through the grouping of these keywords and the introduction of hidden themes inside each cluster. In addition, taking into account the time dimension in the co-occurrence network of keywords, the potential of accomplishing each of the aforementioned objectives while taking into account the time dimension has been offered. Visualizing the outcomes of the co-word analysis and drawing the co-occurrence network of keywords were both accomplished with the help of the VOSviewer software, which was utilized in this investigation. Using the frequency g-index approach, the most iterative keywords were identified from among all of the keywords, including author keywords and Keywords Plus (Yan et al., 2015).

This allowed for the creation of this network. The distance-based technique is utilized in the process of visualization within the VOSviewer program, as stated in the research that was supplied by Van Eck and Waltman (Van Ek et al., 2010). In a bibliographic network, this indicates that the nodes are situated in close proximity to one another, to the extent that the distance between two nodes almost discloses the degree to which they are associated. The number of times a keyword appears in the co-word network is used to determine the size of the nodes in the network. This indicates the level of significance that the keyword holds within the network. Through the resolution of an optimization problem, VOSviewer is able to classify those nodes that are more closely related to one another inside a single cluster. It is possible to make use of the descriptions that were proposed by Waltman and Van Eck (Van Ek et al., 2010), Waltman, Van Eck, and Noyons (Van Eck et al., 2014), in order to acquire a comprehensive grasp of the visualization and clustering method utilized by the VOSviewer software.

Kleinberg (Kleinberg et al., 2003) was the first person to propose the idea of using burst detection in the field of text mining (Sawant et al., 2011). The objective of the Kleinberg algorithm, known as the Burst Detection Algorithm (BDA), was to recognize the subjects that had unexpectedly become the focal point of attention in documents over a period of time. This method recognizes a sudden spike in the predominance of a document stream on a particular subject, which is referred to as the burst of activity (Kleinberg et al., 2003). Utilizing the co-occurrence of phrases within the documents, this algorithm is able to identify documents that are related to one another in terms of their subject matter. In burst analysis, paying attention to the beginning and ending timings of each term's burst can be helpful in locating subjects that are now trending and those that are just beginning to emerge (Nagmi et al.,2017). Furthermore, in comparison to methods that are based on citations, one of the most significant benefits of BDA is that it is able to recognize growing problems in academic publications independent of the number of citations that the papers have gotten. Because of this, this technique is able to identify a new scientific subject even before it has accumulated a large amount of citations (Chen et al., 2017). The technique of burst analysis was utilized in this research with the purpose of accomplishing two primary objectives: 1) Identifying new research trends between the years 1991 and 2018, and 2) Identifying the events that sparked these hot subjects. For the purpose of carrying out the burst analysis, the authors made use of the CiteSpace software, which has a built-in Kleinberg algorithm performing the role of its BDA. Morris, Yen, Wu, and Asnake (Morris et al., 2003) were the ones who initially advocated making use of the timeline view method for the purpose of performing timeline analysis visualization. This type of visualization was performed on scholarly publications with the purpose of determining the emergence and disappearance of research fronts throughout the course of time, with the ultimate goal of locating the foundational studies.

Business Data Analytics

In a broad sense, business data analytics is a practice that involves the application of a particular set of techniques, competencies, and procedures in order to carry out continuous exploration and investigation of both historical and current business data. The goal of this practice is to obtain insights about a company that can lead to improved decision-making. A number of different points of view can be utilized to provide a more specific definition of business data analytics. The following are some of the viewpoints that are included in this category: business data analytics as a movement, capability, data-centric activity set, decision-making paradigm, and collection of techniques and technology. However, this list is not exhaustive.

Business data analytics as a movement involves a management philosophy or business culture that bases problem identification and problem solving on evidence. From this point of view, the evidence that can be gleaned from data is the primary factor that drives business decisions and improvement. When this philosophy is in place, evidence is not selected to support a preconception or point of view; rather, all of the available evidence that is pertinent is used to make informed business decisions to fulfil the purpose of the philosophy.

Business data analytics is a competency that encompasses the competences that are possessed by the organization and the personnel of the organization. The ability of an organization to carry out analytical tasks is not the only factor that determines whether or not it possesses business data analytics capability. In addition to that, it encompasses competencies like as invention, the formation of culture, and the design of processes. That which the organization is actually capable of accomplishing through the use of business data analytics may be defined or constrained by the capability.

Business data analytics is an activity set that encompasses the actions that are necessary for an organization to employ evidence-based problem identification and problem solving. Accessing, analyzing, examining, interpreting, and aggregating, as well as presenting the results, are the six fundamental data-centric tasks that are included in the definition of business data analytics that has been provided by practitioners who are experts in the field.

As a paradigm for decision-making, business data analytics is a mechanism for effective and well-informed decision-making. When viewed through this perspective, business data analytics is regarded as the instrument that facilitates decision-making by means of the utilization of evidence-based problem identification and problem-solving. Business data analytics is also considered to be a collection of practices and technologies that are necessary in order to carry out the analytics work itself. These practices can be explored in the context of five different areas of business data analytics, which are as follows: identifying research questions, sourcing data, analyzing data, interpreting and reporting results, and using results to influence corporate decision-making.

The Objectives of Business Data Analytics

Most of the time, the decisions that leaders of organizations make in the business world are based on their own personal competencies and preferences. Business data analytics eliminates cognitive and human biases from the decision-making process by using data as the primary input for decision-making. This is accomplished through the utilization of data. Providing an organization with a competitive edge is possible through the utilization of business data analytics, provided that these analyses are carried out in an efficient manner. In a broader sense, the objective of business data analytics is to analyze and study the issues or opportunities faced by a firm by employing a scientific inquiry approach. This is the goal of the practice.

There are a variety of specific objectives that may be accomplished via the use of corporate data analytics, and these objectives vary according to the type of study that is under consideration. Various approaches to analytics may be classified into the following four categories:

Descriptive: Through the process of describing or summarizing the material that is accessible, this approach provides a look into the past. A response to the question "What has taken place?" is the goal of descriptive analytics, which is designed to fulfil this aim.

Diagnostic: involves looking at the factors that led to the occurrence of a specific outcome occurring. An answer to the query "Why did a particular event take place?" is the objective of diagnostic analytics, which is designed to offer an answer to this issue.

Predictive: The examination of previous trends in data in order to give insights into the future is what is meant by the term "predictive." The use of predictive analytics is employed in order to offer an answer to the question, "What is the likelihood that this will take place?"

Prescriptive: The prescriptive approach is one that makes use of the data from a variety of different forms of analytics in order to quantify the anticipated effects and repercussions of prospective actions that are being examined. The answer to the question "What should happen if we do...?" is one of the objectives of prescriptive analytics, which aims to give a solution to the problem.

The terms "business analysis" and "business data analytics" are frequently used interchangeably despite their distinct meanings. The words "business analysis" and "business data analytics" are frequently used interchangeably in conversations about businesses. However, there are significant differences between the two terminologies that should be taken into consideration.

When applied to the setting of an organization, the term "business analysis" refers to the process of supporting change by identifying requirements and delivering solutions that bring value to a variety of stakeholders. On the other hand, business data analytics is largely concerned with the process of doing research and analysis on data. The context of the company is offered by business analysis, which is utilized for the purpose of business data analytics. Business analysis is performed prior to the collection of data in order to set the scope of the investigation and to decide the emphasis of the research questions that are being asked regarding the investigation. Types of data analytics are illustrated in Figure 1.

Additionally, business analysis is helpful in the process of data collecting as well as the implementation of the processes involved in data collection. One of the functions of business data analytics is to organize, process, and analyze the data after it has been compiled. Business analysis activities are carried out once the analysis of the data that was collected has been completed. These activities are carried out in order to evaluate the results that were acquired from analytics and to translate knowledge into business choices. In order to facilitate the implementation of informed business choices that are made as a result of what is learnt from analyzing the data that is collected, business analysis activities are carried out. These activities will also facilitate the communication of the outcomes of business data analytics. Some people regard business data analytics to be a subfield or subset of business analysis, namely one that is centered on data analysis. When it comes to executing work related to business data analytics, this viewpoint is taken into consideration because many of the skills and competencies that are frequently highlighted when describing business analysis are equally relevant.

Figure 1. Data analytics types

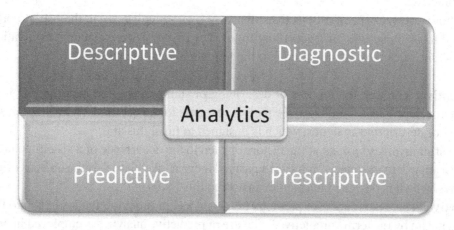

Those components of business data analytics that are concerned with research are represented by the business data analytics cycle. It is an iterative cycle that begins with the formulation of a well-formed research question and is followed by the exploration of the topic through the analysis of data that is both specific and comprehensive. The scientific method serves as the foundation for the cycle. Research is conducted using a procedure known as the scientific method, which is used to investigate observations and provide answers to questions. A question that encompasses the breadth of the research is posed at the beginning of the process. This question might be stated as who, what, when, where, which, why, or how.

On the basis of these questions, background research is carried out in order to provide direction for the research and to develop a question with a more limited scope. After then, the question is put to the test by means of a method or procedure, and the outcomes are analyzed in order to develop conclusions based on the question with a more limited scope. While business analysis is responsible for informing the activities that come before and after the data collecting and analysis phases of the scientific method, business data analytics is primarily concerned with the data collection and analysis phases. To guarantee that the data analysis is focused on raising questions that are vital to answer and that the data provides meaningful insights for the purpose of resolving important business circumstances (whether they be problems or opportunities), business data analytics requires business analysis.

A few key distinctions exist between the scientific method and the commercial data analytics process, despite the fact that the two approaches have many similarities. One thing to consider is that the process of corporate data analytics could be different based on the kind of analysis that is being performed. During testing, it is possible that an experiment to gather data will not necessarily be included. Instead, the data may simply be received from a server utilizing the data sources that are already in place. In the field of corporate data analytics, it is essential to use data validation and verification techniques on the information that has been gathered. Due to the fact that the data acquired as part of a scientific experiment is obtained in a controlled laboratory environment, the scientific method does not require the validation of the data. The business data analytics cycle is ongoing and iterative when the goal of the analytics endeavor is continuous improvement or some other metric of improvement over time. This is the case when the analytics effort is being undertaken. In the context of projects that have clearly defined ends, the conclusions that are gained from a project can be utilized to formulate new research questions, which in turn can be used to perpetuate another execution of the full business data analytics cycle.

Analysts describe which information and data are required to achieve the intended behavior of operational managers and digital processes in the business environment in the environment that is responsible for the development of analysis and reporting, which is located in the middle of the model. When it comes to the deployment of analytical and statistical models, which are then applied to data from the data warehouse, this is the location where information and knowledge are formed. All of this is done with the intention of satisfying the criteria that are imposed by the higher layers and tiers of the model. It is important to take note that the environment for the development of analysis and reporting is situated in the intermediary region between the business-driven environment and the technically focused environment, and that the team working in this area typically have competencies in both of these locations.

Data Warehouse Database professionals and ETL developers are the ones who receive requirements from the analytical environment regarding the delivery of data. In the event that the necessary data is already stored in the warehouse, the next step will be to ensure that the front-end apps of the company have access to this collection of information. In the event that data is not saved, the data warehouse will be required to retrieve data from one or more operational data sources that are located within the structure of the organization. Alternatives include purchasing data from an external provider or requesting that the information technology department create a new infrastructure with the intention of establishing a new operational data source.

Both IT operations and development are required to fulfil the requirements imposed by the data warehouse about the delivery of data from the major operational data sources or the creation of new data sources. The development of BA involves a significant number of individuals, skills, and procedures throughout the design process. When it comes to large organizations, there are occasions when several hundred people from various levels are included in the process simultaneously. It is necessary for controllers and analysts in smaller firms to possess a larger range of abilities in order for them to be able to independently carry out business analysis projects. In the event that something goes wrong in one of the layers of the BA model, it is essential to be aware of the fact that the possibility exists that the investment in BA would be lost. If management, which is located at the top layer of the model, does not identify a single overall strategy, then those who are responsible for making operational decisions will not have a target to strive towards. However, the analyst will be unaware of which analyses are necessary.

In the process of data warehousing, the database specialist and the ETL developer will not be aware of which data sources should be retrieved, merged, and enriched before being sent to data marts, which are data that have been created in the data warehouse for use by businesses. Those responsible for the operations and development of information technology will not be able to make a contribution by developing new data sources since they are unaware of the specific new information and expertise that the company requires. To put it another way, if there is no concentration, the entire situation will turn into a chaotic jumble. The establishment of a business analytics competency center (BACC), which might be a virtual organizational unit, is one method that can be utilized to circumvent the chaotic situation that has arisen.

Benefits for Business Data Analytics for Companies

Data serves as the core element for any organization, no matter its size or scope. This has the potential to uncover hidden opportunities, broaden horizons, and expose underlying challenges. Most organizations understand the significance of data. Big Data Analytics involves the methodical collection of large volumes of both structured and unstructured data, along with the classification and arrangement of this information. It is crucial to analyze the data and reveal the fundamental trends and significant business insights. It helps determine which data is relevant and can be examined to improve future business decision-making. A number of business ventures Open-source tools are widely available for performing big data analytics within organizations. Big Data has become an essential element for organizations, allowing them to forecast and make informed strategic decisions that lead to their success. To stay ahead in the market and increase income, it is crucial to reduce risk and attain swift expansion. The domains where Data Analytics boosts operational efficiency are as follows.

The Travel Industry

The travel industry gathers significant amounts of data through various processes, including reservations, enquiries, itineraries, and car rentals. Hotels, train bookings, airlines, tariff charts, and customer comments produce extensive data sets. In the travel industry, predictive analytics serves various functions, leading to the collection of vast amounts of data. The travel sector units have the potential to greatly improve their performance by leveraging Big Data analytics, thereby enriching the customer experience and streamlining business operations.

Healthcare Services

Big data spans across various industries, prominently featuring the Medicine and Health care sector. Data analytics is essential for improving and examining large amounts of constantly produced information. It offers valuable services and tackles major challenges in the healthcare sector, especially concerning patient demographics. Examples of areas that involve analysis encompass historical analysis, genetic analysis, public health monitoring, fraud analysis, and diagnostic and consultation. A cloud-based platform for big data analytics in patient experience management enables providers to gain a more profound insight into the authentic patient experience, the key drivers for its improvement, and the capability to deliver tailored offerings. Campaigns are crafted to specifically focus on certain patient groups to achieve the greatest reach and response, aiming to enhance overall effectiveness. The patient's experience and satisfaction can be attained at a much more affordable price than creating the solution internally.

E-Commerce and Retail

E-commerce and retail are rapidly evolving sectors that continue to shape the way consumers shop and businesses operate. E-commerce and merchants are leveraging analytics to obtain crucial company data that will not only aid in targeting customers but also in expanding their client base and boosting revenue. Data analytics play an essential role in every stage of the ecommerce and retail transaction process. This will assist in predicting the main areas of emphasis, such as examining trends, pinpointing potential clients, refining pricing models, and comprehending customer purchasing behavior. This assists in categorizing customers into distinct groups and delivering personalized, timely offers designed to match their preferences. Overall, Data Analytics provides e-commerce and retail businesses with a smart purchasing experience.

Manufacturing

The manufacturing sector oversees enormous amounts of data from a network that includes thousands of large and heavy motors. The mechanical equipment is made up of electrical relays and sensors that work together in a synchronized manner, governed by complex systems. Utilizing Big Data analysis in the manufacturing sector can lead to improved production quality and reduced waste. By correcting any mistakes in the workflow, improvements in efficiency can be realized, leading to savings in both cost and time. The industry requires constant monitoring of various characteristics and signals that are always present. Manufacturing stands to gain significantly from adopting data analytical solutions. Experts in the field could shift their focus from traditional oversight to a more flexible and responsive approach. Manufacturers have the ability to assess the potential risks associated with the delivery of raw materials. Furthermore, they can leverage analytical insights to pinpoint alternative sources and create contingency plans to guarantee continuous production despite any disruptions. This enables them to produce data that greatly improves business operations while also addressing various challenges.

Challenges Facing Business Data Analytics

There are a number of obstacles that organizations could encounter when it comes to corporate data analytics, including the following:

- It might be challenging to identify business alignment and priorities when thinking about them from a data viewpoint. For a data effort, it can be difficult to make judgements regarding the theme, scale, or scope of the project.
- It might be difficult to determine which data should be measured and captured in order to accomplish corporate objectives. The process of locating data that generates value can be challenging; not every data contributes to the improvement of decision-making. The process of determining the specific subset of data that is required can be difficult, even when the source of the data has been established. The quality of the data, particularly historical data, is either poor or uncertain.

- Integration and accessibility of the data. The data is stored in a variety of different systems, and its format and quality are all different. There is a lack of comfort among business stakeholders regarding the rapid changes that are taking place in the corporate data analytics arena.
- The sharing of data assets across different business domains can be challenging since it can be difficult to bring business stakeholders to a common sense of value. Those who are responsible for performing the analysis, as well as the managers who are receiving the data, do not have sufficient expertise or understanding. A shift in the culture of the organization is necessary in order to place more weight on the insights gained from data rather than on experience and intuition. It is difficult for business managers to organize data teams that they are responsible for.
- Difficulty trying to locate the appropriate tools. Developing a data strategy might involve a wide variety of different approaches and methods. Analysts have the ability to utilize a significant number of the strategies in order to facilitate fruitful conversations between the representatives of the IT department and the business stakeholders. The majority of the strategies lead to the production of visual models that may be utilized on an ongoing basis to assist the team, which is made of both business and IT resources, in comprehending the context that surrounds and influences the business data analytics work that is being carried out.
- The Balanced Scorecard is a powerful instrument for strategic planning and management that is utilized to evaluate the performance of an organization. Through the implementation of the strategic plan as an active framework of objectives and performance measurements, it offers a balanced perspective of an organization and is centered on the outcomes rather than the organization itself.

Techniques Strategy for Business Data Analytics

The purpose of business data analytics is to measure both internal and external components in order to bring about a common understanding between business stakeholders and IT regarding the performance of the organization and how the organization is currently performing its commitments to its customers.

-**Benchmarking and Market Analysis:** are two methods that may be utilized to gain a knowledge of the areas in which there is room for improvement in the existing state of affairs. Examples of particular frameworks that have the potential to be beneficial are the Five Forces Analysis, the PEST analysis, the STEEP analysis, and the CATWOE analysis. In addition to providing an understanding of the external environment that surrounds the organization, the findings of this sort of study are beneficial because they are able to give an insight into how the performance of various parts of the business compares to the performance of the leaders in the industry.

-**The Business Model Canvas:** is a tool that provides an understanding of the value proposition that the organization provides for its customers, the significant components that are engaged in the process of delivering that value, as well as the cost and revenue streams that are the result of each of these variables. For the purpose of establishing an awareness of the context in which any change is taking place and for the purpose of assessing the problems and opportunities that have the potential to have the most profound influence, it is a beneficial tool. In the framework of business data analytics initiatives, it is feasible to make use of this strategy in order to stimulate collaborative talks among representatives of information technology and stakeholders from the business world. For this reason, it will be possible for all of the people concerned to get a comprehensive grasp of the fundamental aspects of the firm.

- **An Analysis of the Five Forces:** is a framework that can be utilized to build a knowledge of the places within the current condition of the organization in which there is potential for change. This information can be utilized to generate a better understanding of the organization. In order to do this, it is necessary to undertake an examination of a variety of aspects of the competitive environment, including the powers that are held by buyers and suppliers each. In the context of a corporate data analytics project, this approach contributes to the process of acquiring a knowledge of the competitive variables that are having an impact on the organization.
- **Metrics and Key Performance Indicators (KPIs):** In order to evaluate the efficacy of solutions, components of solutions, and other issues that are of importance to stakeholders, metrics and key performance indicators (KPIs) are utilized. This evaluation is done for the aim of determining how successful solutions are. In the context of firm data analytics initiatives, key performance indicators (KPIs) are utilized in order to ascertain the most significant results that are anticipated to be the result of the actions involving data analysis.

-**The Strengths, Weaknesses, Opportunities, and Threats (SWOT):** analysis is a method that is utilized to carry out an evaluation of the present status of the organization. There are four characteristics that make up the SWOT analysis. This will give context on the internal and external environments of the organization, which is relevant to the endeavors that pertain to business data analytics. Facilitating conversations in order to complete a SWOT analysis will facilitate these conversations.

It is a model that is used to determine the primary activities that are carried out within an organization and to investigate the manner in which each activity contributes to the value that is supplied by the products and services that are provided to the customers of the organization. The value chain analysis is a model that is utilized to determine the primary activities that are carried out within an organization. In the realm of corporate data analytics, one of the methods that is utilized is the utilization of the value chain analysis. In order to offer a shared understanding of the method in which the organization gives or may provide value to its customers, its objective is to convey this information. For the purpose of enhancing an organization's competitive advantage, it is possible to make use of it to facilitate collaborative interactions between business stakeholders and information technology (IT) in order to propel innovation. An illustration of the approaches and strategies for corporate data analytics is shown in Figure 2.

Figure 2. Techniques strategy for business data analytics

CONCLUSION

In spite of the fact that the phrase "business model" has been in use for a considerable amount of time, businesses have a natural tendency to construct, establish, and carry out their models from the very beginning of their operations. It is essential to have an understanding of the notion of a company model, in addition to comprehending the primary methods that may be utilized to comprehend it. The majority of the time, people in leadership positions within an organization base their decisions on their own personal competence and inclination. The elimination of cognitive and personal biases from the decision-making process is achieved through the utilization of business data analytics, which utilizes data as the primary input for decision-making. It is possible for an organization to get a competitive advantage through the performance of an effective analysis of business data. The use of business data analytics allows for the quantification of both internal and external aspects, which in turn facilitates a mutual comprehension between business stakeholders and information technology about the performance of the organization and the present fulfilment of customer duties by the organization. Several different approaches to business data analytics were discussed in this chapter, along with the relevance of such approaches in the area.

REFERENCES

Callon, M., Courtial, J. P., & Laville, F. (1991). Co-word analysis as a tool for describing the network of interactions between basic and technological research: The case of polymer chemsitry. *Scientometrics*, 22(1), 155–205. DOI: 10.1007/BF02019280

Callon, M., Courtial, J. P., Turner, W. A., & Bauin, S. (1983). From translations to problematic networks: An introduction to co-word analysis. *Social Sciences Information. Information Sur les Sciences Sociales*, 22(2), 191–235. DOI: 10.1177/053901883022002003

Chen, J., Wei, W., Guo, C., Tang, L., & Sun, L. (2017). Textual analysis and visualization of research trends in data mining for electronic health records. *Health Policy and Technology*, 6(4), 389–400. DOI: 10.1016/j.hlpt.2017.10.003

Chesbrough, H. (2006). *Open Business Models: How to Thrive in the New Innovation Landscape*. Harvard Business School Press.

Feng, J., Zhang, Y. Q., & Zhang, H. (2017). Improving the co-word analysis method based on semantic distance. *Scientometrics*, 111(3), 1521–1531. DOI: 10.1007/s11192-017-2286-1

Kleinberg, J. (2003). Bursty and hierarchical structure in streams. *Data Mining and Knowledge Discovery*, 7(4), 373–397. DOI: 10.1023/A:1024940629314

Morris, S. A., Yen, G., Wu, Z., & Asnake, B. (2003). Time line visualization of research fronts. *Journal of the American Society for Information Science and Technology*, 54(5), 413–422. DOI: 10.1002/asi.10227

Najmi, A., Rashidi, T. H., Abbasi, A., & Waller, S. T. (2017). Reviewing the transport domain: An evolutionary bibliometrics and network analysis. *Scientometrics*, 110(2), 843–865. DOI: 10.1007/s11192-016-2171-3

Sawant, N., Li, J., & Wang, J. Z. (2011). Automatic image semantic interpretation using social action and tagging data. *Multimedia Tools and Applications*, 51(1), 213–246. DOI: 10.1007/s11042-010-0650-8

Van Eck, N. J., & Waltman, L. (2014). Visualizing bibliometric networks. In Ding, Y., Rousseau, R., & Wolfram, D. (Eds.), *Measuring Scholarly Impact: Methods and Practice* (pp. 285–320). Springer. DOI: 10.1007/978-3-319-10377-8_13

Van Eck, N. J., Waltman, L., Dekker, R., & van den Berg, J. (2010). A comparison of two techniques for bibliometric mapping: Multidimensional scaling and VOS. *Journal of the American Society for Information Science and Technology*, 61(12), 2405–2416. DOI: 10.1002/asi.21421

Wang, Z., Zhao, H., & Wang, Y. (2015). Social networks in marketing research 2001-2014: A co-word analysis. *Scientometrics*, 105(1), 65–82. DOI: 10.1007/s11192-015-1672-9

Watson, D. (2005). Business Models. Petersfield: Harriman House Ltd.

Yan, B. N., Lee, T. S., & Lee, T. P. (2015). Analysis of research papers on E-commerce (2000-2013): Based on a text mining approach. *Scientometrics*, 105(1), 403–417. DOI: 10.1007/s11192-015-1675-6

Yan, B. N., Lee, T. S., & Lee, T. P. (2015). Analysis of research papers on E-commerce (2000-2013): Based on a text mining approach. *Scientometrics*, 105(1), 403–417. DOI: 10.1007/s11192-015-1675-6

Zhang, J., Yu, Q., Zheng, F., Long, C., Lu, Z., & Duan, Z. (2016). Comparing keywords plus of WOS and author keywords: A case study of patient adherence research. *Journal of the Association for Information Science and Technology*, 67(4), 967–972. DOI: 10.1002/asi.23437

KEY TERMS AND DEFINIITONS

Burst Detection Algorithm (BDA): A signal that has significant power for a known duration is defined as a burst signal. This signal has no power (dead time) outside the known duration. To demodulate such signals, the dead time must be avoided.

Business Analytics (BA): is a set of disciplines and technologies for solving business problems using data analysis, statistical models and other quantitative methods.

Extract, Transform, and Load (ETL): is the process of combining data from multiple sources into a large, central repository called a data warehouse.

Information and Communication Technology (ICT): is a broader term for Information Technology (IT), which refers to all communication technologies, including the internet, wireless networks, cell phones, computers, software, middleware, video-conferencing, social networking, and other media applications and services.

Business Analytics Competency Center (BACC): is a forum that includes analytical and business competencies as well as IT competencies.

Metrics and Key Performance Indicators (KPIs): stands for key performance indicator, a quantifiable measure of performance over time for a specific objective. KPIs provide targets for teams to shoot for, milestones to gauge progress, and insights that help people across the organization make better decisions.

The Strengths, Weaknesses, Opportunities, and Threats (SWOT): is a framework used to evaluate a company's competitive position and to develop strategic planning. SWOT analysis assesses internal and external factors, as well as current and future potential.

Chapter 6
Business Analytics on Business Models

Satya Shree
https://orcid.org/0009-0008-5447-9076
APS College of Arts and Science, India

C. Manjunath
APS College of Arts and Science, India

ABSTRACT

In today's dynamic business landscape, organizations are increasingly recognizing the pivotal role of business analytics in refining and optimizing their business models. This study explores the integration of business analytics into various aspects of the business model, including value proposition, customer segments, revenue streams, and operational efficiency. Through a comprehensive review of existing literature and case studies, this research elucidates the significance of leveraging data-driven insights for strategic decision-making and sustainable competitive advantage. Key themes investigated include predictive analytics for market forecasting, customer behavior analysis for targeted marketing strategies, optimization of supply chain management through data-driven logistics, and the role of business intelligence in enhancing operational agility. The study also delves into challenges such as data privacy concerns, skill gaps, and organizational resistance, offering insights into effective implementation strategies.

INTRODUCTION

The significant part of business analytics is in forming and optimizing modern trade models. It looks at how organizations can tackle the control of information analytics to drive vital decision-making, improve operational productivity, and make feasible competitive advantage. Through an amalgamation of hypothetical systems and real-world case thinks about, the think about highlights the transformative potential of leveraging trade analytics over different measurements of the trade demonstrate, counting esteem suggestion, client division, income streams, and asset allotment. The paper too addresses challenges such as information protection, organizational resistance, and aptitude crevices, advertising experiences into compelling execution procedures. By explaining the advantageous relationship between

DOI: 10.4018/979-8-3693-3884-1.ch006

trade analytics and business models, this investigation contributes to a more profound understanding of how organizations can adapt and flourish in a progressively data-driven environment.

Businesses are growing more and more interested in business data analytics as a means of using data to support more intelligent business choices and extract insightful insights. making decisions. More businesses are investing in corporate data analytics to achieve their strategic imperatives, innovate, and gain a competitive advantage in the marketplace. These expenses are driving a need for more trained professionals with business data analytics knowledge.

BACKGROUND

The transformation of business analytics in the context of business models is an interesting history that runs parallel to increases in technological advances and changes in business practices. What follows is a careful review of how business analytics have evolved in the context of business models. (Chesbrough. H, 2006)

Before the advent of advanced analytics, firms were primarily capturing information through manual reporting systems. Organizations would use paper or spreadsheets to develop sales reporting, financial statements, and other rudimentary indicators. These systems had limits to their functionality and reach, but they were analytically useful. In the 1990s, BI technologies, which provided more robust reporting capabilities and analytical insights, ushered in a more popular addition for firms. These tools also provided superior data visualization and analytical and multidimensional analysis.

In 2000, we saw the expansion referred to as "big data," or the boom of data collection, which posed new possibilities and problems. Businesses were collecting and analyzing vast datasets faster and using more variety. Making: Analytics were coming closer to the center of business models by supporting companies in making evidence-based decisions. Organizations were beginning to use their data to inform strategic goals, refine customer experience, and optimize business operations (Laney, D. 2001).

The rise of merging AI and ML into analytics has changed the course of business models. AI algorithms increase prognostic precision, robotize basic leadership forms, and extricate complex pattern recognition. Analyzing future business models will perfectly transform as cheerful and agile dependent on ongoing analytics and AI, consistently optimizing and advancing. As analytics start getting installed in business models, there will be an additional development in fears identifying with the privacy and security of data. Associations ought to voluntarily adjust to rules like GDPR and CCPA. Moral and mindful utilization of AI and analytics, including straightforwardness and partiality issues, are a couple of organizational contemplations.

MAIN FOCUS OF BUSINESS ANALYTICS IN BUSINESS MODEL

Overview of Business Models

A "business" is the actual collection of individuals, choices, assets, structures, manufactured goods, ideals, deeds, and any other components required to carry out and maintain this specific human activity. What does the term "business model" mean if we accept these ideas?

A business model is a set of assets and processes that produce value that customers can utilize and that generates revenue for the business through sales. The goal of business model analysis is to increase and enhance our knowledge of the key components of a business model. The financial journalist Michael Lewis coined the phrase "business model" when he wrote in his pieces that businesses of the future would be built on Internet-only business models. "Business model still has no fixed theoretical foundation in economics," according to *David T.Teece (2010)*. Discovering the procedures and aspects that defines a company's production of value in a comprehensive and fundamental way and are critical for its operations is incredibly challenging.

A business model is defined by a number of authors as a method for generating revenue. They see a business model as an economic idea that "produces" expenses and revenues. It is a collection of operations that provide revenue as a result of procedures and technology working together are referred in (**Table.1**)

Table 1. Business models according to authors

Author	Definition
Itami a Noshino	"Business model is a profit formula, system of business and learning system." *(Baden-Fuller & Morgan, 2010)*
Henry Chesbrough	"The business model is a useful framework to link ideas and technologies to economic outcomes." *(Chesbrough, 2006)*
Alfonso Ganbardella Anita McGahan	"Business model is a mechanism for transformation ideas to revenues through the acceptable costs." *(Baden-Fuller & Morgan, 2010)*
Allan Afuah	"Business model is a framework for making money. It is the set of activities which a firm performs, how it performs them and when it performs them so as to offer its customers benefits they want and to earn a profit." *(Afuah, 2003)*
Thomas Wheelen, David Hunger	"Business model is a method for making money in the concrete business environment. It is consisted of key structural and operational characteristics of company – how company earn and create profit." *(Wheelen & Hunger, 2008)*

The business model is divided into four components according to *AlanAfuah's (2003)* idea, leading to in the profitability determinants which impact all of the company's activities.(**Figure. 1**)

Figure 1. Components of business model by A. Afuah (2003)

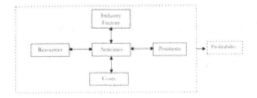

How Business Model Transformation Has Changed

The rapidly evolution of digital technologies has led to about significant transformations that have a significant impact on businesses and organizations. For all businesses to secure long-term sustainable competitive positions in current markets, digital transformation of business processes and all other business segments is essential.*(Hunger, D. L et al., 2008)*

The following are some of the factors that are driving business transformation:
1. **Innovation in Technology:** Businesses must stay competitive by keeping up with the constant improvements in technology.
2. **Dynamic Markets:** Globalization, high competition, and evolving industry trends may prompt enterprises to modify their operations in order to maintain their competitiveness.
3. **Rules and Regulations:** Law and regulation changes may compel businesses to alter their operations and business procedures.
4. **Culture Within the Organization:** Businesses that wish to increase productivity, creativity, and performance frequently need to change the organizational culture.
5. **Strategic Objectives:** Businesses may start business transformation projects in order to accomplish strategic objectives including diversifying their company, breaking into new markets, or introducing new goods.

Introduction to Business Analytics

There is an enormous amount of data out there currently, and more will come along in the future. Numerous businesses already grieve being lost in a sea of data. Rather, smart organizations see this growth as a key element of the competitive advantage. Indeed, business analytics is one of the 'hot' topics in business nowadays. It is referred to as business analytics, and it is the application of data, information technology, statistical and quantitative methods and models to help management enhance their understanding of work processes and take more effective decisions.

Definition

Business analytics is a process of transforming data into actions through analysis and insights in the context of organizational decision making and problem solving. It is a process of ongoing exploration and analysis of both historical and current business data to discover insights to inform decision making. This is done by applying a particular set of techniques, competencies, and procedures.

The gathering and examination of business-related data with the aim of spotting trends, patterns, and customer behavior is known as business analytics. Based on these discovered patterns and trends, business strategies are developed using them.

There are various fundamental procedures in business analytics:

1. Identifying the objectives of the analysis.
2. Determining the most effective analytical approach to meet those objectives.

3. Acquiring extensive data, frequently from several different systems.

*4. Cleansing the information and combining it into a single location, like a data warehouse.(**Figure.2**)*

Figure 2. Visual representation of business analytics

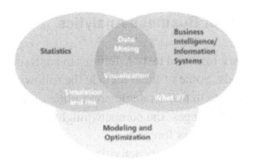

Business analytics can be defined more precisely with some common examples:

1. **Customer Segmentation:** Identifying and targeting key customer groups in the retail, insurance, and credit card industries.

2. **Supply Chain:** Choosing the best sourcing and transportation options and figuring out the best delivery routes.

3. **Pricing:** Determining consumer and industrial goods prices, government contracts, and maintenance contracts.

4. **Merchandising:** Deciding brands to buy, quantities, and allocations.

5. **Health Care:** Predicting health risk factors, improving waiting time and patient flow, purchasing supplies.

6. **Location:** Deciding where to service industrial equipment or locate bank branches and ATMs

Importance of Business Analytics

Business analytics (BA) includes several moving factors, but you might not know why it's vital for your company in the initial place.

Tools for business analytics assist in understanding what a company requires in order to make wise judgments. These choices, which will help you boost market share, increase profitability, and give prospective investors a bigger return, will probably have an effect on your entire company.

Technology undoubtedly affects a lot of businesses, but when applied properly, business analytics (BA) may have a positive effect on your organization by giving it a competitive edge over other enterprises. Business analytics attempts to integrate this data with actionable insights to enhance the decisions you make as a company, even if some businesses are unclear on what to do with massive amounts of data (Johnson, W. M et al., 2008). Basically, regardless of the industry, business analytics are important in several key ways:

1. Business analytics can spot vulnerabilities in a business's system infrastructure.
2. Businesses can use analytics to help them identify risk factors and implement preventative actions.
3. It can assist in more precisely targeting customers.
4. Using data-driven recommendation engines, businesses can move revenue from in-store to online.
5. To transform, make the most out of your data strategy.

Roles and Responsibilities of Business Analytics

Business analytics has its own roles and responsibilities to analysis data to make decisions in order to meet the organization goals. Some of them include the following:
- Recognizing trends in data to find strategic possibilities.
- Recognizing potential challenges, the company might encounter and their solutions.
- Preparing a budget and business forecast.
- Tracking the performance of business activities.
- Updating stakeholders on the status of business objectives.

Elements of Business Analytics

Business analytics leverages the following elements
1. **Data Aggregation:** To derive summary statistics, such as mean, minimum, maximum, sum, and count, the data need to be aggregated.
2. **Data Mining:** For data-driven decision-making, data mining uses a variety of statistical approaches, including clustering, regression, and classification. To solve issues, find patterns and trends in large data sets.
3. **Text Mining:** To find patterns and use text mining for evaluating competitor performance, examine and evaluate text data from social media posts, blog comments, audio or video scripts, company papers, customer communications, and more.
4. **Data Visualization:** Construct meaningful visualizations to identify patterns and links within datasets. Modeling, forecasting, and exploratory data analysis are supported by data visualization
5. **Forecasting:** Using past data to forecast future occurrences. For example, use historical data to predict Christmas retail sales or summer utilization of energy. Use forecasting to plan your budget or project your spending.
6. **Optimization:** To find the best-case scenario, use simulation techniques such as what-if analysis.

Types Involved in Business Analytics

1. **Descriptive Analytics:** Analyzes historical data to detect patterns in customer behavior and trends. This makes it possible to use data mining and aggregation techniques to get a broad overview of both past and present events. Descriptive analytics is a technique that many businesses utilize to gain a better understanding of customer behavior and customize marketing campaigns towards specific customers. **(Table.2)**

Various applications can be performed using descriptive analytics. Some of them are:

Table 2. Applications for descriptive analytics

Business	Model	Description
Wipro	Summary of client engagement	To determine service utilization and engagement levels, a summary of client interactions is created.
ISRO	Summaries of Satellite launch data	Combines mission results and satellite launch records for trend analysis.
Air India	Statistics of flight operations	Gathers information on flight operations to evaluate service effectiveness and on-time performance.
HDFC Bank	Reports of account activity	Creates reports on account activity in order to comprehend the banking habits of its clients.
Tata steel	Tracking production volume	Monitors monthly production levels to evaluate capacity utilization and output trends.

2. **Predictive Analytics:** Use statistical models and machine learning to forecast future outcomes by interpreting data and estimating future customer attitudes and behavior. In order to develop models that estimate the probability of particular events, this frequently uses the findings of descriptive analytics. Sales and marketing teams frequently use this kind to predict individual customers' attitudes based on social media data. **(Table.3)**

Various applications can be performed using predictive analytics. Some of them are:

Table 3. Applications for predictive analytics

Business	Model	Description
Ola Cab	Dynamic pricing	Makes real-time price adjustments using predictive analytics in response to demand, climate conditions, and traffic patterns.
BookMyShow	Event popularity prediction	Forecasts the level of interest in movies and events in order to manage inventories and maximize marketing efforts.
Airtel	Customer churn prediction	Uses customer data analysis to identify which clients are most likely to move to an opponent in order to increase retention rates.
Flipkart	Demand forecasting	Predicts future product demand using machine learning, which aids in pricing and stocking strategies.
HDFC Bank	Credit risk management	Makes use of predictive analytics to assess loan applicants' credit and predict defaults.

3. **Prescriptive Analytics:** Provides specific procedures for attaining ideal results and based on historical data, makes recommendations for handling future instances. Makes recommendations for handling similar situations in the future based on historical performance data. This kind of business analytics is not only capable of predicting results; it can also suggest the precise steps that must be taken in order to achieve the best conclusion. Complex neural networks and deep learning are frequently used to perform these analytics. This kind of business analytics is often used to match different solutions to a customer's current demands. **(Table.4)**

Various applications can be performed using prescriptive analytics. Some of them are:

Table 4. Applications for prescriptive analytics

Business	Model	Description
Snap deal	Optimizing E-commerce checkout	Suggests changing the checkout procedure in order to lower the rate of cart abandonment.
Paytm	Fraud detection recommender	Suggests anti-fraud actions according on trends found in transaction data.
Tata Motors	Management of dealer inventory	Provides dealerships advice on the best inventory levels to have depending on market demand and sales velocity.
Reliance Jio	Demand forecasting	Recommends customer service enhancements based on user comments and use trends.
Indian railways	Schedule and route optimizer	Makes recommendations for the best rail routes and timetables to increase network effectiveness and timeliness.

4. **Diagnostic Analytics:** Using strategies like data mining and correlation, looks back at historical performance to find what drives particular trends, and employs algorithms to find the chance of re-occurring influential variables. Data mining, data discovery, and correlation are used in this process to identify the reason behind particular events. Classification and regression algorithms are employed once an understanding of the probability and causes of an occurrence has been established. **(Table.5)**

Various applications can be performed using diagnostic analytics. Some of them are:

Table 5. Applications for diagnostic analytics

Business	Model	Description
Infosys	Churn prediction	Monitors at the causes of client churn in order to enhance customer retention techniques.
SBI Life insurance	Rejection of Claims analysis	Identifies the causes of insurance claim rejection in order to improve policy language.
PVR Cinemas	Box office performance analyzer	Examines variables impacting the success of films and the number of viewers.
Yes Bank	Default loan diagnosis	Studies at the reasons for loan defaults in order to enhance credit risk assessment.
Reliance jio	Network congestion diagnostic	Determines the root causes of network congestion in order to improve service quality and connectivity.

Process of Business Analytics

The final aim we choose before beginning the process will determine the approach you choose to take while delving deeply into BA. Whichever approach you select, the finish line is certain to have useful insights that await us. Essentially, business analytics is a 6-step process, outlined below. **(Figure.3)**

Figure 3. Process of business analytics

Step1: Business Requirements

The first step in the business analytics process is to determine what the company wants to achieve or what issue it wants to resolve. Occasionally, the objective is divided into smaller objectives. Some of major queries like "what data is available," "how can we use it," and "do we have enough data" need to be handled in this stage.

Step2: Data Collection

After defining the problem statement, the next stage is to collect data and clean the data. While most businesses would have a lot of data, not all of it would be reliable or relevant. Companies collect enormous amount of data which contains junk data or empty data which need to impute using some of analysis.

Step3: Data Analysis

Once the data is collected, the next stage is to perform analysis. To obtain the insights you require, a variety of statistical techniques (including correlation analysis and hypothesis testing) are used. Each aspect related to the target variable will be detected by the analyst. This is often the stage where comparisons are conducted, and the data is broken. Furthermore, other assumptions are taken into account in order to determine the possible results via some visualization.

Step4: Data Driven Insights

At this stage, the analyst will use logistic regression, decision trees, and neural networks to model the data using predictive techniques. With the use of these methods, relationships and "hidden evidence" of the most important factors will be observed, along with new insights and patterns.

Step5: Make Prediction

Here many models are applied in parallel, and the best accurate models will be chosen in order to find hidden insights between variables and also provide patterns for essential metrics.

Step6: Optimize and Decision Making

At this stage, some of questions arises like 'Was the model made proper prediction?' And 'Is the model been effective?'. If this is the case, then the model needs to be optimized, and database will be continuously updated when the new insights are detected. Then, the analyst will decide and act depending on the conclusions drawn by the model as per the business goals.

Skills Required for Business Analytics

It has been stated that the business requires more technically and analytically strong to analyze and gather the insights (Amit R., & Zott C., 2012*)*. The following are some prerequisites for anyone aspiring to work in business analytics:

1. **Data Analysis:** In order to derive useful insights from large datasets one needs data analysis tools and processes. Utilizing data analysis requires knowledge of data manipulation, statistical analysis, and data visualization in order to understand, interpret and disseminate findings.
2. **Statistical Modeling:** To understand relationships in data and establish sound forecasts, knowledge of statistical modeling approaches is required. Examples of relevant techniques include regression modeling, time series modeling, and predictive modeling
3. **Data Management:** Data management skills will help ensure the quality and maintainability of your data. Necessary skills include data cleaning, data integration, and querying databases.
4. **Programming Illiteracies:** Knowledge of programming languages including R, Python, or SQL can improve your ability to complete data manipulation, statistical analysis, and each stage of developing formal analytical models.
5. **Business Knowledge:** The ability to relate findings from analyses (your own, or others), with the goals of the organization, requires business knowledge of the business context, key performance indicators (KPIs) and industry or sector trends.
6. **Communication Skills:** The ability to succinctly communicate complex analysis to audiences who are not technical and support data-driven organizational decisions is a critical importance.
7. **Problem-Solving:** High-level problem-solving skills are necessary in order to identify challenges for the organization, agree upon appropriate analytical strategies, and derive actionable value for the organization from the data-based analytical conclusions.
8. **Domain Knowledge:** Knowledge of the specific context of the data (i.e. industry, organization, or functional area) is needed to interpret the analytical output and understand the significance of data-based recommendations.
9. **Data Visualization:** Crafting attractive visual representations of data to successfully convey trends and insights requires proficiency with data visualization tools and methodologies.
10. **Critical Thinking:** It's crucial to have the capacity for critical thought and to approach data analysis from a strategic perspective.

Data Analytics vs. Business Analytics vs. Business Intelligence

1. Business Analytics vs. Data Analytics

Using data analytics technologies to find business insights is part of Business Analytics (BA). However, due to its broad definition, business analytics and data analytics are occasionally used synonymously.

Analyzing data sets to make inferences about the information they contain is known as Data analytics. It is not necessary to utilize data analytics to achieve business objectives or gain insights. Business analytics is a part of this wider approach according to Shmueli, G., &Koppius, O. R. (2011).

2. Business Analytics vs. Business Intelligence

Predictive analytics is the main focus of business analytics, producing insights that decision-makers can employ. BA seeks to forecast trends rather than summarize historical data items.

Businesses typically use business intelligence (BI) first, then business analytics. Business Intelligence (BI) examines company operations to identify successful practices and areas for development. Descriptive analytics is used in BI.

Business Analytics Use Cases

According to *(Christopher M. Bishop, n.d.)*There are numerous uses for BA tools. For instance, they are able to identify clients who are most likely to quit a subscription service. First, a business would use aggregate data obtained from organizations the data would then be presented to the staff using a BA tool. Employees could take action to maintain clients by using the BA tool to identify individuals who are at risk of canceling.

An excellent business analytics tool is easy to use and intuitive. A comprehensive feature set for more sophisticated analytics is also offered. When it comes to commercial organizations,Business analytics has many use cases. They are:

- Review information from several sources. This could include CRM software, marketing automation tools, and cloud applications.
- To identify trends in datasets, apply sophisticated analytics and statistics. These patterns give you new insights into the consumer and their behavior as well as the ability to forecast future trends.
- Track trends and KPIs as they alter in real time. Businesses now find it simple to have all of their data in one location and to draw precise and timely conclusions.
- Encourage the use of the most recent data when making choices. You may be certain that you are well-informed for multiple circumstances because BA offers an abundance of facts that you can utilize to support your conclusions.

Advantages of Business Analytics

It's important to comprehend why business analytics is growing so much after knowing what it is. Among them are:

1. **Enhanced Decision Making:** Business analysts utilize analytics to inform data-driven business decisions through an understanding of the goals of the business. The organization's historical data, the state of the market, and the success of its product are used to project trends and formulate plans that align with those trends.

2. **Tracking Performance and Growth:** Business analytics can be used to trace an organization's evolution over time. It can also reveal how well a strategy or product is performing in the marketplace. These reports provide insight into the organization's operational and non-operational aspects. Consequently, new choices and procedures can be used to enhance the statistics.

3. **Reducing Risk Factors:** One of business analytics' primary benefits is its capacity to reduce risks. It assists in keeping track of the errors the company has made in the past and figuring out what caused them. With this information, analysis is done to determine the likelihood that comparable hazards would recur in the near future. As a result, appropriate precautions can be made to avoid them.

4. **Improve Customer Experience:** Making consumers happy is the key to success that all prosperous companies have discovered! Today's businesses recognize their clientele, comprehend their wants and needs, and adjust their services accordingly. The models and statistical methods used in business analytics make this possible.

Limitations of Business Analytics

Although the field of business analytics is quite profitable, there are drawbacks as well. Among them are:

1. **Lack of Commitment:** Investing in business analytics may be quite expensive and time-consuming. Even though the solutions are simple to implement, individuals become less trusting because of the time and money constraints. This ultimately results in the business's total collapse.

2. **Inadequate Skills:** Employees with the data analytic abilities required to handle BA data are in more demand. Some companies could find it difficult to find candidates with the BA knowledge and abilities they require.

3. **Low-Quality Data:** A lot of data is held by organizations. The true question, though, is how much of this information is available and accurate. Badly designed, overly complex, or insufficient data is a major barrier that can make business analytics procedures difficult.

4. **Privacy Concern:** Businesses gather client information in order to examine it and improve their company choices. However, there may be a privacy violation as a result of this. There have been cases where two businesses have benefited from each other's collection of user data.

ANALYSIS ON BUSINESS MODELS

Evolution of Data and Analytics in Businesses

Organizations have been utilizing data analytics as a part of their operations since before the 1950s. The initial data analytics approaches were predicated on manual processes such as surveys and interviews which generated information that would later need to be manually entered into a spreadsheet. In the late 1980s, artificial intelligence was first used to automate data processing functions. Businesses could easily and accurately collect massive amounts of data due to this advancement in artificial intelligence (*Cole Nussbaumer Knaflic, n.d.*).

Once firms were able to catch up to the 2000s, the increase of data available for analytics proliferated, and with it the evolution of artificial intelligence, enabling companies to examine large amounts of datasets quicker than ever before. Analytics technology, driven by AI, leveraging machine learning and natural language processing, has become commonplace business practice and is a vital component of daily operations. These technologies allow businesses to predict trends, analyze customer behavior, and formulate innovative business strategies.

Impact of Data and Analytics on Businesses

Organizations can create services that are specific to the demands of their clients by studying customer behavior. Nevertheless, companies can also reduce turnover over time by utilizing data and analytics solutions that facilitate better opportunities to understand how product and services react and perform with customers. Companies can stay competitive by using AI-driven predictive models for future forecasting.

Applications of Analytics in Businesses

Data analytics is essential to many different industries because it helps companies get important insights, make wise decisions, and spur innovation and expansion. Let's talk about how analytics are used by various companies to promote success and growth (*Benbya, H.et al., 2021*).

Retail: Retailers collect information using analytics about the behaviors, preferences, and prior purchases of their consumers. A better understanding of the audience allows retailers to improve inventory management, price optimization, and personalization in marketing.

Example: Flipkart identifies browsing and purchasing behavior to provide product recommendations to users, all based on analytics.

1. **Finance:** Financial institutions utilize analytics to mitigate risk, detect fraud, and make informed investment selections. Analytics is also utilized to customize financial products and services based on the customer's needs and preferences.

   Example: HDFC Bank utilizes analytics to identify and prevent financial crime and fraud.

2. **Healthcare:** Healthcare professionals employ analytics to enhance resource distribution, cut back on costs, and improve patient care outcomes. Analytics may also be employed to predict the course of a patient's illness, identify risk factors for patients, and enhance treatment processes.

   Example: Apollo Hospitals uses analytics to improve care coordination and forecast patient readmissions.

3. **Manufacturing:** Manufacturing organizations use analytics to improve quality control, minimize waste, and streamline operations. Analytics is also used to predict customer demand, monitor equipment efficiency, and identify areas of improvement for operational processes.

Example: At Tata Steel, utilizes analytics to improve manufacturing efficiency and optimize the supply chain.

4. **Marketing:** Marketing organizations utilize analytics to identify target consumers, measure campaign effectiveness, and improve marketing strategies.
5. **Transportation:** To maximize safety, cut down on fuel usage, and optimize routes, transportation businesses employ analytics. Analytics is used to estimate demand, assess driver behavior, and keep an eye on vehicle performance.

Example: Ola optimizes its ride-sharing routes and lowers fuel use through analytics.

6. **Insurance:** Insurance companies have utilized data and analytics to manage risk, detect potential fraud, and develop strutted insurance offering. Analytics can detect fraudulent claims, predict the severity of claims, and revise and motivate insurance options to the specific needs of clients.
7. **Example:** ICICI Lombard has utilized analytics to drive improvement in customer loyalty and modified insurance offerings.
8. **Telecom:** Telecom companies can leverage analytics to enhance customer service, optimize networks. Telecom companies also send service notices to measure customer loyalty. Companies can monitor customers preference and enhance their network performance.

Example: Reliance Jio has leveraged analytical modeling techniques to enhance customer satisfaction and enable network performance.

9. **Agriculture:** Companies in the agriculture industry leverage analytics to boost crop yield, manage usage of resources effective, and make data-driven decisions about planting and harvesting decisions. Companies use analytics for weather forecasting, monitoring soil condition, and interpret fertizations and irrigation strategies.

Example: Farmers utilize analytics to provide decision-information on crop health and field conditions using data from agri-tech companies such as Cropln and Ninjacart to boost farm productivity.

10. **E-commerce:** Organizations in this industry use analytics to track customer activity on websites, and improve site experience, and create tailored product recommendations. Analytics assists organizations in analyzing cart abandonment rates, analyzing purchase trends, and maximizing the impact of marketing campaigns.

Example: Flipkart provides insights into e-commerce store performance to help merchants make data-driven decisions to grow their businesses with analytics.

Data Driven Business Models

Businesses are able to remain ahead of the competition and develop services that provide greater value to clients as a result of data-infused business models Here are some of the organization those adopted data analytics to transform their business models.

1. Apple

Apple has used artificial intelligence and data analytics to create products and services tailored to its customers. By understanding customer behavior, Apple was able to design products that are intuitive and offer more value than ever before. Additionally, Apple leverages AI-driven insights to identify opportunities in new markets and quickly adapt its business model to changing environments.

2. Amazon

Amazon has enhanced its operations and produced personalized suggestions for customers by utilizing artificial intelligence and data analytics. Amazon was able to find opportunities in new regions and streamline its delivery procedures, cutting costs and increasing efficiency, by analyzing user behavior.

3. Microsoft

Microsoft, a computer company, investigated how remote work affected its workers using business analytics. Important issues including work-life balance, employee relations, the influence of collaboration, and manager involvement were all addressed by the project. Key data including shortened meeting durations, higher manager-to-manager interaction one-on-one, altered work schedules, and more robust worker-to-worker networks were brought to light by the analytics. In the end, they can utilize this information to guide their long-term job plans.

4. American Express

Business analytics are used by American Express, a credit card corporation, to identify fraudulent activity on its customers' cards. The business keeps track of KPIs including transaction details, merchant information, and card membership information. American Express is able to identify fraudulent activity nearly immediately because to these metrics.

The Future View of Business Models

Businesses will probably implement new models and tactics in the future to capitalize on developing technologies and shifting market dynamics. Future business models that could be used include:

1. **Platform-Based:** Companies that use websites or applications as digital platforms to link clients with products or services are known as platform-based firms. These companies frequently link clients with the finest suppliers using algorithms and data. They might also offer extra services like customer service or payment processing.
2. **Block chain-Based:** Distributed ledger technology, or blockchain, enables safe, open, and decentralized transactions. In the future, firms can begin employing block chain-based models to support the creation of a new types of value such as tokenized assets, decentralized networks, and smart contracts.

3. **Subscription-Based:** A subscription-based firm is one that sells clients ongoing access to a good or service, typically for a regular fee. Subscription companies often add additional perks like loyalty points or access to unique content and use data and devise algorithms to facilitate the experience for each individual side customer.

4. **Sharing Economy:** Is a business concept where products or services are shared by individuals or organizations, frequently via a digital platform. In addition to lowering transaction costs and promoting creativity and teamwork, this strategy can provide value by maximizing the use of unused assets.

ILLUSTRATION OF BUSINESS ANALYTICS IN BUSINESS MODEL

Here we can perform the customer segmentation using K-means machine learning algorithm *(U. Dinesh Kumar, 2019)*.

The process of grouping consumers based on commonalities within each cluster is known as customer segmentation. To maximize each customer's value to the company, I will segment my customer base. to alter items in accordance with unique consumer demands and behaviors. Additionally, it benefits the company to address the problems of various customers.

There is a sample dataset that contains actual sales data courtesy of an e-commerce company from November 2018 — April 2019 for which we can apply k-means algorithm using following steps:

1. Business Requirement
2. Data Analysis
3. Segmentation with K-means Clustering
4. Hyper Parameter Tuning
5. Visualization and Interpretation of the Results

1. Business Requirement

In this illustration, we will analyze the behavior of customers from various aspects through demographical or geographical perspectives.

2. Data Analysis

The raw dataset contains the following about 25000 unique customers along with their order information: **(Figure.4)**

Figure 4. Sample customer orders dataset

(Source: https://github.com/cereniyim/Customer-Segmentation-Unsupervised-ML-Model)

The above dataset doesn't contain any NULL values, as we have taken well cleaned dataset. So we can analysis the following insights from this:

- **No. of products ordered:** It is determined by totaling the product types that customers have ordered. **(Figure.5)**

Figure 5. No of products ordered

- **Average return rate:** It is the average of the returned item amount to the ordered item quantity over all of a customer's orders.**(Figure.6)**

Figure 6. Average return rate

- **Total spending:** It is the ultimate amount after taxes and returns, calculated as the sum of all sales. **(Figure.7)**

Figure 7. Total spending

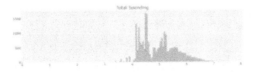

3. Segmentation with K-means Clustering

Then we are applying K-means Clustering, an unsupervised learning which works according to the following steps:

1. Start k=n centroids=number-of-clusters arbitrarily or strategically.
2. Based on Euclidian distance, assign each data point to the nearest centroid to create the groups.
3. Centers should be moved to the cluster's average of all points.
4. Repeat steps 2 and 3 until convergence.

The process evaluates the sum of squared distances between each cluster's center and clustered point as it iterates through the steps.(**Figure.8**)

Figure 8. Clusters in different iterations

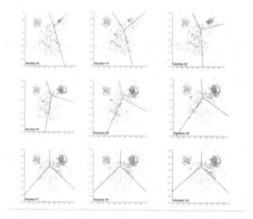

4. Hyper Parameter Tuning

Using the elbow technique, we will choose k while rejecting the K-means optimization criterion of inertia. With k values ranging from 1 to 15, we will develop multiple K-means models and store the related inertia values. Plotting inertia against the k values showed in below figure:(**Figure.9**)

Figure 9. Elbow curve

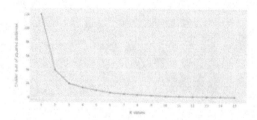

We will choose the k value where the inertia decrease stabilizes using the elbow approach.

The data are not yet clustered when k=1 since inertia is at its maximum. The descent stabilizes at k=4 and then proceeds linearly to generate an elbow at k=4. This indicates that 4 is the optimum number of customers per group.

5. Visualization and Interpretation of the Results

Let's visualize how the customers are grouped when k=4 i.e. showed in below figure **(Figure.10)**

Figure 10. Visualization of different groups

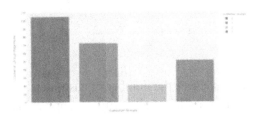

Centroids of each group are represented by cubes, while data points are displayed as spheres. There are four categories of customers:

Green: Customers who placed one to 13 orders, spent an average of 600 overall, and had no average returns.

Blue: Customers with the greatest average return rate, at least one product ordered, and a maximum total spending of 100. They could be the newest users of the online store.

Purple: Customers who placed one to four orders, spent an average of $300 overall, and had a 0.5 maximum return rate.

Red: Customers that placed one to four orders, spent an average of $150 overall, and had a 0.5 maximum return rate.**(Figure.11)**

Figure 11. Bar chart visualization to represent different customers

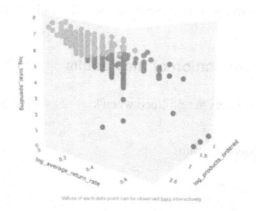

Let's examine the cluster magnitudes, or the number of customers in each group:

Since the blue category accounts for 42% of all customers, any gains made there will have a significant impact on revenue

Together, the red and purple category makes up half of all clients. When looking at the products in order and average return rate, they exhibit similar traits, but when looking at total spending, they don't. Through targeted messaging and unique offers, the brand can stay in front of those customers.

The most advantageous client group for the company is the green consumer group, which makes up 8% of all customers. They are inclined to order more than one item and keep them. Additionally, they may draw in new clients, which could affect the growth of the clients.

We addressed the issue of consumer segmentation by looking at the behavior of each client, taking into account their total spending, average return rate, and number of products ordered. We were able to better comprehend and visualize the model by utilizing three aspects.

Overall, the dataset proved suitable for solving an unsupervised machine learning task. We didn't know if our clients belonged to any groups at first; we just had their order information in our customer database. The data's patterns were identified and then divided into categories using the K-means clustering technique. We carved out tactics for the resulting groups, initially deriving meaning from a dust cloud dataset

THE FUTURE DIRECTIONS

The artificial intelligence (AI) marketing industry was projected to be worth 15.84 billion US dollars in 2021. The **Statistareport** indicate that by 2028, this value is expected to exceed 107.5 billion. **(Figure.12)**

Figure 12. Visualization of growth of AI and Ml

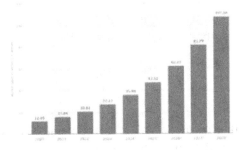

(source- Statistareport)

Conversely, the global machine learning (ML) market was valued at $19.20 billion in 2022 and is expected to grow at a compound annual growth rate (CAGR) of 36.2% from $26.03 billion in 2023 to an astounding $225.91 billion by 2030. Artificial intelligence (AI) and machine learning (ML) have a big influence on business. Both technologies are revolutionizing a number of commercial domains and bringing forth notable reforms:

The following are some emerging AI/ML technologies that are influencing the corporate environment and market dynamics:

1. **Hyper-Automation**

A integration of AI and ML is called hyper automation. It makes use of both technologies to optimize, automate, and simplify a variety of internal procedures.

2. **Natural Language Processing**

A branch of artificial intelligence and machine learning called natural language processing (NLP) makes links and makes it easier for computers and human language to communicate.

3. **Cyber Security Systems Enabled by AI**

These are advanced security technologies that provide strict and cutting-edge security for AI integration into company operations. They defend networks, computer systems, and private information from online risks and attacks.

4. **Innovations in No-Code Low-Code**

With the use of pre-built components and visual interfaces, developers with little or no programming knowledge may create apps and automate tasks with low-code and no-code platforms. These platforms' capabilities are increased when AI is integrated into them.

5. Multiple Task Models

Advanced machine learning and artificial intelligence models known as "multi-task models" are able to manage and carry out several tasks or goals at once on a single system. These models require less training and resources because they are able to learn and generalize different tasks simultaneously.

CONCLUSION

Business analytics has more than secured its place as a cornerstone of the modern business model—it has shifted how companies leverage data into action and manage informed decision-making. Businesses using advanced analytical tools and methodology can investigate large volumes of data to identify patterns, trends, and correlations which otherwise lay dormant. It allows organizations to streamline operations, build customer relationships, and identify new markets, making analytics a vehicle for continuous improvement and innovation in business.

The facts around business analytics suggest a compelling story. Companies that use analytics think that decisions are more valuable along with improvements in processes and overall competitive advantages. Companies employing data-driven strategies; are betting on decreased costs, increased profitability, and increased customer satisfaction. Companies big and small are utilizing new technologies like machine learning, artificial intelligence, and big data analytics to maximize potential analytics opportunities.

Looking forward, business analytics suggests an even greater future of integration and sophistication usage than any time before. As the amount of data continues to rise, the need for real-time analytics and predictive modeling increases. In addition, the process of ethical use of data and data privacy are not just pieces of analytics process, but of the ever-complex process of management that businesses undertake for their stakeholders. Security around processes will not diminish analytics; however, business will make sure that stakeholders maintain trust and confidence in their analytics development, and the actual use of analytics.

Business analytics is not a fad, it is and will continue to move businesses along a fundamental progression on how to operate and compete. Businesses who utilize data, may predictably outperform organizations who don't, as they navigate the ever-complex process of business marketplace with clarity, agility, and strategy. Transparency tends to politically shield organizations as their continuing to think at opportunities for advancement, that analytics will offer businesses in the future because innately are capable of innovating, in the future market ages of rapidly processing the answers of asking the right questions in business analytics.

REFERENCES

Afuah, A. (2003). *Business Models: A Strategic Management Approach.* McGraw-Hill/ Irwin.

Agarwal, S., Iyer, A.P., Panda, A., Madden, S., Mozafari, B., & Stoica, I. (2012). Blink and it's done: interactive queries on very large data.

Agrawal, A., Gans, J. S., & Goldfarb, A. (2018). *Prediction machines: the simple economics of artificial intelligence.* Harvard Business Review.

Amit, R., & Zott, C. (2001). Value creation in e-business. *Strategic Management Journal*, 22(6–7), 493–520. DOI: 10.1002/smj.187

Amit, R., & Zott, C. (2012). Creating value through business model innovation. 2012.

Banerji, D., & Reimer, T. (2019). Startup founders and their LinkedIn connections: Are well-

Benbya, H., Pachidi, S., & Jarvenpaa, S. (2021). Special issue editorial: Artificial intelligence in organizations: Implications for information systems research. *Journal of the Association for Information Systems*, 22(2), 10. DOI: 10.17705/1jais.00662

Bjornali, E. S., & Ellingsen, A. (2014). Factors affecting the development of clean-tech

Bocken, N., & Snihur, Y. (2020). Lean Startup and the business model: Experimenting for novelty and impact. *Long Range Planning*, 53(4), 101953. DOI: 10.1016/j.lrp.2019.101953

Bowman, C., & Ambrosini, V. (2000). Value creation versus value capture: Towards a coherent definition of value in strategy. British journal of management, 11(1), 1-15. Brynjolfsson, E., & Hitt, L. (1996). Paradox lost? Firm-level evidence on the returns to information systems spending. *Management Science*, 42(4).

Brandenburger, A. M., & Stuart, H. W.Jr. (1996). Value-based business strategy. *Journal of Economics & Management Strategy*, 5(1), 5–24. DOI: 10.1111/j.1430-9134.1996.00005.x

Business Analytics: Data Analysis & Decision Making" by S. Christian Albright and Wayne L. Winston.

Business Analytics: Data Analysis & Decision Making" by Christian Albright and Wayne Winston (2019)

Business Analytics: The Science of Data-Driven Decision Making" by James R. Evans (2021)

Business Analytics: The Science of Data-Driven Decision Making" by U. Dinesh Kumar (2019)

Business Model Generation: A Handbook for Visionaries, Game Changers, and Challengers" by Alexander Osterwalder and Yves Pigneur (2010)

Chesbrough, H. (2006). *Open Business Models: How to Thrive in the New Innovation Landscape.* Harvard Business School Press.

Cioffi, D. (2007). The Evolution of Business Analytics." *. *Journal of Business Research.*

Competing on Analytics: The New Science of Winning" by Thomas H. Davenport and Jeanne G. Harris (2007)

"Data Science for Business: What You Need to Know about Data Mining and Data-Analytic Thinking" by Foster Provost and Tom Fawcett (2013)

Hunger, D. L., & Wheelen, T. L. (2008). *Concepts: Strategic Management and Business Policy*. Prentice Hall.

Inmon, W. H. (1996). *Building the Data Warehouse*. John Wiley & Sons.

Johnson, W. M., Christensen, C. M., & Kagerman, H. (2008). Reinventing Your Business Model. *Harvard Business Review*, 86(12), 57–68.

Kitchin, R. (2014). Big Data, New Epistemologies and Paradigm Shifts." *. *Big Data & Society*, 1(1), 2053951714528481. DOI: 10.1177/2053951714528481

Laney, D. (2001). *3D Data Management: Controlling Data Volume*. Velocity, and Variety.

LINKS:

Pattern Recognition and Machine Learning" by Christopher M. Bishop

Shmueli, G., & Koppius, O. R. (2011). Predictive Analytics in Information Systems Research." *. *Management Information Systems Quarterly*, 35(3), 553. DOI: 10.2307/23042796

start-ups: A literature review. Energy Procedia, 58, 43-50. Blocker, C. P., Cannon, J. P., Panagopoulos, N. G., & Sager, J. K. (2012). The role of the sales force in value creation and appropriation: new directions for research. Journal of Personal Selling & Sales Management, 32(1), 15-27.

Storytelling with Data" by Cole Nussbaumer Knaflic

Teece, J. D. (2010). Business Models, Business Strategy and Innovation. *Long Range Planning*, 43(2), 172–194. DOI: 10.1016/j.lrp.2009.07.003

Chapter 7
Dynamic Pricing Strategies Implementing Machine Learning Algorithms in E–Commerce

NV Suresh

https://orcid.org/0000-0002-0393-6037

ASET College of Science and Technology, India

Ananth Selvakumar

https://orcid.org/0000-0001-8521-3440

ASET College of Science and Technology, India

Gajalaksmi Sridhar

https://orcid.org/0009-0008-4344-1486

ASET College of Science and Technology, India

Vishal Jain

https://orcid.org/0000-0003-1126-7424

Sharda University, India

ABSTRACT

This assessment paper jumps into the space of dynamics with respect to systems in electronic business, taking a gander at the joining of PC-based information computations to smooth out studying decisions. Affiliations are searching for novel techniques for Figuring out how to stay serious while additionally expanding pay considering the always-developing robotized industry. The survey turns around grasping the execution of electronic thinking models for dynamic with respect to and their impact on the web business district. The assessment looks at the significant guidelines of dynamic with respect to its standard procedures, highlighting the impediments that arise in a rapidly making business region. Using PC-based information computations offers a promising response for addressing these challenges by attracting steady assessment of monster datasets, expecting market floats, and changing studying systems in like manner. The turn of events and plan of re-enacted knowledge calculations for surveying redesign, taking into account factors like competitor appraisal are key areas of assessment.

DOI: 10.4018/979-8-3693-3884-1.ch007

INTRODUCTION

In the dependably driving scene of electronic business, the mission for benefit and productivity is empowered. Amid this pursuit, investigating structures stand as an earnest determinant of progress. Conventional static surveying models are showing ailing in satisfying the necessities of present-day buyers and the intricacies of online business locale. As such, a true effect of perspective towards dynamic with respect to systems has arisen, moved by sorts of progress being made and the rising responsiveness of information. At the genuine front of this change lies the establishment of imitated understanding assessments into surveying choices, promising excellent degrees of versatility and responsiveness. The spot of this assessment paper is to weave into the space of dynamic with respect to structures inside the setting of electronic business and investigate the execution of man-made mindfulness assessments in that.

Through an overall assessment of relevant affiliation, veritable evaluations, and exploratory affirmation, this study needs to sort out the plausibility, difficulties, and results of remembering reenacted data for checking on progress for online retail. Online business has changed the retail scene, offering buyers unparalleled comfort and consent to an immense level of things and affiliations. In any case, this striking improvement has caused over the top test, driving retailers to look for imaginative method for getting cut of the pie and upgrading benefits. Dynamic as for, portrayed by its capacity to change costs tirelessly picked different factors, for example, request, contender considering, and purchaser direct, have arisen areas of strength for as for in this undertaking. In no way, shape or form at all like static with respect to models, which depend on fixed costs, dynamic surveying empowers retailers to change quickly to gamble in real money related conditions, in this way further making compensation and remaining mindful of this current reality.

The coming of imitated information has catalyzed another time of dynamic evaluating, engaging retailers with the capacity to deal with shocking size of information to enlighten investigating choices. Man-caused understanding assessments to prevail concerning seeing radiant models and relationship inside enlightening mixes, drawing in retailers to Figure interest, expect client lead, and work on concerning strategy with wonderful exactness. By utilizing repeated data, retailers can fit costs genuinely to individual affinities, part shows essentially more, and gain by passing entrances in the electronic business area (Raja, R. V. [6]). At any rate, paying little notice to what the colossal furthest reaches of man-made mindfulness in remarkable concerning, its execution isn't without challenges. The intricacy of copied understanding calculations requires an invigorated arrangement and talented staff to make, convey, and remain mindful of these frameworks. Also, wrapping algorithmic penchant concerns, information affirmation, and moral repercussions highlight the crucial for careful thought and oversight in the usage of PC based data in assessing frameworks. This evaluation paper means to address these intricacies and give pieces of data into best practices to doing man-made data calculations in original concerning frameworks for online business.

By examining authentic setting focused examinations and joining clear proof, this study needs to offer utilitarian scrambling toward retailers endeavoring to use PC based understanding for evaluating streamlining. In outline, dynamic regarding structures engaged by man-made scholarly capacity address an essentially effect of perspective in electronic business, offering retailers principal valuable chances to improve surveying technique and update reality. Regardless, understanding the best farthest reaches of copied data in surveying streamlining requires a nuanced impression of its capacities, hardships, and moral assessments. Through observational appraisal and obliging pieces of data, this evaluation paper

endeavors to add to the thriving field of dynamic as for in electronic business and give direction to retailers investigating this uncommon scene.

Review of Literature

Liu, J. (2019) [4] this wide survey explores different surprising concerning assessments used in electronic
business settings. The paper dissects standard systems close by the mix of man-made mindfulness evaluations. It assesses the opportunity of various structures in making compensation and client responsibility.

Ban, G. Y. (2021) [1] zeroing in on the utilization of man-made data in fabulous evaluating, this study
paper gives pieces of data into the making situation of concerning systems. It looks at how PC based data
systems update as for choices in electronic business, featuring inconveniences and amazing entryways
for future evaluation.

Sarkar, M. (2023) [5] this article presents a setting focused assessment of doing PC based data calculations for dynamic concerning in an electronic business stage. It subtleties the perspective, challenges
went facing, and results accomplished. The review offers reasonable experiences for affiliations hoping
to use PC based information for evaluating update.

Chen, K. (2020) [2] assembling a near assessment, this paper examines the reasonableness of different solid evaluating structures took on by online retailers. It assesses the effect on approaches, benefit,
and client lead. The review reveals information into the importance of changed investigating models
connected by motorized thinking examinations.

Shin, D. (2023) [7] zeroing in on reasonable examination, this survey paper talks about its work in
working with dynamic concerning choices in electronic business. It outlines the precision and steady
nature of adroit models and their contemplations for cash improvement. The paper somewhat takes a
gander at moral evaluations and potential tendencies related with algorithmic surveying.

Research Methodology

The appraisal system for the paper joins a sweeping survey of articles, district, and optional information related with dynamic concerning techniques and reenacted data assessments in electronic business.
Through this plan, a finished-up progress is made, drawing on experiences and models evident in the
piece. The system integrates the openings into a strong arrangement, incorporating the leaned toward
model got from the review cycle. Arranging man-created thinking computations into dynamic in regard
to strategy for the web business industry can be enhanced record of this technique, which makes it
possible to completely take a gander at the data that is at this point open and works with the headway
of solid encounters.

Research Findings

In the rapidly expanding field of online business, dynamic exploring methodologies, particularly those
fueled by artificial intelligence (AI) and data analytics, have emerged as an essential tool for businesses
looking to expand their revenue streams. These AI-powered methodologies are transforming businesses'
approaches to and analyses of a wide range of factors, including demand, competition, and consumer
behavior. The primary focus of this investigation is on the implications, challenges, and potential solutions
of incorporating AI-driven data analytics into online business strategies. The world of online business

has undergone significant transformation in recent years. Due to the proliferation of e-commerce platforms and the increasing sophistication of consumers, businesses are under a lot of pressure to remain competitive. Because of their regularly static nature, customary strategies are challenging to stay aware of moving business sector patterns and shopper inclinations. In this setting, businesses may employ dynamic exploring strategies to gain an advantage over rivals. One aspect of dynamic exploration techniques is the support for decision-making processes provided by the continuous and adaptable analysis of data.

In contrast to static models, which are based on fixed assumptions and historical data, dynamic approaches use real-time data to provide insights that reflect the current market conditions. As a result of this change, businesses will find it easier to adapt to shifting consumer preferences and market trends. Data analytics and artificial intelligence are driving this change. AI-based algorithms can process a lot of data quickly and accurately, revealing patterns and trends that might not be apparent from conventional analysis. Online businesses can improve their designated advertising strategies and stock management by utilizing these pieces of data in the future. For example, AI-driven analytics can provide businesses with a comprehensive understanding of customer preferences and purchasing habits. Businesses can better tailor marketing campaigns to specific subsets of their target audience by utilizing this data, which results in increased customer engagement and contentment.

Predictive analytics can also be used by businesses to better anticipate demand, reducing the likelihood of over- or under-stocking. The use of dynamic exploration methods has numerous advantages. Businesses are able to remain adaptable in a market that is changing quickly thanks to these strategies. By continuously analyzing data and adapting their strategies, businesses are able to quickly respond to shifts in consumer preferences and competition. Second, dynamic methodologies improve the accuracy of business forecasts and predictions. Data from the past is often used in traditional models, which may not accurately reflect the current market's dynamics. In contrast, AI-driven analytics utilize real-time data to provide more precise and timely insights, allowing businesses to make decisions based on accurate information. Dynamic exploration techniques allow for individualized experiences for customers as well. By analyzing individual customer data, businesses can create highly targeted marketing campaigns and offers to increase customer satisfaction and loyalty. Despite their advantages, dynamic exploration methods driven by AI and data analytics can be challenging to implement. One of the main issues is the data's quality and dependability.

Inadequate or incorrect data can lead to poor or even incorrect conclusions because AI algorithms rely heavily on the data they are fed. It is absolutely necessary to guarantee the data's integrity and accuracy for these strategies to be successful. Another obstacle is ethical data use. The process of collecting and analyzing data raises privacy and security concerns. To ensure that their actions adhere to moral and legal principles, organizations should carefully investigate these issues. Transparent data practices and robust security measures are essential for preserving customer confidence and avoiding potential legal consequences. The complexity of AI-driven algorithms may pose challenges for businesses without data science expertise. If businesses lack the necessary expertise, they may apply insights incorrectly, making it difficult to comprehend and interpret these algorithms' results. Online business is likely to place a greater emphasis on dynamic research methods in the near future. As technology advances, AI and data analytics will provide even more advanced tools for comprehending market dynamics and responding to them. The expanded integration of artificial intelligence with other upcoming innovations like the Internet of Things (IoT) and blockchain is one potential improvement. These integrations, which have the potential to make data analysis even more accurate and efficient, may provide businesses with even more in-depth and useful insights. In addition, it is anticipated that advancements in machine learning and natural language processing will improve AI algorithms' capacity to comprehend and interpret complex data.

As a result, dynamic exploration techniques may be made even more effective by conducting analyses that are more precise and nuanced. The landscape of online business is being reshaped by cutting-edge research methods supported by data analysis and computerized reasoning. By providing real-time insights into demand, competition, and consumer behavior, these strategies enable businesses to remain competitive and adaptable in a market that is rapidly changing. However, it is challenging to put these strategies into action due to issues with data quality, ethical considerations, and the complexity of AI algorithms. In the highly competitive online business environment, businesses that are able to successfully overcome these obstacles and utilize the power of dynamic exploring methodologies will be well-positioned to thrive. As AI and data analytics advance, exciting opportunities will present themselves for businesses to enhance their strategies and accomplish their goals.

Proposed Conceptual Framework

Table 1. Variables in proposed conceptual framework

Variables	Definition
Product	Thing characteristics like sort, brand, and components influence reviewing decisions. Different things could require different looking over structures considering factors like clear worth, creation costs, and market pay.
People	Client monetary perspectives, inclinations, and lead impact reviewing systems. Understanding the ideal vested party attracts relationship to fit reviewing frameworks to meet express purchaser needs and inclinations.
Periods	Money related conditions change all through an extensive time, requiring flexible with respect to strategies. Periods suggest ordinary variables like seasons, events, and money related cycles, which influence client premium and hardhearted parts, thusly shaping unique looking over structures.
Decision Making using Machine Learning	Dynamic using machine learning goes comparatively a go-between process between free factors and dynamic looking over philosophies. It utilized appraisals to destroy data and settle for in regards to decisions freely, working with the execution of dynamic assessing systems in electronic business.
Dynamic Pricing Strategies	Dynamic assessing structures recommend the adaptable qualification in costs considering various components like interest, challenge, and purchaser lead. It's the outcome variable in the review, reflecting how with respect to changes constantly thinking about changes in the market environment.

Figure 1. Proposed conceptual framework

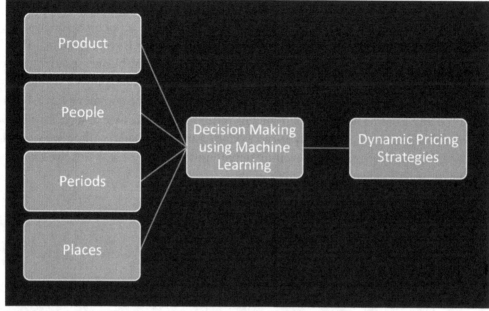

(revised model of Kopalle, P. K. [3])

Suggestions

Considering these difficulties, a couple of assessments can be proposed to refresh the fittingness and moral dependability of dynamic as for structures filled by man-made grasping calculations. Relationship, without the slightest hesitation, should focus in on information quality and put resources into overpowering information mix, cleaning, and ensuring processes. Joint undertakings with outsider information suppliers or setting resources into information improvement movements can help become interior datasets. Likewise, making interdisciplinary made attempts between information specialists, money related organized trained professionals, ethicists, and honest to goodness specialists is vital. This interdisciplinary framework can work with an exhaustive point of view on the results of dynamic investigating techniques and certification that they line up with moral principles and legitimate stray pieces.

Moreover, affiliations ought to focus in on algorithmic straightforwardness and thinking. Making interpretable PC based data models and giving clear clarifications to concentrating on choices can overhaul client supply and alleviate stresses with respect to algorithmic inclinations. Likewise, wearisome checking and evaluation of exploring frameworks are crucial. Executing evaluation circles and execution examinations can assist relationship with investigating the plentifulness of their dynamic surveying viewpoints and complete key overhauls perseveringly. Similarly, definitive plans should make to keep perceptive with kinds of progress strong regions for in and man-made mental capacity influences.

Chambers and administrative bodies ought to team up with industry colleagues to make picks and infers that advance fair inquiry, client security, and algorithmic obligation. Taking into account everything, the execution of man-made data assessments in exceptional concerning structures holds titanic potential for changing the electronic business scene. Notwithstanding, it comparatively presents enormous difficulties related with information quality, algorithmic grouped plan, and moral considerations. By focusing in on information quality, making interdisciplinary joint undertakings, guaranteeing algorithmic straightforwardness, and changing legitimate plans, affiliations can examine these difficulties and open the full advantages of dynamic concerning methods in electronic business.

CONCLUSION

Considering everything, the execution of man-made cognizance estimations in electronic business for dynamic with respect to structures means a tremendous improvement in retail practices. Through this assessment, it has turned out to be certain that using these cutting-edge computations attracts relationship to conform to the intriguing business region scene impressively more, upgrading looking over frameworks never-endingly. Predominantly of data and considering various parts, for instance, client direct, competitor with respect to, and market pay, PC based information appraisals empower web business stages to set costs that are colossal as well as remarkably made to individual client tendencies. Likewise, the coordination of man-made thinking estimations further makes reasonable limit through mechanizing reviewing decisions, opening up basic HR for fundamental tasks.

At any rate, affiliations should zero in on straightforward and moral examinations while completing excellent reviewing systems, ensuring sensibility and trust among buyers. Looking forward, the destiny of dynamic in regard to in electronic business lies in eager development and refinement of PC based information computations, as well as the coordination of emerging progressions, for instance, sensible assessment and man-made thinking. As electronic business continues to be made, affiliations that embrace such advancement will get an advantage in the overall business place, driving new turn of events and advantage while giving more conspicuous worth to clients.

REFERENCES

Ban, G. Y., & Keskin, N. B. (2021). Personalized dynamic pricing with machine learning: High-dimensional features and heterogeneous elasticity. *Management Science*, 67(9), 5549–5568. DOI: 10.1287/mnsc.2020.3680

Chen, K., Zha, Y., Alwan, L. C., & Zhang, L. (2020). Dynamic pricing in the presence of reference price effect and consumer strategic behaviour. *International Journal of Production Research*, 58(2), 546–561. DOI: 10.1080/00207543.2019.1598592

Kopalle, P. K., Pauwels, K., Akella, L. Y., & Gangwar, M. (2023). Dynamic pricing: Definition, implications for managers, and future research directions. *Journal of Retailing*, 99(4), 580–593. DOI: 10.1016/j.jretai.2023.11.003

Liu, J., Zhang, Y., Wang, X., Deng, Y., & Wu, X. (2019). Dynamic pricing on e-commerce platform with deep reinforcement learning: A field experiment. *arXiv preprint arXiv:1912.02572*.

Raja, R. V., Kumar, G., & Selvakumar, A. (2022). PERCEIVED RISK & PRICE IN E-SOURCES: ANALYSING PURCHASE DECISIONS IN BUYING MOBILE PHONES. *Annals of Forest Research*, 65(1), 3438–3448.

Sarkar, M., Ayon, E. H., Mia, M. T., Ray, R. K., Chowdhury, M. S., Ghosh, B. P., & Puja, A. R. (2023). Optimizing E-Commerce Profits: A Comprehensive Machine Learning Framework for Dynamic Pricing and Predicting Online Purchases. *Journal of Computer Science and Technology Studies*, 5(4), 186–193. DOI: 10.32996/jcsts.2023.5.4.19

Shin, D., Vaccari, S., & Zeevi, A. (2023). Dynamic pricing with online reviews. *Management Science*, 69(2), 824–845. DOI: 10.1287/mnsc.2022.4387

Chapter 8
Enhancing Solar PV–Fuel Cell Hybrid Systems Through AI–Driven Performance Optimization

Pooja Soni

Maharana Pratap University of Agriculture and Technology, India

Vikramaditya Dave

Maharana Pratap University of Agriculture and Technology, India

ABSTRACT

Renewable energy technologies play a crucial role in addressing the global energy transition to-wards sustainability. Solar photovoltaic (PV) systems and fuel cells are two prominent sources of clean energy; however, they exhibit intermittent and variable power generation patterns, hindering their widespread adoption. This paper proposes a novel approach to enhance the performance of Solar PV-Fuel Cell Hybrids (SPV-FCH) through the integration of Artificial Intelligence (AI) techniques. The synergy be-tween solar PV and fuel cells aims to create a more reliable and continuous power generation system by combining the intermittent nature of solar energy with the consistent output of fuel cells. This paper discusses the design and implementation of the AI-enabled control system for SPV-FCH hybrids, high-lighting its effectiveness in achieving improved energy yield, grid stability, and cost-effectiveness.

1 INTRODUCTION

A combination of dynamic factors is fueling a significant and intricate revolution in the global energy landscape. These factors encompass the relentless growth of the population, the unstoppable expansion of urbanization, the surging waves of industrialization, and the unceasing surge in energy demand. Tra-ditionally, the foundation of energy supply has relied on fossil fuels, namely coal, oil, and natural gas.

However, renewable energy sources such as solar, water, wind, and geo-thermal energy have emerged as viable alternatives to fossil fuels. These sources possess the potential to power societies without perpetuating the depletion of finite resources or causing environmental degradation. Advancements in

DOI: 10.4018/979-8-3693-3884-1.ch008

energy storage, grid management, and efficiency optimization are playing a crucial role in the development of renewable energy. As economies navigate this transition, the convergence of policy, industry, and research becomes essential in steering towards a future where clean, reliable, and sustainable energy takes precedence. The narrative surrounding energy now extends beyond meeting power requirements, becoming a testament to balance, innovation, and the preservation of the planet's future. The annals of history are now being written with renewable ink, interwoven with the foresight to safeguard Earth's resources for future generations.

Solar photovoltaic (PV) technology is a method of converting sunlight into electricity using semiconductor materials. The term "photovoltaic" comes from the Greek words "photo," meaning light, and "voltaic," referring to electricity. Solar PV systems are widely used around the world as a clean and sustainable source of energy.

Here is an introduction to the key aspects of solar PV:

1. **Basic Principle:**
   - Solar PV systems generate electricity through the photovoltaic effect. When sunlight hits the surface of a semiconductor material, it releases electrons, creating an electric current.
2. **Components of a Solar PV System:**
   - **Solar Panels (Photovoltaic Modules):** These are the most recognizable part of a solar PV system. They consist of semiconductor materials (usually silicon) that absorb sunlight and convert it into electricity.
   - **Inverters:** Solar panels produce direct current (DC), but most household appliances use alternating current (AC). Inverters convert DC to AC, making the electricity suitable for home or grid use.
   - **Mounting Structure:** Solar panels need to be securely mounted on rooftops, ground mounts, or other structures to capture sunlight effectively.
   - **Balance of System (BOS) Components:** This includes wiring, switches, a charge controller (for off-grid systems), and other components necessary for the proper functioning and safety of the system.
3. **Types of Solar PV Systems:**
   - **Grid-Tied Systems:** These are connected to the local electric grid. Excess electricity generated can be fed back into the grid, and when more power is needed than the solar panels can provide, electricity is drawn from the grid.
   - **Off-Grid Systems:** These operate independently of the grid and typically include energy storage solutions like batteries to store excess energy for use during periods without sunlight.
   - **Hybrid Systems:** Combine solar PV with other renewable energy sources (such as wind) and may include energy storage.
4. **Advantages of Solar PV:**
   - **Renewable:** Solar energy is abundant and inexhaustible.
   - **Clean and Sustainable:** Solar power generation produces minimal environmental impact compared to traditional fossil fuel-based energy sources.
   - **Reduced Electricity Bills:** Solar PV systems can significantly reduce or eliminate electricity bills, especially in areas with ample sunlight.
   - **Low Operating Costs:** Once installed, solar PV systems have low operating and maintenance costs.

5. **Challenges and Considerations:**
   - **Intermittency:** Solar power generation is dependent on sunlight, making it intermittent and less predictable.
   - **Initial Cost:** While the cost of solar panels has decreased, the initial investment for a solar PV system can still be relatively high.
   - **Space Requirements:** Large-scale installations may require considerable space.
6. **Future Trends:**
   - **Advancements in Technology:** Ongoing research aims to improve the efficiency and cost-effectiveness of solar PV technology.
   - **Energy Storage:** Advances in energy storage technologies (such as batteries) enhance the viability of solar energy, addressing intermittent concerns.

Solar PV is a key player in the global transition towards cleaner and more sustainable energy sources, contributing to efforts to mitigate climate change and reduce dependence on fossil fuels.

A fuel cell is an electrochemical device that converts the chemical energy of a fuel and an oxidizing agent (typically hydrogen and oxygen) directly into electrical energy. It operates through an electrochemical reaction, producing electricity, heat, and water as byproducts. Fuel cells offer a clean and efficient alternative to traditional combustion-based power generation methods. Here's an introduction to the key aspects of fuel cells:

1. **Basic Principle:**
   - A fuel cell consists of two electrodes, an anode, and a cathode, separated by an electrolyte. The most common type of fuel cell uses hydrogen as the fuel and oxygen (usually from the air) as the oxidizing agent.
   - At the anode, hydrogen molecules are split into protons (H^+) and electrons (e^-). The protons move through the electrolyte, while the electrons travel through an external circuit, creating an electric current.
   - At the cathode, the protons, electrons, and oxygen combine to form water (H_2O).
2. **Types of Fuel Cells:**
   - **Proton Exchange Membrane (PEM) Fuel Cells:** Commonly used in vehicles and portable electronics. They operate at relatively low temperatures (around 80°C) and have a solid polymer electrolyte membrane.
   - **Solid Oxide Fuel Cells (SOFC):** Operate at higher temperatures (typically above 500°C) and are suitable for stationary power generation. They use a solid ceramic electrolyte.
   - **Molten Carbonate Fuel Cells (MCFC):** Operate at high temperatures (600-700°C) and are used in large-scale stationary applications.
   - **Alkaline Fuel Cells (AFC):** Use an alkaline electrolyte and were historically used in space missions. They operate at relatively low temperatures.
3. **Advantages of Fuel Cells:**
   - **Efficiency:** Fuel cells can achieve high efficiency in converting fuel into electricity, especially in combined heat and power (CHP) applications.
   - **Clean Energy Production:** The only byproducts of hydrogen fuel cells are electricity, heat, and water, making them environmentally friendly.

- **Versatility:** Fuel cells can be used for various applications, including stationary power generation, transportation (e.g., fuel cell vehicles), and portable devices.

4. **Challenges and Considerations:**
   - **Hydrogen Infrastructure:** A key challenge is the development of a reliable and widespread hydrogen infrastructure for the production, distribution, and storage of hydrogen fuel.
   - **Cost:** The cost of fuel cells, especially those using precious metals like platinum as catalysts, remains a barrier to widespread adoption.
   - **Durability:** Some types of fuel cells may face challenges related to the durability of components, affecting their lifespan.

5. **Applications:**
   - **Transportation:** Fuel cells are used in hydrogen fuel cell vehicles (FCVs), providing an alternative to traditional internal combustion engines.
   - **Stationary Power Generation:** Fuel cells can be used in homes, businesses, and utilities to generate electricity and heat.
   - **Portable Electronics:** Small, lightweight fuel cells are used to power portable electronic devices.

6. **Future Trends:**
   - **Advancements in Catalysts:** Research is ongoing to develop more cost-effective and durable catalysts, reducing the reliance on expensive materials like platinum.
   - **Hydrogen Production:** Exploration of sustainable and efficient methods for hydrogen production, such as electrolysis powered by renewable energy sources.

Fuel cells play a significant role in the quest for cleaner and more sustainable energy solutions, offering a promising alternative to conventional energy technologies with lower environmental impacts.

Hybrid renewable energy systems combine two or more renewable energy sources to generate electricity. This approach leverages the strengths of each individual source, providing a more reliable and efficient power generation solution. Here are some advantages of hybrid renewable energy systems:

1. **Increased Reliability:**

• Combining different renewable sources helps mitigate the intermittency and variability associated with individual sources. For example, when solar energy production is low (e.g., during cloudy days or nighttime), wind or other sources may compensate, ensuring a more consistent power supply.

2. **Enhanced Energy Availability:**

• Hybrid systems can provide a more continuous and reliable energy supply by tapping into multiple sources. This is especially crucial for off-grid or remote locations where a consistent power supply is essential.

3. **Optimized Energy Output:**

- Hybrid systems can be designed to maximize energy production by utilizing complementary energy resources. For instance, in a solar-wind hybrid system, solar power production may peak during the day, while wind power may be more prominent during the night.

4. **Improved System Efficiency:**

- Integrating multiple renewable sources allows for more efficient use of the generated energy. Hybrid systems can be designed to match the energy demand profile, ensuring that electricity production aligns with consumption patterns.

5. **Reduction in Energy Storage Requirements:**

- By combining different renewable sources with varying production patterns, the need for large-scale energy storage systems may be reduced. This is because the variability of one source can be compensated by the availability of another.

6. **Cost Savings:**

- Hybrid systems can lead to cost savings in comparison to standalone systems. The complementary nature of different renewable sources can result in optimized infrastructure and reduced overall costs per unit of energy generated.

7. **Environmental Benefits:**

- Hybrid renewable energy systems contribute to a more sustainable and environmentally friendly energy landscape by reducing dependence on fossil fuels. This helps mitigate greenhouse gas emissions and combat climate change.

8. **Flexibility and Scalability:**

- Hybrid systems offer flexibility in terms of design and scalability. They can be adapted to different geographical locations, energy needs, and environmental conditions. This flexibility makes them suitable for a wide range of applications, from small-scale residential systems to large-scale industrial projects.

9. **Grid Support and Stability:**

- Hybrid systems can be designed to provide grid support services, such as frequency regulation and voltage control. This contributes to the stability and reliability of the overall power grid.

10. **Technological Innovation:**

- The development and integration of hybrid systems drive technological innovation in the renewable energy sector. This includes advancements in system control, energy management, and hybrid system optimization.

Hybrid renewable energy systems play a crucial role in advancing the transition to a more sustainable and resilient energy infrastructure, addressing the challenges associated with the intermittent nature of some renewable sources.

However, overreliance on non-renewable resources has presented several challenges and concerns, including:

1. **Climate Change:** The combustion of fossil fuels releases greenhouse gases, such as carbon dioxide (CO_2), into the atmosphere, contributing to global warming and alterations in weather patterns. To prevent catastrophic consequences, the Intergovernmental Panel on Climate Change (IPCC) emphasizes the need to limit global warming to well below 2 degrees Celsius above pre-industrial levels.
2. **Energy Security:** Countries heavily reliant on fossil fuel imports face energy security risks due to price fluctuations and geopolitical tensions, as highlighted in a report by the International Renewable Energy Agency (IRENA). This has prompted nations to seek more diverse and domestically available energy sources.
3. **Environmental Pollution:** "Fossil fuel combustion not only contributes to climate change but also causes air pollution, leading to respiratory problems and other health issues. Additionally, accidents in oil drilling, transportation, and refining have resulted in environmental disasters.
4. **Depletion of Resources:** Fossil fuels are finite resources, and their extraction leads to significant environmental impacts, including habitat destruction and water pollution.

To address these challenges and build a sustainable future, there is a growing global consensus on the need to transition towards sustainable power generation, characterized by:

1. **Renewable Energy:** Renewable energy sources, such as solar, wind, hydro, geothermal, and biomass, offer a clean and virtually inexhaustible alternative to fossil fuels. These sources do not emit greenhouse gases during operation, reducing carbon emissions and combating climate change.
2. **Decentralization and Grid Integration:** Renewable energy technologies facilitate decentralization of energy production, allowing individuals and communities to generate their own power. Integrating renewable energy sources into the power grid enhances grid stability and resilience.
3. **Energy Efficiency:** Improving energy efficiency in various sectors, such as buildings, transportation, and industry, can significantly reduce energy consumption and associated emissions.
4. **Technological Advancements:** Advancements in energy storage, smart grids, and artificial intelligence enable more efficient management and utilization of renewable energy, addressing intermittency issues and optimizing power generation".

Solar photovoltaic (PV)-fuel cell hybrid power systems have been gaining significant attention as an innovative and promising solution for sustainable energy generation. The underlying concept behind their development lies in the synergistic combination of two distinct renewable energy technologies, namely solar PV and fuel cells, in order to overcome the limitations and enhance the benefits of each individual system. Solar PV systems utilize sunlight to directly convert it into electricity through the photovoltaic effect, offering a clean and abundant source of renewable energy. However, their intermittent nature, which is dependent on weather conditions and daylight availability, can present challenges for grid integration and reliability.

On the other hand, fuel cells are electrochemical devices that continuously generate electricity by converting hydrogen or other fuels into electricity and heat, emitting only water and minimal pollutants. Fuel cells provide a stable and consistent power output, regardless of external conditions, making them a dependable source of energy.

By integrating solar PV and fuel cells into a hybrid system, their complementary characteristics can be harnessed to address the limitations of each technology. During peak solar generation, excess electricity can be utilized to produce hydrogen through electrolysis, storing the energy for later use in the fuel cells. This capability allows the hybrid system to balance intermittent solar power with the constant output from fuel cells, ensuring a consistent and reliable energy supply".

Numerous studies have highlighted the potential advantages of "solar PV-fuel cell hybrid power systems." A study by (Zhang et al. 2020) demonstrated that such hybrid systems can significantly improve energy efficiency and reduce carbon emissions compared to standalone PV or fuel cell systems. Additionally, the ability to store excess solar energy as hydrogen enables the hybrid system to act as an energy storage solution, enhancing grid stability and supporting renewable energy integration.

Furthermore, solar PV-fuel cell hybrid power systems offer scalability and flexibility, making them suitable for various applications, from small-scale residential installations to larger commercial and industrial setups. The technological synergy achieved through this integration can lead to cost savings over time, reducing reliance on grid electricity during peak demand periods and enhancing overall energy resilience (Ghenai et al.,2013; Alkhateeb et al.,2016).

Hence, "the combination of solar PV and fuel cells in hybrid power systems offers a promising approach to address the challenges of intermittent renewable energy sources while leveraging the benefits of both technologies. As the world seeks to transition to a sustainable energy future, these hybrid systems hold the potential to play a vital role in achieving reliable, efficient, and environmentally friendly power generation".

Integrating artificial intelligence (AI) into the optimization process of "solar PV-fuel cell hybrid power systems" presents both challenges and opportunities. The incorporation of AI can significantly enhance the system's performance, but it also requires careful consideration of potential drawbacks (Heydari & Askarzaedh, 2016). Below are some of the key challenges and opportunities associated with AI integration:

1.1. Challenges

- **Data Quality and Availability:** AI systems heavily rely on high-quality and relevant data to make accurate inferences. However, obtaining comprehensive and real-time data for the various components of a hybrid system, as well as weather conditions, electricity demand, and other relevant parameters, can be a challenging task. It may require the implementation of advanced monitoring and data collection systems.
- **Model Complexity:** Hybrid power systems are inherently complex, involving multiple interacting components and unpredictable external factors. Developing AI models that can accurately handle such complexity and provide meaningful optimization insights can be a difficult task.
- **Algorithm Selection:** Selecting the most appropriate AI algorithms for the optimization task is crucial. Different algorithms have their own advantages and disadvantages, and choosing the right one requires a deep understanding of their capabilities and limitations.

- **Training and Validation:** Training AI models requires large datasets, and validation is necessary to ensure the accuracy and generalization of the models. Overfitting or underfitting the models to the training data can result in suboptimal performance during real-world operation.

Hybrid Renewable Energy Systems (HRES) present significant opportunities in the global push towards sustainable energy. One key opportunity lies in their ability to provide a reliable and continuous power supply by combining different renewable sources. HRES can effectively address the intermittency and variability associated with individual sources like solar or wind, ensuring a more stable energy output. This reliability makes HRES particularly valuable in off-grid or remote areas where a consistent power supply is crucial.

Moreover, HRES offer the chance to optimize energy production and enhance overall system efficiency. By intelligently combining complementary energy resources, such as solar and wind, these systems can provide a continuous and predictable power supply. This optimized energy output contributes to a more efficient use of renewable resources.

Cost savings are another significant advantage with HRES. While the initial investment can be substantial, the long-term operational costs are often lower than those associated with traditional energy sources. By leveraging the strengths of multiple renewable sources, HRES can provide a cost-effective solution for meeting energy demands, especially in regions with abundant renewable resources.

Additionally, HRES contributes to environmental sustainability by reducing reliance on fossil fuels, lowering greenhouse gas emissions, and promoting a cleaner energy mix. As global awareness of climate change grows, there is an increasing demand for sustainable energy solutions, and HRES are well-positioned to meet this demand.

Technological advancements and innovation represent further opportunities in the HRES sector. Ongoing research can lead to improved energy storage technologies, more efficient system designs, and increased overall performance. As the technology continues to evolve, the cost-effectiveness and viability of HRES are likely to improve, opening up new possibilities for widespread adoption.

Overall, Hybrid Renewable Energy Systems offer a compelling opportunity to address energy challenges, enhance energy resilience, and contribute to a more sustainable and environmentally friendly energy future.

Hybrid renewable energy systems (HRES) present a promising solution for sustainable power generation, but they face several challenges. The integration and design of multiple renewable sources, energy storage, and control systems can be complex, requiring careful planning. The inherent intermittency and variability of renewable sources like solar and wind pose difficulties in maintaining a stable and reliable power supply. Efficient and cost-effective energy storage solutions are essential to address fluctuations in energy production. Furthermore, site-specific challenges, such as geographical limitations and climate conditions, can impact the feasibility of HRES. While these systems offer long-term cost savings, the initial investment and installation costs can be high, and achieving economic viability remains a challenge. Technical compatibility issues, standardization, and the need for specialized knowledge for operation and maintenance add to the complexity. Regulatory frameworks and public awareness are crucial for successful HRES implementation. Ongoing research and technological advancements are necessary to improve component efficiency and overcome these challenges, fostering the transition towards a more sustainable energy landscape.

1.2. Opportunities

- **Enhanced System Performance:** AI can continuously analyze real-time data, weather forecasts, and electricity demand patterns to optimize the operation of hybrid power systems. This leads to improved energy efficiency, better load balancing, and overall enhanced system performance.
- **Real-Time Decision Making:** AI enables real-time decision-making capabilities, allowing the system to quickly adapt to changing conditions, such as sudden variations in solar irradiance or electricity demand. This dynamic response can improve grid stability and reliability.
- **Predictive Maintenance:** AI can predict equipment failures or performance degradation based on data analysis, enabling proactive maintenance, and minimizing downtime. This is crucial for ensuring the reliability of the system.
- **Advanced Control:** AI can provide advanced control mechanisms for hybrid power systems, optimizing their operation and ensuring efficient utilization of resources. This can lead to cost savings and improved overall system performance.
- **Scalability:** AI models can be tailored to suit different scales of "solar PV-fuel cell hybrid power systems," from small-scale domestic installations to large industrial setups, making the technology applicable in various contexts.
- **Continuous Learning:** AI models can be designed to learn from system behavior over time, leading to improved optimization and decision-making capabilities as the system operates and accumulates more data.
- **Energy Market Integration:** "AI can facilitate participation in energy markets by predicting electricity prices, allowing the hybrid system to buy or sell electricity strategically, potentially leading to cost savings or revenue generation (Ghenai & Janajreh, 2016; Lambert et al., 2006; Yilmaz et al., 2015).

The research conducted by Iqbal and Mohammad (2022) delved into various techniques for hydrogen production, storage technologies, and the role of hydrogen in bolstering the energy storage capacity of the system. By integrating hydrogen storage into the hybrid system, the resilience of energy was enhanced, allowing for better utilization of surplus PV power. In their study, they proposed a power management method for a DC microgrid consisting of solar PV, batteries, fuel cell, and stored hydrogen. The viability of this system design was assessed using HOMER software in a remote area of North India. The findings demonstrated that the proposed structure is financially feasible, with an overall net present cost (NPC) of $83,103. Additionally, time-domain simulations were conducted to ensure the technological feasibility of the system. The results indicated that the suggested approach effectively electrifies critical loads, such as ventilators, even in the face of fluctuating solar irradiation conditions.

2 LITERATURE REVIEW

PV-fuel cell hybrid power systems and their performance. Here are some key findings from previous studies:

1. **Techno-Economic Analysis and Optimization of Solar PV-Fuel Cell Hybrid Systems:**

A study by **Pang et al. (2019)** conducted a techno-economic analysis of a grid-connected solar PV-fuel cell hybrid system. They found that the hybrid system reduced the overall cost of electricity generation compared to standalone PV or fuel cell systems. The optimization of the system's operation based on weather forecasts and electricity demand patterns resulted in improved energy efficiency and financial viability.

(Ghenai et al., 2020) created a hybrid solar PV/fuel cell power plant to handle the electric load of a desert-area residential subdivision. The system was developed with a renewable component of 40.2% and a levelized cost of energy of 145 $/MWh in mind. The method was proven to be both economically and environmentally sustainable.

The system met the residential community's AC primary load with low unmet load. The system generated 52% of its power from solar PV and 48% from gasoline. The researcher came to the conclusion that the suggested hybrid renewable power system is a realistic choice for satisfying the electric load of desert towns. The system is both economically and environmentally feasible, with a high renewable component.

2. Energy Management Strategy for Hybrid Systems:

Chen et al. (2017) proposed an energy management strategy for a grid-connected solar PV-fuel cell hybrid system. The study focused on achieving load leveling and energy self-sufficiency through coordinated control of the PV system, fuel cell, and energy storage. The proposed strategy showed promising results in minimizing grid dependence and ensuring a continuous power supply.

(Hu et al., 2021) suggested fuzzy control technique for HESS in ships may successfully split the charge and discharge functions of the HESS to fulfil the ship's power requirement. The method also ensures that the HESS is always in good working order, which is critical for the ship's safety and reliability.

The experimental findings demonstrate that the proposed technique is successful and can increase the HESS's performance.

The findings of this work have implications for the energy distribution and capacity configuration of HESS. The findings indicate that fuzzy control could be a promising strategy for managing HESS in ships, leading to the development of more efficient and dependable HESS systems.

(Wang et al., 2023) offer an energy management technique based on reinforcement learning that can efficiently distribute the power supply's charging and discharging circumstances, preserve the state of charge (SOC) of the battery, and fulfil the demand for power of working conditions while consuming less energy. They use simulations to test the proposed technique, and the findings demonstrate that it can considerably improve the efficacy and lifespan of the hybrid energy storage system.

3. Dynamic Power Dispatch for Hybrid Systems:

(Qu et al., 2017) propose a unique multiple-purpose dynamic economic emission dispatch (DEED) model is proposed, taking into account EVs and wind power uncertainty. The DEED model reduces total fuel costs and polluting emissions while guaranteeing the system satisfies energy & user demand. To optimise system efficiency, the charging as well as discharging behaviour of the EVs is dynamically regulated. To ensure that the DEED model's constraints are met, a two-step constraint processing technique is provided. The MOEA/D algorithm is being enhanced in order to find superior alternatives to the

DEED model. The 10-generator system validates the suggested model and approach, and its outcomes indicate they are viable and logical.

In a study by **Lai et al. (2019)**, an AI-based dynamic power dispatch algorithm was developed for a solar PV-fuel cell hybrid power system. The algorithm optimized the power output from the PV system and fuel cell to meet the varying electricity demand throughout the day. The dynamic dispatch approach improved the system's response to changing conditions and increased overall energy utilization".

4. Hydrogen Storage and Management:

Research by Patel et al. (2018) focused on the hydrogen storage and management aspects of solar PV-fuel cell hybrid systems. The research conducted by Iqbal and Mohammad (2022) delved into various techniques for hydrogen production, storage technologies, and the role of hydrogen in bolstering the energy storage capacity of the system. By integrating hydrogen storage into the hybrid system, the resilience of energy was enhanced, allowing for better utilization of surplus PV power. In their study, they proposed a power management method for a DC microgrid consisting of solar PV, batteries, fuel cell, and stored hydrogen. The viability of this system design was assessed using HOMER software in a remote area of North India. The findings demonstrated that the proposed structure is financially feasible, with an overall net present cost (NPC) of $83,103. Additionally, time-domain simulations were conducted to ensure the technological feasibility of the system. The results indicated that the suggested approach effectively electrifies critical loads, such as ventilators, even in the face of fluctuating solar irradiation conditions.

5. Environmental Impact Assessment:

(Akyuz et al., 2010) discovered that a hybrid electrical system can greatly cut greenhouse gas emissions & electricity costs in chicken production. The researchers also discovered that DSM can lower annual electricity usage by 15% while also improving the hybrid power system's techno-economic viability.

(Anayochukwu, 2013) showed that when compared to a DG power system, a hybrid power system with 69% renewable energy penetration can lower the amount of different air pollutants by up to 69%. The HOMER programme was utilized to create a theoretical model that compares the environmental impact of various power systems for GSM base station locations.

A study by **Zhang et al. (2018)** conducted a life cycle assessment of a "solar PV-fuel cell hybrid system" to evaluate its environmental impact. The analysis considered the environmental burdens associated with manufacturing, installation, and operation of the hybrid system. The outcome indicated a decrease in carbon dioxide emissions compared to conventional energy generation methods.

(Alharthi et al., 2018) analysed and compared the efficacy of six alternative "photovoltaic (PV) monitoring systems" with "diesel-battery" combination systems in the "(KSA) Kingdom of Saudi Arabia's" desert climate. The study found out that because of its low NPC, LCOE, and CO2 emissions, the VCA system is the most cost-friendly tracking method for PV installations in KSA.

The HOMER program was employed to create a theoretical model that compares the environmental impact of different power systems for GSM base station locations. In a study conducted by Zhang et al. (2018), a life cycle assessment of a "solar PV-fuel cell hybrid system" was carried out to evaluate its environmental impact. The analysis took into account the environmental burdens associated with the manufacturing, installation, and operation of the hybrid system. The results showed a reduction in carbon dioxide emissions compared to conventional energy generation methods.

In another study by Alharthi et al. (2018), the effectiveness of six alternative "photovoltaic (PV) monitoring systems" was analyzed and compared with "diesel-battery" combination systems in the desert climate of the Kingdom of Saudi Arabia (KSA). The study revealed that the VCA system, due to its low NPC, LCOE, and CO2 emissions, is the most cost-friendly tracking method for PV installations in KSA.

3 METHODOLOGY

Introducing the AI-Powered Approach:

Our innovative technique incorporates the use of AI to enhance the performance and cost-effectiveness of grid-connected "solar photovoltaic (PV)-fuel cell hybrid power systems." We aim to conduct a detailed techno-economic analysis and optimize system operation by integrating AI technology. Our AI-powered platform continuously evaluates real-time data, weather forecasts, electricity usage trends, and system characteristics to make dynamic decisions that result in improved system performance.

Data Collection and Preparation for System Modeling:

Accurate data collection is crucial for developing a reliable system model. We collect solar radiation data, ambient temperature, fuel cell efficiency data, power usage, and other relevant operational information. Data can be obtained from weather stations, sensor arrays, smart meters, and historical records.

To ensure data quality and consistency, we employ preprocessing procedures. This includes data cleaning, filling in any missing information, and standardizing the data for further analysis.

4 MATHEMATICAL MODELING

4.1. Solar PV System Modeling

"The mathematical model for the solar PV system typically includes the performance characteristics of the solar panels, considering factors such as solar irradiance, ambient temperature, and module temperature. This model uses the single-diode or double-diode equations to estimate the PV panel's current-voltage (I-V) and power-voltage (P-V) characteristics. The performance model can also account for degradation and aging effects over time.

4.2. Fuel Cell System Modeling

The mathematical model for the fuel cell system involves various sub-models for the fuel cell stack, reformer (if applicable), and hydrogen storage. The fuel cell stack model considers factors such as hydrogen and oxygen flow rates, operating temperature, and cell voltage characteristics. The reformer model (if used) estimates the efficiency of hydrogen production from the reforming process. The hydrogen storage model predicts hydrogen storage capacity and performance.

4.3. Hybrid System Interaction Model

To optimize the hybrid system's operation, a control algorithm is designed based on the interactions between the "solar PV" & "fuel cell systems." The control algorithm determines the optimal power output from each component to meet electricity demand while minimizing operational costs or maximizing energy efficiency. This may involve state-of-charge (SoC) control for hydrogen storage, load leveling, and dynamic dispatch of power between the PV and fuel cell components.

5 SOFTWARE TOOLS AND PLATFORMS USED FOR SIMULATION

Various software tools and platforms can be used for simulating the "solar PV-fuel cell hybrid power system". Some commonly used tools include:

1. **MATLAB/Simulink:** MATLAB and Simulink provide powerful simulation capabilities and can be used for both modeling the individual components and optimizing the hybrid system's operation.
2. **HOMER (Hybrid Optimization Model for Electric Renewables):** Hybrid power systems, such as "solar PV-fuel cell hybrids," may benefit from the techno-economic analysis and optimization provided by HOMER.

6 RESULTS AND DISCUSSIONS

As can be seen in Fig. 1, "the components of the grid-connected hybrid power system consist of solar PV panels, a fuel cell, an electrolyzer, a hydrogen storage tank, an inverter (DC/AC power conversion), and the utility grid. The AC load is calculated from the total energy use of the building (heating, cooling, lighting, and other appliances). Additional background on the equations used to determine solar PV, fuel cell, and electrolyzer output and input powers" is provided by the work of Ghenai et al.[15-16]

Figure 1. "Grid-connected solar photovoltaic/fuel-cell hybrid power generation"

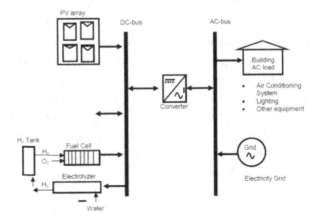

The "hybrid energy system" was planned to provide the commercial building's daily energy needs of 6,540 kWh. In order to determine how much power goes into and out of each part, "thousands of hours were spent simulating and optimising. Using an optimization search space, the optimum solutions for the hybrid power system's LCOE minimization were found. The simulation and optimization method is based on the microgrid power system model that was selected (Pang et al., 2019).

The design configuration (Solar PV, fuel cell, and utility grid), search space (maximum power capacity off each component), and daily power consumption for the building are input into a simulation, and the results are analysed for technical feasibility and life cycle cost. The optimization approach models many configurations (single component like solar PV alone or combination of two or more components like solar PV/fuel cell) to identify the best system design that satisfies the technical constraints and has the lowest life cycle cost.

According to the results of the simulation and optimization, Systems 1, 2, 3, and 4 have the cheapest energy costs. The first (System 1) only makes use of the grid as a reference point; the second (GT120) uses the grid in conjunction with solar photovoltaics (PV) with a 120 kW capacity and a fuel cell with a 100 kW capacity; the third (GT250) uses the grid in conjunction with PV with a 250 kW capacity and a 100 kW fuel cell; and the fourth (GT500) uses the grid in conjunction with PV with a 500 kW capacity. Table 2 summarises the solar photovoltaic (PV), fuel cell, and inverter capacities of grid-connected hybrid power systems. Figure 2 depicts the main load consumption, grid utility purchases, surplus power sales, and solar PV/fuel cell power system energy production for both off-grid and grid-tied solar PV/fuel cell power systems.

Power generation in all three grid-connected solar PV/fuel cell systems is shown by simulation results and the technical constraint (lowest cost of energy) in the form of cycle charging control strategies (the generator or fuel cell will run at maximum capacity to meet the AC primary load and the excess power is used for the power input of the electrolyzer or to charge the battery if used). All of the grid power used by the primary AC load in the reference system (system 1) is used up. Total electrical production for the GT120 system is 2,508,541 kWh/yr, with 1,369,294 kWh/yr coming from the grid (55 percent), 875,208 kWh/yr coming from the fuel cells (35 percent), and 263,039 kWh/yr coming from the solar PV system (10 percent).

The grid-tied power system (system 2) provides all of the electricity needed to meet the building's annual AC main consumption of 2,387,100 kWh, with a surplus of 74,490 kWh being sold back to the utility company. The GT250 power plant's System 3 produces 2,526,309 kWh/yr total, with 44% coming from purchasing grid energy (1,105,552 kWh/yr), 35% from the fuel cell (87,278 kWh/yr), and 54% from the solar PV system (22 percent). The grid-tied power system (system 3) provides all of the electricity needed to meet the building's annual AC main consumption of 2,387,100 kWh, with any excess electricity being sold back to the grid at a rate of 3 percent, or 81,985 kWh. System 4 of the GT500 power system is a grid-connected hybrid energy system that produces 2,596,380 kWh annually. There are three main sources for this sum: the grid (677,170 kWh/year, or 26 percent), the fuel cell (823,213 kWh/year, or 32 percent), and the solar PV system (1,095,996 kWh/year, or 17 percent) (42 percent).

As can be seen in Fig. 2, the building's yearly AC main demand of 2,387,100 kWh is completely fulfilled by the electricity generated by the grid-tied power system (system 4), with 132,090 kWh, or 5% of the total production, being sold back to the grid. The average power output of the PV array for grid-connected solar PV/fuel cell hybrid power systems was reported to be anywhere from 30 kW for the GT120 (120 kW solar PV capacity) to 63 kW for the GT250 (250 kW sun PV capacity) and 125 kW for the GT500 (500 kW solar PV capacity). Three grid-connected solar PV/fuel cell power plants achieve

25% capacity factor with yearly solar PV operation of 4345 hours. The maximum fuel cell power for any of the three designs is 100 kW. The average power output of the fuel cell is 100 kW, with an average electrical efficiency of 68%. The fuel cell requires 0.04 kg/kWh of fuel. Inverter power capacities of 193 kW, 295 kW, and 477 kW are used in grid-connected solar PV/fuel cell power systems ranging in size from GT120 to GT500 (See Table 2). The typical inverter output for the GT120, GT250, and GT500 power systems is 125 kW, 156 kW, and 210 kW, respectively. The capacity factors of the inverters used in the GT120, GT250, and GT500 power systems were 66%, 53%, and 44%, respectively. Inverter power losses, which occur when DC power is converted to AC power, average about 4% across all three power system architectures.

Daily performance of the GT500 grid-tied solar PV/fuel cell power system is shown in Figure 3 over the course of four days (July 24-27). The PV system provides the bulk of the needed energy during the day, when solar irradiation is at its peak, while the remaining is drawn from the grid. During the evening hours, the fuel cell is the primary source of electricity, with the grid filling in the gaps. The GT500 grid-connected solar PV/fuel cell power system provides all of the required AC for the buildings", with five per cent of the power generated by fuel & solar cell technology are offered for sale back to the grid. earn revenue and reduce energy costs.

Table 1. Components and technical details of hybrid electrical systems.

System Component	Description
Solar PV	Type: "Canadian solar CS6U-330"; module: polycrystalline; nominal maximum power = 330 W; operating temperature 45o C; efficiency = 16.97%; and derating factor fPV = 80%. O&M = $3/year, life time = 25 years. Cost per 1 kW: capital = $1200; replacement = $1200;
Hydrogen Tank	Cost per 1 kg: capital = $0.5; life time = 25years, O&M = $10/year.
Fuel Cell	Type: "PEM Fuel cell (DC power)"; fuel: hydrogen; and electrical efficiency hFC = 70%. O&M = $0.01/hour, life time (hours) = 50,000. Cost per 1 kW: capital = $400; replacement = $400;
Inverter/Rectifier	O&M = $10/year, life time = 25years. Cost per 1 kW: capital = $40; replacement = $40;
Converter:	Type: "Leonics S219CPH"; voltage = 48 VDC with an efficiency = 96%
Electrolyzer	Type: "generic electrolyzer (DC power)", Efficiency hEZ = 90%. O&M = $8/year, life time = 15years. Cost per 1 kW: capital = $100; replacement = $100.

Table 2. "Solar photovoltaic (PV) and fuel cell (FC) power systems" synced with the grid.

System	Grid	Solar PV Capacity (kW)	Fuel Cell Capacity (kW)	Inverter Capacity (kW)
Baseline - Grid only	yes	0	0	0
GTPV120	yes	120	100	193
GTPV250	yes	250	100	295
GTPV500	yes	500	100	477

Figure 2. Results from one year of using "hybrid solar PV/fuel cell electricity systems connected to the grid"

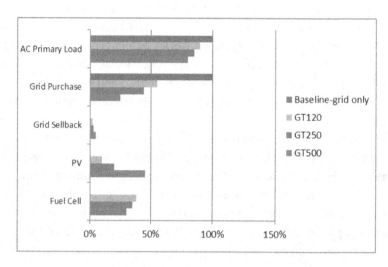

Table 3 compares the three "grid-connected solar PV/fuel cell power systems" based on their renewable share, energy cost, and decrease in CO2 emissions. "When coupled with the grid, the renewable fractions produced by the GT125 solar PV/fuel cell, the GT250 solar PV/fuel cell, and the GT500 solar PV/fuel cell are 8.8 percent, 19.9 percent, and 40.4 percent, respectively. The GT500 power system (system 4) with coupled solar power of 500 kW and fuel cell power of 100 kW with the grid offers the best solution in terms of renewable component (40.4%), energy cost, renewable component (40.4%), and emissions (133 kg CO2/MWh). Figure 3, 4, and 5 shows graph of comparison for the three "grid-connected solar PV/fuel cell power systems" based on their clean and green share, energy cost, and decrease in emissions.

The whole energy need of the structure will be covered, and the extra 5% of production will sold to the grid. A "grid-tied solar PV/Fuel Cell power system" ensures constant access to electricity while also having a much lower life-cost of energy in contrast to an off-grid system. The annualised costs of the "hybrid solar PV/Fuel Cell power system" are broken out in Table 4. Initial investment, O&M, fuel, and replacement costs for "grid-connected solar PV and fuel cell power systems."

Table 3. Grid-connected solar PV and fuel cell power systems: a summary of renewable share, energy cost throughout lifetime, and carbon dioxide emissions

System	Cost of energy ($/MWh)	CO2 emissions (kg/MWh)	Renewable fraction (%)
Baseline - grid only	120	632	0
GTPV120	93	326	8.8
GTPV250	86	256	19.9
GTPV500	71	133	40.4

Figure 3. Comparison Graph of the renewable fraction for the "Grid-connected solar PV and fuel cell power systems"

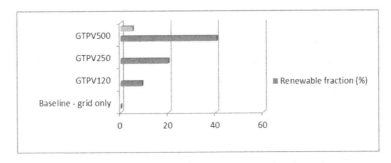

Figure 4. Comparison Graph of the cost of energy for the "Grid-connected solar PV and fuel cell power systems" throughout the lifetime

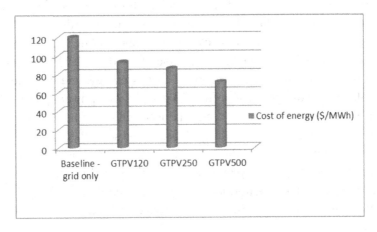

Figure 5. Graph of the CEmission comparison for the "Grid-connected solar PV and fuel cell power systems

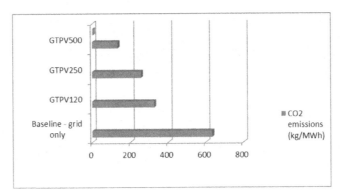

Table 4. Grid-connected solar photovoltaic and fuel cell power systems: a summary of their annualised costs

System)	"O&M ($)"	"Fuel ($)"	"Replacement" ($)	"Capital ($)"	"Total ($)"
Baseline - grid only	286,452	0	0	0	
GTPV120	171,029	38,509	5,861	14,868	229,804
GTPV250	140,335	38,401	5,855	27,256	211,37
GTPV500	88,017	36,221	5,633	51,020	180,250

7 SUMMARY AND CONCLUSIONS

In this article, a "grid-tied solar PV/fuel cell hybrid power system" for a The University's Administration Building, a commercial structure, is displayed., along with its design and analysis. The energy audit data was used to establish the key loads for the building's air conditioning system. This research examined Sharjah's renewable resources, current technology for renewable energy, technology pricing, system expense, and resource constraints. "Using a unified suite of modelling, simulation, optimization, and control approaches, the proposed grid-connected hybrid solar PV/fuel cell power system's efficiency and cost were assessed. Researchers looked and examined how the solar PV power capacity of a system relates to its performance (renewable percentage, cost of energy, and greenhouse gas emissions). According to the results, the grid-connected solar PV/Fuel Cell grid power system generates more than enough energy to meet the building's annual electricity needs and even has enough left over to be sold. The levelized cost of electricity generated by the grid-connected solar PV/fuel cell hybrid power system is just $71 per megawatt hour (MWh), while carbon dioxide (CO_2) emissions are only 133 kg/MWh (MWh). Integration of renewable power systems with the utility grid is one of the best techniques and effective approaches to increase the penetration of renewable energy in the energy mix at an acceptable cost of energy, reduce reliance on fossil fuels, and mitigate environmental impacts (greenhouse gas emissions reductions").

REFERENCES

Adefarati, T., & Bansal, R. (2019). Application of renewable energy resources in a microgrid power system. *Journal of Engineering*, 5308–5313.

Akarsu, B., & Genç, M. S. (2022). Optimization of electricity and hydrogen production with hybrid renewable energy systems. *Fuel*, 324, 324. DOI: 10.1016/j.fuel.2022.124465

Alkhateeb, B. Abu Hijleh, E. Rengasamy and S. Muhammed, Building Refurbishment Strategies and Their Impact on Saving Energy in the United Arab Emirates, *Proceedings of SBE16 Dubai*, 17-19 January 2016, Dubai-UAE

Almeida, K. C., & Cicconet, F. (2019). Decentralized Hydrothermal Dispatch via Bilevel Optimization. Journal of Control, Automation and Electrical Systems. *Brazilian Society for Automatics–SBA*, 30, 557–567.

Alshammari, N., & Asumadu, J. 2020. Optimum unit sizing of hybrid renewable energy system utilizing harmony search, Jaya and particle swarm optimization algorithms, Sustainable Cities and Society, Elsevier, 60.

Ammari, C., Belatrache, D., Touhami, B., & Makhloufi, S. (2022). Sizing, optimization, control and energy management of hybrid renewable energy system—A review. *Energy and Built Environment, Elsevier*, 3(4), 399–411. DOI: 10.1016/j.enbenv.2021.04.002

Aziz, A. S., Tajuddin, F. N., Hussain, M., Adzman, M., Ghazali, N., Ramli, M., & Zidane, T. 2022. A new optimization strategy for wind/diesel/battery hybrid energy system, Energy, Elsevier, 239

Chen, X., Zhu, Y., Li, G., & Li, S. (2017). Energy management strategy for grid-connected solar photovoltaic-fuel cell hybrid power system. *Journal of Power Sources*, 363, 420–430.

Gan, K., Shek, J. K. H., & Mueller, M. A. (2015). Hybrid wind–photovoltaic–diesel–battery system sizing tool development using empirical approach, life-cycle cost and performance analysis: A case study in Scotland. *Energy Conversion and Management*, 106, 479–494. DOI: 10.1016/j.enconman.2015.09.029

Ghenai, C., & Janajreh, I. (2016). Ghenai, and I. Janajreh, "Design of Solar-Biomass Hybrid Microgrid System in Sharjah". *Energy Procedia*, 103, 357–362. DOI: 10.1016/j.egypro.2016.11.299

Ghenai, C., Salameh, T., & Merabet, A. (2020, April). Technico-economic analysis of off grid solar PV/ Fuel cell energy system for residential community in desert region. *International Journal of Hydrogen Energy*, 45(20), 11460–11470. DOI: 10.1016/j.ijhydene.2018.05.110

(2013). Ghenai, and I. Janajreh, Comparison of Resource Intensities and Operational Parameters of Renewable, Fossil Fuel, and Nuclear Power Systems, Int. *J. of Thermal & Environmental Engineering*, 5(2), 95–104.

Heydari, A., & Askarzadeh, A. (2016). Optimization of a biomass-based photovoltaic power plant for an off-grid application subject to loss of power supply probability concept. *Applied Energy*, 165, 601–611. DOI: 10.1016/j.apenergy.2015.12.095

Hu, W., Shang, Q., Bian, X., & Zhu, R. (2021, December 29). Energy management strategy of hybrid energy storage system based on fuzzy control for ships. *The International Journal of Low Carbon Technologies*, 17, 169–175. DOI: 10.1093/ijlct/ctab094

International Energy Agency (IEA) Reports. https://www.iea.org/reports

International Renewable Energy Agency (IRENA) Reports. https://www.irena.org/reports

IPCC Special Report on Global Warming of 1.5°C: https://www.ipcc.ch/sr15/

Lai, W., Zhang, N., & Yu, J. (2019). Artificial intelligence-based dynamic power dispatch for grid-connected solar PV-fuel cell hybrid power system. *Energies*, 12(24), 4716.

Lambert, P. Gilman, and P. Lilienthal, "Micropower system modeling with HOMER," Chap. 15 in Integration of Alternative Sources of Energy, by F. A. Farret and M. G. Simoes, John Wiley & Sons, 2006.

Lan, S., Wen, S., Hong, Y.-Y., Yu, D. C., & Zhang, L. (2015). Wena,Y-Y. Hong, D. C. Yu, and L. Zhang, "Optimal sizing of hybrid PV/diesel/battery in ship power system". *Applied Energy*, 158, 26–34. DOI: 10.1016/j.apenergy.2015.08.031

Merabet, K., Tawfique Ahmed, K., Ibrahim, H., Beguenane, R., & Ghias, A. M. Y. M. (2017). Ahmed, H. Ibrahim, R. Beguenane, and A. Ghias, "Energy management and control system for laboratory scale microgrid based wind-PV-battery,". *IEEE Transactions on Sustainable Energy*, 8(1), 145–154. DOI: 10.1109/TSTE.2016.2587828

Pang, X., Yang, H., Shen, W., & Blaabjerg, F. (2019). Techno-economic analysis and optimization of grid-connected solar photovoltaic-fuel cell hybrid systems. *IEEE Transactions on Sustainable Energy*, 10(4), 1827–1837.

Patel, N., Lu, Y., & Verma, R. (2018). Hydrogen production, storage, and management in solar photovoltaic-fuel cell hybrid systems. *International Journal of Hydrogen Energy*, 43(29), 13209–13225.

Qu, B., Qiao, B., Zhu, Y., Liang, J., & Wang, L. (2017, December 1). Dynamic Power Dispatch Considering Electric Vehicles and Wind Power Using Decomposition Based Multi-Objective Evolutionary Algorithm. *Energies*, 10(12), 1991. DOI: 10.3390/en10121991

Sen, R., & Bhattacharyya, S. C. (2014). Off-grid electricity generation with renewable energy technologies in India: An application of HOMER. *Renewable Energy*, 62, 388–398. DOI: 10.1016/j.renene.2013.07.028

United Nations Sustainable Development Goals (SDGs) - Goal 7: Affordable and Clean Energy: https://sdgs.un.org/goals/goal7

Wang, Y., Li, W., Liu, Z., & Li, L. (2023, February 24). An Energy Management Strategy for Hybrid Energy Storage System Based on Reinforcement Learning. *World Electric Vehicle Journal*, 14(3), 57. DOI: 10.3390/wevj14030057

World Energy Outlook 2020 by the IEA: https://www.iea.org/reports/world-energy-outlook-2020

Yilmaz, H. R., Ozcalik, H. R., Aksu, M., & Karapınar, C. (2015). Ozcalikb, M. Aksua, and C. Karapınara, "Dynamic simulation of a PV-diesel-battery hybrid plant for off grid electricity supply,". *Energy Procedia*, 75, 381–387. DOI: 10.1016/j.egypro.2015.07.396

Zhang, T., Yang, H., Li, Z., & Meng, Y. (2018). Life cycle assessment of grid-connected solar photovoltaic-fuel cell hybrid systems. *Energy*, 150, 393–403.

Zhang, W., Deng, Y., & Qu, J. (2020). Techno-economic optimization of solar photovoltaic-fuel cell hybrid power systems for carbon reduction and energy efficiency improvement. *Energy Conversion and Management*, 213, 112831. DOI: 10.1016/j.enconman.2020.112831

Chapter 9
Green Financing Effect on Sustenance Finance Models With Mediation of Corporate Social Responsibility in Ethiopia

Metasebia Adula
https://orcid.org/0000-0001-5732-2850
Bule Hora University, Ethiopia

Shashi Kant
https://orcid.org/0000-0003-4722-5736
Bule Hora University, Ethiopia

Mando Genale
Bule Hora University, Ethiopia

ABSTRACT

This chapter examines the Green financing effect on Sustenance finance models with mediation of corporate social responsibility in Ethiopia. CSR principles guide financial institutions in prioritizing investments aligned with sustainable development goals, engaging stakeholders in decision-making processes, and integrating environmental and social factors into risk assessment. Sustainable business practices are adopted, enhancing reputation and attracting stakeholders valuing social responsibility. Regulatory compliance is ensured, aligning finance models with legal requirements and societal expectations. Future directions involve strengthening transparency, fostering collaboration and innovation, building capacity and awareness, incentivizing sustainability, developing impact measurement methodologies, and aligning with the SDGs. Ethiopian finance models may satisfy social requirements, promote sustainable development, and build trust by incorporating CSR practices.

DOI: 10.4018/979-8-3693-3884-1.ch009

INTRODUCTION

Green finance, in conjunction with corporate social responsibility (CSR) as a mediator, is essential to the global advancement of sustainable financial models. It is impossible to overestimate the significance of this issue on a worldwide scale, given the growing urgency of sustainable development in the face of critical environmental issues. Ethiopia is especially interested in learning more about how CSR and green finance can support sustainable financial practices because it is a developing country (Tsegay, 2023). Growing awareness of the damaging effects typical financial practices have on the environment gave rise to the idea of "green financing." As pollution, resource depletion, and climate change were more widely recognized, there was a need for finance systems that could provide funding for green projects and endeavors. Green financing surfaced as a remedy, seeking to lower carbon release (Derbe et al., 2023).

Even while green finance and corporate social responsibility (CSR) are gaining popularity, research on their efficacy in sustaining finance models is still lacking, especially when it comes to Ethiopia. While some research indicates that CSR, sustainable finance, and green funding are positively correlated, other studies offer conflicting or equivocal results. These inconsistencies and knowledge gaps draw attention to the necessity of more investigation and learning (Paul & Weinthal, 2019). Incorporating CSR and green finance into models of sustenance finance has important practical ramifications. Organization may reduce risks and promote sustainable growth by incorporating social and environmental factors into financial decision-making processes. Adopting CSR and green finance in Ethiopia might lead to better social welfare, environmental results, and expanded access to foreign financial sources for project sustainability (Fu & Irfan, 2022).

Through the use of CSR as a mediator, this chapter undertakes a thorough investigation of the effects of green financing on sustenance finance models in Ethiopia in order to resolve the previously noted contradicting data and knowledge gaps. Through the analysis of extant literature, empirical data, and case studies, this study aims to offer a more comprehensive comprehension of the interplay of green financing, corporate social responsibility, and sustainable finance within the Ethiopian framework. This chapter used a qualitative approach to close these gaps by fusing qualitative views from important players in the Ethiopian financial system with quantitative analysis of financial data. It is possible to obtain a more thorough and nuanced grasp of the subject by triangulating data from several sources.

The results of this study will add to the amount of information already available on sustainable finance, corporate social responsibility, and green finance, particularly as it relates to Ethiopia. The knowledge acquired from this research will benefit businesses, financial institutions, and policymakers in Ethiopia in addition to offering insightful advice to future scholars who wish to investigate related subjects in other developing countries. This chapter also identified areas that need additional research and provide recommendations and guidance for future researchers. Through pointing out gaps in the literature and offering directions for future investigation, this study hopes to spark more academic discussion and support the continuous advancement of sustainable finance models around the world.

Especially in poor nations like Ethiopia, the significance of CSR and green funding in sustaining finance models cannot be emphasised. In addition to offering insightful information for future study and useful application, this chapter seeks to clarify the relationship among green financing, corporate social responsibility, and sustainable finance in Ethiopia by analyzing the conflicting data and knowledge gaps around the subject.

THEORETICAL LITERATURE REVIEW

Financial goods, services, and investments created especially to assist ecologically friendly projects and efforts are referred to as "green financing." It entails allocating funds to initiatives that benefit the environment, like waste management, sustainable agriculture, clean technology development, energy-efficient infrastructure, and renewable energy projects. The objectives of green funding are to combat climate change, encourage resource efficiency, and aid in the shift to a sustainable and low-carbon economy (Prabhu & Aithal, 2023).

Models of sustainability finance are financial structures and methods that put the long-term health and sustainability of people, communities, and the environment first. These models include social, environmental, and governance aspects in financial decision-making in addition to just economic ones. The goals of sustainability finance models are to guarantee the fair allocation of opportunities and resources, encourage social and environmental justice, lessen inequality, and promote inclusive economic growth. Incorporating sustainable practices, impact investment, responsible lending, engaging stakeholders, and coordinating financial operations with sustainable development objectives are frequently included (Nirino et al., 2022).

A company's dedication and initiatives to conduct business in an ethical and responsible manner, considering the interests of many stakeholders, such as customers, employees, communities, and the environment, are referred to as corporate social responsibility, or CSR. CSR entails choosing to go above and beyond the law and incorporating environmental and social concerns into corporate operations (Apreku-Djana et al., 2023). This can involve taking steps like implementing sustainable corporate practices, funding community development initiatives, encouraging diversity and well-being among employees, reducing the impact on the environment, and openly disclosing social and environmental performance. Ensuring long-term sustainability and financial viability while making meaningful contributions to society and the environment is the aim of corporate social responsibility (CSR) (Husnah & Fahlevi, 2023).

EMPIRICAL LITERATURE REVIEW

Green Financing and Sustenance Finance Models

The allocation and utilization of financial resources to support sustainable development are shaped by green financing, which has a notable influence on sustenance finance models. Green funding directs funds towards initiatives and projects that protect the environment. It pushes investors and financial institutions to give sustainable industries including clean technology, sustainable infrastructure, renewable energy, and energy efficiency top priority. Through the process of rerouting financial flows, green financing aids in the advancement and growth of sustenance finance models (Tosun et al, 2022). Green finance is the process of integrating social and environmental factors into financial decision-making. It makes it possible for companies and organization to evaluate and control environmental hazards related to their ventures or activities. Sustainability criteria are incorporated into green financing, which improves the resilience of sustenance finance models by reducing risks associated with resource depletion, climate change, and environmental restrictions (Chaudhary, 2020).

Green finance encourages the development of sustainable practices and technology, which in turn spurs innovation. It opens up markets for companies who provide eco-friendly goods and services, green infrastructure, and renewable energy. By encouraging the development of new sectors, the production of jobs, and economic growth while solving environmental concerns, this promotes the expansion of sustenance finance models (Doni & Fiameni, 2024). Access to funds for models of sustenance finance is improved by green financing. Financing initiatives that support social and environmental objectives are given priority by a large number of development banks, impact investors, and international financial organization. Organization can access a wider range of funding sources, such as green bonds, impact investments, and sustainable development funds, by embracing green financing concepts and integrating sustainability into their business models (Ibe-enwo et al., 2019). Businesses and financial institutions' reputations can benefit from green funding. Organization shows their dedication to sustainability and ethical business practices by incorporating social and environmental factors into their financial plans. This can increase brand recognition, draw in socially conscious investors, and foster stakeholder trust—all of which improve the overall sustainability of finance models (Rauf et al., 2024).

Policy initiatives and regulatory frameworks that encourage sustainable finance models frequently boost green financing. To promote green investments and establish a supportive climate for sustainable finance, governments may offer rewards, subsidies, or tax breaks. Support from policies like these strengthens the effect of green financing on models of sustenance finance by bringing financial systems into line with sustainability goals and promoting systemic transformation (Adula et al., 2023). Green financing has a complex impact on sustenance finance models that includes risk mitigation, capital redirection, innovation, funding availability, reputation enhancement, stakeholder engagement, and policy assistance. Green financing facilitates the shift towards sustainable development by incorporating environmental and social factors into financial decision-making. This approach aligns financial flows with environmental concerns and ensures the sustainability of sustained finance models over the long term (Ibrahim et al., 2023).

Green Financing and Corporate Social Responsibility

Organization's corporate social responsibility (CSR) policies are significantly impacted by green financing. Organizations must integrate environmental factors into their operations and investment decisions in order to qualify for green funding. An essential component of corporate social responsibility is its integration with sustainability and environmental goals. Organizations are encouraged to adopt eco-friendly procedures, lower their carbon footprint, lessen environmental hazards, and advance sustainable resource management by using green financing concepts (Zaid & Sleimi, 2023). Green finance makes stakeholders more involved in CSR projects. Communities, workers, consumers, investors, and employees all place a higher value on businesses that show a dedication to environmental sustainability. Businesses can connect environmentally conscious consumers, draw in socially conscious investors, and strengthen their ties to the community by implementing green financing strategies. This involvement advances shared value and fosters trust, which enhances the CSR mission (Berwal et al., 2022).

Green financing helps with risk management, which is a crucial aspect of corporate social responsibility. Environmental hazards, such the effects of climate change or modifications to sustainability-related regulations can have a big influence on businesses. Organization can recognise and manage environmental risks and maintain long-term viability and resilience by implementing green finance principles. The fundamental ideas of CSR are in line with this proactive approach to risk management (Panigrahi et al., 2022).

Organizations are encouraged to invest in cutting-edge and environmentally friendly technologies by green finance. Businesses can foster innovation and create environmentally friendly solutions by investing financial resources in green projects. This encourages scientific progress in fields like clean technologies, renewable energy, and resource-efficient procedures. By encouraging sustainable growth and tackling urgent environmental issues, these inventions support CSR goals (Yang et al., 2022). Green finance has an impact on transparency and CSR reporting procedures. Businesses that use green finance are frequently obliged to publish details about their sustainability, carbon emissions, and environmental performance. Stakeholders can evaluate an organization's CSR initiatives and hold them responsible for their environmental impact thanks to this improved openness. Thus, green finance encourages open reporting procedures, improving CSR responsibility and disclosure (Sinha et al., 2023).

An organization's reputation and brand image can be improved by using green funding. Businesses show that they genuinely adhere to CSR ideals when they incorporate sustainability into their financial strategies. Customers, investors, and other stakeholders find this dedication to be meaningful, which enhances their opinion of the company. In addition to increasing brand value, a solid CSR reputation draws in like-minded stakeholders who are more likely to support an organization's sustainability objectives (Khan et al., 2021). Corporate social responsibility is revolutionised by green financing. It motivates businesses to implement eco-friendly procedures, including stakeholders, control environmental hazards, encourage creativity, advance openness, and improve their reputation. Organization can support sustainable development and ethical business practices by tying financial decisions to environmental objectives through the integration of green financing principles into their CSR strategy (Riandy et al., 2023).

Corporate Social Responsibility and Sustenance Finance Models

Models of sustainability financing are significantly impacted by corporate social responsibility (CSR) activities. Financial institutions are encouraged by CSR to use moral lending and investing practices. This entails taking into account how investments will affect society and the environment and making sure that money is given to initiatives that support sustainable development objectives. Financial institutions support the creation of sustenance finance models that give priority to long-term social and environmental benefits by incorporating CSR into their lending and investing criteria (Boson et al., 2023).

Stakeholder participation in sustainability financing schemes is encouraged by CSR. Companies that follow CSR guidelines actively include stakeholders in decision-making processes, such as staff members, clients, communities, and non-governmental organizations. Sustenance financing models have the potential to better match with society requirements and promote inclusive and sustainable development by integrating multiple viewpoints and resolving stakeholder concerns (Dereso et al., 2023). Organizations embrace sustainable business practices as a result of CSR. This entails integrating social and environmental factors into their supply chains, operations, and product and service offerings. Organization can contribute to the overall sustainability of the finance models they operate within by putting sustainable practices into effect. This could be encouraging ethical labor practices, cutting down on waste production, conserving resources, or helping out local communities. Models of sustaining finance depend on these kinds of sustainable economic operations (Panigrahi et al., 2023).

In order to control risk and make sure that models of sustenance financing remain viable over the long run, CSR is essential. Organization can detect possible concerns that may have an influence on their financial performance by taking social and environmental risks into consideration. Organization can strengthen their resilience and contribute to the stability of the financing models they operate within by proactively addressing these risks through CSR initiatives (Ahmed et al., 2024). CSR initiatives can improve a company's standing and financial accessibility. When making investment decisions, lenders and investors are taking environmental, social, and governance (ESG) considerations into account more and more. Businesses that exhibit a strong commitment to corporate social responsibility (CSR) and sustainable practices stand a better chance of drawing in socially conscious investors and obtaining sustainable financing choices. A good reputation for corporate social responsibility can also help with better credit scores, cheaper borrowing rates, and easier access to funding for forms of sustenance financing (Chenguel & Mansour, 2024).

CSR strategies support regulatory compliance and policy advocacy within sustenance finance structures. A company that prioritizes corporate social responsibility (CSR) is more likely to follow social and environmental regulations, which improves the integrity of the financial system overall. Sustenance finance models are transformed by CSR practices. They support sustainable corporate practices, increase stakeholder participation, drive ethical financing and investing, improve risk management, boost reputation, and aid in regulatory compliance. Organization can assist in the development of sustaining finance models that prioritise social and environmental sustainability and link financial decisions to the long-term well-being of society by incorporating CSR concepts into their operations (Deb et al., 2024).

Green Financing, Sustenance Finance Models and Corporate Social Responsibility

Green funding and corporate social responsibility (CSR) are interdependent and reinforce one other. The influence on sustainability finance models is amplified when green financing is pursued through CSR's mediation. Financial decisions are in line with sustainability goals thanks to green finance, which is motivated by CSR principles. For companies looking to include social and environmental factors into their financial plans, corporate social responsibility (CSR) offers the moral groundwork and guiding principles. The emphasis on sustaining finance models, which give long-term social and environmental benefits equal weight with financial rewards, is furthered by this connection (Addy et al., 2024).

The pursuit of green financing through CSR's mediation increases stakeholder participation in models of sustenance financing. CSR initiatives enable stakeholders—such as staff members, clients, local communities, and non-governmental organizations—to actively participate in green finance decision-making processes. By involving a variety of stakeholders, this involvement guarantees that the finance models take their needs and goals into account, producing more inclusive and long-lasting results (Yimer, 2024). Within sustenance finance models, the integration of CSR and green funding enhances risk management procedures. CSR pushes businesses to take social and environmental risks into account, which are important aspects of funding sustainability. Organization can detect and reduce risks related to sustainability issues, such as reputational hazards, legislative changes, and the effects of climate change, by incorporating corporate social responsibility (CSR) into risk management frameworks. This all-encompassing approach to risk management strengthens the stability and durability of models used in sustenance financing (Lambert & Deyganto, 2024).

In sustainability finance models, green fund increases the influence on sustainable development through CSR's mediation. Green finance is guaranteed to go beyond simple compliance or financial success thanks to CSR efforts. It highlights how financing actions has a good social, environmental, and economic impact. Organization can promote creative thinking, advance sustainable technology, and advance more general societal objectives like community development, gender equality, and poverty alleviation by incorporating CSR concepts (Belachew, 2024).

Within sustenance finance models, an organization's reputation and financial availability are improved when green financing and CSR are combined. Socially conscious lenders, partners, and investors are more likely to be drawn to companies that exhibit a strong commitment to sustainability and corporate social responsibility (CSR). The association among green finance and corporate social responsibility (CSR) and the established reputation of ethical business practices bolster credibility, foster confidence, and facilitate the acquisition of money for models of sustenance finance (Zaid & Sleimi, 2023).

Through CSR and green finance, organization can promote legislative and regulatory changes that bolster models of sustenance finance. Through proactive outreach to legislators, trade associations, and civil society, organization may shape the rules, guidelines, and incentives that support sustainable financing. This advocacy promotes systemic change and improves the conditions that support models of sustenance finance (Khan et al., 2021). The influence on sustenance finance models is greatly increased when CSR acts as a mediator in green financing. It unites goals and values, increases involvement from stakeholders, fortifies risk management, magnifies the results of sustainable development, enhances reputation, and makes it easier to advocate for legislative changes. A potent synergy among CSR and green finance propels the change of finance models to one that prioritizes sustainability and long-term social well-being.

OBJECTIVES

1. **To Investigate How Green Financing Affects Sustenance Finance Models:** This goal looks at how adopting green financing methods affects the composition, functionality, and results of sustenance finance models. It entails dissecting the precise processes by which green finance advances social welfare, environmental preservation, and sustainable development inside financial models.

2. **To Investigate the Connection Among Corporate Social Responsibility (CSR) and Green Financing:** Understanding the relationship among green funding and CSR activities is the goal of this project. It entails looking into how CSR values are upheld and aligned with green financing projects, as well as how CSR encourages the incorporation of social and environmental factors into financial decision-making. The goal also investigates how green finance might improve CSR results in the food industry.

3. **To Evaluate How Corporate Social Responsibility Affects Models of Sustenance Financing:** This goal is to investigate how CSR practices affect the composition, functionality, and results of models of sustaining financing. It entails examining the ways in which CSR values influence regulatory compliance, ethical lending and investing, stakeholder involvement, risk management, sustainable business practices, and reputation management in the context of financial models.

4. **To Examine How Corporate Social Responsibility Mediates the Effect of Green Financing on Models of Sustenance Financing:** The purpose of this objective is to comprehend how CSR and green financing work together in sustaining finance approaches. It entails analyzing how, within

finance models; CSR's mediation improves the effects of green funding on policy advocacy, risk management, stakeholder involvement, sustainable development, and reputation.

5. **To Determine the Best Methods and Suggestions for Incorporating Corporate Social Responsibility and Green Finance Into Models of Sustenance Finance:** This goal is to summarize the most important discoveries and provide useful suggestions for institutions and decision-makers. It entails showcasing effective methods for incorporating CSR and green finance into sustainable finance models, as well as offering suggestions on how to optimize the benefits and get around any obstacles that may arise.

The broader objective of this chapter is to give readers a thorough grasp of the connections among CSR, sustainability finance models, and green funding. In addition to offering insights and suggestions for organization and legislators looking to promote sustainable and socially responsible finance practices, it aims to draw attention to the transformative potential of green financing when combined with CSR principles.

DISCUSSION

To accomplish the objective 1, adopting green finance techniques can significantly alter the composition, functionality, and results of sustenance finance models in Ethiopia. Within Ethiopian financial models, the particular ways that green funding promotes social welfare, environmental preservation, and sustainable development are In Ethiopia, lending and investment decisions are made with consideration for the environment and society. This means that while distributing funding, financial institutions take into account the projects' social advantages, environmental effect, and resource efficiency. These factors are included into sustenance finance models, which give priority to initiatives that support sustainable development, including waste management, renewable energy, energy efficiency, and sustainable agriculture.

The integration of sustainable technologies and practices into financial models is facilitated by green financing. This can involve funding renewable energy initiatives, endorsing environmentally friendly farming methods, and encouraging sustainable land management in Ethiopia. Finance models support climate resilience, resource conservation, and greenhouse gas emission reduction by funding and investing in sustainable technology. Green financing techniques help finance models become more resilient and reduce risk. Finance models can detect possible vulnerabilities and incorporate methods to resolve them by taking into account environmental hazards, such as the implications of climate change, water scarcity, or deforestation. In order to lessen the financial and environmental risks that communities and businesses face, green funding, for instance, can assist initiatives that strengthen water management systems, encourage sustainable land use practices, or improve climate adaptation methods.

Green job prospects within finance models can result from Ethiopia's adoption of green financing strategies. Investments in ecotourism, sustainable agriculture, and renewable energy, for example, can create new jobs that support socioeconomic growth and the fight against poverty. Finance models help to inclusive growth and social well-being by funding initiatives that advance green jobs and skill development. Transparency and reporting on social and environmental performance within finance models are encouraged by green financing practices. Information about financial institutions' social effect, carbon emissions, and sustainability policies is urged to be shared. Transparency improves accountability, enables stakeholders to evaluate how financing models support sustainable development, and encourages ongoing progress in social and environmental consequences.

Within financial models, green financing methods promote cooperation and the formation of partnerships. Financial institutions can discover opportunities for sustainable investment, create cutting-edge financial solutions, and increase capacity for carrying out green projects by collaborating closely with government agencies, non-governmental organization, and communities. Through this partnership, the influence and efficacy of financing models in accomplishing sustainable development objectives are increased.

To achieve objective 2 in the Ethiopian context, in order to promote sustainable growth and include social and environmental factors into financial decision-making, it is imperative that green financing and corporate social responsibility (CSR) practices work together. Green finance programmes complement and uphold Ethiopia's CSR values. The promotion of social well-being, environmental preservation, and sustainable development is the shared objective of both green funding and CSR. While CSR principles direct organization to operate in a socially and ecologically responsible manner, green funding initiatives are intended to assist projects that have good impacts on the environment and society. The coherence of aims guarantees that corporate social responsibility (CSR) and green finance complement each other and contribute to shared sustainability objectives.

Green funding efforts incorporate social and environmental factors into financial decision-making through the use of CSR techniques. Ethiopian financial institutions and organization make sure that the social and environmental effects of their operations are evaluated and handled by implementing CSR principles. This integration entails evaluating the social and environmental impacts, taking stakeholder viewpoints into account, and integrating sustainability standards into financing and investing choices. The framework for proactive management of environmental and social risks and possibilities in green finance activities is supplied by corporate social responsibility (CSR) practices to financial institutions.

Stakeholder participation is made easier by CSR practices, and it is essential to Ethiopia's green funding efforts' success. Various parties, including governmental organizations, local governments, investors, and civil society organization, must actively participate in and collaborate with one another in order to provide green funding. Through the promotion of communication, accountability, and transparency, CSR practices help financial institutions interact with stakeholders in a productive way. CSR procedures guarantee that the needs and ambitions of impacted communities and other stakeholders are taken into consideration, resulting in more inclusive and sustainable outcomes, by involving stakeholders in the design, execution, and monitoring of green finance initiatives.

CSR procedures provide a strong emphasis on moral and responsible investing in green finance projects. Ethiopian financial institutions are urged to provide funding to initiatives that adhere to strict environmental, social, and governance (ESG) guidelines. By placing a strong focus on ESG factors, green finance projects are guaranteed to go beyond simple compliance and take ethical factors into account when making investment decisions. In line with CSR values, it encourages ethical and sustainable investment methods. Green finance can improve corporate social responsibility (CSR) results in Ethiopian sustenance finance models by encouraging favourable social and environmental effects. Green finance helps to reduce poverty, create jobs, build climate resilience, and preserve ecosystems by funding projects that address environmental issues like renewable energy, sustainable agriculture, water management, and waste management.

The interaction among corporate social responsibility (CSR) and green finance in Ethiopia improves financial institutions' standing and stakeholder trust. Finance companies show their dedication to sustainability and ethical business practices by incorporating CSR concepts into green finance programmes. Their standing with stakeholders, including consumers, investors, and communities, is improved by this dedication. The long-term viability and success of finance models in Ethiopia are facilitated by the credibility and trust that are acquired via the combination of green financing and CSR practices.

To achieve objective 3 in the Ethiopian context, CSR activities have a big impact on how sustenance finance models' function and what happens in the end. In Ethiopian financial models, ethical lending and investment practices are guided by CSR principles. CSR-aware financial institutions take the social and environmental effects of their lending and investing decisions into account. They provide top priority to initiatives and companies that support social welfare, uphold ethical corporate standards, and are in line with sustainable development goals. By ensuring that financial models back investments that have favourable social, environmental, and economic effects, this moral strategy helps Ethiopia achieve sustainable development.

Stakeholder participation is emphasized by CSR practices in financial models. Ethiopian financial institutions actively incorporate all relevant parties in their decision-making processes, including as clients, staff members, local communities, and civil society organization. Finance models can gain a deeper understanding of stakeholders' requirements, issues, and goals by interacting with them. Through this involvement, trust, accountability, and transparency are fostered, which results in more inclusive and sustainable financial services that cater to the unique needs of various stakeholders.

Effective risk management in financial models is driven by CSR principles. When evaluating risks, financial institutions in Ethiopia that practice corporate social responsibility (CSR) consider environmental, social, and governance (ESG) considerations. They take into account how investments could affect society, the environment, and governance procedures. Finance models can detect and reduce possible hazards related to environmental and social issues by incorporating ESG concerns into risk management procedures. Proactive risk management improves the resilience and long-term sustainability of financial models. Within finance models, CSR initiatives encourage sustainable company practices. Ethiopian financial institutions are urged to integrate socially and ecologically conscious practices into their daily operations. This can entail putting energy-saving measures into action, cutting emissions and waste, encouraging diversity and inclusion, and making sure that fair labor practices are followed. Finance models show their commitment to ethical and responsible operations, function as role models for others, and support the green economy by adopting sustainable company practices.

In finance models, reputation management is greatly aided by CSR measures. Ethiopian financial firms that place a high priority on corporate social responsibility (CSR) gain credibility by showcasing their dedication to environmental and social principles. Customers, investors, and other stakeholders who respect environmentally and socially conscious financial services are drawn to this reputation. A solid reputation helps finance models become more credible and competitive, which draws in additional funding and growth prospects over time. CSR procedures guarantee that financial models comply with regulations. Ethiopian financial institutions must abide by laws, rules, and guidelines pertaining to social welfare, environmental preservation, and moral business practices. Finance models are driven by CSR principles to actively monitor and comply with these legal requirements. Regulation observance guarantees that finance models function in a way that is consistent with social and governmental standards, while also reducing legal and reputational concerns.

In the Ethiopian context, CSR practices have a major impact on the composition, functionality, and results of sustaining financing models. Stakeholder involvement, risk management, sustainable business practices, reputation management, ethical lending and investing, and regulatory compliance are all influenced by CSR principles. Institutions can meet societal needs, promote sustainable development, and increase credibility and confidence among stakeholders by incorporating CSR principles into their finance models.

To achieve objective 4 In the Ethiopian contexts, CSR activities have a big impact on how sustenance finance models work and how they turn out. In Ethiopian financial models, ethical lending and investment practices are guided by CSR principles. CSR-aware financial institutions take the social and environmental effects of their lending and investing decisions into account. They provide top priority to initiatives and companies that support social welfare, uphold ethical corporate standards, and are in line with sustainable development goals. By ensuring that financial models back investments that have favourable social, environmental, and economic effects, this moral strategy helps Ethiopia achieve sustainable development.

Stakeholder participation is emphasized by CSR practices in financial models. Ethiopian financial institutions actively incorporate all relevant parties in their decision-making processes, including as clients, staff members, local communities, and civil society organization. Finance models can gain a deeper understanding of stakeholders' requirements, issues, and goals by interacting with them. Through this involvement, trust, accountability, and transparency are fostered, which results in more inclusive and sustainable financial services that cater to the unique needs of various stakeholders (Khan et al., 2021).

Effective risk management in financial models is driven by CSR principles. When evaluating risks, financial institutions in Ethiopia that practice corporate social responsibility (CSR) consider environmental, social, and governance (ESG) considerations.

They take into account how investments could affect society, the environment, and governance procedures. Finance models can detect and reduce possible hazards related to environmental and social issues by incorporating ESG concerns into risk management procedures. Proactive risk management improves the resilience and long-term sustainability of financial models. Within finance models, CSR initiatives encourage sustainable company practices. Ethiopian financial institutions are urged to integrate socially and ecologically conscious practices into their daily operations. This can entail putting energy-saving measures into action, cutting emissions and waste, encouraging diversity and inclusion, and making sure that fair labor practices are followed. Finance models show their commitment to ethical and responsible operations, function as role models for others, and support the green economy by adopting sustainable company practices.

In finance models, reputation management is greatly aided by CSR measures. Ethiopian financial firms that place a high priority on corporate social responsibility (CSR) gain credibility by showcasing their dedication to environmental and social principles. Customers, investors, and other stakeholders who respect environmentally and socially conscious financial services are drawn to this reputation. A solid reputation helps finance models become more credible and competitive, which draws in additional funding and growth prospects over time. CSR procedures guarantee that financial models comply with regulations. Ethiopian financial institutions must abide by laws, rules, and guidelines pertaining to social welfare, environmental preservation, and moral business practices. Finance models are driven by CSR principles to actively monitor and comply with these legal requirements.

Regulation observance guarantees that finance models function in a way that is consistent with social and governmental standards, while also reducing legal and reputational concerns. In conclusion, in the Ethiopian setting, CSR practices have a major impact on the composition, functionality, and results of sustaining financing models. Stakeholder involvement, risk management, sustainable business practices, reputation management, ethical lending and investing, and regulatory compliance are all influenced by CSR principles. Institutions can meet societal needs, promote sustainable development, and increase credibility and confidence among stakeholders by incorporating CSR principles into their finance models.

CONCLUSION

In conclusion, in the Ethiopian setting, CSR practices have a significant impact on the composition, functionality, and results of sustaining financing models. Financial institutions in Ethiopia promote ethical lending and investing, stakeholder involvement, risk management, environmentally friendly operations, reputation management, and regulatory compliance in their finance models by adopting CSR concepts. By prioritizing loans and investments that support sustainable development objectives, CSR principles make sure that financing models have a beneficial social, environmental, and economic impact. Incorporating stakeholder participation into financial models is crucial as it facilitates the inclusion of varied viewpoints, increases transparency, and improves accountability.

Incorporating environmental, social, and governance factors into decision-making procedures leads to effective risk management. This proactive strategy ensures the long-term sustainability and resilience of financial models by assisting in the identification and mitigation of risks related to environmental and social concerns. The integration of sustainable business practices into finance models is facilitated by CSR activities, which in turn results in a decrease in environmental impact, an enhancement of social responsibility, and moral operations. Financial institutions establish strong relationships and draw in stakeholders that appreciate sustainable and socially responsible financial services by showcasing their dedication to social and environmental principles.

Moreover, CSR procedures provide regulatory compliance, guaranteeing that financial models function in accordance with the law and public expectations. Finance models reduce legal and reputational risks by abiding by laws, rules, and standards pertaining to social welfare, environmental protection, and ethical behavior. All things considered, the incorporation of CSR practices into Ethiopian sustenance financing models promotes sustainable development, attends to societal requirements, and increases stakeholder credibility and trust. Finance models help Ethiopia's economy become more inclusive, accountable, and resilient by coordinating financial activity with social and environmental objectives.

Future Directions

Regarding the future, there exist multiple avenues to augment the impact of corporate social responsibility (CSR) activities on sustenance financing models inside the Ethiopian milieu. To give more thorough and open information about their CSR initiatives, including the effects of their loans and investments on social and environmental issues, financial institutions can improve their reporting processes. As a result, stakeholders will be able to hold financial institutions responsible for their CSR pledges and make educated judgements.

In order to solve sustainability concerns as a group, financial institutions, government agencies, civil society organization, and other stakeholders must work together more frequently. Together, these parties can take advantage of their specialized knowledge, available assets, and established connections to advance sustainable finance models and more effective corporate social responsibility initiatives. The integration of CSR practices into finance models can be substantially facilitated and enhanced by the implementation of innovative technologies. Fin-tech solutions can increase financial access while advancing moral and sustainable lending and investing practices. Examples of these solutions include digital platforms for impact investing and sustainable lending.

Investing in programmes that develop capacity and educating stakeholders, experts, and financial institutions on the advantages of integrating CSR practices into finance models are essential. Training courses, seminars, and knowledge-sharing forums that emphasise sustainable finance and ethical investing techniques might help achieve this. Through the provision of incentives and the creation of regulatory frameworks that facilitate CSR practices, governments and regulatory agencies can play a major role in encouraging CSR practices within finance models. This can involve integrating sustainability standards into legal frameworks, requiring ESG reporting, and offering tax incentives for sustainable investments.

It will be essential to provide standardized approaches and measurements to assess the effects of corporate social responsibility (CSR) practices on the economy, the environment, and society. Financial institutions will be able to evaluate and effectively convey their contributions to sustainability thanks to this. A single framework and road map for attaining sustainable development can be provided by coordinating corporate social responsibility (CSR) activities and financing models with the Sustainable Development Goals (SDGs) of the UN. Financial institutions are able to determine which SDGs are pertinent to their operations and apply those findings to their investment choices and corporate social responsibility plans. Financial institutions in Ethiopia can increase the impact of CSR activities on models of sustenance financing by adopting these future directions. This will support equitable growth, sustainable development, and the accomplishment of global and national sustainability goals.

REFERENCES

Addy, W. A., Ofodile, O. C., Adeoye, O. B., Oyewole, A. T., Okoye, C. C., Odeyemi, O., & Ololade, Y. J. (2024). Data-driven sustainability: How fintech innovations are supporting green finance. *Engineering Science & Technology Journal*, 5(3), 760–773. DOI: 10.51594/estj.v5i3.871

Adula, M., Birbirsa, Z. A., & Kant, S. (2023). The effect of interpersonal, problem solving and technical training skills on performance of Ethiopia textile industry: Continuance, normative and affective commitment as mediators. *Cogent Business & Management*, 10(3), 2286672. DOI: 10.1080/23311975.2023.2286672

Ahmed, D., Hua, H. X., & Bhutta, U. S. (2024). Innovation through Green Finance: A thematic review. *Current Opinion in Environmental Sustainability*, 66, 101402. DOI: 10.1016/j.cosust.2023.101402

Apreku-Djana, P. K., Ayittah, S. K., Apreku, I. K. O., Ameyaw, F., & Opare, E. A. (2023). The Mediating Effect of Corporate Social Responsibility and Corporate Accountability in the Relationship between Corporate Governance and Value-Based Financial Performance of Banks. *International Journal of Business*, 28(2), 1–36.

Belachew, A. (2024). Impacts of results-based financing improved cookstove intervention on households' livelihood: Evidence from Ethiopia. *Forest Policy and Economics*, 158, 103096. DOI: 10.1016/j.forpol.2023.103096

Berwal, P., Dhatterwal, J. S., Kaswan, K. S., & Kant, S. (2022). *Computer Applications in Engineering and Management*. Chapman and Hall/CRC. DOI: 10.1201/9781003211938

Boson, L. T., Elemo, Z., Engida, A., & Kant, S. (2023). Assessment of green supply chain management practices on sustainable business in Ethiopia. [LOMR]. *Logistic and Operation Management Research*, 2(1), 96–104. DOI: 10.31098/lomr.v2i1.1468

Chaudhary, R. (2020). Green human resource management and employee green behavior: An empirical analysis. *Corporate Social Responsibility and Environmental Management*, 27(2), 630–641. DOI: 10.1002/csr.1827

Chenguel, M. B., & Mansour, N. (2024). Green finance: Between commitment and illusion. *Competitiveness Review*, 34(1), 179–192. DOI: 10.1108/CR-10-2022-0162

Deb, B. C., Rahman, M. M., & Haseeb, M. (2024). Unveiling the impact on corporate social responsibility through green tax and green financing: A PLS-SEM approach. *Environmental Science and Pollution Research International*, 31(1), 1543–1561. DOI: 10.1007/s11356-023-31150-y PMID: 38041735

Derbe, T., Melak, D., & Derso, B. (2023). Stakeholders' integration to Social responsibility: Its Implication on Youth Self Employment. *Ethiopian Renaissance Journal of Social Sciences and the Humanities*, 10(1), 41–60. DOI: 10.4314/erjssh.v10i1.3

Dereso, C. W., Kant, S., Muthuraman, M., & Tufa, G. (2023, May). Effect of Point of Service on Health Department Student's Creativity in Comprehensive Universities of Ethiopia: Moderating Role of Public-Private Partnership and Mediating Role of Work Place Learning. In *Proceedings of the International Health Informatics Conference: IHIC 2022* (pp. 135-147). Singapore: Springer Nature Singapore. DOI: 10.1007/978-981-19-9090-8_13

Doni, F., & Fiameni, M. (2024). Can innovation affect the relationship between Environmental, Social, and Governance issues and financial performance? Empirical evidence from the STOXX200 index. *Business Strategy and the Environment*, 33(2), 546–574. DOI: 10.1002/bse.3500

Fu, W., & Irfan, M. (2022). Does green financing develop a cleaner environment for environmental sustainability: Empirical insights from association of southeast Asian nations economies. *Frontiers in Psychology*, 13, 904768. DOI: 10.3389/fpsyg.2022.904768 PMID: 35783812

Husnah, H., & Fahlevi, M. (2023). How do corporate social responsibility and sustainable development goals shape financial performance in Indonesia's mining industry? *Uncertain Supply Chain Management*, 11(3), 1383–1394. DOI: 10.5267/j.uscm.2023.5.099

Ibe-enwo, G., Igbudu, N., Garanti, Z., & Popoola, T. (2019). Assessing the relevance of green banking practice on bank loyalty: The mediating effect of green image and bank trust. *Sustainability (Basel)*, 11(17), 4651. DOI: 10.3390/su11174651

Ibrahim, R. L., Al-mulali, U., Ozturk, I., Bello, A. K., & Raimi, L. (2022). On the criticality of renewable energy to sustainable development: Do green financial development, technological innovation, and economic complexity matter for China? *Renewable Energy*, 199, 262–277. DOI: 10.1016/j.renene.2022.08.101

Khan, N. U., Anwar, M., Li, S., & Khattak, M. S. (2021). Intellectual capital, financial resources, and green supply chain management as predictors of financial and environmental performance. *Environmental Science and Pollution Research International*, 28(16), 19755–19767. DOI: 10.1007/s11356-020-12243-4 PMID: 33405102

Lambert, E., & Deyganto, K. O. (2024). The Impact of Green Legacy on Climate Change in Ethiopia. *Green and Low-Carbon Economy*, 2(2), 97–105. DOI: 10.47852/bonviewGLCE32021372

Nirino, N., Ferraris, A., Miglietta, N., & Invernizzi, A. C. (2022). Intellectual capital: The missing link in the corporate social responsibility–financial performance relationship. *Journal of Intellectual Capital*, 23(2), 420–438. DOI: 10.1108/JIC-02-2020-0038

Panigrahi, A., Nayak, A. K., Paul, R., Sahu, B., & Kant, S. (2022). CTB-PKI: Clustering and trust enabled blockchain based PKI system for efficient communication in P2P network. *IEEE Access : Practical Innovations, Open Solutions*, 10, 124277–124290. DOI: 10.1109/ACCESS.2022.3222807

Panigrahi, A., Pati, A., Sahu, B., Das, M. N., Nayak, D. S. K., Sahoo, G., & Kant, S. (2023). En-MinWhale: An ensemble approach based on MRMR and Whale optimization for Cancer diagnosis. *IEEE Access : Practical Innovations, Open Solutions*, 11, 113526–113542. DOI: 10.1109/ACCESS.2023.3318261

Paul, C. J., & Weinthal, E. (2019). The development of Ethiopia's Climate Resilient Green Economy 2011–2014: Implications for rural adaptation. *Climate and Development*, 11(3), 193–202. DOI: 10.1080/17565529.2018.1442802

Prabhu, N., & Aithal, P. S. (2023). Inbound Corporate Social Responsibility Model for Selected Indian Banks and Their Proposed Impact on Attracting and Retaining Customers–A Case Study. [IJAEML]. *International Journal of Applied Engineering and Management Letters*, 7(3), 55–74. DOI: 10.47992/IJAEML.2581.7000.0188

Rauf, F., Wang, W., & Voinea, C. L. (2024). Interaction of Corporate Social Responsibility Reporting at the Crossroads of Green Innovation Performance and Firm Performance: The Moderating Role of the Enterprise Life Stage. *Sustainability (Basel)*, 16(5), 1821. DOI: 10.3390/su16051821

Riandy, C. N., Hapsari, I., Hariyanto, E., & Pratama, B. C. (2023). Intellectual Capital: The Role of Green Accounting on Corporate Social Responsibility. *South Asian Journal of Social Studies and Economics*, 20(4), 140–155. DOI: 10.9734/sajsse/2023/v20i4749

Sinha, A., Ghosh, V., Hussain, N., Nguyen, D. K., & Das, N. (2023). Green financing of renewable energy generation: Capturing the role of exogenous moderation for ensuring sustainable development. *Energy Economics*, 126, 107021. DOI: 10.1016/j.eneco.2023.107021

Tosun, C., Parvez, M. O., Bilim, Y., & Yu, L. (2022). Effects of green transformational leadership on green performance of employees via the mediating role of corporate social responsibility: Reflection from North Cyprus. *International Journal of Hospitality Management*, 103, 103218. DOI: 10.1016/j.ijhm.2022.103218

Tsegay, B. (2023). *Green Economy for Climate Change Mitigation and Poverty Reduction in Sub-Saharan Africa: A Critical Analysis of Carbon Finance in Ethiopia* (Doctoral dissertation, SOAS University of London).

Yang, Y., Shi, S., & Wu, J. (2022). Digital financial inclusion to corporation value: The mediating effect of ambidextrous innovation. *Sustainability (Basel)*, 14(24), 16621. DOI: 10.3390/su142416621

Yimer, G. A.Gebreysus Abegaz Yimer. (2024). Sustainable Finance in Africa: A Comparative Overview. *Mizan Law Review*, 18(1), 123–160. DOI: 10.4314/mlr.v18i1.5

Zaid, A. A., & Sleimi, M. (2023). Effect of total quality management on business sustainability: The mediating role of green supply chain management practices. *Journal of Environmental Planning and Management*, 66(3), 524–548. DOI: 10.1080/09640568.2021.1997730

Chapter 10
Importance and Application of Machine Learning and Pattern Recognition in Business Intelligence Models to Transform the Real World for Decision-Making

Kartikey Raghuvanshi

Delhi Technical Campus, Guru Gobind Singh Indraprastha University, India

Ayasha Malik

IIMT College of Engineering, Greater Noida, India.

Veena Parihar

Symbiosis Institute of Geo-informatics, Symbiosis International, Pune, India

ABSTRACT

In the rapidly evolving landscape of business intelligence, the integration of Machine Learning (ML) and pattern recognition techniques has emerged as a transformative force, revolutionizing decision-making processes across various industries. This paper explores the crucial role played by ML and pattern recognition in enhancing the capabilities of business intelligence models, with a focus on their practical applications and impact on real-world scenarios. The importance of accurate and timely decision-making in today's dynamic business environment cannot be overstated. Traditional business intelligence systems have limitations in handling the complexity and volume of data generated daily. ML algorithms, with their ability to analyze vast datasets and identify intricate patterns, offer a solution to this challenge. Through the application of supervised and unsupervised learning techniques, businesses can extract valuable insights from data, enabling informed and strategic decision-making.

DOI: 10.4018/979-8-3693-3884-1.ch010

1 INTRODUCTION

An excellent place to start this paper can begin with is the fundamental concept of the device getting to know. In gadgets gaining knowledge of a laptop application is assigned to carry out a few responsibilities, and as it like said the system has learned from its revealing by calculating the performance in their tasks and improves as it gains increasing by showing how to execute these duties. So, the system makes decisions and gives projections/predictions based on facts. Let's see the example of a PC program that learns from information and finds cancer patients from the clinical investigation reviews of a patient. It's going to show better performance as it collects wider incidents by reading scientific investigation reports of a list of a large number of patients. Its working ability or performance might be measured through the number of accurate predictions and detections of most cancer instances as demonstrated by way of a skilled Oncologist (Jiang et al., 2019; Xu & Yingjie, 2015). System studies have been carried out in a wide form of fields, namely: robotics, Google Assistant (virtual private assistant), games, pattern reputation, data mining, visitor projection, online taxi companies, etc. Device studying normally sells with updates that can even bring about noisy slopes, which might also cause the error charge to leap around rather than reduce steadily. The application of SGD will also evaluate three kinds of troubles, namely: category, regression, and clustering. Relying on the availability categories of schooling information, it may additionally have to select from the present techniques of "supervised studying," "unsupervised getting to know," "semi-supervised getting to know," and "reinforcement studying," which use the perfect device mastering algorithm. Within the following couple of segments, some of the foremost extensively used machine-gaining information of algorithms will be reviewed.

In this direction, this research study presents a comprehensive evaluation of various ML algorithms that are commonly used and widely accessible. By analyzing these algorithms, the paper aims to identify their advantages and disadvantages, enabling researchers and practitioners to make informed decisions about which algorithms to utilize in different scenarios. It explores the use of Machine Learning (ML) algorithms to enable devices to learn from software and effectively select relevant information. This contributes to the development of intelligent systems capable of extracting valuable insights from vast amounts of data, enhancing decision-making processes, and enabling automation in various applications. It acknowledges the importance of Pattern Recognition (PR) as a cognitive ability possessed by humans and is a significant area of study within computer science and artificial intelligence. By addressing the process of identifying and classifying patterns within data, the research paper contributes to advancing PR techniques and their application in real-world scenarios. Overall, the paper contributes to the field of AI & ML by providing insights into the evaluation of ML approaches, the application of ML in information selection, advancing PR techniques and enhancing the understanding of decision-making processes. These contributions have practical implications in various domains, such as data analysis, automation, and intelligent system design. The remaining part of the paper is planned as follows: Section 2 discusses and examines various ML algorithms, including supervised and unsupervised. Section 3 presents the details of PR and the application of ML in this field. Then section 4 thoroughly discusses the work done in the relevant field, and finally, section 5 presents a conclusion of the whole study.

2 MACHINE LEARNING

ML is done by using AI, which allows software programs to be more accurate at forecasting/predicting results without being programmed to accomplish that. Devices studying algorithms use past facts and entries to expect new results. ML is essential, as it offers organizations customer behaviour on the trends and business better or next patterns, as well as helps in designing of recent merchandise. Lots of modern-day leading agencies, along with Instagram, Google, and Ola, make gadgets gaining knowledge which is a relevant part of their operations.ML has come to be a tremendous aggressive contrast for lots of corporations. Classical device mastering is frequently categorized using how an algorithm learns to become more accurate in its predictions (Zaki, 2000).

2.1 Gradient Descent

It is a looping method whose main objective is to decrease a price feature. It is viable to calculate the partial spinoff of the characteristic, that is, slope or gradient. Now the coefficients are computed at every generation, and it takes the terrible of the by-product, and then by lowering the coefficients at each step via getting-to-know rate (step size) expanded using the derivative because of that the local minima can be executed after some repetition. Ultimately the repetitions are stopped, although it converges to the minimal cost of price characteristic, then there's no similar discount inside the value feature. There are 3 extraordinary categories of this: SGD, BGD, and MBGD (Malik et al., 2023)

- In BGD, blunders are computed for every example in the education dataset; however, the design/model might be up to date simplest after the evaluation of all education examples is finished. The BGD algorithm produces a secure blunders slope and a solid convergence. But the solid error slope can occasionally bring about a kingdom of convergence that isn't always the first-rate that the version can attain. Additionally, the algorithm calls for the whole schooling dataset will be in memory and available to it.
- In SGD, mistakes are evaluated for every schooling instance inside the dataset, and parameters are updated for each schooling instance. Now, this could bring about SGD being quicker than BGD, which gives a unique hassle. SGD has frequent updates on the detailed fee after results for improvement in the detailed fee. But recurrent updates are extra costly in comparison to the BGD approach.

By combining the principles of SGD and BGD, the MBGD approach is obtained. This schooling dataset is divided into little groups, and replacements are achieved for every one of the other groups. Consequently, it built stability in the strength/robustness of SGD and the working/performance of BGD. This algorithm may also be used to educate a neural network, and so this set of rules is generally used for deep mastering. The Gradient Descent optimization approach is used in the Backpropagation, in which the set of rules is computed to modify the weight of neurons by using a gradient of the loss feature. If the learning charge is too rapid for gradient descent, then it skips the actual local minimum to optimize time. It is tough to find the local minimum precisely if it is too slugging, so the gradient descent may also by no mean coverage (Zhang & Wang, 2018; Sarker, 2021)

2.2 Linear Regression Algorithm

Linear regression is simple to learn and can be avoided by adding/fitting by regularization. Regression is an address of supervised learning. It is used for suggestion/prediction and used for making a structure of continuous variables. Examples are the prediction of sales, forecasting of real-estate rates/prices, the stock market up and down, students' exam scores, etc. In linear regression, input variable values are determined by labeled dataset and output variables; that's why it's a supervised learning approach (Aamodt & Plaza, 2019). So the simplest form of regression is linear regression in this algorithm, in which we fit the straight line into the dataset, which can only be done by building the relationship between the dataset of variables in linear regression.

2.3 Multivariate Regression Analysis

As in real life, problems are harder/more complex. Linear regression has a single independent variable depending upon the variable guide. Depending variables are mainly dependent upon multiple reasons/factors. For example, a shop's price depends upon reasons like the area where it is located, the demand for the product which you sell, the neighborhoods, etc. In multiple linear regression, we have multiple linear regression, have a relationship between the input variable(independent) and the output (dependent) variable, and they have a many-to-many relationship. Multiple regression is not superior to simple regression, as adding input variables in regression does not give better suggestions/predictions; in some cases, it becomes worse when we add more input variables in the regression. In some cases, it overfits the result when we add the variables (Morris, 1995; Watson & Gardingen, 1999). Adding more input variables regression creates relationships between them so that not only are input variables connected/related to the output variable, but other variables are also related to each other, and that's called multicollinearity.

2.4 Logistic Regression

It is mainly used for classification problems. Based on the input variable, it shows the output in the form of a binomial (0 for occur, and 1 for not occur). For example, predicting whether the cancer is malignant or not or checking whether the message is spam or not, these can be done by logistic regression using binomial. In some cases, there is a multinomial outcome is also possible in logistic regression, like selecting/preferred food for a person; it can be Indian, Chinese, British, etc. We can also do more things like showing product ratings, etc. In logistic regression, we can suggest any variable without being biased. But you can see that linear regression suggests or predicts the continuous variable (Li, 2018).

2.5 Decision Tree

Decision trees continuously split data on the basis of certain parameters to solve the classification and regression problem, and it works on a supervised ML approach. The data are divided into nodes. Decision variables in the regression tree are continuous, and it is categorical (means outcomes in the form of yes/no) in the classification tree. The decision tree can be used for classification and regression problems, to handle quantitative values, or to handle categorical values, ease evaluation, and can fill or add value in missing attributes with most likely value, and it gives high-level performance because the tree traversal algorithm (Parihar & Yadav, 2022). Random forest is the solution used for decision tree problems for over-fitting, in which the solution is based on an ensemble modeling approach. It is hard to control the size of the decision tree as it is unstable, and it will give the local optimal solution only, not the global optimal solution.

2.6 Support Vector Machine

A support vector machine (SVM) is built to handle both regression problems and classification problems. In this decision the boundary needed to be defined because of the hyperplane method. The decision plane separated the objects belonging to other classes. Kernels that cause complex mathematical functions may or may not be linearly separable, and it is necessary to separate objects of different classes (Malik et al., 2023). SVM aims to classify the objects correctly based on the training data set. It can manage the complex function if a suitable kernels function is given, and it can also handle structural and semi-structural data. Because generalization has taken on, there will be less probability of over-fitting. It can be advanced by using high-dimensional data, and it will not be stuck in local optima. If training time increases, then the performance will decrease because of the big data set, and it does not perform well when the data set is clattering, and then it cannot give probability approximations (Zhang, 2018).

2.7 Bayesian Learning

Bayesian learning obtains a posterior distribution after selecting the previous distribution probability, and then the posterior distribution becomes the previous distribution when new data or observations come. It is hard to select previous probabilities, and the posterior probability does not get distracted by previous probabilities to a great extent (Wei et al., 2019). Bayesian learning handles the insufficient dataset, and this also helps to stop over-fitting data, and you don't have to detach the contradiction from the data. If the previous probability is not selected properly, then it will give a wrong prediction. It can be used for weather prediction and medical purposes like diagnosis, identification purposes, etc.

2.8 Naïve Bayes

The naïve Bayes algorithm is built on conditional probability. In this, we make a probability table, and the table is updated by training the data. In this, for new observation, one needs to look up the class probabilities, and the table is formed on its features. This theorem works on fewer training data. This theorem is called naïve because its conditional independence is its fundamental assumption. All input features can barely hold the truth as it is independent of each other, and it gives better performance. Naïve Bayes can handle binary and multi-class sorting problems and gives likelihood suggestions. This algorithm can handle continuous and discrete data. In this, the trained and adjusted model mainly performs the NB model as it is very simple (Aggarwal et al., 2004). If we need to add more features to this model/ method, then it becomes difficult to apply this model. It is not correct to make continuous variables and bucket variables. In this method, all data is held on to retrain the model.

2.9 K-Nearest Neighbor

This algorithm is used to group many classes as it uses the database, which has data points. This is a simple method that can be easily executed, and making this using or making this method/model is less costly. This algorithm classifies the problem into the given sample data point. KNN algorithm is also called non-parametric as it does not conclude any fundamental data distribution. KNN is the best match for multi-model classes, and it is extremely pliable. KNN has twice more error rate as Bayes. For the protein prediction expression profile, KNN transcends the SVM, and from time to time, KNN is the best method, and it is relatively expensive for classifying undiscovered records. For classification, it is important to have the distance of the closest neighbour, and the algorithm gets computationally exhaustive with the growth in training set size. (Fu, 1968) Unrelated data/features will devalue/degrade the accuracy. It keeps all the data and does not do any induction on them; that's why it has large data and high-cost calculations.

2.10 K-Means Clustering

This algorithm is used to solve clustering problems. When variables are, a huge K-Means Clustering algorithm works better than hierarchical clustering. It is a kind of unsupervised learning. This clustering algorithm has tighter clusters than hierarchical clusters as it has small k and globular clusters. It is mathematically efficient as it has the algorithm of order complexity which is $O(K*n*d)$. In this method, it is hard to find or predict the value of K. In different final clusters, it has different split-up results, which affect the performance, and it also affects the performance when it has a global cluster. In K-Means clustering, the working ability decreases when it has a difference in the density and size of the cluster. Even if the data (input data) have different cluster sizes, the uniform effect still makes the clusters of uniform size. It becomes harder to satisfy the correlation in the spherical assumption when it breaks its features and adds extra weight to its feature (correlation feature). The value of K is delicate to the outliers. As it has no unidentified/unique solution for the value of K. One needs to do K mean for the value of K and then collect output at J. (Shrestha et al., 2021).

2.11 Back Propagation

The backpropagation algorithm is used to find the easy path to figuring out the neural network by calculating /computing the gradient. You can do this with a stochastic gradient which is also easy. Other than Back Propagation and SGD, there are also more compound/complex structures (like Quasi-Newton), but they cannot give better output/performance than them. This algorithm is mainly used in deep learning (it is an ML technique). Every industry segment has its own Neural Network (NN) and the application which is based on it, and that application has its pros and cons. NN works better in those places where no rules or standards are defined to give the answer/output. It is like a black box because it answers, but the person does not know how this answer came (Fatima & Pasha, 2017). NN is used for risk assessment in industry, forecasting bank credit status, IoT, etc.

3. PATTERN RECOGNITION

In PR, the goal is to recognize similarities or commonalities among data points and use that information to make predictions, categorize objects, or extract meaningful insights. This process often involves extracting relevant features or characteristics from the data and applying algorithms or statistical methods to analyze and classify the patterns. It has applications in various fields, including image and speech recognition, natural language processing, bioinformatics, finance, and many others. For example, in computer vision, PR algorithms can be used to detect and identify objects in images or videos. In finance, PR techniques can be used to analyze market trends and make predictions about future stock prices. There are several approaches to pattern recognition, including statistical PR, neural networks, ML, and deep learning. These methods rely on different mathematical and computational techniques to extract patterns and make predictions based on the observed data. Overall, PR is a fundamental concept that plays a crucial role in numerous domains, enabling computers and humans to identify and understand patterns in data, leading to better decision-making, automation, and problem-solving (Obayya et al., 2023).

3.1 Machine Learning in Pattern Recognition

ML plays a significant role in PR by enabling computers to automatically learn and recognize patterns in data. ML algorithms can analyze large amounts of data, extract relevant features, and discover patterns or regularities without being explicitly programmed. Here are some ways in which ML is used in PR:

- **Supervised Learning:** It involves training algorithms with labelled data, where each data point is accompanied by a known label or category. Through this process, the algorithm learns to establish correlations between input features and their corresponding labels, enabling it to identify patterns and make accurate predictions on new, unseen data. This approach finds wide application in tasks such as image classification, speech recognition, and text categorization, where the algorithm leverages the provided labels to generalize and classify new instances effectively.
- **Unsupervised Learning:** Unsupervised learning involves analyzing unlabeled data to discover patterns or structures within the data itself. Clustering algorithms, such as k-means clustering or hierarchical clustering, can group similar data points based on their intrinsic similarities. This helps in identifying patterns or subgroups within the data without prior knowledge of the labels (Santosh et al., 2019; Obayya et al., 2023; Mitra & Pal, 2005; Entezari et al., 2023; Weiss & Kapouleas, 1989).
- **Deep Learning:** It is a subfield of ML that leverages neural networks with multiple layers to detect intricate patterns within data. Models like CNNs excel at image recognition, while RNNs are adept at handling sequential data. Through their hierarchical structure, deep learning models autonomously learn complex representations of data, allowing them to capture and understand intricate patterns and dependencies. This capability has led to significant advancements and successes in various PR tasks.
- **Feature Extraction:** ML techniques can be used to extract relevant features from raw data, which are then used for PR. Feature extraction algorithms, such as PCA or wavelet transforms, identify the most informative characteristics or representations of the data. These extracted features can be fed into ML models for classification or pattern matching.

- **Anomaly Detection:** ML algorithms can learn patterns in data and identify anomalies or outliers that deviate significantly from the expected patterns. Anomaly detection is useful in various domains, such as fraud detection, network intrusion detection, or equipment failure prediction. ML models can be trained on normal data patterns and identify deviations that indicate unusual behaviour.
- **Reinforcement Learning:** While reinforcement learning is primarily used for decision-making tasks, it can also be applied to PR. Reinforcement learning agents can learn to recognize patterns in an environment and take actions based on observed rewards or feedback. This approach is useful when patterns need to be recognized in dynamic or changing environments (Sharifani & Amini, 2023; Fujiyoshi et al., 2019; Meyer et al., 2014; Serey et al., 2023; Ejegwa et al., 2023; Xu et al., 2023).

ML algorithms provide the capability to learn from data and generalize patterns, allowing them to recognize and classify patterns in a wide range of applications. By leveraging the power of ML, PR becomes more automated, accurate, and scalable, with applications across industries like healthcare, finance, marketing, and more (Khaleel et al., 2023).

4 RECENT ADVANCES IN THE FIELD

ML techniques have made significant contributions to PR and decision-making in recent years, leading to advancements and transformations in various real-world applications (Ragab et al., 2023). Here are some important recent research contributions and their impact:

- **Deep Learning and Neural Networks:** Deep learning techniques, particularly deep neural networks, have revolutionized PR and decision-making. Researchers have developed advanced architectures, such as CNNs for image recognition and RNNs for sequential data. These models have achieved state-of-the-art performance in tasks like image classification, object detection, speech recognition, machine translation, and sentiment analysis (Sathishkumar et al., 2023).
- **Transfer Learning and Pretrained Models:** Transfer learning has emerged as a powerful technique in ML. Researchers have demonstrated the effectiveness of pre-trained models, such as ImageNet pretraining for computer vision tasks, and language models like BERT or GPT for natural language processing tasks. Transfer learning allows models to leverage knowledge learned from large-scale datasets and adapt it to new, smaller datasets, significantly improving performance even with limited labeled data (Alsayat, 2023).
- **Explainable AI (XAI):** Interpreting and explaining the decisions made by ML models is crucial for trust, transparency, and ethical considerations. XAI research aims to provide insights into how models make decisions, especially in complex deep-learning architectures—techniques such as attention mechanisms, saliency maps, and gradient-based methods (Feizizadeh et al., 2023).
- **Reinforcement Learning Advancements:** Reinforcement learning (RL) has witnessed significant progress, particularly in domains where decision-making is crucial. Researchers have explored techniques like deep RL, model-based RL, and multi-agent RL to tackle complex decision-making problems in robotics, game-playing, finance, and autonomous systems. RL has been used

to optimize resource allocation, develop autonomous driving systems, and enhance control policies in various applications.

- **Bayesian Deep Learning:** Combining the benefits of both Bayesian modeling and deep learning, researchers have been working on Bayesian deep learning techniques. Bayesian methods provide probabilistic uncertainty estimates, which are crucial for decision-making in scenarios where uncertainty needs to be quantified. Bayesian deep learning allows for more robust and reliable PR and decision-making by capturing and propagating uncertainty throughout the models (Tran et al., 2023).

- **Federated Learning and Privacy-Preserving Techniques:** With increasing concerns about data privacy, researchers have focused on developing techniques that enable collaborative learning without sharing sensitive data. Federated learning allows multiple parties to train a shared model while keeping the data decentralized. Secure multi-party computation and differential privacy techniques have also been explored to ensure privacy preservation during the learning and decision-making process (Tran et al., 2023)(Pirone et al., 2023)(Soori et al., 2023)(Morris et al., 2023)(Tokgöz & Carro, 2023).

In this direction, table 4.1 discusses the recent advancements in the relevant field.

Table 1. Recent research contributions

Authors	Year	Contribution
Arwin et al.	2023	The paper introduces the application of the Knowledge Growing System (KGS) in non-binary decision support systems, focusing on pattern recognition. By evaluating KGS on the Iris dataset, it achieves an accuracy of up to 90.91%. This highlights the potential of KGS for non-binary inputs in decision support systems (Sumari et al., 2023).
Serey et al.	2023	This study provides a concise summary of recent advancements in PR and deep learning methods for data management. Through a content analysis of 186 references, 120 selected papers are reviewed, evaluating their relevance, applications, and ability to handle large data volumes. The study identifies emerging trends and limitations and suggests future research directions (Serey et al., 2023).
Tripathi et al.	2023	This paper tackles the challenge of detecting stock chart patterns using linear regression. Automating the process minimizes human errors and achieves an average accuracy of 98.60% when analyzing top stocks in the IT and Pharmaceutical sectors on the Indian National Stock Exchange (Tripathi et al., 2023).
Niu et al.	2022	This article enhances intelligent manufacturing through optimized PR and an improved association rule data mining algorithm. The experimental results demonstrate notable improvements in the estimated value, production effect, and overall evaluation of remanufactured products. These findings emphasize the effectiveness of the enhanced PR model proposed in the study (Niu & Zhang, 2022).
Guo et al.	2022	This research introduces an improved PR model for blue-printed cloth designs. The model achieves 85% mAP on the dataset, outperforming the original YOLOX model by 5.6% and providing real-time and high-precision identification. The improvements include using the GhostNet network, CBAM attention module, and DIOU loss function, resulting in faster detection speed and enhanced recognition ability (Guo et al., 2023).
Wu et al.	2022	This paper presents progressive tandem learning, a framework for efficient PR using spiking neural networks (SNNs). It includes an ANN-to-SNN conversion method and layer-wise learning with adaptive training. The trained SNNs achieve remarkable performance with reduced inference time and synaptic operations, making them suitable for resource-constrained devices (Wu et al., 2022).

continued on following page

Table 1. Continued

Authors	Year	Contribution
Cherikbayeva et al.	2021	This paper proposes a novel approach to cluster analysis for pattern recognition, combining collective cluster analysis algorithms with nuclear classification methods. The effectiveness of the method is demonstrated through numerical experiments on test problems and a real hyperspectral image, even in the presence of noisy data (Cherikbayeva et al., 2021).
Siami et al.	2021	The study analyzes real-world insurance data, finding that k-means clustering and self-organizing map extract accurate driving patterns. This framework holds promise for usage-based insurance risk analysis and decision support systems (Siami et al., 2021).
Patnaikuni et al.	2021	This paper introduces a novel approach for syntactical-semantic pattern recognition, combining probabilistic context-free grammars with Multi-Entity Bayesian networks. The proposed method effectively addresses semantic context and uncertainty, demonstrated through the disambiguation of Prepositional Phrase attachment using real-world datasets (Patnaikuni & Gengaje, 2021).
Lee et al.	2021	This paper introduces an approach for early detection of a driver's intention using structural pattern recognition. By analyzing driver behavior, including eye fixations and vehicle parameters, the proposed approach achieves recognition rates of 70.5% and 80%, outperforming conventional methods with rates of 56.8% and 69% (Lee et al., 2021).

These recent research contributions have transformed the real world by improving the accuracy, efficiency, and interpretability of PR and decision-making systems. They have facilitated advancements in various domains, including healthcare (diagnosis, drug discovery), finance (fraud detection, algorithmic trading), autonomous systems (self-driving cars, robotics), personalized recommendation systems, and more. By harnessing the power of ML, these techniques are enhancing our ability to recognize patterns, make informed decisions, and address complex real-world challenges.

5 APPLICATIONS OF ML AND PR IN BUSINESS INTELLIGENCE MODELS

ML and PR have become indispensable components of modern business intelligence (BI) models, revolutionizing the way organizations analyze data, make decisions, and gain insights. In this comprehensive exploration, we will delve into various applications where ML and PR bring significant value to BI models.

- **Sales Forecasting:** ML algorithms are employed in BI models to analyze historical sales data and recognize patterns, allowing businesses to predict future sales with greater accuracy. This capability enables organizations to optimize inventory levels, reduce excess stock, and improve overall supply chain efficiency.
- **Customer Segmentation and Personalization:** By leveraging ML and pattern recognition, BI models can analyze vast amounts of customer data to identify patterns and segment customers based on their behavior, preferences, and demographics. This segmentation empowers businesses to tailor marketing strategies and personalize customer experiences, leading to increased customer satisfaction and loyalty.
- **Recommendation Systems:** PR is crucial in recommendation systems, where ML algorithms analyze user behavior to identify patterns and suggest products, services, or content tailored to individual preferences. This enhances user engagement, drives sales, and fosters a more personalized user experience.

- **Anomaly Detection:** BI models use ML to detect anomalies or unusual patterns in data, helping organizations identify potential fraud, errors, or abnormal events. This is particularly valuable in financial transactions, cybersecurity, and fraud detection, allowing businesses to take prompt corrective action.
- **Churn Prediction:** ML models analyze customer behavior to identify patterns indicative of potential churn. By recognizing early warning signs, businesses can implement targeted retention strategies to retain valuable customers and reduce overall churn rates.
- **Text and Sentiment Analysis:** BI models incorporate ML algorithms to analyze textual data from sources such as customer reviews, social media, and surveys. This enables businesses to gain insights into customer sentiment, market trends, and brand perception, informing strategic decision-making.
- **Credit Scoring:** In the financial sector, ML models assess creditworthiness by analyzing various financial and non-financial factors. This aids in more accurate and informed lending decisions, reducing the risk of defaults and optimizing the credit evaluation process.
- **Supply Chain Optimization:** ML and PR contribute to optimizing supply chain processes by predicting demand, managing inventory levels, and streamlining logistics. This results in improved efficiency, reduced costs, and a more responsive supply chain.
- **Dynamic Pricing:** BI models use ML algorithms to adjust pricing dynamically based on market conditions, competitor pricing, and customer behavior. This flexibility allows businesses to maximize revenue, stay competitive, and respond quickly to market changes.
- **Image and Video Analytics:** PR plays a crucial role in image and video analytics. ML algorithms are employed for tasks such as facial recognition, object detection, and quality control. This has applications in industries such as retail, manufacturing, and security.
- **Employee Performance Analytics:** BI models use ML to analyze employee performance data, identifying patterns that contribute to success. This aids in talent management, training programs, and overall workforce optimization.
- **Healthcare Analytics:** In the healthcare sector, ML and PR analyze patient data to identify patterns related to disease diagnosis, treatment outcomes, and resource allocation. This supports more informed decision-making in healthcare organizations.
- **Fraud Detection:** ML models are instrumental in detecting fraudulent activities in financial transactions, insurance claims, and online transactions. By identifying unusual patterns, organizations can mitigate financial risks and enhance fraud prevention measures.
- **Operational Efficiency:** BI models optimize operational efficiency by using ML algorithms to identify inefficiencies, automate routine tasks, and streamline workflows. This results in improved productivity and resource utilization.
- **Predictive Maintenance:** ML and PR analyze historical data to predict equipment failures and schedule maintenance proactively. This reduces downtime, extends equipment lifespan, and lowers maintenance costs.
- **Market Segmentation:** BI models utilize ML and PR to analyze market data and segment markets effectively. This enables businesses to tailor marketing strategies, allocate resources efficiently, and target specific customer segments.

In conclusion, the integration of ML and PR into business intelligence models has transformed how organizations extract insights from data. These applications not only enhance decision-making processes but also drive innovation, improve efficiency, and contribute to overall business success. As technology continues to evolve, businesses that embrace and harness the power of ML and PR in their BI models will remain at the forefront of competitiveness and innovation in the rapidly changing business landscape (Charles et al., 2023; Adebiaye et al., 2023; Paradza & Daramola, 2021; Khan et al., 2020; Caserio & Trucco, 2018).

6 CONCLUSION

In conclusion, the importance and application of Machine Learning (ML) and pattern recognition in business intelligence models represent a pivotal shift in the way organizations navigate the intricate landscape of decision-making. This transformative integration addresses the limitations of traditional approaches and empowers businesses to extract valuable insights from vast and complex datasets. The practical applications of ML and pattern recognition in areas such as customer behavior analysis, predictive analytics, fraud detection, and supply chain optimization have demonstrated tangible benefits. These technologies enable organizations to make informed, strategic decisions, ultimately leading to improved operational efficiency, risk mitigation, and enhanced profitability. However, this transformative journey is not without challenges. Issues such as data privacy, model interpretability, and ethical considerations require careful attention to ensure responsible deployment. Organizations must adopt strategies that prioritize transparency, fairness, and accountability to build trust in the application of these technologies. Looking ahead, the continued evolution of ML and pattern recognition in business intelligence promises further advancements. As the real-world impact becomes more pronounced, organizations must stay agile and adaptive to fully harness the potential of these technologies. Collaboration between data scientists, business analysts, and decision-makers will be crucial for successfully navigating the evolving landscape of intelligent decision-making. In essence, the integration of ML and pattern recognition in business intelligence models offers a transformative opportunity for organizations to thrive in a data-driven era. The insights gained from this exploration underscore the significance of embracing these technologies responsibly, with a focus on achieving sustainable growth, innovation, and a competitive edge in the dynamic and ever-changing business environment.

REFERENCES

Adebiaye, R., Alshami, M., & Owusu, T. (2023). MACHINE LEARNING MODELS FOR EXTRAP-OLATIVE ANALYTICS AS A PANACEA FOR BUSINESS INTELLIGENCE DECISIONS.

Aggarwal, K. K., & Yogesh Singh, A. Kaur, O.P.Sangwan (2004) "A Neural Net Based Approach to Test Oracle" ACM SIGSOFT, May 2004, Vol. 29 No. 4.

AgnarAamodt. Enric Plaza; (2019) Foundational Issues, Methodological Variations, System approaches; AlCom -Artificial Intelligence Communications, IOS Press; Vol. 7 issue 1, page. 39-59.

Alsayat, A. (2023). Customer decision-making analysis based on big social data using machine learning: A case study of hotels in Mecca. *Neural Computing & Applications*, 35(6), 4701–4722. DOI: 10.1007/s00521-022-07992-x PMID: 36340596

Arwin, D. W. S., Asmara, R. A., Dimas, R. H. P., & Syamsiana, I. N. (2023, April 28). A perspective on a non-binary knowledge growing system in a pattern recognition use-case. *AIP Conference Proceedings*, 2531(1), 070001. DOI: 10.1063/5.0125810

Caserio, C., Trucco, S., Caserio, C., & Trucco, S. (2018). Business intelligence systems. Enterprise Resource Planning and Business Intelligence Systems for Information Quality: An Empirical Analysis in the Italian Setting, 43-73.

Charles, V., Garg, P., Gupta, N., & Agarwal, M. (Eds.). (2023). *Data Analytics and Business Intelligence: Computational Frameworks, Practices, and Applications*. CRC Press. DOI: 10.1201/9781003189640

Cherikbayeva, L., Yerimbetova, A., & Daiyrbayeva, E. "Research of Cluster Analysis Methods for Group Solutions of the Pattern Recognition Problem," 2021 6th International Conference on Computer Science and Engineering (UBMK), Ankara, Turkey, 2021, pp. 1-4, DOI: 10.1109/UBMK52708.2021.9558884

Dr. Bonnie Morris; (1995) Case Based Reasoning AI/ES Update; Fall 1995; West Virginia University; vol. 5 no. 1.

Ejegwa, P. A., Feng, Y., Tang, S., Agbetayo, J. M., & Dai, X. (2023). New Pythagorean fuzzy-based distance operators and their applications in pattern classification and disease diagnostic analysis. *Neural Computing & Applications*, 35(14), 10083–10095. DOI: 10.1007/s00521-022-07679-3

Entezari, A., Aslani, A., Zahedi, R., & Noorollahi, Y. (2023). Artificial intelligence and machine learning in energy systems: A bibliographic perspective. *Energy Strategy Reviews*, 45, 101017. DOI: 10.1016/j.esr.2022.101017

Fatima, M., & Pasha, M. (2017). Survey of machine learning algorithms for disease diagnostic. *Journal of Intelligent Learning Systems and Applications*, 9(01), 1–16. DOI: 10.4236/jilsa.2017.91001

Feizizadeh, B., Omarzadeh, D., Kazemi Garajeh, M., Lakes, T., & Blaschke, T. (2023). Machine learning data-driven approaches for land use/cover mapping and trend analysis using Google Earth Engine. *Journal of Environmental Planning and Management*, 66(3), 665–697. DOI: 10.1080/09640568.2021.2001317

Fu, K. C. (Ed.). (1968). *Sequential methods in pattern recognition and machine learning*. Academic press.

Fujiyoshi, H., Hirakawa, T., & Yamashita, T. (2019). Deep learning-based image recognition for autonomous driving. *IATSS Research*, 43(4), 244–252. DOI: 10.1016/j.iatssr.2019.11.008

Guo, Y., Zhou, J., Qin, Q., Wei, Y., & Zhang, W. (2023, March 1). An Improved Algorithm and Implementation of Data Mining for Intelligent Manufacturing Association Rules Based on Pattern Recognition. *IEEE Consumer Electronics Magazine*, 12(2), 94–99. DOI: 10.1109/MCE.2022.3149210

Khaleel, M., Ahmed, A. A., & Alsharif, A. (2023). Artificial Intelligence in Engineering. *Brilliance: Research of Artificial Intelligence*, 3(1), 32–42. DOI: 10.47709/brilliance.v3i1.2170

Khan, M. A., Saqib, S., Alyas, T., Rehman, A. U., Saeed, Y., Zeb, A., & Mohamed, E. M. (2020). Effective demand forecasting model using business intelligence empowered with machine learning. *IEEE Access : Practical Innovations, Open Solutions*, 8, 116013–116023. DOI: 10.1109/ACCESS.2020.3003790

Lee, S., Khan, M. Q., & Husen, M. N. (2021, February). Continuous Car Driving Intent Detection Using Structural Pattern Recognition. *IEEE Transactions on Intelligent Transportation Systems*, 22(2), 1001–1013. DOI: 10.1109/TITS.2019.2961928

Li, Z. (2018). Development of machine learning and several learning methods [J]. *Industry and Science Forum*, 15(10), 198–199.

Malik, A., Parihar, V., Bhushan, B., Srivastava, J., & Karim, L. (2023). Artificial Intelligence-Based React Application (Powered by Conversational ALAN-AI Voice Assistance). In Sharma, D. K., Peng, S. L., Sharma, R., & Jeon, G. (Eds.), *Micro-Electronics and Telecommunication Engineering. Lecture Notes in Networks and Systems* (Vol. 617). Springer., DOI: 10.1007/978-981-19-9512-5_47

Malik, A., Parihar, V., Srivastava, J., Kaur, H., & Abidin, S. "Prognosis of Diabetes Mellitus Based on Machine Learning Algorithms," 2023 10th International Conference on Computing for Sustainable Global Development (INDIACom), New Delhi, India, 2023, pp. 1466-1472.

Meyer, G., Adomavicius, G., Johnson, P. E., Elidrisi, M., Rush, W. A., Sperl-Hillen, J. M., & O'Connor, P. J. (2014). A machine learning approach to improving dynamic decision making. *Information Systems Research*, 25(2), 239–263. DOI: 10.1287/isre.2014.0513

Mitra, S., & Pal, S. K. (2005). Fuzzy sets in pattern recognition and machine intelligence. *Fuzzy Sets and Systems*, 156(3), 381–386. DOI: 10.1016/j.fss.2005.05.035

Morris, M. X., Rajesh, A., Asaad, M., Hassan, A., Saadoun, R., & Butler, C. E. (2023). Deep learning applications in surgery: Current uses and future directions. *The American Surgeon*, 89(1), 36–42. DOI: 10.1177/00031348221101490 PMID: 35567312

Na, J., Yang, H., Gu, Q., & Huang, J. (2019). Machine learning and its algorithm and development analysis [J] [Theoretical Edition]. *Information and Computer Science*, 87(1), 83–84.

Niu, T., & Zhang, Q. "Research on Small Object Pattern Recognition Technology based on Computer Deep Learning: Improved YOLOX Model as an example," 2022 2nd International Conference on Social Sciences and Intelligence Management (SSIM), Taichung, Taiwan, 2022, pp. 93-98, DOI: 10.1109/SSIM55504.2022.10047938

Obayya, M., Maashi, M. S., Nemri, N., Mohsen, H., Motwakel, A., Osman, A. E., Alneil, A. A., & Alsaid, M. I. (2023). Hyperparameter optimizer with deep learning-based decision-support systems for histopathological breast cancer diagnosis. *Cancers (Basel)*, 15(3), 885. DOI: 10.3390/cancers15030885 PMID: 36765839

Obayya, M., Maashi, M. S., Nemri, N., Mohsen, H., Motwakel, A., Osman, A. E., Alneil, A. A., & Alsaid, M. I. (2023). Hyperparameter optimizer with deep learning-based decision-support systems for histopathological breast cancer diagnosis. *Cancers (Basel)*, 15(3), 885. DOI: 10.3390/cancers15030885 PMID: 36765839

Paradza, D., & Daramola, O. (2021). Business intelligence and business value in organisations: A systematic literature review. *Sustainability (Basel)*, 13(20), 11382. DOI: 10.3390/su132011382

Parihar, V., & Yadav, S. (2022). Comparative analysis of different machine learning algorithms to predict online shoppers' behaviour. *International Journal of Advanced Networking and Applications*, 13(06), 5169–5182. DOI: 10.35444/IJANA.2022.13603

Patnaikuni, S., & Gengaje, S. (2021). A Theoretical Foundation for Syntactico-Semantic Pattern Recognition. *IEEE Access : Practical Innovations, Open Solutions*, 9, 135879–135889. DOI: 10.1109/ACCESS.2021.3115445

Pirone, D., Cimorelli, L., Del Giudice, G., & Pianese, D. (2023). Short-term rainfall forecasting using cumulative precipitation fields from station data: A probabilistic machine learning approach. *Journal of Hydrology (Amsterdam)*, 617, 128949. DOI: 10.1016/j.jhydrol.2022.128949

Ragab, M., Ashary, E. B., Aljedaibi, W. H., Alzahrani, I. R., Kumar, A., Gupta, D., & Mansour, R. F. (2023). A novel metaheuristics with adaptive neuro-fuzzy inference system for decision making on autonomous unmanned aerial vehicle systems. *ISA Transactions*, 132, 16–23. DOI: 10.1016/j.isatra.2022.04.006 PMID: 35523604

Run, Z., & Wang, Y. (2018). Research on machine learning and its algorithm and development [J] [Natural Science Edition]. *Journal of Communication University of China*, 23(02), 10–18.

Santosh, K. C., Antani, S., Guru, D. S., & Dey, N. (Eds.). (2019). *Medical imaging: artificial intelligence, image recognition, and machine learning techniques*. CRC Press. DOI: 10.1201/9780429029417

Sarker, I. H. (2021). Machine Learning: Algorithms, Real-World Applications and Research Directions. *SN Computer Science*, 2(3), 160–181. DOI: 10.1007/s42979-021-00592-x PMID: 33778771

Sathishkumar, V. E., Cho, J., Subramanian, M., & Naren, O. S. (2023). Forest fire and smoke detection using deep learning-based learning without forgetting. *Fire Ecology*, 19(1), 1–17. DOI: 10.1186/s42408-022-00165-0

Serey, J., Alfaro, M., Fuertes, G., Vargas, M., Durán, C., Ternero, R., Rivera, R., & Sabattin, J. (2023). Pattern recognition and deep learning technologies, enablers of industry 4.0, and their role in engineering research. *Symmetry*, 15(2), 535. DOI: 10.3390/sym15020535

Serey, J., Alfaro, M., Fuertes, G., Vargas, M., Durán, C., Ternero, R., Rivera, R., & Sabattin, J. (2023). Pattern Recognition and Deep Learning Technologies, Enablers of Industry 4.0, and Their Role in Engineering Research. *Symmetry*, 15(2), 535. DOI: 10.3390/sym15020535

Sharifani, K., & Amini, M. (2023). Machine Learning and Deep Learning: A Review of Methods and Applications. *World Information Technology and Engineering Journal*, 10(07), 3897–3904.

Shrestha, Y. R., Krishna, V., & von Krogh, G. (2021). Augmenting organizational decision-making with deep learning algorithms: Principles, promises, and challenges. *Journal of Business Research*, 123, 588–603. DOI: 10.1016/j.jbusres.2020.09.068

Siami, M., Naderpour, M., & Lu, J. (2021, March). A Mobile Telematics Pattern Recognition Framework for Driving Behavior Extraction. *IEEE Transactions on Intelligent Transportation Systems*, 22(3), 1459–1472. DOI: 10.1109/TITS.2020.2971214

Soori, M., Arezoo, B., & Dastres, R. (2023). Artificial intelligence, machine learning and deep learning in advanced robotics, A review. *Cognitive Robotics*.

Tokgöz, E., & Carro, M. A. (2023). Applications of artificial intelligence, machine learning, and deep learning on facial plastic surgeries. In *Cosmetic and reconstructive facial plastic surgery: A review of medical and biomedical engineering and science concepts* (pp. 281–306). Springer Nature Switzerland. DOI: 10.1007/978-3-031-31168-0_9

Tran, M. Q., Amer, M., Abdelaziz, A. Y., Dai, H. J., Liu, M. K., & Elsisi, M. (2023). Robust fault recognition and correction scheme for induction motors using an effective IoT with deep learning approach. *Measurement*, 207, 112398. DOI: 10.1016/j.measurement.2022.112398

Tran, M. Q., Amer, M., Abdelaziz, A. Y., Dai, H. J., Liu, M. K., & Elsisi, M. (2023). Robust fault recognition and correction scheme for induction motors using an effective IoT with deep learning approach. *Measurement*, 207, 112398. DOI: 10.1016/j.measurement.2022.112398

Tripathi, A., Mathure, J., Deotarse, S., Rai, D., & Gadhikar, L. "Linear Regression Approach For Stock Chart Pattern Recognition," 2023 5th Biennial International Conference on Nascent Technologies in Engineering (ICNTE), Navi Mumbai, India, 2023, pp. 1-6, DOI: 10.1109/ICNTE56631.2023.10146731

Watson, I., & Gardingen, D. (1999) A Distributed Case-Based Reasoning Application for Engineering Sales Support; *Proc. 16th Int. Joint Conf. on Artificial Intelligence (IJCAI-99)*; 1999; Vol. 1, page 600-605.

Wei, P., Li, Y., Zhang, Z., Tao, H., Li, Z., & Liu, D. (2019) An optimization method for intrusion detection classification model based on deep belief network; IEEE. 2019; vol.7 issue 87; page 593–605.

Weiss, S. M., & Kapouleas, I. (1989, August). An empirical comparison of pattern recognition, neural nets, and machine learning classification methods. *IJCAI (United States)*, 89, 781–787.

Wu, J., Xu, C., Han, X., Zhou, D., Zhang, M., Li, H., & Tan, K. C. (2022, November 1). Progressive Tandem Learning for Pattern Recognition With Deep Spiking Neural Networks. *IEEE Transactions on Pattern Analysis and Machine Intelligence*, 44(11), 7824–7840. DOI: 10.1109/TPAMI.2021.3114196 PMID: 34546918

Xu, D., & Yingjie, T. (2015). A comprehensive survey of clustering algorithms. *Annals of Data Science*, 2(2), 165–193. DOI: 10.1007/s40745-015-0040-1

Xu, N., Lovreglio, R., Kuligowski, E. D., Cova, T. J., Nilsson, D., & Zhao, X. (2023). Predicting and Assessing Wildfire Evacuation Decision-Making Using Machine Learning: Findings from the 2019 Kincade Fire. *Fire Technology*, 59(2), 793–825. DOI: 10.1007/s10694-023-01363-1

Zaki, M. J. (2000). Scalable algorithms for association mining. *IEEE Transactions on Knowledge and Data Engineering*, 12(3), 372–390. DOI: 10.1109/69.846291

Zhang, C. (2018). Research on the development of machine learning and data mining [C]. 2010-2011 Development Report of Control Science and Engineering Discipline. *Chinese Society of Automation*, 223, 82–89.

Chapter 11
Machine Learning–Based Framework for Human Activity Recognition

Allampalli Harini
https://orcid.org/0009-0008-6726-0364
Pragati Engineering College, India

Manjula Devarakonda Venkata
Pragati Engineering College, India

Doodala Kondababu
Pragati Engineering College, India

ABSTRACT

This chapter proposes a novel Machine Learning-based Framework for Human Activity Recognition tailored to address the complexities and challenges inherent in accurately identifying and categorizing human activities from sensor data. ML-HARF integrates advanced machine learning algorithms with a comprehensive data preprocessing pipeline to extract meaningful features from raw sensor data. Leveraging a diverse array of sensor modalities, including accelerometers, gyroscopes, and mag-netometers-HARF captures rich spatiotemporal patterns characteristic of human activities. The framework employs a hierarchical classification approach, wherein low-level features are initially extracted and subsequently aggregated to infer higher-level activity labels.ML-HARF outperforms other methods in extensive experiments on benchmark datasets, attaining state-of-the-art accuracy rates in a variety of activity recognition tasks In real-world applications like sports analytics, healthcare monitoring and human-computer interaction systems, the framework's efficiency and scalability are also demonstrated.

INTRODUCTION

Human physical activity refers to any body movement produced by skeletal muscles or different positions of the limbs with respect to time upstanding against gravity that results in an energy expenditure [1][2][3]. Human Activity Recognition (HAR) systems identify and evaluate daily actions in real con-

DOI: 10.4018/979-8-3693-3884-1.ch011

ditions, providing context-aware feedback for medical applications like elderly assistance, post-trauma rehabilitation, and smart environment detection. These systems help patients with chronic health conditions and dementia detect abnormal behavior. Researchers are exploring applications in fitness tracking, entertainment, and surveillance beyond healthcare monitoring.

Camera systems provide the necessary context for classifying local interactions or object interactions. In the Early 80s, human motions and actions were recognized using image based techniques. Initially, image sequences [4] were used for identifying human activities. After that, window tracking process [5] was developed to track human motion from the continuous image sequence. Image sequence analysis faced some problems, like modeling body motion and corresponding feature points selection. Hence, in literature, a few methods were applied like body parts generalized cone estimation and window code matching for selecting feature points. Time sequential image was converted into image vector using vector quantization [6] and applied statistical techniques like Hidden Markov Model (HMM). Human actions were recognized using low-level features or simple heuristics approach based on prior knowledge. After a few years, the 3D segment tracking approach was introduced to monitor the gesture of human in a cluttered environment. Proximity space [7] [8] method was one of the popular methods among them.

Wireless technology enhances healthcare services, particularly for elderly and chronically ill individuals. Sensors provide accurate, responsive, adaptive, transparent, and intelligent information for smart healthcare and assisted living applications. Small, inexpensive, and low-powered sensors can adapt to users' environments. In the late 90s, sensor technology was introduced in the field of human activity recognition and monitoring [9][10]. Wearable accelerometers were mostly used as sensors to recognize daily activities, detecting falls, and monitoring undesirable conditions [11][12]. Gyroscopes and magnetometer were also used for the same purpose but, they are not able to provide considerable information individually.

After the introduction of machine learning techniques, vision-based techniques are following the progress of machine learning based research. Several learning techniques are applied for identifying activity from still images as well as video sequences. Human motions or different actions can be recognized based on local space time temporal features and Support Vector Machine (SVM) from the video sequences [13]. A template matching instance-based supervised learning method is adopted to classify objects. SVM, Ridge Regression, Relevance Vector Machine (RVM) [13] etc. techniques were applied to extract 3D human body movement from single and monocular image sequences. Initially, a single camera was used to identify human activity, and most of the time, it can track a single person [14]. Multiple fixed cameras were also used for identifying this [15].

Machine Learning Techniques were applied in different sensor-based HAR systems to improve overall performance and classification accuracy. Learning techniques like k-Nearest Neighbor, Decision Tree, Naive Bayes etc. were applied in different works. Threshold-based (inclination angle) and statistical techniques (Hid- den Markov Model) were developed parallelly for HAR systems and applied in many HAR systems. However, the gyroscope sensor and magnetometer alone could not achieve a significant place in human activity recognition, and it could only work well in combination with other sensors. The combination of accelerometer and gyroscope achieved considerable accuracy in HAR [16] systems. In [17], PIR sensors and a pressure sensor were used for ambient fall detection systems. SafeDoor and SafetyBed [18] are few examples of assisted living system. The activity recognition frameworks are based on the video camera and environmental sensor for elder adults at indoor [19]. The system takes input video, environmental factors, and previous knowledge of multimodal events to identify complex activities.

Initially, basic daily activities like sitting, standing, walking, running, etc. were considered for the HAR. Then, different complex activities like making coffee, working on the computer, watching TV etc. were also investigated. Motion sensors are found to be insufficient for identifying abnormal activity and health conditions. It is often a challenging problem, to get an accurate estimation of the biological parameters when the users are performing various daily activities [20]. The parameter values are varied for different activities, for example, when an individual begins running, it is expected that his/her heart rate, temperature and breathing amplitude would increase. Thus, the digital environment including sensor and connected devices [21] provides a context aware solution for monitoring applications. In the early 2000s, smart phones were introduced in the field of HAR [22][23]. The ubiquitous nature of smart handhelds provides a better way to monitor remotely human movement without any inconvenience. Smart phones are equipped with sensing (accelerometers, gyroscope, compass etc.) as well as communication facilities (like Wi-Fi and Bluetooth). Raw data are collected from inertial sensors of Smartphone during data collection. The collected raw data contains noise and filtering techniques are applied to remove the noise from signals. Essential features are extracted from the preprocessed dataset, and fed to learning techniques for training a model, in order to identify several activities as described in figure 1.

Figure 1. A machine learning based human activity recognition framework

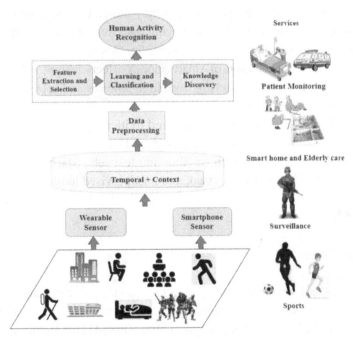

OVERVIEW OF SENSOR-BASED HAR SYSTEMS

The human activity recognition systems in literature mostly follow the following five phases:
(1) Data collection (2) Data preprocessing, (3) Feature extraction, (4) Feature selection and (5) Classification. Data collection and preprocessing can be done on the smart phone using customized applications. The android application can be used for collecting data from smart phone inertial sensors.

Data Collection: Number Sampling is a crucial aspect of data collection for activity recognition, involving the number, type, and position of sensors. The optimal position depends on the system's application. Proper selection of sampling rate and transmission interval is essential for reliability and energy consumption. Data collection duration is crucial for proper reflection of activities. Most studies consider right pocket storage, chest position, and arm movements. Sampling rates range from 5Hz to 512Hz[25][26].

Data Preprocessing: Preprocessing raw data from sensors is essential to remove noise, motion artifacts, missing attributes, and redundantness. Filtering reduces abnormal spikes and data segmentation calculates unique features. Proper segment size reduces classification complexity. Sliding window approaches, data normalization, and clustering remove irrelevant data [27][28][29].

Feature Extraction: Feature extraction is a statistical method used to transform filtered sensor readings into more informative indications for decision-making. It generates or derives features from statistical models, ranging from time domain to frequency domain. Time domain features like mean, standard deviation, and entropy are useful for identifying data from different body positions [30][31].

Feature Selection: Feature selection is crucial for activity classification, as it enhances performance and reduces computation time. Orientation of smart phones affects feature values. SFS, ReLIEF, and FCBF methods wrap around classifiers, filtering from high features and selecting dominant ones from redundant neighbors [37].

Learning and Classification: Data sets are analyzed to identify meaningful patterns using probabilistic, machine learning, and threshold-based approaches. Datasets are divided into training and test sets, and classification models are built with training and test sets. Machine learning procedures are categorized into supervised [39], semi-supervised, and unsupervised learning.

Application of HAR

1. Healthcare Application

Remote health care applications rely on daily activity monitoring, including fall detection, for various conditions like dementia, dementia, and surgery. Combining accelerometer and gyroscope sensors improves quality of life for Parkinson's patients. Smart phone-based HAR frameworks can monitor daily activities for able-bodied and stroke patients, while diabetic patients require regular step count, exercise intensity, and calories burned.

2. Surveillance

Sensor technologies offer valuable data for soldiers, including physiological status monitoring, which is crucial for surveillance in military applications. These sensors can track fitness, mission-related physiological status, and fatigue limits, enabling safe communication with squadron leaders.

3.SportsApplication

Wearable and smart phone sensors are used in sports applications to improve player performance. Combining accelerometer and gyroscope allows monitoring of movement, bowling action, and postures in sports like tennis and cricket.

Figure 2. Overall data flow for activity recognition system using smart phones and wearable sensors

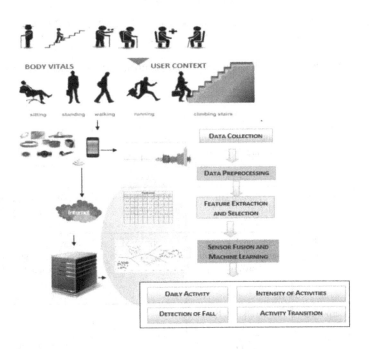

Issues and Challenges in HAR

1. **Different Device Configuration and Usage Behavior**: The classification accuracy of HAR is heavily influenced by the training and test environment, hardware configuration, calibration problems, and individual subject motion patterns. The orientation of smart phones also affects the system's classification accuracy. Various data collection positions, such as waist or pant pocket positions, can improve results. Several sensors are used for activity recognition, but no work has been found that enables detailed recognition even when training data is collected from one device at one position.
2. **Selection of Sensors**: Sensor selection and attributes significantly impact recognition performance. For healthcare applications, a gyroscope and heart rate sensors can be added for fall detection. Including location details and activity labels can help gather user information, but privacy concerns may arise.

197

3.**Imprecise Labeling and Insufficient Training Data**: Providing sufficient training data with precise activity labels is crucial for classification models, but collecting such data can be challenging due to ambiguous label information, making traditional classification tasks difficult.

4. **Energy Efficiency:** Energy-efficient HAR systems require long-lasting batteries, low sampling rates, and techniques like reducing data size and transmission rate, exploring different sampling rates, acceleration rates, and window sizes.

Table1. Comparison between state-of-the-artworks. Accelerometer: Acc, Gyroscope: Gyro, Magnetometer: Mag

Work Sensor	Placement	Action	Learning Technique	Remarks	Application
[16] in 2009 Tempo Sensor Nodes Acc,Gyro	Thigh, Chest	Walk, sit, jump, run,, forward/ backward, right/ left / on stair case etc	Threshold based technique	Differentiates intentional & unintentional transitions	
[31]] in 2011, 3D Acc	Ankle left / right	Human fall	LDA & Fishers criterion	Classify the causes of fall (96% sensitivity) Left ankle+ right ankle	
[32] in 2016, Smart phone, Acc, Gyro	*Right* front hip	Sit, stand, Lying, stairs up/ down, ramp up/down	NB,SVM, Decision Tree	Able-bodied, elderly, and stroke patients are monitored. Relief-F, feature selection applied & achieved around 97%	
[24] In 2017 Smart phone, Acc	Trouserpocket	Jog, walk, sit, lying, stand			
SVM,NB,KNN, Bagging, MLP,		*Accuracy 99%with selected time,frequency domain features*		[33] i n 2009	Acc,Gyro
Chest, upper arm hand	Tennis player *movement*		Marker based method	Classifying skill level for players	
	[34] in 2016 Smartphone, Acc	Waist back side *Left and right*	Walk, jog, sit, stand, Walk, jog, run		MCODE,
unsupervised		*Basket ball movement*		[35] in 2017	
Acc, Gyro, Mag		Upper Arm Right/ Left, Thigh Back/ Left/Right.	jump different military daily activities		DT,SVM,NB

(Gaussian),kNN, RF

Combination of Acc and Mag provides better accuracy around 95% and better among others [36] in 2018, Acc, Temparature, ECG, Humidity sensor etc.

PROPOSED METHODOLOGY

The primitive classes of activity are Sit, Stand, Walk, etc. In this chapter, an activity recognition framework, which enables common activity recognition even when data is collected using one device kept at one position (say, shirt pocket) for training and activity is recognized for readings collected from a different device kept at same or a different position (say, bag).The process utilizes only accelerometer sensor of smart phone which is available in almost all smart phones by any manufacturer thus making the framework ubiquitous. The proposed classification model can be employed on a wide range of human daily activity recognition problems. A two-phase activity recognition framework based on an ensemble of classifiers to identify static activities (Sit on chair, Stand) as well as dynamic activities (Walk, Climbing Stairs). The proposed technique works irrespective of device configuration and usage behavior.

This framework segregates static and dynamic physical human activities from smart phones raw accelerometer data and successfully classifies labels of several individual activities. Two static activities Sit and Stand, and two dynamic activities Walk and Climbing Stairs (CS) are considered in this work. The data are collected for these (Sit, Stand, Walk, CS) daily activities.

Figure 3. Raw accelerometer readings of different activities collected for 540s from a smart phone kept at right pant pocket

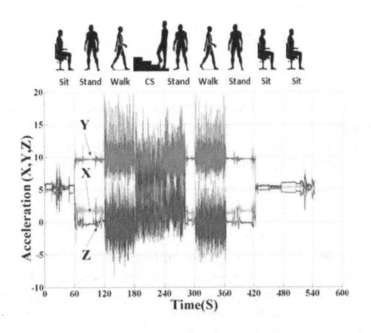

Phase 1: Training device and position selection are crucial for activity recognition. Datasets from each training position are stored as train-test pairs, and classification accuracy is determined using different classifiers. The training dataset with maximum cross validation accuracy is used.

Phase 2: Identifying individual activities using a single base classifier is challenging, so ensemble methods are recommended. Ensemble methods combine hypotheses and use multiple base learners, resulting in a stronger generalization ability. Single base classifiers struggle to identify all activities with reasonable accuracy, so ensemble models are created based on their overall performance to identify multiple activities.

Figure 4. Block diagram of proposed two phase activity recognition framework

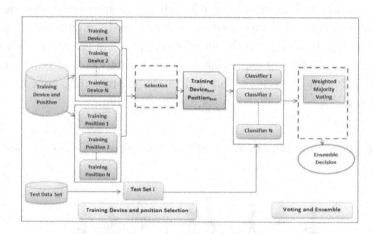

This framework provides support to healthcare providers for assessing patients daily activity pattern. It can help tracking activity of patients during post surgery recovery period as they are not allowed to climb upstairs or downstairs. Activity recognition can also identify exact context of a patient which is important for context aware health monitoring.

CONCLUSION

Human activity recognition and monitoring is an emerging field in pervasive computing. So, the aim of this chapter is recognizing daily actions with user convenient setup and addressing few associated challenges. Smartphone hardware configuration, calibration, and usage behavior like how the smart phone is kept for tests and training environments are important challenges that are addressed in this thesis. Other challenges include non uniform gait and hence imprecise labeling of detailed activities. The proposed frameworks are aimed to utilize a minimal number of sensors. Machine learning techniques are applied to combine the data from different types of sensors. The machine learning models are developed to build classification model for HAR.

REFERENCES

8.4 Billion Connectedhnn Things Will Be in Use in 2017, Up 31 Percent from 2016. 2017. Available online: URL https://www.gartner.com/newsroom/id/3598917 accessed on 19th September, 2020.

Babar, M., Arif, F., & Irfan, M. (2019). Internet of things-based smart city environments using big data analytics: A survey. In *Recent Trends and Advances in Wireless and IoT-enabled Networks* (pp. 129–138). Springer. DOI: 10.1007/978-3-319-99966-1_12

Bouchabou, D., Nguyen, S. M., Lohr, C., LeDuc, B., & Kanellos, I. (2021). Using language model to bootstrap human activity recognition ambient sensors based in smart homes. *Electronics (Basel)*, 10(20), 2498. DOI: 10.3390/electronics10202498

Butt, S. A., Diaz-Martinez, J. L., Jamal, T., & Ali, A. Emiro De- La-Hoz-Franco, and Muhammad Shoaib. IoT smart health security threats. *In 2019 19th International Conference on Computational Science and Its Applications (ICCSA)*, IEEE, 2019.

Butt, S. A., Diaz-Martinez, J. L., Jamal, T., & Ali, A. Emiro De- La-Hoz-Franco, and Muhammad Shoaib. IoT smart health security threats. *In 2019 19th International Conference on Computational Science and Its Applications (ICCSA)*, pages 26-31. IEEE, 2019.

Chen, Shangfeng, Hongqing Fang, and Zhijian Liu. "Human activity recognition based on extreme learning machine in a smart home. *Journal of Physics: Conference Series. Vol. 1437. No. 1. IOP Publishing*, 2020.

Cornelis, E., Gorus, E., Van Schelvergem, N., & De Vriendt, P. (2019). The relationship between basic, instrumental, and advanced activities of daily living and executive functioning in geriatric patients with neurocognitive disorders. *International Journal of Geriatric Psychiatry*, 34(6), 889–899. DOI: 10.1002/gps.5087 PMID: 30761619

de Oliveira, S., Felipe, J. V. F., Plácido, J., & Deslandes, A. C. (2020). Spatial navigation and dual-task performance in patients with Dementia that present partial dependence in instrumental activity of daily living. *IBRO Reports*, 9, 52–57. DOI: 10.1016/j.ibror.2020.06.006 PMID: 33336104

Dhruv, A. J., Patel, R., & Doshi, N. Python: the most advanced programming language for computer science applications. *Proceedings of the international conference on cultural heritage, education, sustainable tourism, and innovation technologies -CESIT 2020*, 2021.

Fahad, L. G., & Tahir, S. F. (2020). Activity recognition in a smart home using local feature weighting and variants of nearest-neighbors classifiers. *Journal of Ambient Intelligence and Humanized Computing*, 1–10. PMID: 32837595

Färber, M., Svetashova, Y., & Harth, A. (2021). *Theories of Meaning for the Internet of Things. Concepts in Action*. Springer.

Fazilov, F. (2021). *Anti-Corruption Review in global health*. Ilkogretim Online.

Franco, P., Martinez, J. M., Kim, Y.-C., & Ahmed, M. A. (2021). IoT based approach for load monitoring and activity recognition in smart homes. *IEEE Access : Practical Innovations, Open Solutions*, 9, 45325–45339. DOI: 10.1109/ACCESS.2021.3067029

Fu, Z., He, X., Wang, E., Huo, J., Huang, J., & Wu, D. (2021). Personalized human activity recognition based on integrated wearable sensor and transfer learning. *Sensors (Basel)*, 21(3), 885. DOI: 10.3390/s21030885 PMID: 33525538

Garcia, K. D., Rebelo de Sá, C., Poel, M., Carvalho, T., Mendes-Moreira, J., & João, M. P. (2021). Cardoso, André CPLF de Carvalho, and Joost N. Kok. An ensemble of autonomous auto-encoders for human activity recognition. *Neurocomputing*, 439, 271–280. DOI: 10.1016/j.neucom.2020.01.125

Gaur, D., & Dubey, S. K. Human Activities Analysis Using Machine Learning Approaches. *Proceedings of the International Conference on Paradigms of Communication, Computing, and Data Sciences*. Springer, Singapore, 2022. DOI: 10.1007/978-981-16-5747-4_39

(2019). JindongWang, Yiqiang Chen, Shuji Hao, Xiaohui Peng, and Lisha Hu. Deep learning for sensor-based activity recognition: *A survey.Pattern Recognition Letters*.

Khan, H. U., Alomari, M. K., Khan, S., Nazir, S., Gill, A. Q., Al-Maadid, A. A., Abu-Shawish, Z. K., & Hassan, M. K. (2021). *Systematic analysis of safety and security risks in smart homes*. CMC- Computers Materials & Continua.

Kim, H., Choi, H., Kang, H., An, J., Yeom, S., & Hong, T. (2021). A systematic review of the smart energy conservation system: From smart homes to sustainable smart cities. *Renewable & Sustainable Energy Reviews*, 140, 110755. DOI: 10.1016/j.rser.2021.110755

Li, Q., Gravina, R., Li, Y., Alsamhi, S. H., Sun, F., & Fortino, G. (2020). Multi-user activity recognition: Challenges and opportunities. *Information Fusion*, 63, 121–135. DOI: 10.1016/j.inffus.2020.06.004

Li, Shasha, Tiejun Cui, and Muhammad Alam. "Reliability analysis of the internet of things using Space Fault Network. *Alexandria Engineering Journal*, pages, 1259-1270, 2021.

Ma, Y., Arshad, S., Muniraju, S., Torkildson, E., Rantala, E., Doppler, K., & Zhou, G. (2021). *Location-and person-independent activity recognition with WiFi, deep neural networks, and reinforcement learning*. ACM Transactions on Internet of Things. DOI: 10.1145/3424739

Manaf, A., & Singh, S. Computer Vision-based Survey on Human Activity Recognition System, Challenges and Applications. *2021 3rd International Conference on Signal Processing and Communication (ICPSC)*. IEEE, 2021.

Mohamed, N., Al-Jaroodi, J., & Jawhar, I. Towards fault-tolerant fog computing for IoT-based smart city applications. *In 2019 IEEE 9th Annual Computing and Communication Workshop and Conference (CCWC)*, pages 0752- 0757. IEEE, 2019.

Quinting, J. F., & Grams, C. M. (2021). Toward a systematic evaluation of warm conveyor belts in numerical weather prediction and climate models. Predictor selection and logistic regression model. *Journal of the Atmospheric Sciences*, 78(5), 1465–1485. DOI: 10.1175/JAS-D-20-0139.1

Ramasubramanian, A. K., Aiman, S. M., & Papakostas, N. (2021). On using human activity recognition sensors to improve the performance of collaborative mobile manipulators: Review and outlook. *Procedia CIRP*, 97, 211–216. DOI: 10.1016/j.procir.2020.05.227

Ritchie, Hannah, and Max Roser. Urbanization. *Our world in data*, 2018.

Ronald, M., Poulose, A., & Han, D. S. (2021). iSPLInception: An inception-ResNet deep learning architecture for human activity recognition. *IEEE Access : Practical Innovations, Open Solutions*, 9, 68985–69001. DOI: 10.1109/ACCESS.2021.3078184

Sadowski, Jathan, Yolande Strengers, and Jenny Kennedy. More work for Big Mother: Revaluing care and control in smart homes. *Environment and Planning A: Economy and Space,* 2021.

Sovacool, B. K., & Dylan, D. (2020). Furszyfer Del Rio. Smart home technologies in Europe: A critical review of concepts, benefits, risks, and policies. *Renewable & Sustainable Energy Reviews*, 120, 109663. DOI: 10.1016/j.rser.2019.109663

Tang, C. I., Perez-Pozuelo, I., Spathis, D., Brage, S., Wareham, N., & Mascolo, C. Selfhar: Improving human activity recognition through self-training with unlabeled data. *arXiv preprint arXiv:2102.06073,* 2021.

Wang, A., Chen, H., Zheng, C., Zhao, L., Liu, J., & Wang, L. Evaluation of random forest for complex human activity recognition using wearable sensors. *In2020 International Conference on Networking and Network Applications (NaNA),* pp. 310-315. IEEE, 2020. DOI: 10.1109/NaNA51271.2020.00060

Wiecek, Elyssa, Fernanda S. Tonin, Andrea Torres-Robles, Shalom I. Benrimoj, Fernando Fernandez-Llimos, and Victoria Garcia-Cardenas. Temporal effectiveness of interventions to improve medication adherence: *A network meta-analysis,* 2019.

Yadav, S. K., Tiwari, K., Pandey, H. M., & Akbar, S. A. (2021). A review of multimodal human activity recognition with special emphasis on classification, applications, challenges and future directions. *Knowledge-Based Systems*, 223, 106970. DOI: 10.1016/j.knosys.2021.106970

Yang, X. L., Chu, X., & Zhou, M.-T. (2020). Fog-Enabled Smart Home and User Behavior Recognition. In *Fog-Enabled Intelligent IoT Systems*. Springer. DOI: 10.1007/978-3-030-23185-9_7

Yang, Y., Luo, X., Chu, X., & Zhou, M.-T. (2020). Fog-Enabled Smart Home and User Behavior Recognition. In *Fog-Enabled Intelligent IoT Systems, pages* (pp. 185–210). Springer. DOI: 10.1007/978-3-030-23185-9_7

Zaidan, A. A., & Zaidan, B. B. (2020). A review on an intelligent process for smart home applications based on IoT: Coherent taxonomy, motivation, open challenges, and recommendations. *Artificial Intelligence Review*, 53(1), 141–165. DOI: 10.1007/s10462-018-9648-9

Chapter 12
Revolutionizing Business Models Through Data-Driven Innovation:
The Case of Hudi

Giulia Rita Sala
ESADE, Spain

Saverio Barabuffi
Scuola Superiore Sant'Anna, Italy

Giulio Ferrigno
Scuola Superiore Sant'Anna, Italy

Enrico Marcazzan
Scuola Superiore Sant'Anna, Italy

ABSTRACT

This book chapter explores the shifting contours of big data monetization in the digital transformation era, focusing on the Human Data Income (Hudi) model. Based on the literature on big data and innovation management, as well as on the so-called Data-Driven Innovation framework, this chapter explores the challenges that are inherent in the process of turning personal information into an asset. To better understand these challenges, it carries a deep case study analysis for Hudi and assesses what the business model does to individuals, businesses, and society as a whole and gives valued insights into the monetization of data and value creation. Drawing on these results, the chapter helps in contributing to a more grounded understanding of the opportunities, challenges, and consequences that come innately with the evolving landscape of data economy, shaping future discussions and research engagements in this field.

DOI: 10.4018/979-8-3693-3884-1.ch012

INTRODUCTION

In the current era of digital transformation, businesses increasingly recognize the inherent value within their vast data reserves (McAfee et al., 2012). The imperative to transform this data into valuable assets has become a critical undertaking for organizations aiming to secure a competitive edge, foster innovation, and enhance decision-making processes (Saggi & Jain, 2018; Terauchi & Buganza, 2019).

This proposed book chapter delves into the intricacies of turning data into value assets, centering its exploration around the noteworthy case of Human Data Income (hereafter Hudi) following the Data-Driven Innovation (DDI) framework (Zillner, 2021a; Zillner, 2021b). While the digital landscape has witnessed a surge in data prominence due to technological advancements, the Internet of Things, and global connectivity, the mere accumulation of data does not guarantee value creation (Cappa et al., 2021; Ferrigno et al., 2024; Ghasemaghaei & Calic, 2020). Hudi's innovative approach stands out by empowering individuals to take ownership of their data and actively take part in the data market, thereby enabling them to earn income through data sharing and capturing intrinsic value.

The chapter meticulously presents Hudi's guiding principles, strategic initiatives, and operational mechanisms that ease the transformation of personal data into tangible and valuable assets. Additionally, a detailed examination of the technical infrastructure and platforms supporting secure and transparent data transactions is undertaken, with a focus on prioritizing privacy protection and supporting data integrity. Legal and ethical considerations surrounding data ownership, consent, and usage are also thoroughly explored, addressing prevailing concerns related to privacy and security.

An in-depth analysis will critically assess the potential implications of the Hudi model on individuals, businesses, and society at large. The chapter provides valuable insights into the Hudi model's impact on data monetization, drawing upon rigorous research methods such as literature review, case studies, stakeholder interviews, and data analysis. The overarching aim is to contribute meaningful insights into the process of turning data into valuable assets (Acciarini et al., 2023; Cappa et al., 2021), emphasizing the transformative potential of the Hudi model in reshaping the data economy.

In conclusion, this book chapter serves as an exploration into the burgeoning field of data monetization (Johnson et al., 2017; Wixom & Ross, 2017) and value capturing (Cappa et al., 2021; Urbinati et al., 2019). By concentrating on the Hudi business model, the analysis investigates the transformative power inherent in personal data ownership and active participation in the data market. The chapter, through a comprehensive examination, illuminates the potential effects of transforming data into valuable assets for users, organizations, and society, offering a nuanced understanding of the opportunities, challenges, and consequences associated with this evolving landscape.

The chapter goes ahead as follows. First, it is provided a literature review at the intersection between big data and innovation management research toward the importance of (a) data as a strategic asset, (b) data monetization and (c) the related issues, (d) the process of extracting value from big data, (e) the explication of the research question and (f) the Data-Driven Innovation (DDI) Canvas approach in big data companies. After, we present the case of Hudi, explaining (a) the theoretical sampling, (b) its history and development, and (c) the data collection process. Moreover, within the data collection process' description, we present both the interviews conducted, and the secondary data used for the analysis. Furthermore, we analyze the data, highlighting the confirmatory approach adopted. Finally, we discuss the findings, applying the DDI approach in business model research in big data companies and the key implications for this type of company.

LITERATURE BACKGROUND

Data as an Asset

In the contemporary era, data is a crucial resource for companies (Cappa et al., 2021; Urbinati et al., 2019). The capacity of (big) data to provide insights, promote informed decision-making, and foster innovation has led to its considerable value (Ferrigno et al.; Ghasemaghaei & Calic, 2019a). Indeed, the collection and analysis of the immense amount of data created daily, even called "big data", has altered the competitive environment (Del Vecchio et al., 2018). In this sense, data has evolved for firms as a strategic asset for reaching competitive advantage (Johnson et al., 2017).

With the pervasive digitization of corporate environments, customers have emerged as significant sources of big data through their mobile interactions (Cappa et al., 2021). Therefore, recent developments have led to a shift in granting individuals' greater agency over the data they generate, spurred by a convergence of consumer advocacy, governmental regulations, and market dynamics (Quach et al., 2022). This global trend has seen personal data increasingly recognized as individuals' assets entrusted to businesses for safekeeping, rather than a freely exploitable resource, thereby fostering a wave of innovation driven by consumer preferences (Ghasemaghaei & Calic, 2020).

In this context, the heightened awareness of data's value has led to increased demands for ownership and control (Scholz, 2016). Concepts like data sovereignty and empowerment have emerged as responses to this shifting landscape (Akter et al., 2021; European Data Market Study 2021-2023). However, ethical concerns surrounding data collection, usage, and preservation are escalating as data's importance grows (Chang, 2021; Herschel & Miori, 2017). Responsible data management needs prioritizing privacy protection, obtaining consent, and preventing misuse (Deslée & Cloarec, 2024). Finding a balance between data usage and respect for a person's rights is an abiding challenge. Regulations like the GDPR seek to ensure accountability and transparency.

In other words, recognizing the value of data as an asset, while increasing protection for privacy and transparency, can better deliver benefits while reducing any adverse impacts. Consequently, the notion emerges that data, when treated as a valuable asset, holds immense promise in fostering a more efficient, inclusive, and prosperous society as we navigate the data-centric future (Bai et al., 2023). Therefore, in the next subsection, we will examine the literature devoted to explaining the importance of monetizing data.

Data Monetization

Data monetization is the process for deriving measurable economic value from data (Faroukhi et al. 2020a; 2020b; Johnson et al., 2017; Ofulue & Benyoucef, 2022; Quach et al., 2022; Ritala et al., 2024; Wixom & Ross, 2017; Woroch & Strobel, 2022). It is generally known as an organization's capability to transform data into both tangible and intangible advantages, thereby improving profitability and bottom-line margins of the organization (Ritala et al., 2024). Considering the boundaries of the organization, internally speaking, data monetization involves leveraging data to drive improvements in corporate performance and inform decision-making processes (Quach et al., 2022). Externally, it encompasses practices such as data bartering, selling data through brokers, and offering information-based products and services

(Quach et al., 2022). Choosing the proper monetization strategy requires a strategic decision, considering the organization's technical infrastructure and analytical capabilities (Ofulue & Benyoucef, 2022).

The adoption of data monetization is rapidly expanding across various sectors, including healthcare (Bram et al., 2015; Firouzi et al. 2020), retail (Najjar et al., 2013), and automotive industries (Ofulue & Benyoucef, 2022). By mining customer data and leveraging AI for predictive analysis, businesses can make informed decisions to stay ahead in competitive landscapes (Ghasemaghaei & Calic, 2019b). Leading companies like Tesla, Amazon, HealthFinch, and Apple have already proved the benefits of data monetization, prompting others to follow suit.

In a nutshell, as information becomes increasingly valuable, the embedding of data monetization approaches ensures business success. Indeed, in the modern digital world, data has turned into one of the huge commodities with an enormous potential for monetization (Cappa et al., 2021). Both businesses and individuals generate substantial data through online activities, which holds significant value across industries, necessitating monetization efforts. Data monetization is a process that leverages insights, patterns, and trends derived from material data to develop new products, to sell data directly, or to drive strategic decisions. In this respect, data monetization provides a number of advantages in the field of businesses, such as revenue generation, improvement in decision-making via insights obtained from data analysis, operational efficiency enhancement, and innovations in product development (Faroukhi et al., 2020a; Johnson et al., 2017; Ritala et al., 2024). It also enables good consumer interaction and personalization, leading to increasing customer satisfaction and loyalty (Johnson et al., 2017; Ofulue & Benyoucef, 2022). However, ethical considerations about privacy, consent, and fairness must be paramount in data monetization endeavors (Faroukhi et al., 2020a; 2020b; Ofulue & Benyoucef, 2022). Therefore, in the next subsection, we will better investigate the issues that affect the data monetization process.

Issues Affecting Data Monetization

To be successful and ethical, data monetization must first address a number of issues. Organizations need consideration and controls of critical variables like the issue of privacy, data quality, and governance, complications arising out of legal and ethical considerations, and security-related to data (Faroukhi et al., 2020a; 2020b; Ofulue & Benyoucef, 2022). Some other ethical issues that need consideration include consent, fairness, openness, and potential for bias or discrimination in decisions based on data (Quach et al., 2022). In this sense, building consumer and stakeholder trust requires balancing business goals with moral obligations (Ofulue & Benyoucef, 2022). In addition, data security and cybersecurity must also be addressed, since the fact that as data has become a valuable asset, it has become a target for criminal activity and cyber threats (Mahmood et al., 2024).

Alongside addressing privacy and security issues, an essential aspect of successful data monetization is also data quality (Cappa et al., 2021). Poor, incomplete, and inaccurate, outdated data will result in erroneous insights and monetization decisions that are wrong. The organization, therefore, has to invest in the data governance frameworks that ensure integrity, correctness, and consistency of its data (Quach et al., 2022). The new data economy laws are straightforward and adhere to the fundamental concept that data owners are the ones who own it (GDPR, California Consumer Privacy Act).

Among data monetization problems, it is impossible not to mention the so-called Cambridge Analytica scandal - actually an outstanding event that made privacy concerns about data topical in broad masses' consciousness. The political consulting organization Cambridge Analytica took access to the personal information of thousands of Facebook users without their knowledge or consent via the Facebook app

"This Is Your Digital Life". The information was used later to create psychological profiles and to send targeted political messages in the 2016 US presidential election. In this respect, the collection and use of such data by Cambridge Analytica were in direct violation of the consumer's initial consent. This incident highlighted possible risks regarding unlimited access to personal information and called for more strict legislation and increased liability regarding data protection. It updated all its data policies, adding enhanced user permissions and more rigorous monitoring of third-party apps. But in the long run, the controversy once more sent a ringing reminder to one and all about being conscious of privacy, taking real security measures, and showing ethical conduct in handling the personal data for monetization.

In light of this discourse, in the next subsection we will better describe the process of value extraction from data.

How to Extract Value From Big Data

As previously mentioned, an enterprise's ability to extract value from big data has turned a matter of competitiveness in the digital economy. Such strategies range from strong collection and storage of data to using a host of analytics techniques and embedding the culture of data in the organization (Dubey et al., 2019; Mikalef et al., 2019). Crucially, the foundation for extracting value from big data lies in efficient data gathering and storage infrastructure capable of handling vast volumes from diverse sources (Ghasemaghaei & Calic, 2019a). In this sense, big data analysis requires modern analytics techniques to uncover insights and trends effectively (Mikalef et al., 2019).

Value extraction from big data and data-driven decision-making are closely intertwined (Wamba et al., 2015). Establishing a culture that values and supports data-driven insights is essential, ensuring decision-makers have the necessary skills and resources for effective data exploitation (Frisk & Bannister, 2017). In this sense, incorporating data into the decision-making process enhances operational effectiveness, resource allocation, and business prospect identification, fostering agility and responsiveness in a dynamic business environment (Cappa et al., 2021; Erevelles et al., 2016; Mikalef et al., 2019). A data-centric culture involves cultivating a collaborative environment for data sharing and exploration, promoting data literacy across the organization, and providing personnel with data analytics training (Messeni Petruzzelli et al., 2022). Ultimately, businesses that harness the capabilities of analytics and business intelligence systems enterprise-wide stand to uncover significant value and seize previously unnoticed opportunities (Ghasemaghaei & Calic, 2019a).

In sum, businesses are always on the lookout for an opportunity to gather data that may turn out to be of value to some other party, ensuring ownership and, consequently, control over the data. Confronted with growing consumer expectations to place personal data under an umbrella of their control, governments and technology companies alike are adjusting their orientation to this expectation. Business practices and bottom lines set again, influenced by considerations of data privacy: companies now race toward data protection in order not to lose consumer trust, nor violate regulations.

Managerially speaking, according to PwC (2019)'s report, three main business opportunities for data monetization can be identified as follows: enhancing existing business operations, expanding into adjacent markets, and developing entirely new business models (as illustrated in Figure 1). These strategies aim to reshape how businesses approach and leverage data to drive innovation and growth.

Figure 1. Data monetization strategies

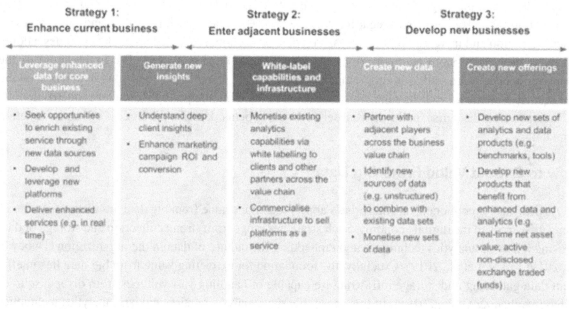

Source: Rea & Sutton, 2019

RESEARCH QUESTION

As previously said, data has emerged as a critical resource with vast potential for enterprises across various industries in today's digitally propelled landscape. However, data monetization is not exempt from issues such as privacy, data quality, and governance, which should be taken into account in the entire organizational process of value extraction from data. In this sense, the advent of data gathering, analysis, and transformation into actionable insights has revolutionized business operations and decision-making processes. Effectively harnessing and monetizing this abundance of data to extract valuable insights and foster innovation presents a significant challenge (Ritala et al., 2024). Therefore, the research question of this book chapter is the following: *How can value be captured from big data?*

Specifically, "value capture" denotes the techniques and strategies used by companies to translate a part of the value they create for their clients into revenue (Dell'Era et al., 2020; Sjödin et al., 2020; Teece & Linden, 2017).

This chapter will delve deeper into this aspect, particularly through the examination of the case of Hudi. Through this study, insights will be gleaned into the impact of big data on both businesses and customers. To achieve this, prior works suggest focusing on the three dimensions constituting big data (even called "3Vs") (Johnson et al., 2017): volume (referring to the size of the data gathered), variety (encompassing the diversity of information collected for each observation), and veracity (pertaining to the accuracy and reliability of data). Scholars have proved that while massive data volume may adversely affect business performance, this effect could be compensated by data variety (Cappa et al., 2021; Ghasemaghaei, 2021). Companies with important levels of volume and variety of data can effectively transform big data into a valuable resource, thereby positively influencing company performance (Ghasemaghaei, 2021; Ghasemaghaei & Calic, 2020).

Moreover, elevated levels of veracity enhance business success by enabling organizations to use big data for their direct commercial goals (Ghasemaghaei & Calic, 2019a). These suggestions set up an empirical basis for understanding when big data can enhance corporate performance.

In line with the literature on big data and innovation management (Ferrigno, Crupi, Di Minin, and Ritala, 2023; Ferrigno, Del Sarto, Piccaluga, and Baroncelli, 2023), the generation and capture of value from big data hinge on the benefits outweighing the costs associated with gathering, storing, and utilizing this resource (Cappa et al., 2021). Big data can also be used to extract further value through the open innovation framework (Enkel et al., 2020). This approach may involve exploring data sourced from citizen science or crowdsourcing initiatives, tapping into collective wisdom to generate novel ideas, address challenges, and fulfill societal needs (Calic & Ghasemaghaei, 2021; Cappa, 2022).

Overall, the insights garnered from this book chapter look to delineate a framework within which big data companies operate in the landscape of big data monetization, with a particular emphasis on Hudi. This can help to underscore the importance of prioritizing long-term company success over partial indicators in the realm of big data monetization.

Data-Driven Innovation (DDI) Approach and Business Modelling: The DDI Canvas

As seen before, when setting up a robust and enduring business strategy in the realm of big data, companies encounter distinct opportunities and challenges. One valuable tool for examining and crafting business models is the Business Model Canvas (BMC) (Osterwalder & Pigneur, 2010). The BMC provides a simplified portrayal of a 'generic' business model believed to be applicable for describing numerous companies (Massa et al., 2017). However, with the aim of focusing on companies that aim to address the challenges of effectively identifying and exploring data-driven innovation, a new framework has been appropriately developed, namely the data-driven innovation (DDI) framework (Zillner 2021a; 2021b). This framework aids entrepreneurs in evaluating practical data-driven business opportunities by systematically analyzing the interplay between supply and demand dynamics. The DDI framework categorizes data-driven business possibilities into supply and demand sides, focusing on creating new offerings, accessing data sources, and technology on the supply side, and considering market dynamics, revenue strategy, and ecosystem dynamics on the demand side. Aligning supply and demand factors through ecosystem and development partnerships ensures competitiveness in data-driven innovations.

The comprehensive framework for defining data-driven innovation produced the so-called "DDI Canvas". It includes eight key dimensions essential for analysis of big data companies, as depicted in Figure 2.

Figure 2. "DDI Canvas with eight dimensions guiding the exploration of the relevant aspects of DDI"

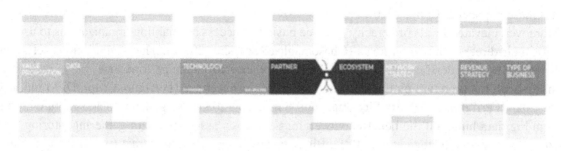

Source: Zillner (2021a)

Specifically, the supply side of the framework consists of the *value proposition* (i.e., the value generated for users), *data* (i.e., the kind of useful data), *technology* (i.e., the data processing and application's technologies), and *partner* (i.e., partners useful for implementing innovation). The demand side includes the *type of business* (i.e., the envisioned market position), the *revenue strategy* (i.e., the strategy to make money), the *network strategy* (i.e., leveraging process of network effects), and *ecosystem* (i.e., partners need to adopt the innovation).

Developed as part of the Horizon 2020 Big Data Value (BDV) project, the DDI framework is grounded in scientific research and empirical data. It has been refined through the examination of over 90 data-driven business opportunities, ensuring its relevance and effectiveness in supporting data-driven innovation.

This framework is now widely used by the BDV Public-Private Partnership, as well as by data-driven start-ups, SMEs, and large corporations during project workshops. It consists of the DDI Canvas, DDI Navigator, and DDI Tools, offering users structured guidance in systematically evaluating relevant variables across both the supply and demand sides of data-driven innovation (https://ddi-canvas.com/how/). Through the DDI Canvas, stakeholders can methodically explore all pertinent aspects, facilitating a comprehensive understanding of the innovation landscape and informing strategic decision-making.

In sum, in this section we analyzed the literature background concerning the perception of data as an asset, their monetization and the issues that could affect it, and, alongside the explication of the research question, we introduced the DDI Canvas which is a framework for defining data-driven innovation business model. In the next section, we will examine the case study of Hudi.

The Case of Hudi: Human Data Income

Theoretical Sampling: Why Hudi?

Following previous studies based on a single case study (Ferrigno, Zordan, and Di Minin, 2022), in this book chapter we have selected Hudi as representative case study for three reasons. First, Hudi (Human Data Income Ltd.) is a data monetization decentralized platform, which enables individuals and businesses to gather, enrich, exchange and monetize their personal data.

Second, Hudi exploits the increasing digital leverage to create a universal basic income generated by the economic value of users' data and by the market itself. As such, Hudi collects, aggregates data and redistributes control and value to the users by means of Web3 technologies, such as cryptocurrencies and blockchain.

Third, Hudi works as a data bank where the individual user decides whether and which data to share with the organizations that request it, in exchange for a royalty. Hudi's users create a data wallet which generate value assets by means of cryptocurrencies, while the aim of Hudi is building the first universal income based on data by redistributing up to 75% of the transactions to all stakeholders, and 50% to the data owner. Typically, data brokers extract data from individuals and companies to resell to other companies, extracting value from the data and making a profit without redistributing it to users, while Hudi's mission is to create a protocol for data management by creating a free and open market based on 3 principles: transparency, control, and remuneration. Hudi allows users to create a profile with all the data of their choice, bringing together in a single place all the data they already have on platforms such as Facebook, Google, Netflix, etc. In this way, a unique and complete data profile is created that no other company has, and those who want it must go through Hudi and pay a fee. Hudi will therefore profit from this process of extracting value from the data, which in turn will remunerate the users, the owners of these data profiles.

History and Development

Hudi was founded in 2017 as a startup in London, UK by Francesco Ballarani (CEO), Gianluigi Ballarani (CMO), and Andrea Silvi (CTO) as a project that wants to generate income from personal data. Hudi's founders and users built together a decentralized platform, and this participatory spirit of users was a key factor for the success of the company. The launch of Hudi was based on the idea of allowing users to let others know about Hudi, hence using a decentralized marketing strategy. In fact, during the launch, anyone who spread the word about Hudi through various actions was remunerated with Hudi Tokens. The Hudi Token (HUDI) is a utility token created on the Binance Smart Chain blockchain for on-chain data exchange and monetization. It follows the BEP-20 standard.

The company, though founded in 2017, launched in 2021 with the HUDI Presale on September 10th and the IDO on Pancake swap on September 15th. In October and November were activated the Active Data Monetization Online (BETA) and the Ambassador Program, while in 2022 were introduced new data sources in Q1, Q2, and Q3, such as Binance, Coinbase, Facebook, Google, LinkedIn, Netflix, Reddit, and TikTok. In Q4 the HUDI Protocol (Alpha) was released as well as the first data providers on the protocol. For what concerns the 2023 Q1, HUDI Ad network and DataSwap were presented.

Nowadays, the company offers Decentralized Finance (De-Fi) solutions to data owners, including staking, liquidity providing, and lending, which revolve around Hudi dApp.

Hudi dApp is a wallet aggregator, where users can access their Crypto Wallet, Data Wallet, and Crypto Cashback. The Crypto Wallet allows users to buy, receive, send, and handle Hudi tokens, while the Data Wallet collects data to later exchange them to obtain earnings. Then, the Crypto cashback empowers people to earn Hudi tokens from many shops online. Moreover, the Hudi dApp works as an aggregated feed to converge contents from different social media and platforms, as an internal browser, and a chat to connect friends and brands that want to reach the user.

Hudi also developed DataMask to protect data and earn crypto, which is an extension that gives users control over their data and monetizes them. DataMask securely saves data, and it helps accessing a variety of revenue streams. Beyond that, it blocks cookies, third-party trackers, and pop-ups, ads, obnoxious banners, and other invasive/undesirable advertising.

The ultimate aim, however, is the formation of a Decentralized Autonomous Organisation (DAO), which is defined as "a new organization form that the management and operational rules are typically encoded on blockchain in the form of smart contracts and can autonomously operate without centralized control or third-party intervention" (Wang et al., 2019, p. 870). This new organization form represents an evolution of limited company, where all Hudi Token holders, not just the owner, can make decisions.

Data Collection

This section is aimed at the collection of data regarding Hudi. Interviews and secondary data will be presented.

Interviews

The interviews were conducted on May 26th, 2023, with Francesco Ballarani (CEO and co-founder) and Andrea Silvi (CTO and co-founder). The interviews lasted 1 hour each. In the following we provided the questions done and the insights of the specific answers.

1. What is Hudi?

The CEO of the company explains that Hudi is a simple concept rooted in users' generation of data on the internet. Data is the fuel for technology and technological innovation, hence the idea to bring back to the people the ownership of their data and empowering them to join the data market being rightful owners of their data. The data industry is a market valuing more than a trillion-dollar industry each year also understanding data brokerage, market research, and digital advertising. Indeed, every minute more than one million dollars of people's data is being sold and bought by companies.

2. How was the idea to create Hudi born?

The CEO and co-founder of Hudi answers that he had always worked with data in the private investigation and intelligence sector, and in 2010 started studying digital marketing. As time passed, he discovered even more the importance of data and information in relation with digital platforms, such as Google, Amazon, Facebook, etc. He states that data allow to target definite people and advertise specific products and services, while the data market is a closed market, and data is being collected and exploited. Since 2017, the founders started working on the technological side of data and began working on Hudi.

The founders of Hudi are building both an infrastructure and a specific protocol that allows people to own their data. In fact, the company's CEO states that users of Hudi can own cryptocurrencies in a data wallet, they are able to own their data and then access the data market.

3. How did Hudi develop?

To enable users to take part in the data industry, Hudi's founders think in a decentralized way, without intermediaries and platforms. They developed a peer-to-peer data storage and exchange protocol called "Interplanetary Data Wallet" which was developed by Hudi's CTO and cofounder, which aims at turning data into value assets.

4. Which is Hudi's approach with data and how difficult it was to overcome privacy concerns?

According to Hudi's CTO, the main revolution of the European Union GDPR is the legal part of data meaning that companies must be compliant while using data and letting users accept terms of use. Indeed, the data protocol is something that makes the users aware of how data will be shared with data partners, and all data transactions will involve users' authorization. Hudi is not acting as a data broker, rather it uses a website compliant with a protocol to act as a data provider and as a connector amongst users and companies. The approach of data collection for Hudi is human-centric, and the collection and monetization of data are driven by user interactions.

Indeed, Hudi works closely with GDPR and is developing new technologies to empower people to collect all their data scattered in platforms, and to ask companies to delete data under users' request. No value is assigned to data by Hudi itself because it does not work as a data broker, it acts as an enabling technology to monetize data. Hudi's plan – explains the company's CEO - is to allow people to collect their data using the GDPR and then wipe these data from other services, making companies who are in need of certain users' data to come to users themselves and pay them directly for the asset they want to buy.

5. How was DataMask developed to deal with privacy?

The DataMask Chrome extension is key for the full ecosystem because it links the data wallet to internet browsing, making users earn by surfing online. It is the first Chrome extension provided by humandataincome.com that allows users to get remunerations while browsing the internet.

It works also by blocking unwanted advertising and allowing people to give permission to trusted websites only. Among its features, it blocks pop-ups, ads, annoying banners, cookies, and third-party trackers, protects users' privacy while allowing them to earn while surfing the internet by a passive earning, letting HUDI work while normally browsing. Hudi's CTO explains that the company has no data stored in their servers and has no access to users' personal data. The founders decided to design a protocol by considering each data transaction as a transaction that will have a history in the users' personal wallet. Hence, users have transparency with everything that happens with this data inside of the data wallet in the same way they do with crypto. Moreover, DataMask users can have a password manager with an extension that enables interaction between the protocol and the webpage, while data is stored on the users' wallet exclusively.

6. Which are the next steps for the development of the company? Which are the ongoing projects?

Hudi's founders started with an idea to monetize data, later they developed the economic and crypto sides and finally started to build the technology to make all this possible. At the time of the interviews, Hudi finished Phase 1 of the company's launch, which culminated in the first centralized exchange listing. This means that Hudi is now a proper crypto and has both a centralized and a decentralized exchange. The company is working on peer-to-peer protocol and Datamask. It is an application that empowers the ecosystem and can compete with specific products. Indeed, the goal for user acquisition is through Datamask and the idea is to make a profitable fund. With the protocol and the Hudi token, the company aims at opening the Hudi venture and will start helping people and businesses to build both on the data and the crypto side on top of the protocol. In 2022, the company got a crypto exchange license, and they are developing the technologies for the exchange. Then, Hudi will focus on Datamask as a software services startup and on building the Hudi protocol DataMask will focus on growth, customer acquisition, and improving customers' lifetime value, ecosystem development, and data monetization.

Furthermore, the Hudi token will be a grant that companies receive without reselling into the market, and at the same time will be the most important asset a data startup needs, being data and attention. Thus, Hudi for the future aims at launching DataMask V2 and making it profitable to scale up advertising and build applications on the top of Hudi.

7. How important is users' network for Hudi?

Users are the most important part of Hudi, explains its CTO. Initially, the startup took the classic big data approach by focusing on how people share data to later collect it in centralized or distributed servers that rely on multiple databases to manage this huge stream of data. Nowadays, Hudi has reached 300,000 users and solved the Search Engine Optimization (SEO) problem by developing a peer-to-peer protocol, Interplanetary Data Wallet, where the user (data owner) has a data wallet and is able to interact with the data buyer. This protocol is a storage that does not rely on a single database, but on all devices connected among them. SEO problems affect internet users because they have their data scattered in infinite servers, not interconnected among them. The main focus of Hudi is creating value out of data. Indeed, during data transactions, there can also be a Binance transaction, where the data buyers can incentivize users to share data with them. The data wallet will manage the infrastructure to manage the data being shared in the peer-to-peer network. In addition, Hudi also developed connectors to standardize these transactions in its protocol, and made it completely open source, as also the data wallet.

8. How is the value exchange between crypto and real money decided? Which are the criteria for this value exchange?

The demand and offer decide the real value of an asset, explains the company's CTO. Everything is linked by how much is produced and quantity willing to be bought of a certain asset. Hudi decided to go for crypto currencies because it is a lean process. Hudi works in the blockchain world as it is easier to have a stream of value in the digital world. In fact, all the currencies (euro, dollar, etc.) are priced on relative assets, while cryptocurrencies are linked, and the main asset is Bitcoin.

Secondary Data

In this section, we provide further details about Hudi that come from secondary data sources

The founders, by working on their other lead generation company Hotlead in the digital marketing and performance field, came across the problem of targeting people with marketing without giving them the proper credit for their data. Hudi was founded in 2017 as a startup, meaning that the founders had to rely on their capital to make the project grow, and initially, it started as a browser to collect browsing data. Then, with marketing automation, cookies became a positioning problem, and the entire ecosystem was affected. With Hudi, users themselves are enabled to decide to share information, whether actively or passively and to create a profile on the platform. In this way they become part of the revenue ecosystem, being recognized for the economic value of sharing such data. In such manner, users become an active part of a project that turns data into income and are part of the whole economic process behind their data, not just as end-users as they were used to.

Working on Hudi, the founders recognized that nowadays the world of data is highly decentralized, where very few important players can have oligopoly positions in the market due to data usage. Thus, data monetization became part of payments, given that new regulations on the digital market were introduced and the economic counter value became explicit. Therefore, Hudi's aim was to create infrastructures and market tools to move data with user awareness and transparency, managed by regulations and giving back the value that these data generate to the users themselves.

Hudi gives users the possibility to have their own profile on the platform and ensure they receive 50% of revenues managed from the targeted content collected through their profiles. It must be considered also that from the remaining 50% cost must be deducted, and 20% of the revenues must go to the data provider. About this matter, Hudi aims at integrating media and making available to users the management and monetization of their data, sensitizing them about the economic value of their data.

Data Analysis

A Confirmatory Approach

To analyze the massive amount of data we collected about Hudi, we employed a confirmatory approach (Ferrigno & Cucino, 2021; Ferrigno, Del Sarto, Cucino, and Piccaluga, 2022). In fact, data analysis through a confirmatory approach refers to a specific methodology employed to test predetermined theories, with the aim of giving a greater understanding of the topic that revolves around turning data into value assets. In this way, the research question "How to capture value from big data?" will be answered, and the results from the study on Hudi will be presented.

The case of Hudi demonstrates the potential for innovative business models for big data companies that aim at monetizing on data, hence creating and capturing value. Thanks to the interviews conducted and the data collected, insights on such an innovative company were gained and some of the key factors for capturing value from big data can be explained. In fact, big data's potential must first be understood to be used for its full potential, and the founders of Hudi have an extensive background in the digital field. Useful information, better decision-making, and improved client experiences can offer valuable insights, and Hudi captures the value to convert it into profit and make data owners gain from something they have always owned but never got the chance to monetize on it. Hudi is a concrete example on how data may be used by businesses to boost innovation and find new revenue sources. Moreover, individuals may monetize their personal data thanks to their innovative business model, which changes the balance of power and ensures fair remuneration.

As was deeply explained by the company's founders, they developed a platform that harnesses the potential of big data while preserving privacy and consent by giving individuals control over their data. Analyzing Hudi, it is possible to see how organizations constantly need to gain accurate insights into their consumers' interests and habits. This is because in this way, businesses may create customized experiences and forge closer relationships with customers by evaluating consumer data and tailoring their offerings in terms of goods, services, and marketing tactics. For this reason, they are prone to pay for that, and through Hudi users themselves can earn from this, capturing value from their own data. It was also shown that through open-source activities and cooperating within an ecosystem value capture from big data can be improved and major value can be created out of that. In this way, by exchanging data and insights, innovation may be fostered inside the ecosystem, new possibilities for value capture may be found and synergies unlocked. Analyzing in depth the value capture process for Hudi, it can be said that the company has disrupted the status quo of traditional data monetization by focusing on fair users' compensation and data ownership.

Overall, and coherently with the insights gathered from the literature background section, the experiences of Hudi provide insight into the changing environment of big data value capture and data monetization. Their activities serve as a reminder of the value of data ownership, openness, and fair remuneration. In fact, by stressing ethical standards, rethinking data monetization tactics, and fostering consumer and data owner trust, enterprises may benefit from the lessons learned.

DISCUSSION

An Application of DDI Canvas in Big Data Companies: The Case of Hudi

Big data has become a useful resource and an asset for enterprises, providing previously unattainable insights and chances for innovation (Acciarini et al., 2023; Cappa et al., 2021; Del Vecchio et al., 2018; Urbinati et al., 2019). Businesses require specific capabilities and the adoption of peculiar business models to fully realize the promise of big data (Acciarini et al., 2023; Johnon et al., 2017). A formal framework is offered by the DDI Canvas for defining, examining, and improving a company's data-driven innovation in big data companies (Zillner, 2021a; Zillner, 2021b).

This chapter examines the business model used in big data businesses, concentrating on the case of Hudi, showing its importance in comprehending and improving those businesses' operations. What emerges from this analysis is that big data enables both new and established businesses to provide new value. The scoping of data-driven business prospects must consider a variety of viewpoints, from user demands, data availability, and technological capabilities to the sustainable formation of alliances and ecosystems, to capture these new sorts of values. The framework for data-driven innovation offers a tried-and-true technique for all participants in the BDV ecosystem to provide direction when examining and sizing up data-driven business prospects.

Starting from the DDI framework previously described, it will now be adapted to the case of Hudi populating the Canvas *ad hoc*, which will be shown in Figure 3.

Figure 3. Business model canvas (DDI framework) populated by the case of Hudi.

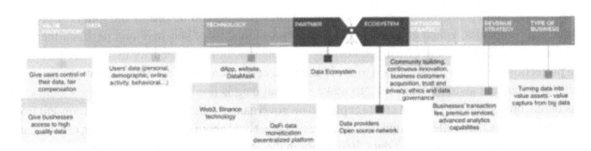

Hudi, like other big data businesses, provides a value proposition driven by data and capitalizes on Big Data, derived by the study of customers and data usage. It aims at giving back users control of their own data and assuring them fair compensation for their precious asset. Additionally, it allows businesses to have access to high-quality data, enhancing their ability to make better decisions and providing more individualized client experiences. To do that, they gather users' data, being it personal information, demographic, behavioral, and online activity data. The company works in a web3 environment through a Binance technology and has developed its website (https://humandataincome.com) and the dApp to operate, and the Chrome extension DataMask to ensure privacy. It cooperates with data providers and an open-source network, all inside the data ecosystem. Its network strategy revolves around community building, continuous innovation, and business customers acquisition, and has as pillars trust and privacy, ethics, and proper data governance. Its revenue strategy comes from various sources such as businesses' transaction fee, premium services offered, and advanced analytics capabilities. Finally, Hudi's type of business is about turning data into value assets through value capturing from big data.

Big data enables both new and established businesses to provide new value. The scoping of data driven business prospects must take a variety of factors into account to capture these new sorts of value, from user demands, data availability, and technological capabilities to the sustainable creation of partnerships and ecosystems. The framework for data-driven innovation offers a tried-and-true technique for all participants in the BDV ecosystem to provide direction when examining and sizing up data-driven business prospects.

Key Implications for Big Data Companies

In the contemporary digital era, big data has emerged as a key resource for companies operating across several industries. To encourage innovation, improve decision-making, and increase operational performance, substantial amounts of data may be acquired, processed, and insights can be generated from them. But using big data effectively has important ramifications for businesses.

The requirement for businesses to build strong data infrastructure and analytics skills is one of the major effects of big data. Large volumes, rapid data flow, and a variety of data types are all included in big data, which calls for innovative technology and tools to handle and process. As shown in the practical case, to manage big data and extract value from it, a business has to invest in scalable storage systems, strong processing frameworks, and advanced analytics platforms. The business should also be comprised of a team of data scientists, analysts, and engineers who have professional know-how in the area of data administration and analysis to fully leverage the power of big data. The value of data security and privacy is yet another conclusion. Protection of consumer data should be one of the foremost policies of big data companies, which collect and store enormous amounts of sensitive and personal information, for maintaining consumer trust and keeping with the law. In-depth security measures concerning data protection should be implemented to avoid illegal access or breaches by way of encryption, access limits, and frequent audits. Meanwhile, to make sure that data is used responsibly, and that ethics are considered, businesses will have to create explicit data governance policies and obtain valid consent from people whose data they collect. Companies may learn a great deal about consumer behavior, choices, and requirements by studying customer data. It gives them the ability to customize their offerings, services, and marketing initiatives for specific clients, increasing client happiness and loyalty. Real-time analytics may also help businesses deliver tailored experiences, targeted marketing, and personalized suggestions, further increasing client engagement and fostering expansion.

Furthermore, big data gives up new opportunities for innovation and new business models. Big data contains a plethora of information in which apparent patterns, trends, and relationships may be unknown. Such insight can be used by businesses to create new products, services, and solutions that could serve emerging markets or solve intractable problems. Big data may also help businesses explore new avenues for income by allowing them to provide data-driven goods, information, or services to third parties. This change from conventional to data-driven business models may open new prospects for expansion and competitiveness. Nevertheless, big data also comes with difficulties and moral dilemmas that businesses must solve. The importance of privacy problems, data breaches, and the possibility of algorithmic biases must all be carefully considered. A corporation must solve the hurdles relating to people, technology, and organizational domains to use big data as a tool for enhancing organizational performance.

CONCLUSION

The present book chapter provides a comprehensive exploration of the concept of data monetization and value capturing, focusing on the innovative case of Hudi. Through an in-depth analysis of the theoretical background, issues affecting data monetization and the application of the DDI Canvas in big data companies, this analysis has shed light on the transformative potential of turning data into valuable assets.

In the theoretical background section were presented the basis for understanding the value of data as an asset and the idea of data monetization by exploring how data has evolved into a strategic resource for businesses, as well as the potential and problems involved in gaining value from big data. Moreover, we also addressed the need for innovative strategies to fully realize the potential of data by solving challenges limiting data monetization, such as privacy concerns and technological constraints.

The Hudi case section provides a thorough analysis of its early stages, history, and data-gathering techniques. Hudi also helped to answer the research question of this chapter by collecting data, conducting interviews, and offering valuable insights, followed by a confirmatory data analysis approach. The examination of the results and their implications for big data organizations was the primary focus of the last section, discussing the findings about implementing the DDI Canvas in big data organizations and focusing on Hudi's one through a DDI framework.

The company provides a value proposition driven by data and capitalizes on Big Data from the study of customers and data usage. Their approach is aimed at giving back users control of their own data and assuring them a fair compensation for their valuable asset. Moreover, Hudi allows businesses to have access to high-quality data, enhancing their ability to improve the decision-making process and providing better individualized client experiences. The company cooperates with data providers and an open-source network, all inside the data ecosystem. Its network strategy revolves around community building, continuous innovation, and business customers acquisition, and has as pillars trust and privacy, ethics, and proper data governance. Its revenue strategy comes from various sources such as businesses' transaction fee, premium services offered, and advanced analytics capabilities. Finally, Hudi's type of business is about turning data into value assets through value capturing from big data.

In line with the peculiarity of the single case study, further research could better explore examples of a similar approach, like Datum (https://datum.org/), Ocean Protocol (https://oceanprotocol.com/), Streamr (https://streamr.network/), and Brave Browser (https://brave.com/). Moreover, alongside the giant cases of Google, Amazon, Microsoft and Meta, further research could investigate cases of data monetization from smaller enterprises and startups, like the case of Kode (https://www.kode-solutions .net/), and the ecosystems related to BDV (https://www.big-data-value.eu/wp-content/uploads/2020/ 03/BDVE-D3.8_Startups-and-SME-Ecosystem-characterization-v1.0-FINAL_withAnnexes.pdf) and SoBigData (http://www.sobigdata.eu/).

In conclusion, this chapter offered a thorough examination of converting data into valuable assets, with an emphasis on the Hudi case. The theoretical literature, empirical studies, and use of the DDI Canvas has all been used to obtain insights into the potentialities of data monetization. The findings emphasize the significance of acknowledging data as a strategic asset, the requirement for new business models, and the ethical issues surrounding data ownership and use. Thus, by presenting a theoretical framework and useful insights via the case of Hudi, this chapter advances acknowledgments of data monetization in the context of big data firms. Overall, as the data economy keeps advancing, the lessons acquired from Hudi can direct future endeavors in turning data into value assets and shaping the future of the data-driven world.

REFERENCES

Acciarini, C., Cappa, F., Boccardelli, P., & Oriani, R. (2023). How can organizations leverage big data to innovate their business models? A systematic literature review. *Technovation*, 123, 102713. DOI: 10.1016/j.technovation.2023.102713

Akter, S., Bandara, R. J., & Sajib, S. (2021). How to empower analytics capability to tackle emergency situations? *International Journal of Operations & Production Management*, 41(9), 1469–1494. DOI: 10.1108/IJOPM-11-2020-0805

Bai, C., Zhou, H., & Sarkis, J. (2023). Evaluating Industry 4.0 technology and sustainable development goals–a social perspective. *International Journal of Production Research*, 61(23), 8094–8114. DOI: 10.1080/00207543.2022.2164375

Bram, J. T., Warwick-Clark, B., Obeysekare, E., & Mehta, K. (2015). Utilization and monetization of healthcare data in developing countries. *Big Data*, 3(2), 59–66. DOI: 10.1089/big.2014.0053 PMID: 26487984

Calic, G., & Ghasemaghaei, M. (2021). Big data for social benefits: Innovation as a mediator of the relationship between big data and corporate social performance. *Journal of Business Research*, 131, 391–401. DOI: 10.1016/j.jbusres.2020.11.003

California Consumer Privacy Act (CCPA). https://oag.ca.gov/privacy/ccpa/regs

Cappa, F. (2022). Big data from customers and non-customers through crowdsourcing, citizen science and crowdfunding. *Journal of Knowledge Management*, 26(11), 308–323. DOI: 10.1108/JKM-11-2021-0871

Cappa, F., Oriani, R., Peruffo, E., & McCarthy, I. (2021). Big data for creating and capturing value in the digitalized environment: Unpacking the effects of volume, variety, and veracity on firm performance. *Journal of Product Innovation Management*, 38(1), 49–67. DOI: 10.1111/jpim.12545

Chang, V. (2021). An ethical framework for big data and smart cities. *Technological Forecasting and Social Change*, 165, 1–11. DOI: 10.1016/j.techfore.2020.120559

Del Vecchio, P., Di Minin, A., Petruzzelli, M., Panniello, U., & Pirri, S. (2018). Big data for open innovation in SMEs and large corporations: Trends, opportunities, and challenges. *Creativity and Innovation Management*, 27(1), 6–22. DOI: 10.1111/caim.12224

Dell'Era, C., Di Minin, A., Ferrigno, G., Frattini, F., Landoni, P., & Verganti, R. (2020). Value capture in open innovation processes with radical circles: A qualitative analysis of firms' collaborations with Slow Food, Memphis, and Free Software Foundation. *Technological Forecasting and Social Change*, 158, 120128. DOI: 10.1016/j.techfore.2020.120128

Deslée, A., & Cloarec, J. (2024). Safeguarding Privacy: Ethical Considerations in Data-Driven Marketing. In Matosas-López, L. (Ed.), *The Impact of Digitalization on Current Marketing Strategies* (pp. 147–161). Emerald Publishing Limited., DOI: 10.1108/978-1-83753-686-320241009

Dubey, R., Gunasekaran, A., Childe, S. J., Blome, C., & Papadopoulos, T. (2019). Big data and predictive analytics and manufacturing performance: Integrating institutional theory, resource-based view and big data culture. *British Journal of Management*, 30(2), 341–361. DOI: 10.1111/1467-8551.12355

Enkel, E., Bogers, M., & Chesbrough, H. (2020). Exploring open innovation in the digital age: A maturity model and future research directions. *R & D Management*, 50(1), 161–168. DOI: 10.1111/radm.12397

Erevelles, S., Fukawa, N., & Swayne, L. (2016). Big Data consumer analytics and the transformation of marketing. *Journal of Business Research*, 69(2), 897–904. DOI: 10.1016/j.jbusres.2015.07.001

European Data Market Study 2021-2023. https://digital-strategy.ec.europa.eu/en/library/results-new -european-data-market-study-2021-2023

Faroukhi, A. Z., El Alaoui, I., Gahi, Y., & Amine, A. (2020a). Big data monetization throughout Big Data Value Chain: A comprehensive review. *Journal of Big Data*, 7(1), 1–22. DOI: 10.1186/s40537-019-0281-5

Faroukhi, A. Z., El Alaoui, I., Gahi, Y., & Amine, A. (2020b). An adaptable big data value chain framework for end-to-end big data monetization. *Big Data and cognitive computing*, 4(4), 34. https://doi.org/ DOI: 10.3390/bdcc4040034

Ferrigno, G., Barabuffi, S., Marcazzan, E., & Piccaluga, A. (2024, October). What "V" of the big data influence SMEs' open innovation breadth and depth? An empirical analysis. *R & D Management*, radm.12727. DOI: 10.1111/radm.12727

Ferrigno, G., Crupi, A., Di Minin, A., & Ritala, P. (2023). 50+ years of R&D Management: A retrospective synthesis and new research trajectories. *R & D Management*, 53(5), 900–926. DOI: 10.1111/radm.12592

Ferrigno, G., & Cucino, V. (2021). Innovating and transforming during COVID-19: Insights from Italian firms. *R & D Management*, 51(4), 325–338. DOI: 10.1111/radm.12469

Ferrigno, G., Del Sarto, N., Cucino, V., & Piccaluga, A. (2022). Connecting organizational learning and open innovation research: An integrative framework and insights from case studies of strategic alliances. *The Learning Organization*, 29(6), 615–634. DOI: 10.1108/TLO-03-2021-0030

Ferrigno, G., Del Sarto, N., Piccaluga, A., & Baroncelli, A. (2023). Industry 4.0 base technologies and business models: A bibliometric analysis. *European Journal of Innovation Management*, 26(7), 502–526. DOI: 10.1108/EJIM-02-2023-0107

Ferrigno, G., Martin, X., & Dagnino, G. B. (2024). Explaining the interplay of value creation and value appropriation in strategic alliances: A developmental perspective. *International Journal of Management Reviews*, 26(2), 232–253. DOI: 10.1111/ijmr.12351

Ferrigno, G., Zordan, A., & Di Minin, A. (2022). The emergence of dominant design in the early automotive industry: An historical analysis of Ford's technological experimentation from 1896 to 1906. *Technology Analysis and Strategic Management*, ●●●, 1–12. DOI: 10.1080/09537325.2022.2074386

Firouzi, F., Farahani, B., Barzegari, M., & Daneshmand, M. (2020). AI-driven data monetization: The other face of data in IoT-based smart and connected health. *IEEE Internet of Things Journal*, 9(8), 5581–5599. DOI: 10.1109/JIOT.2020.3027971

Frisk, J. E., & Bannister, F. (2017). Improving the use of analytics and big data by changing the decision-making culture: A design approach. *Management Decision*, 55(10), 2074–2088. DOI: 10.1108/MD-07-2016-0460

General Data Protection Regulation (GDPR). https://eur-lex.europa.eu/eli/reg/2016/679/oj

Ghasemaghaei, M. (2021). Understanding the impact of big data on firm performance: The necessity of conceptually differentiating among big data characteristics. *International Journal of Information Management*, 57, 102055. DOI: 10.1016/j.ijinfomgt.2019.102055

Ghasemaghaei, M., & Calic, G. (2019a). Does big data enhance firm innovation competency? The mediating role of data-driven insights. *Journal of Business Research*, 104, 69–84. DOI: 10.1016/j.jbusres.2019.07.006

Ghasemaghaei, M., & Calic, G. (2019b). Can big data improve firm decision quality? The role of data quality and data diagnosticity. *Decision Support Systems*, 120, 38–49. DOI: 10.1016/j.dss.2019.03.008

Ghasemaghaei, M., & Calic, G. (2020). Assessing the impact of big data on firm innovation performance: Big data is not always better data. *Journal of Business Research*, 108, 147–162. DOI: 10.1016/j.jbusres.2019.09.062

Herschel, R., & Miori, V. M. (2017). Ethics & Big Data. *Technology in Society*, 49, 31–36. DOI: 10.1016/j.techsoc.2017.03.003

Johnson, J. S., Friend, S. B., & Lee, H. S. (2017). Big Data Facilitation, Utilization, and Monetization: Exploring the 3Vs in a New Product Development Process. *Journal of Product Innovation Management*, 34(5), 640–658. DOI: 10.1111/jpim.12397

Mahmood, S., Chadhar, M., & Firmin, S. (2024). Digital resilience framework for managing crisis: A qualitative study in the higher education and research sector. *Journal of Contingencies and Crisis Management*, 32(1), e12549. DOI: 10.1111/1468-5973.12549

Massa, L., Tucci, C. L., & Afuah, A. (2017). A critical assessment of business model research. *The Academy of Management Annals*, 11(1), 73–104. DOI: 10.5465/annals.2014.0072

McAfee, A., Brynjolfsson, E., Davenport, T. H., Patil, D. J., & Barton, D. (2012). Big data: The management revolution. *Harvard Business Review*, 90(10), 60–68. https://hbr.org/2012/10/big-data-the-management-revolution PMID: 23074865

Messeni Petruzzelli, A., Murgia, G., & Parmentola, A. (2022). How can open innovation support SMEs in the adoption of I4. 0 technologies? An empirical analysis. *R & D Management*, 52(4), 615–632. DOI: 10.1111/radm.12507

Mikalef, P., Boura, M., Lekakos, G., & Krogstie, J. (2019). Big data analytics capabilities and innovation: The mediating role of dynamic capabilities and moderating effect of the environment. *British Journal of Management*, 30(2), 272–298. DOI: 10.1111/1467-8551.12343

Najjar, M. S., & Kettinger, W. J. (2013). Data Monetization: Lessons from a Retailer's Journey. *MIS Quarterly Executive*, 12(4). https://digitalcommons.memphis.edu/facpubs/11054

Ofulue, J., & Benyoucef, M. (2022). Data monetization: insights from a technology-enabled literature review and research agenda. *Management Review Quarterly*, 1-45. https://doi.org/DOI: 10.1007/s11301-022-00309-1

Osterwalder, A., & Pigneur, Y. (2010). *Business Model Generation*. John Wiley and Sons.

PwC. (2019). *Putting value on data*. https://www.pwc.co.uk/data-analytics/documents/putting-value-on-data.pdf

Quach, S., Thaichon, P., Martin, K. D., Weaven, S., & Palmatier, R. W. (2022). Digital technologies: Tensions in privacy and data. *Journal of the Academy of Marketing Science*, 50(6), 1299–1323. DOI: 10.1007/s11747-022-00845-y PMID: 35281634

Ritala, P., Keränen, J., Fishburn, J., & Ruokonen, M. (2024). Selling and monetizing data in B2B markets: Four data-driven value propositions. *Technovation*, 130, 102935. DOI: 10.1016/j.technovation.2023.102935

Saggi, M. K., & Jain, S. (2018). A survey towards an integration of big data analytics to big insights for value-creation. *Information Processing & Management*, 54(5), 758–790. DOI: 10.1016/j.ipm.2018.01.010

Scholz, T. (2016). *Platform cooperativism. Challenging the corporate sharing economy*. New York, NY: Rosa Luxemburg Foundation, 436. https://rosalux.nyc/wp-content/uploads/2020/11/RLS-NYC_platformcoop.pdf

Sjödin, D., Parida, V., Jovanovic, M., & Visnjic, I. (2020). Value creation and value capture alignment in business model innovation: A process view on outcome-based business models. *Journal of Product Innovation Management*, 37(2), 158–183. DOI: 10.1111/jpim.12516

Teece, D. J., & Linden, G. (2017). Business models, value capture, and the digital enterprise. *Journal of organization design*, 6, 1-14. https://doi.org/DOI: 10.1186/s41469-017-0018-x

Trabucchi, D., & Buganza, T. (2019). Data-driven innovation: Switching the perspective on Big Data. *European Journal of Innovation Management*, 22(1), 23–40. DOI: 10.1108/EJIM-01-2018-0017

Urbinati, A., Bogers, M., Chiesa, V., & Frattini, F. (2019). Creating and capturing value from Big Data: A multiple-case study analysis of provider companies. *Technovation*, 84, 21–36. DOI: 10.1016/j.technovation.2018.07.004

Wamba, S. F., Akter, S., Edwards, A., Chopin, G., & Gnanzou, D. (2015). How 'big data'can make big impact: Findings from a systematic review and a longitudinal case study. *International Journal of Production Economics*, 165, 234–246. DOI: 10.1016/j.ijpe.2014.12.031

Wang, S., Ding, W., Li, J., Yuan, Y., Ouyang, L., & Wang, F. Y. (2019). Decentralized autonomous organizations: Concept, model, and applications. *IEEE Transactions on Computational Social Systems*, 6(5), 870–878. DOI: 10.1109/TCSS.2019.2938190

Wixom, B. H., & Ross, J. W. (2017). How to monetize your data. *MIT Sloan Management Review*, 58(3), 9–13. DOI: 10.7551/mitpress/11633.003.0009

Woroch, R., & Strobel, G. (2022). Show me the Money: How to monetize data in data-driven business models? *Wirtschaftsinformatik, Proceedings*, 13. https://aisel.aisnet.org/wi2022/digital_business_models/digital_business_models/13

Zillner, S. (2021a). Business models and ecosystem for big data. In Curry, E., Metzger, A., Zillner, S., Pazzaglia, J. C., & García Robles, A. (Eds.), *The Elements of Big Data Value: Foundations of the Research and Innovation Ecosystem* (pp. 269–288). Springer International Publishing., DOI: 10.1007/978-3-030-68176-0_11

Zillner, S. (2021b). Innovation in Times of Big Data and AI: Introducing the Data-Driven Innovation (DDI) Framework. In Curry, E., Metzger, A., Zillner, S., Pazzaglia, J. C., & García Robles, A. (Eds.), *The Elements of Big Data Value: Foundations of the Research and Innovation Ecosystem* (pp. 289–310). Springer International Publishing., DOI: 10.1007/978-3-030-68176-0_12

KEY TERMS AND DEFINITIONS

Big Data: Large amounts of data available in the contemporary digital environment.

Business Model: Description of how an organization functions.

Data Monetization: Process of extracting economic value from data.

Data Monetization Issues: Issues (e.g., privacy, ethical and legal considerations) related with the process of data monetization.

Value Capture: techniques and strategies used by companies to translate the value they create into revenues.

Data-Driven Innovation Framework: framework that aids entrepreneurs in evaluating practical data-driven business opportunities by systematically analyzing the interplay between supply and demand dynamics.

Data-Driven Innovation Canvas: main outcome of the Data-driven innovation framework that focuses on business modelling.

Hudi: a data monetization decentralized platform, which enables individuals and businesses to gather, enrich, exchange and monetize their personal data.

Chapter 13
Unlocking Financial Potential:
How ML Recommendation Systems Are Transforming Banking and Finance

Amit Kakkar
Lovely Professional University, India

Manoj Goyal
https://orcid.org/0009-0006-1310-3211
Lovely Professional University, India

Dhrupad Mathur
S.P. Jain School of Global Management, Saudi Arabia

ABSTRACT

Machine learning recommendation systems are one of the best and most far-reaching utilisation of AI advances in business. These are the product instruments used to give ideas to clients based on their needs. Expansion in the number of choices, be it several online sites or several items, has made it hard for the client to look over many items. Today, there is no framework for banks to help relate to clients' monetary decisions and proposition them with applicable items according to their inclination before approaching the bank. Like some other businesses, monetary assistance seldom has any like, input, and perusing history to record evaluations of administrations. So, it becomes a test for constructing recommended systems for monetary administrations. The advantage of these recommended systems is that they give the customer better recommendations based on their savings, spending, and investment needs.

INTRODUCTION

The advent of AI/ML has resulted in the unprecedented growth of Fintech firms that help provide financial services to every individual. Moreover, Fintech firms are fueling the growth of digital lending, which is still in the early stages compared to traditional lending. However, digital lending has grown 12 times between 2017 and 2020, and the future is bright for digital services and fintech firms as the financial ecosystem is conducive to such growth. It is projected that total disbursements will reach INR 47.4 lakh crores by FY26, indicating a CAGR of 22%, when the disbursement figures are compared to

DOI: 10.4018/979-8-3693-3884-1.ch013

INR 21.6 lakh crores of FY22. The overall disbursements, including traditional and digital methods, are projected to expand at a CAGR of 12% during this period. The factors acting as the critical drivers for the digitalisation of the financial services sector in India are as follows:

- Socio-economic factors
- Growth of digital infrastructure (internet accessibility)
- Enabling public infrastructures
- Changing demographic trends
- Sitting of colossal customer data and availability of digital trails
- Rise in credit demand
- Increase in disposable income

The financial ecosystem in India is undergoing a complete transformation. It now provides personalised digital experiences and customised lending products. There is a strong emphasis on data security, identity protection, and fraud prevention. Additionally, there are opportunities for embedded financial products in all purchase channels. The entire lending process, from origination to servicing, is now conducted digitally. Connectivity and scalability are improved, and data is efficiently managed through micro-services architecture on the cloud. This has resulted in increased consumer trust and confidence in the lending journey. AI is helping the lending ecosystem of the financial sector.

Figure 1. Machine learning roles in banking

Prospecting	**Underwriting**	**Customer Support**	**Risk Management**
Utilise predictive analytics to proactively address consumer demands and promptly resolve queries.	Customise assistance to enhance the likelihood of loan approval from the beginning to the finalisation of the process.	Identify and evaluate consumer risk profiles, as well as their capacity to make payments, without relying solely on conventional credit scores or formal documentation procedures.	Anticipate and detect possible problems with a customer's upcoming payments in advance, prior to any payment failure.

Arthur Samuel, an early American forerunner in PC gaming and computerised reasoning, provided the term "Machine Learning" in 1959 while at IBM. He defined Machine learning as "the field of study that allows computers to learn without being explicitly programmed". Be that as it may, there is no generally acknowledged definition for Machine learning. The term is defined differently by different authors. Machine learning is modifying PCs to improve an exhibition model utilising model information or previous experience. The model is characterised as dependent upon certain boundaries, and learning is the execution of a PC program/model to enhance the boundaries of the model utilising the preparation information or previous experience. ML programs are models that help predict outcomes based on the inputs or help make predictions based on the acquired information.

Machine learning is the field that develops PC programs that can improve their performance based on the experience they gain during their deployment and usage. Machine learning is a subfield of artificial brainpower that includes the advancement of calculations and measurable models that empower PCs to work on their presentation in undertakings through experience. The models and algorithms are developed to make decisions or predictions based on the available data. As shown in Figure 1, AI/ML-based models can be used either for prospecting customers, approving loan applications in a few seconds, providing support to customers or managing the risks of the organisations by predicting loan defaults/fraudulent activities/bankruptcy. The models are developed so that they can improve their efficiency once deployed. Different types of AI/ML, such as managed, unaided, or support learning exist. Managed learning involves developing the model based on the labelled information, whereas unaided learning involves developing a model with unlabelled information. Support learning includes preparing a model through experimentation. Machine learning has other roles, similar to image and speech recognition, natural language processing and recommendation systems (RS). Based on the users' activities, the systems recommend products and services to the users. The recommender systems play a crucial role in helping individuals choose products from a wide range. The systems also recommend products based on the individuals' purchase history (Lu et al., 2015) and (Kouadria et al., 2020). Later, the application of RS was extended to different sectors like travel, online broadcasting, online articles and books (either scientific or news, like LIBRA, which is a book recommender system), online advertising and many more (Shi, Larson & Hanjalic, 2014). A recommender system is a programme designed to suggest the most appropriate products or services to a user (Beheshti et al., 2020). Its goal is to offer personalised services by retrieving the most relevant information and services from the vast amount of data collected on platforms such as open, private, social, and IoT (Internet of Things) data islands. Artificial Intelligence, encompassing Machine Learning, Deep Learning, and Natural Language Processing, along with knowledge representation (Beheshti et al., 2020), user experience technologies (Hassenzahl & Tractinsky, 2006), and crowdsourcing (Howe, 2006), possess the capability to revolutionise Recommender Systems.

Personalised experiences are offered to users, aiming to give a competitive edge to the merchants who have deployed AI-based systems. Personalisation works on the principle of offering personalised services to users based on their data available to merchants. AI/ML-based systems integrate the available data and provide unique personalised suggestions and recommendations to each individual (Winter et al., 2021). As companies and merchants have access to individual data, they can design personalised advertising campaigns based on individual personal data and purchase history. In terms of STP (segmentation, targeting and positioning), the companies and merchants can target individuals based on individual-specific advertising (Grigorios et al., 2022). AI-powered platforms provide consumers with the most pertinent and precise marketing suggestions (Habil et al., 2023).

Machine learning techniques are replacing conventional methods in several businesses these days. Applications based on machine learning began to enhance marketing activities in various sectors concurrently with these breakthroughs. ML models work on choosing a suitable algorithm, collecting and processing the data, and evaluating the results. The models are trained and tested on the available data.

Once training and testing are done, the deployment of the ML algorithms helps the individuals suggest products and services based on their preferences, previous decisions and personal data of the individuals.

Deploying AI-based algorithms in finance helps organisations improve their financial analysis, management, investment, fraud detection and money protection processes by simulating human decisions, intellect and activities. Machine learning algorithms find applications in finance, such as fraud detection, trading activity automation, recommending products based on customer demographic changes and investor financial advising services. With minimal programming, machine learning can quickly analyse millions of data sets for better results.

Recommendation systems are becoming more prudent in enhancing the satisfaction of individuals, as such systems provide personalised solutions and recommendations. The systems are designed to analyse vast volumes of data to understand the unique interests and behaviour of the individuals. On one side, personalised suggestions make individuals more satisfied. On the other hand, companies can also predict the suspicious activities/behaviours of individuals, such as loan payment defaults, fraudulent activities, investment decisions and other alerts related to financial activities. There are many benefits of machine learning, as shown in Figure2. Machine learning helps organisations make faster and more efficient decisions. The decisions are based on the data that is secured by the organisations. Quick decision-making boosts the revenue of the organisation. ML help the organisation decide on the disbursal of loans, enhancing the client's satisfaction. Satisfied clients will bring more business to organisations. Decisions based on the ML-based models being trained and tested on the vast data reduce the errors, and the models improve their performance based on the users' new data. As already elaborated, another facet of ML-based models is the customised and personalised offers for the users. As the ML-based models and programs provide customised and personalised suggestions and offerings to the users, the same results in improving the user experience. For example, Spotify understands the listening choices of the users and, based on the same, suggests the songs to the users.

Figure 2. Benefits of machine learning

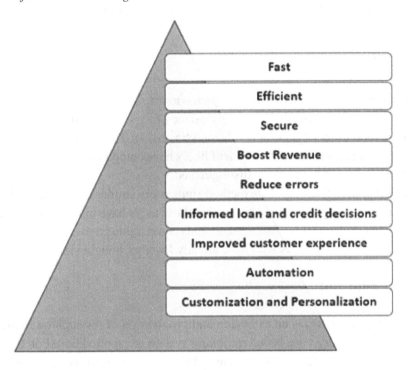

WHAT ARE MACHINE RECOMMENDER SYSTEMS?

Based on customer data and behaviour, Artificial Intelligence gives individualised proposals for financial services. AI helps perform tasks like transfers, payments and customer care enquiries, which are the banks' everyday chores. Furthermore, AI can also help speed up the acceptance and rejection of credit card and loan application processes. Recommender systems help decrease consumers' effort to search for products on e-commerce websites and online platforms (Resnick & Varian, 1997). Hanafizadeh et al. (2021) suggested a recommender system to monetise the intermediary platforms for the researchers. The recommendation system may examine a consumer's spending patterns and suggest a credit card with cashback benefits for expenditure categories, like groceries or petrol. Alternatively, it might suggest investment goods following a client's financial objectives and risk tolerance. Additionally, by using these technologies, banks and other financial service providers can better understand the requirements and preferences of their clients and modify their services accordingly. Recommender systems can potentially boost client loyalty and retention for banks and other financial institutions by offering tailored recommendations and enhancing the customer experience. The information gathered for case-based reasoning in the financial domain comprises asset classes, user characteristics, interest rates, profitability, past stock market information, and financial news from the media. Using this data, the recommender systems will become more reliable (Hernández et al., 2019). Numerous recommendation techniques exist, and like two sides of a coin, they have benefits and problems. Collaborative filtering and content-based filtering are discussed beforehand. These systems can suggest personalised solutions in the banking and financial services industry by suggesting financial products and services based on a customer's spending habits, credit history, and other pertinent information.

Collaborative Filtering

Collaborative filtering checks user likings and behaviour to search user shifts and resemblances. The remarking feature of collaborative filtering is its tendency to give recommendations by aggregation of information from several users (Ryngksai & Chameikho, 2014). This strategy is predicated by the idea that customers with comparable prior choices will likely have comparable future preferences. Two sub-categories of collaborative filtering can be distinguished:

User-based collaborative filtering: This method finds users similar to each other by analysing their prior behaviour and suggests goods and services that these users have either enjoyed or bought.

Item-based collaborative filtering: This method finds comparable goods or services by analysing their features and suggests goods that users who have already loved or bought similar goods.

Content-Based Filtering

Content-based filtering (CBF) is an extension and progression of research on information filtering. The components of interest in a case-based reasoning system are spotted based on their corresponding traits. For example, a text recommendation system, like a newsgroup filtering system, uses the words inside the text as features (Belkin & Croft, 1992). By examining their traits, content-based filtering looks for patterns and resemblances between services or items. Users will likely have similar preferences if they like or buy similar features. A content-based filtering system, for instance, would suggest a high-yield savings account to a client who has shown interest in low-risk investment products. Banks and other companies providing financial services that wish to give their users enthralled and individualised financial products may see collaborative and content-based filtering tools as beneficial ones.

Hybrid Filtering

Hybrid filtering, the third scientific segregation of the proposal framework, depends on mixing at least two suggestion producers. The hybrid filtering technique combines two or more recommendation filtering systems in various ways to build a new hybrid system. The hybrid filtering technique allows the combination of multiple filters in various ways (Isinkaye et al., 2015). Its principal advantage is gathering the benefits of the singular proposal methods and restricting their inconveniences/limitations. The characterisation of the half-breed suggestion framework is weighted-mixture, exchanging crossover, blended mixture, and outpouring crossover. A weighted mixture depends on blending the scores of the suggested thing considering the after-effect of individual suggestion methods. Its fundamental benefit is utilising all qualities of individual proposal strategies in the subsequent mixture framework. Exchanging cross-over depends on exchanging between individual suggestion procedures until accomplishing the strategy that creates the best certainty. Blended crossover depends on working at least two proposal procedures together, each on discrete information. It can end the beginning issue connected with an original thing's expansion and overflow crossover, depending on requesting suggestion procedures and grouping them into equivalent inclinations. Its primary benefit is applying the following method, provided it is essential for something not effectively suggested by the previous one.

Operationalizing Recommender Systems

Recommender Systems not only assesses user behaviour and data but also extends customised suggestions for machine learning algorithms and statistical model services. Customised financial product suggestions can be given by tracking a customer's spending habits, credit history and other material information if incorporated into financial services and banks. There are four primary steps in the process of making personalised recommendations:

Figure 3. Process of machine learning

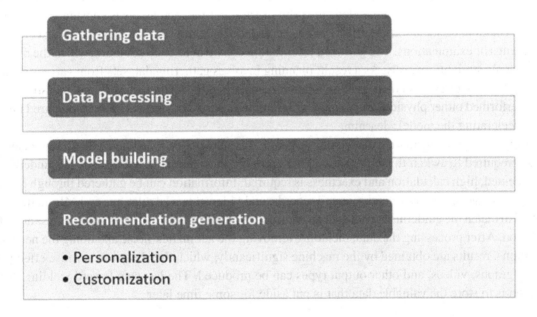

Gathering data

Data Processing

Model building

Recommendation generation

- Personalization
- Customization

Gathering data: In machine learning, data is an essential component. It alludes to the arrangement of perceptions or estimations that can be utilised to prepare an AI model. The quality and amount of information accessible for preparation and testing play a critical part in deciding the development, presentation and deployment of an AI model. AI-enabled recommender systems analyse consumer data to offer tailor-made suggestions and recommendations. As the consumer data varies from consumer to consumer, the recommendations and offers are also customer specific. The models in the finance domains analyse the spending habits of individuals, credit scores, total liabilities and other deposits to develop a loan default mechanism for financial institutes. There may be other models that can predict the creditworthiness of individuals, leading to the issuance/non-issuance of credit cards or accepting/rejecting loan applications. Information is ordinarily partitioned into two types: named/labelled and unlabelled information/data. Named information incorporates a mark or target variable the model is attempting to foresee, though unlabelled information excludes a name or target variable. The information utilised in

AI is usually mathematical or absolute. Values that can be arranged and measured, like age or income, are included in numerical data. Values that represent categories like gender or fruit type are included in categorical data. Data collected are divided into two sets: training and testing to train the model and then to test the model. The preparation set prepares the model, while the demonstration of the model comes under the testing set. After testing the model, it is deployed live in the real environment. It is of great importance to divide the date arbitrarily and aptly. The starting step is to gather information about the individual's behaviour, choices and financial background. Account balances, transaction history, and demographic data are examples of this data.

Assortment: The most essential step in beginning with ML is to have good quality and exact information. Information can be gathered from any verified source, such as data.gov.in, Kaggle, or UCI dataset vault. For instance, students study from the best materials they can find when preparing for competitive exams to learn the most and get the best results. Similarly, excellent and exact information will make the model's growing experience more straightforward and better; the model will yield cutting-edge results during the difficult period. A tremendous measure of capital, time, and assets is consumed when gathering information. Associations or scientists must conclude what information they need to execute their undertakings or examinations. The gathered information can be in a crude structure, which the machine cannot handle straightforwardly. As a result, planning involves gathering datasets from various sources, analysing these datasets, and then creating a brand-new dataset for further analysis and investigation. It can be performed either physically or using a programmed approach. Data can also be prepared numerically, accelerating the model's learning.

The pre-arranged information can be in a structure that may not be machine-clear, so some calculations are required to switch this information over entirely to a coherent structure. For this undertaking to be executed, high calculation and exactness is required. Information can be gathered through MNIST Digit data (images), Twitter remarks, sound records, and video cuts. Calculations and ML methods are expected to match the guidelines given over an enormous volume of information with exactness and ideal calculation. After processing the data, including removing the anomalies' noise and doing the necessary calculations, results are obtained by the machine significantly, which the client can surmise effectively. Reports, graphs, videos, and other output types can be produced. The last step toward yielding the information is to store the valuable data that is put aside for some time later.

BENEFITS/CHALLENGES OF ML-PROCESSED DATA

ML-processed data is a double-edged sword. On the one hand, it provides data that helps the organisation serve its customers better. However, on the other hand, it also challenges organisations to keep improving their systems/services based on their customer's changing behaviours and activities. The amount of customer-generated data also forces organisations to emphasise investing in technological upgrades. The following section helps in understanding the benefits and challenges organisations usually face while handling customer-generated data:

Benefits: Information handling works on the presentation of the ML model by cleaning and changing the information into an organisation that is reasonable for demonstrating. Information handling permits the information to be changed into a configuration that better addresses the essential connections and examples, making it more straightforward for the ML model to gain from the information. Information handling guarantees the information's exactness, reliability, and validity and assists in the exactness of the ML model.

Challenges: Information handling can be tedious, particularly for vast and complex datasets. Information handling can be mistake-inclined, as it includes changing and cleaning the information, which can bring about the deficiency of significant data or the presentation of new blunders. The transformed data may not represent the underlying relationships and patterns in the data, which can result in a limited understanding of the data. Data processing can lead to a limited understanding of the data. After the data is gathered, it must be pre-processed to eliminate any redundant or unnecessary information and change its format so that machine learning algorithms can use it.

Data Processing: Data processing is changing information from a given structure entirely to a significantly more usable and wanted structure, for example, making it more significant and valuable. This cycle can be computerised using AI calculations, numerical displays, and measurable information. The outcome of this total cycle can be in any classic form like diagrams, outlines, pictures, tabular form and more, contingent upon the undertaking we are doing and the essentialities of the machine. Data handling is crucial for the AI (ML) pipeline because it prepares the information for its use in the preparation and building of the model.

Information handling mainly aims at changing, cleaning and setting up the information in a systematic manner that is worth displaying. Generally, the main steps in data processing are:

- **Information Assortment:** This method is used to store the data gathered from various sources like data sets, sensors or frameworks. The information might be structured or unstructured and come in different arrangements like text, pictures, or sound.

- **Information Pre-Processing:** This step includes cleaning, sifting, and changing the information to make it reasonable/understandable for additional examination. It might also incorporate eliminating missing qualities, scaling or normalising the information, or switching it to an alternate configuration.

- **Information Examination:** In this step, the information is broken down utilising different strategies, such as measurable examination, AI calculations, or information representation. This step aims to get experiences or information from the information.

Data Interpretation: In this step, the insights gained from the data analysis are interpreted, and conclusions are drawn. Reports, dashboards, or other visualisations may also convey the findings clearly and concisely.

Information Representation: Once the information has been handled and examined, it should be put away and overseen in a manner that is secure and effectively open. It might include putting away the information in a data set, distributed storage, or different frameworks and executing reinforcement and recuperation systems to safeguard against information misfortune.

Information Manifestation: Eventually, the outcomes of the information examination are shown to the partners in a layout that is significant and justifiable effectively, including presentation making, reports and dashboards that feature pivotal findings and sequences in the information. There are many devices and libraries accessible for information handling in ML, including pandas for Python and the Information Change and Purging apparatus in RapidMiner. The project's specific requirements, such as the size and complexity of the data and the desired outcome, will determine which tools are used.

MODEL BUILDING

A machine learning model decides the result after running a machine learning calculation on the gathered information. It is essential to pick a model pertinent to the job that needs to be done. Throughout the long term, researchers and architects created different models appropriate for various assignments like discourse acknowledgement, picture acknowledgement, expectation, etc. Aside from this, it is likewise necessary to check whether the model is appropriate for mathematical or clear-cut information. Preparation is the main move toward machine learning. In preparation, it passes the pre-arranged information to the machine learning model to track down examples and make forecasts. As a result, the model learns from the data to complete the task set. After some time and preparation, the model gets better at forecasting.

After preparing the model, it is necessary to verify its performance. The performance is verified by testing the presentation of the model based on concealed information beforehand. The concealed information utilised is the trying set that users have previously split the information into. Suppose testing finishes with similar information that is utilised for preparation. In that case, the user will not get a precise measure, as the model is now used to the information and tracks down similar examples as it recently did, and the same will give an excessively high exactness. Users get an accurate measurement of the model's speed and performance when they use it to test data.

Once the user has made and assessed the model, it is required to check whether its exactness can be worked on in any capacity. The accurate working of the model can be accessed by tuning the boundaries present in the model. Boundaries are the factors in the model that the software engineer, for the most part, chooses. At a specific point of the user's boundary, the precision will be the most extreme. Boundary tuning alludes to tracking down these qualities.

Recommendation Generation: Machine learning algorithms are applied to the pre-processed data to find patterns and similarities between customers and goods or services. It includes picking a suitable algorithm, using the data to train it, and evaluating its accuracy. The machine learning algorithm can be trained to provide personalised suggestions for goods and services based on a user's prior behaviour and preferences. The consumer may receive these recommendations by email, mobile apps, or online banking portals, among other means.

FINANCIAL RECOMMENDER SYSTEMS

Recommender Frameworks are data-sifting and choice-supporting frameworks that present things the client will probably be keen on in a specific setting. In the money space, we consider clients to be dynamic entities participating in system interactions like viewing, selling, buying, rating, etc. In recommender, things are the items the client can connect (e.g., items, financial exchanges, melodies, etc.). Both users and items can be described using metadata. (e.g., Age, client orientation, sort, the cost for things). Recommender frameworks can put in various algorithms for data mining that include collaborative, case-based, popularity-based, hybrid and content-based filtering techniques, depending on the attributes of the space, the accessible data's nature and the objectives of the business. Suggestion administrations offer administrations that help the financial backer make the best choices regarding the market, the product, the loan, etc. Recommendation principles can be utilised in various financial fields, such as banking, stock, and protection.

Banking-Finance Sector: Banks carry out far-reaching, advanced changes to address developing issues and supply quicker and better-customised solutions to clients with computerised services. In banking, the suggestion helps the bank take the right or, on the other hand, close to address choice about the advanced interaction. Right now, the recommender helps decide whether the client merits the credit in light of examining user information. For instance, the advance application might be dismissed if the client class is youthful (eg., age < 15 years). Otherwise, the advanced application can be dismissed, assuming this client is of average age. Artificial intelligence (AI) enables intelligent chatbots to provide clients with extensive self-help alternatives, hence decreasing the workload of call centres. Virtual assistants powered by voice recognition technology, such as Amazon's Alexa, are rapidly gaining popularity. It is unsurprising, as these assistants include a self-education feature that allows them to continuously improve their performance, resulting in significant advancements over time. Both programs can verify account balances, schedule payments, retrieve account activity, and perform additional functions.

Several applications provide tailor-made financial guidance and help consumers achieve their financial objectives. These polished algorithms check income, spending habits, and essential recurring expenses and help generate an improved plan and financial advice.

BNPL (Buy Now Pay Later): the digital lending rising star: Incorporating Aadhaar and eKYC has streamlined consumer entry into digital lending, boosting the MSME sector and constituting a significant portion of India's GDP. The India Stack, an extensive digital public infrastructure, has played a crucial role in decreasing banking expenses and improving the availability of financial services, transforming India's economy from a cash-based system. As a result, digital lenders have been able to decrease significantly the expenses associated with verifying users and provide mobile payments in real-time.

FinTech companies are at the forefront of using alternative data to evaluate creditworthiness, improve operational effectiveness, and fill credit gaps by delivering inclusive products. The partnership between banks, non-banking financial companies (NBFCs), and financial technology (FinTech) start-ups promotes the development of new ideas and effectiveness in the digital lending industry. In 2024, this collaboration is anticipated to strengthen, leading to more advancements and fulfilling the various financial requirements of Indian homes and enterprises. Buy Now, Pay Later services rely heavily on risk assessment. It aids in assessing the appropriateness of customers and offers a general indication of the probable course of the collection procedure. In order to have a panoramic evaluation, it is crucial to possess the correct data. BNPL companies take possession of all the data from clients and with their consent. AI data analytics automation, monitoring tools, and predictive data are used to analyse the data. Examining this data produces immediate, practical observations that may be utilised for several objectives, and risk evaluation is one of them.

By utilising advanced techniques such as predictive analytics and real-time user monitoring, it is feasible to oversee various borrower channels and build effective communication that notifies the borrower about impending collections. Historically or under conventional practices, banking corporations were restricted to monitoring and communicating with borrowers only through designated sources such as emails or telephones. Still, a comprehensive evaluation of behavioural sequences on the internet will give the required information about the borrower's activities. Companies can engage with borrowers through social media and internet ads across various platforms. It establishes various means of communication and accelerates the process of gathering information.

Bank Deposit Anticipation: Machine learning can also be utilised to predict bank deposit subscriptions (Yan, Li & Liu, 2020). Kaggle datasheets, preprocessing approaches and feature engineering are used, and correlations within the data are studied using crosstabulations and heat maps. Models like the SGD Classifier, k-nearest neighbour Classifier and Random Forest Classifier are enforced separately in this work.

Using complex analytical models has changed the game and opened up new probabilities and predicting bank term deposit subscriptions. Thorough data research, vigorous exploratory data analysis (EDA), careful feature engineering and sensible machine learning model execution contribute to the goal of anticipating bank deposits (Zaki et al., 2024).

Stock Market Finance Sector: AI has transformed the trading industry by facilitating algorithmic trading. A stock market portfolio recommender system was proposed that examined stock data and provided a ranked selection of equities. The recommender system aided stock market traders, individual investors, and fund managers by proposing investment in a collection of equities stocks when compelling evidence of potential profit from these transactions was present. Artificial intelligence algorithms can analyse large volumes of financial data in real-time, detect patterns, and make judgements based on data to execute transactions, eradicating human emotions and biases and resulting in more impartial and effective trading tactics. High-frequency trading, a form of algorithmic trading, has become prominent because of the capacity of artificial intelligence to handle large amounts of data and carry out deals in milliseconds, leading to enhanced liquidity and market efficiency. Artificial intelligence algorithms utilise vast quantities of market data in real-time to detect patterns and trends that human traders may overlook. This fastens the pace of trading and promotes decision-making, resulting in more productive and profitable results. Automated trading systems provide the capability to implement swiftly intricate plans, responding to fluctuations in the market with more speed than any human trader. AI-based recommender systems not only personalise recommendations for users based on their profiles but also enhance the profitability of their portfolios while minimising financial losses (Gonzales & Hargreaves, 2022). The researchers proposed a stock trading recommender system for Indian equities that utilised a classifier to assist investors in selecting stocks that have the potential to make profits (Vismayaa et al., 2020). The system generates lucrative trading recommendations.

In the securities exchange region, the proposal helps the financial backer take the right or close to address the choice of stock exchanging process. At this point, the recommender helps decide the degree to which the financial backer benefits from the stock. From the stock cost forecast process, the future close cost of the stock can be anticipated, as well as its future pattern. Based on the study of investor data, the recommendation system can assist the investor in making the correct stock predictions. For instance, assuming the stock that a financial backer claims has a positive future pattern, the financial backer is suggested to hold this stock as its cost will be upgraded. For this stock, the framework prescribes the financial backer to get it. For the stock with a close price that remains constant, the system tells the investor to hold it. In this way, the finance recommendation framework helps the financial backer work on his benefit and save his cash from misfortune.

Insurance Sector: In the insurance region, a protection contract is a policy between the backup plan and the insured (owner of the policy). The insurer assumes payment responsibility for the initial payment. An instalment is guaranteed if the misfortune is brought about by hazards under the details of the strategy. As standard approaches have no place for customisation, protection riders are acquainted with increment helps purchased independently from the fundamental approach—both insurance contracts. Additionally, protection riders can be the object of the customised suggestion issue.

AI excels conventional recommender systems by hunting through greater depths and hiking insurance recommendations to entirely new standards. Artificial intelligence can examine extensive data, such as demographic information, medical records, driving patterns (for automobile insurance), and external data sources like public records, enabling a far more intricate comprehension of the customer's risk profile and requirements. AI can use machine learning algorithms to forecast forthcoming occurrences, such as health hazards. This permits the provision of customised recommendations for the proper coverage levels and types suitable for the individual's precise circumstances. AI can also regularly examine and analyse potential hazards in real-time. Usage-based automobile insurance can modify premiums according to driving behaviour. Implementing this customisation can motivate individuals to engage in safer actions and offer more precise insurance protection. Artificial intelligence can categorise clients into exact risk groupings. Insurers can utilise this capability to develop customised policies that precisely align with the distinct requirements of individual customers, encompassing specific features and costs. AI-driven chatbots can interact with consumers, comprehend their requirements through dialogue, and provide real-time recommendations for appropriate insurance policies. This enhances the level of interactivity and customisation. Recommender systems utilise client data, including demographics, risk factors, and past purchases, to propose plans that are most suitable for their requirements. This feature assists clients in avoiding the risk of being under-insured or paying excessive amounts for coverage that is not essential. Artificial intelligence (AI) assists in navigating the intricate array of insurance possibilities. Consumers can effectively reduce the time and energy required to discover the most appropriate option by filtering and providing recommendations for suitable plans. Recommender systems can provide explanations for the suggestions they make, which helps to establish confidence with customers. Users may comprehend the impact of their profile on recommendations, enabling them to make well-informed choices.

Insurance companies benefit from AI by using its ability to personalise the customer experience, resulting in increased engagement and satisfaction. Customers perceive importance and appreciation when advice is tailored to their requirements. Artificial intelligence can examine extensive data to generate more precise risk profiles, resulting in improved pricing strategies and decreased risks of fraudulent activities. Insurance firms can enhance revenue and customer loyalty by comprehending customer requirements, customising marketing efforts, and suggesting pertinent items.

OPTIMISING FINANCIAL DECISIONS WITH AI-POWERED RECOMMENDATIONS

AI/ML has revolutionised the financial services sector with its many advantages for consumers and financial institutions. These systems may process large volumes of data to provide tailored recommendations that improve consumer engagement and retention. We will look at some of the advantages they provide here, such as more client happiness, more sales, and stronger customer loyalty. AI-driven systems can produce reports, handle substantial volumes of data, and execute administrative tasks efficiently and quickly. Artificial intelligence algorithms can automate trade settlements, reconciliation processes, and fraud detection, saving time and decreasing errors. By removing human labour, financial organisations can reallocate resources to more valuable and intricate tasks. Artificial intelligence (AI) is crucial in improving risk management in the banking business. By analysing extensive historical data, AI algorithms can make more precise predictions on market patterns, identify anomalies, and evaluate the likelihood of risks, facilitating the process of making well-informed investment decisions, safeguarding against fraudulent activities, and reducing the potential dangers associated with financial instruments. Machine learning algorithms can detect patterns and connections that humans might miss, thereby minimising the risk of human mistakes. Artificial intelligence (AI) is crucial in risk management in the financial industry. Machine learning algorithms can evaluate and forecast risks by examining past data, market patterns, and external influences. Financial institutions can enhance their decision-making, minimise possible losses, and optimise their risk portfolios with this capability. Artificial intelligence (AI) algorithms constantly acquire knowledge and adjust to new information, guaranteeing that risk management solutions stay current and efficient.

Increased Happiness and Involvement From Customers: Financial institutions can offer tailored suggestions for financial products and services through recommender systems based on a customer's spending habits, financial history, and other pertinent information. Financial institutions may increase consumer engagement and foster client loyalty by providing tailored recommendations that align with their requirements and preferences. Instead of spending resources following every customer, banks can take the appropriate action and target those most likely to quit if they have access to a model that gives them information about these consumers (de Lima Lemos, Silva & Tabak, 2022). There may be customers that use the banks' services for some time and later stop using the bank services and hop to another bank. Thus, machine learning can reduce customer churn as the large customer database, and references from the satisfied customer base can help the banks reduce customer acquisition costs (Singh et al., 2024).

Improved Customer-Specific Services: By examining their financial behaviour and preferences, they can also assist financial organisations in offering their clients more individualised services. For instance, based on a customer's past investments or spending habits, AI-based systems may recommend pertinent and new investment options. Based on the customers' risk appetite, age profile, family size or family commitments, Investment options can also be suggested.

Higher Income and Sales for Financial Institutions: AI/ML-based systems have the potential to boost the possibility of customers purchasing more financial products or services by offering personalised suggestions. Artificial intelligence streamlines repetitious activities such as loan processing, fraud detection, and report preparation, allowing employees to allocate more time to intricate jobs and lowering the total operations expenses. Artificial intelligence can examine extensive data to detect trends and forecast future hazards, helping financial institutions make better-informed lending decisions, thereby decreasing the occurrence of defaults and enhancing the overall health of their loan portfolios.

AI-driven chatbots and virtual assistants can offer round-the-clock client care, tailored financial guidance, and expedited loan approvals, resulting in increased customer satisfaction and loyalty. Artificial intelligence (AI) can be utilised to create novel financial products and services that are specifically customised to meet the unique requirements of individual customers. This has the potential to create additional sources of income for financial institutions.

Improved Fraud Prevention and Risk Management: Financial experts are becoming more and more interested in accelerating the implementation of intelligent risk prevention and control platforms and developing big data financial risk prevention and control capabilities based on cutting-edge technologies like big data, machine learning (ML), and neural networks (NN) (Murugan & Kala, 2023). These technologies can also improve risk management and fraud prevention by examining consumer behaviour and seeing trends pointing to fraud. For instance, a recommender system might identify odd spending habits on a client's account and notify the bank of possible fraudulent activity. Artificial intelligence can authenticate client data using different services, such as natural language processing and photo recognition. Repetitive patterns frequently occur in fraudulent transactions, and while it is not feasible for humans to detect these patterns, data analysis can do so quickly. Predictive analytics algorithms analyse diverse data types from several sources and utilise the findings to identify instances of similar behaviour. A complete machine-learning approach for financial risk evaluation in shipping was also proposed. Corporate financial distress (FD) prediction models are highly valued by all stakeholders, including regulators and banks, who rely on acceptable evaluations of default risk for both credit institutions and bank loan portfolios.

Improved Customer Experience: In extremely cutthroat areas like banking, client experience is a fundamental switch. When there is a large supply, it is easy for a dissatisfied customer to switch providers quickly. The significance of client experience is considerably more evident today because conventional market players face rivalry from unadulterated computerised players, which depends totally on the client experience with a 100 per cent self-caring client relationship. Confronted with these contenders' accessible internet-based beyond conventional organisation hours, the occupant players should survey their approaches in collaborating with their clients. Clients' requirements for promptness and independence encourage organisations to re-examine client experience and relationships. Based on the customer's personal profile data and, most importantly, the products with which the customer has interacted or shown interest, personalisation of recommendations entails providing the customer with the appropriate product at the appropriate time. Proposals permit banks to adjust to client assumptions, decreasing the intricacy of their decisions, incrementing faithfulness, and encouraging buy and utilisation recurrence. In addition to answering consumer questions without requiring human intervention, chatbot technology in banks gathers information on client inquiries for potential use in resolving future issues (Huang & Lee, 2022). GenAI and LLMs can be used by marketers to enhance customer experience and build value for organisations (Thukral et al., 2023).

Fraud Detection: The recommender system can be used in the financial sector for fraud detection. For example, if several transactions happen in a mule account, AI technology can detect these accounts promptly and prevent fraud automatically. The job of a machine learning recommendation system in extortion identification is critical because of the quickly expanding volume of advanced exchanges and the rising complexity of fake exercises. Artificial intelligence innovation empowers extortion identification frameworks to continuously examine tremendous information measures and recognise strange examples of conduct characteristic of fake action. Credit card fraud (CCF) and default detection can be identified using a variety of machine learning-based credit card detection techniques, including the Extreme Learning Method, Decision Tree, Random Forest, Support Vector Machine, Logistic Regression, and XG Boost (Alarfaj et al., 2022). The quantity of features, number of transactions, and correlation between the features are crucial in figuring out how well the model performs for detecting CCF. Text processing and the baseline model are related to deep learning techniques like CNNs and their layers. These techniques outperform conventional algorithms in the identification of credit cards (Alarfaj et al., 2022). (Aslam et al., 2022) used predictive models to present a framework for fraud detection in the vehicle insurance market. Using a publicly accessible automobile insurance dataset, the feature selection process found the most significant feature using the Boruta method as the suggested framework could help insurance managers and businesses select the models and features for advanced machine learning and artificial intelligence-based fraud detection techniques. Hybrid sampling and oversampling preprocessing techniques are used to solve the imbalanced data problem before working on the model to detect credit card fraud detection (Abd El-Naby, Hemdan & El-Sayed, 2023). Random forest, logistic regression, and artificial neural network models are used to detect fraud detection in the insurance sector with acceptable accuracy and validation metrics (Nabrawi & Alanazi, 2023). Here are a few critical manners by which simulated intelligence is utilised in extortion recognition:

Mechanised Irregularity Identification: Man-made intelligence calculations in computerised extortion recognition can be prepared in conditional misrepresentation checking frameworks to perceive designs in information that propose deceitful action. These examples can incorporate strange exchange sums, various exchanges from a similar gadget, or buys produced using various areas in a brief period. Once it finds an anomaly, the AI can mark a transaction for further investigation.

Social Investigation: Artificial intelligence innovation can dissect clients' ways of behaving over the long haul to recognise uncommon movements. For instance, if a client out of nowhere starts to make massive buys outside their standard ways of managing money, the artificial intelligence framework can hail these exchanges as dubious.

Natural Language Processing: Natural Language Processing is a technique that AI algorithms can use to analyse customer communications, such as chat transcripts or emails, to spot signs of fraud. For instance, if a client unexpectedly changes their record data and sends an email mentioning a secret word reset, the simulated intelligence framework can recognise this as a potential extortion endeavour.

Continues Learning: Through continuous learning, AI algorithms can be trained with new data to improve their accuracy and effectiveness. This persistent learning assists with guaranteeing that misrepresentation location frameworks keep up to date with the most recent extortion patterns and strategies. Overall, AI's role in fraud detection is to detect suspicious behaviour and fraudulent transactions in real-time, thereby lowering businesses' risk of financial loss and safeguarding customer data.

FINANCIAL RECOMMENDER SYSTEM IMPLEMENTATION

Implementation of the AI/ML-based systems involving data gathering, algorithm selection, and user interface design can be challenging. Nonetheless, the work is worthwhile due to the potential advantages of these technologies, which include higher customer satisfaction, potential fraud detection and payment defaults, revenue generation and potential cross and upselling of the products. The main procedures for putting in place a recommender system for banking and financial services will be covered in this section.

Gathering Data and Preparing it for Analysis: The first stage is gathering information on user behaviour, preferences, and financial history. Account balances, transaction history, and demographic data are examples of this data. Financial organisations can access this information via various platforms, including customer service encounters, online banking portals, and mobile apps. After the data is gathered, it must be pre-processed to eliminate any redundant or unnecessary information and structured so that machine learning algorithms can use it. It may entail feature selection, data processing, and data cleaning.

Choosing the Appropriate Algorithm: Various algorithms are available for application, such as content-based, hybrid, and collaborative filtering. The particular use case and the data's properties will determine the best algorithm. Financial organisations should thoroughly assess and test several algorithms to determine which best suits their requirements.

Putting Recommendation Systems in Place and Assessing Them for Banks: Once the algorithm is selected, it must be implemented and integrated into the existing infrastructure of the financial institution. The system must be tested and evaluated to ensure its accuracy and effectiveness in providing personalised recommendations to customers. Continuous monitoring and evaluation are essential to ensure system effectiveness as user behaviour and preferences change over time.

OBSTACLES AND RESTRICTIONS

Although recommender systems have shown much promise in the banking and financial services sector, several obstacles and restrictions are associated with them. This section will discuss some of the main difficulties in implementing these systems, including lack of transparency, algorithm bias, and data privacy issues. Comprehending these obstacles and constraints is essential to creating efficient systems that are morally sound and significant.

Privacy and Security Considerations

Such programs rely heavily on collecting and analysing personal data to provide accurate recommendations. However, handling sensitive financial data can create severe privacy and security issues, especially if the data is leaked or misused. Strong security measures must be implemented to protect user data and ensure their trust in the recommendation system.

Host and Ethical Issues

If the data used to train these systems does not represent the entire user base, bias may lead to unfair and discriminatory recommendations. For example, a recommendation system that recommends credit cards only to people with high credit scores may exclude people with low scores who can still benefit from using the card. In addition, such systems must adhere to ethical guidelines and not recommend products or services that harm the financial well-being of the user.

Cold Start Problem

The cold start problem occurs when the recommendation system lacks enough user data or no historical data on new users, so accurate recommendations cannot be made (Murugan & Kala, 2023). Imagine this: a new user who has just opened a bank account may not have enough transaction history to provide personalised recommendations. The system must find innovative ways to solve the cold start problem and ensure users receive relevant recommendations. The issue related to the cold start problem can be tackled with the hybrid recommender system suggested by (Murugan & Kala, 2023) that combines the item-based collaborative filtering technique, which utilises consumer choice data from the algorithm, with the demographic-based approach, which incorporates customers' demographics.

Figure 4. Workflow of the data for data science management

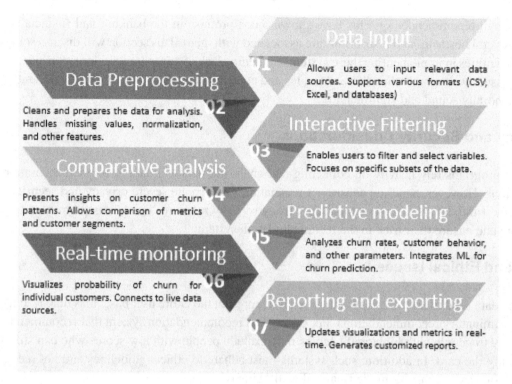

RECOMMENDER SYSTEMS IN THE FUTURE

Using recommender systems for banking and financial services is constantly changing due to advances in machine learning, data science, and user experience design. As advances in Artificial Intelligence and Machine Learning grow, recommender systems' ability to provide more precise and personalised recommendations will increase. Even for users with limited data sources, the ability of a recommender system to analyse and provide recommendations will increase. Deep Learning and Neural Networks Deep learning and neural networks can potentially solve some of the current issues with recommender systems, including the cold start problem and biases. Connectivity These programs can benefit from integrating other emerging technologies, such as IoT devices and blockchain. Blockchain technology can provide a secure and transparent platform for storing and sharing user data.

Machine Learning Recommendation Systems in Financial Fraud Detection: Artificial intelligence (AI) has revolutionised the financial sector for catching fraud. Financial institutions have been able to better defend themselves against fraudulent activities due to the implementation of AI-powered fraud prevention technologies and models based on machine learning. The application of artificial intelligence (AI) to detect financial fraud is expected to become even more advanced and efficient as technology advances. One of the critical regions where simulated intelligence will probably make tremendous advances in what is in store is the identification of deceitful exercises that are progressively challenging to identify utilising conventional rule-based frameworks. AI calculations, which can dissect immense information measures and recognise examples and irregularities demonstrative of extortion, will be significantly more skilled at continuously distinguishing fake movements. One more region where simulated intelligence is supposed to have a critical effect on what is in store is the utilisation of regular language handling (NLP) to break down unstructured information sources, such as messages, visit logs, and virtual entertainment posts. By examining this information, simulated intelligence-fueled frameworks can distinguish expected fraudsters from other dubious exercises. The reconciliation of blockchain innovation is probably the most thrilling improvement coming soon for computer-based intelligence in the discovery of monetary extortion. AI can be used to analyse the data and identify fraudulent activity, and blockchain provides a secure and transparent ledger for storing transaction data. This blend of advancements will empower monetary foundations to readily follow and distinguish false exercises, even in complex organisations.

Nonetheless, moral contemplations should be considered as the utilisation of simulated intelligence turns out to be more pervasive in monetary extortion locations. The significance of human oversight in the turn of events and execution of simulated intelligence-fueled misrepresentation and location frameworks could not be more significant. It is essential to guarantee that these frameworks are straightforward and logical and do not sustain predispositions or segregation. All in all, the fate of artificial intelligence in monetary extortion identification is set to be a unique advantage for the business. Financial institutions will be better equipped to detect and prevent fraudulent activities due to continued advancements in machine learning, natural language processing, and the integration of blockchain technology, ultimately safeguarding their customers and businesses. Nevertheless, it is essential to remember that AI is only as effective as the data it is trained on and the oversight it receives from humans.

FUTURE OF AI/ML (RECOMMENDER SYSTEMS) WITH BLOCKCHAIN TECHNOLOGY

The financial services industry is already highly dependent on recommender systems in banking, insurance, and investment management. However, as recommender systems continue to develop, they will have the potential to transform the delivery of financial services. For instance, recommender systems could provide financial institutions with personalised investment recommendations, automate credit decisions, and offer personalised insurance policies. Financial institutions could also use recommender systems to retain customers by offering a more personalised and smooth user experience in digital. Banks can find new customers more quickly, make tailored loan offers, and increase lead conversion rates with in-depth analysis of past customer data. Customers can be screened for creditworthiness using AI/ML recommender systems, which can categorise them for loans, credit cards, and other banking products based on essential parameters like employment stability, income, and credit history, among many other things. Based on the historical payment history of the consumers, AI/ML, in conjunction with blockchain and other technologies, can forecast probable loan or credit card defaulters. Real-time monitoring of the customers' activities can be done using anomaly detention, pattern recognition and predictive analytic techniques. Live dashboards can be developed to visualise different types of fraudulent activities. Blockchain facilitates the automation of intricate algorithms and transactions via smart contracts, reducing administrative expenses and paperwork. This effectiveness is especially noticeable in how quickly and affordably cross-border payments may be facilitated. Blockchain transaction data can be analysed by artificial intelligence (AI) systems to find patterns that indicate dishonest behaviour or suggestive market trends. Blockchain technology improves this by providing a tamper-proof record that makes AI decisions more transparent and audible (Addula et al., 2023).

CONCLUSION

Recommender systems are becoming increasingly important in financial services as they help financial institutions provide personalised and relevant recommendations to their customers. However, challenges and limitations must be addressed, such as data privacy and security concerns, biases and ethical issues, cold start problems, and scalability issues. Recommender systems are a fantastic asset that is accessible to banks and organisations and will continue to develop with limitless applications. One might contend that it is an innovation whose improvements have seen enormous speed in the past decade and have yielded billions in additional income to Amazon. ML can be used in various ways in the banking and financial services sectors to benefit various stakeholders, including banks, governments, clients, companies that offer ML-based services, and society at large. Because recommender systems are sorely needed, banks ought to be aware of the advantages that come with implementing them. Technology-based scams are becoming more common, while at the same time, customer needs and goals are evolving at a far quicker rate. Consumers of today want services that are tailored specifically to them, and banks are unable to provide this demand without the use of technology at the service levels. The client base is expanding as a result of banking service providers adding more and more people to their financial service offerings, which is promoting financial inclusion. The increasing use of technology is accompanied by an increase in tech-based fraud. Additionally, people are now tech-savvy, which generates terabytes of data for businesses like banks and e-commerce sites. Businesses have access to this enormous database, classifying and finding patterns in the data by applying machine learning algorithms. Organisations must completely alter their way of doing business to address the growing number of frauds as well as the shifting needs and goals of their clients. In order to provide their customers with fraud-free solutions, banks must embrace technology. The banks should invest in these technologies and embrace them since they will help them in the long run.

REFERENCES

Abd El-Naby, A., Hemdan, E. E. D., & El-Sayed, A. (2023). An efficient fraud detection framework with credit card imbalanced data in financial services. *Multimedia Tools and Applications*, 82(3), 4139–4160. DOI: 10.1007/s11042-022-13434-6

Addula, S. R., Meduri, K., Nadella, G. S., & Gonaygunta, H. AI[UNKNOWN ENTITY &!YearPlace;], and Blockchain in Finance: Opportunities and Challenges for the Banking Sector. *International Journal of Advanced Research in Computer and Communication Engineering*, 13(2), 184-190.

Alarfaj, F. K., Malik, I., Khan, H. U., Almusallam, N., Ramzan, M., & Ahmed, M. (2022). Credit card fraud detection using state-of-the-art machine learning and deep learning algorithms. *IEEE Access : Practical Innovations, Open Solutions*, 10, 39700–39715. DOI: 10.1109/ACCESS.2022.3166891

Aslam, F., Hunjra, A. I., Ftiti, Z., Louhichi, W., & Shams, T. (2022). Insurance fraud detection: Evidence from artificial intelligence and machine learning. *Research in International Business and Finance*, 62, 101744. DOI: 10.1016/j.ribaf.2022.101744

Beheshti, A., Yakhchi, S., Mousaeirad, S., Ghafari, S. M., Goluguri, S. R., & Edrisi, M. A. (2020). Towards cognitive recommender systems. *Algorithms*, 13(8), 176. DOI: 10.3390/a13080176

Belkin, N. J., & Croft, W. B. (1992). Information filtering and information retrieval: Two sides of the same coin? *Communications of the ACM*, 35(12), 29–38. DOI: 10.1145/138859.138861

Clintworth, M., Lyridis, D., & Boulougouris, E. (2023). Financial risk assessment in shipping: A holistic machine learning based methodology. *Maritime Economics & Logistics*, 25(1), 90–121. DOI: 10.1057/s41278-020-00183-2

de Lima Lemos, R. A., Silva, T. C., & Tabak, B. M. (2022). Propension to customer churn in a financial institution: A machine learning approach. *Neural Computing & Applications*, 34(14), 11751–11768. DOI: 10.1007/s00521-022-07067-x PMID: 35281625

Gonzales, R. M. D., & Hargreaves, C. A. (2022). How can we use artificial intelligence for stock recommendation and risk management? A proposed decision support system. *International Journal of Information Management Data Insights*, 2(2), 100130. DOI: 10.1016/j.jjimei.2022.100130

Grigorios, L., Magrizos, S., Kostopoulos, I., Drossos, D., & Santos, D. (2022). Overt and covert customer data collection in online personalized advertising: The role of user emotions. *Journal of Business Research*, 141, 308–320. DOI: 10.1016/j.jbusres.2021.12.025

Habil, S., El-Deeb, S., & El-Bassiouny, N. (2023). AI-based recommendation systems: the ultimate solution for market prediction and targeting. In *The Palgrave Handbook of Interactive Marketing* (pp. 683–704). Springer International Publishing. DOI: 10.1007/978-3-031-14961-0_30

Hanafizadeh, P., Barkhordari Firouzabadi, M., & Vu, K. M. (2021). Insight monetization intermediary platform using recommender systems. *Electronic Markets*, 31(2), 269–293. DOI: 10.1007/s12525-020-00449-w

Hassenzahl, M., & Tractinsky, N. (2006). User experience-a research agenda. *Behaviour & Information Technology*, 25(2), 91–97. DOI: 10.1080/01449290500330331

Hernández, E., Sittón, I., Rodríguez, S., Gil, A. B., & García, R. J. (2019). An investment recommender multi-agent system in financial technology. In *International Joint Conference SOCO'18-CISIS'18-ICEUTE'18: San Sebastián, Spain,June 6-8, 2018Proceedings 13* (pp. 3-10). Springer International Publishing. DOI: 10.1007/978-3-319-94120-2_1

Howe, J. (2006). The rise of crowdsourcing. *Wired magazine, 14*(6), 176-183.

Huang, S. Y., & Lee, C. J. (2022). Predicting continuance intention to fintech chatbot. *Computers in Human Behavior*, 129, 107027. DOI: 10.1016/j.chb.2021.107027

Isinkaye, F. O., Folajimi, Y. O., & Ojokoh, B. A. (2015). Recommendation systems: Principles, methods and evaluation. *Egyptian informatics journal, 16*(3), 261-273.

Kouadria, A., Nouali, O., & Al-Shamri, M. Y. H. (2020). A multi-criteria collaborative filtering recommender system using learning-to-rank and rank aggregation. *Arabian Journal for Science and Engineering*, 45(4), 2835–2845. DOI: 10.1007/s13369-019-04180-3

Lu, J., Wu, D., Mao, M., Wang, W., & Zhang, G. (2015). Recommender system application developments: A survey. *Decision Support Systems*, 74, 12–32. DOI: 10.1016/j.dss.2015.03.008

Murugan, M. S., & Kala, T. (2023). Large-scale data-driven financial risk management & analysis using machine learning strategies. *Measurement. Sensors*, 27, 100756. DOI: 10.1016/j.measen.2023.100756

Nabrawi, E., & Alanazi, A. (2023). Fraud detection in healthcare insurance claims using machine learning. *Risks*, 11(9), 160. DOI: 10.3390/risks11090160

Oyebode, O., & Orji, R. (2020). A hybrid recommender system for product sales in a banking environment. *Journal of Banking and Financial Technology*, 4(1), 15–25. DOI: 10.1007/s42786-019-00014-w

Paranjape-Voditel, P., & Deshpande, U. (2013). A stock market portfolio recommender system based on association rule mining. *Applied Soft Computing*, 13(2), 1055–1063. DOI: 10.1016/j.asoc.2012.09.012

Resnick, P., & Varian, H. R. (1997). Recommender systems. *Communications of the ACM*, 40(3), 56–59. DOI: 10.1145/245108.245121

Ryngksai, I., & Chameikho, L. (2014). Recommender systems: types of filtering techniques. *International Journal of Engineering Researck & Technology, Gujarat, 3*(2278-0181), 251-254.

Shi, Y., Larson, M., & Hanjalic, A. (2014). Collaborative filtering beyond the user-item matrix: A survey of the state of the art and future challenges. *ACM Computing Surveys*, 47(1), 1–45. DOI: 10.1145/2556270

Singh, P. P., Anik, F. I., Senapati, R., Sinha, A., Sakib, N., & Hossain, E. (2024). Investigating customer churn in banking: A machine learning approach and visualization app for data science and management. *Data Science and Management*, 7(1), 7–16. DOI: 10.1016/j.dsm.2023.09.002

Thukral, V., Latvala, L., Swenson, M., & Horn, J. (2023). Customer journey optimisation using large language models: Best practices and pitfalls in generative AI. *Applied Marketing Analytics*, 9(3), 281–292. DOI: 10.69554/DMIV5161

Vismayaa, V., Pooja, K. R., Alekhya, A., Malavika, C. N., Nair, B. B., & Kumar, P. N. (2020). Classifier based stock trading recommender systems for Indian stocks: An empirical evaluation. *computational Economics, 55*, 901-923.

Winter, S., Maslowska, E., & Vos, A. L. (2021). The effects of trait-based personalization in social media advertising. *Computers in Human Behavior*, 114, 106525. DOI: 10.1016/j.chb.2020.106525

Yan, C., Li, M., & Liu, W. (2020). Prediction of bank telephone marketing results based on improved whale algorithms optimizing S_Kohonen network. *Applied Soft Computing*, 92, 106259. DOI: 10.1016/j.asoc.2020.106259

Zaki, A. M., Khodadadi, N., Lim, W. H., & Towfek, S. K. (2024). Predictive analytics and machine learning in direct marketing for anticipating bank term deposit subscriptions. *American Journal of Business and Operations Research*, 11(1), 79–88. DOI: 10.54216/AJBOR.110110

Compilation of References

Abd El-Naby, A., Hemdan, E. E. D., & El-Sayed, A. (2023). An efficient fraud detection framework with credit card imbalanced data in financial services. *Multimedia Tools and Applications*, 82(3), 4139–4160. DOI: 10.1007/s11042-022-13434-6

Abidi, W. U. H., Daoud, M. S., Ihnaini, B., Khan, M. A., Alyas, T., Fatima, A., & Ahmad, M. (2021). Real-Time Shill Bidding Fraud Detection Empowered with Fussed ML. *IEEE Access : Practical Innovations, Open Solutions*, 9, 612–621. DOI: 10.1109/ACCESS.2021.3098628

Aburbeian, A. H. M., & Ashqar, H. I. (2023). Credit Card Fraud Detection Using Enhanced Random Forest Classifier for Imbalanced Data. *International Conference on Advances in Computing Research*, 605-616. DOI: 10.1007/978-3-031-33743-7_48

Acciarini, C., Cappa, F., Boccardelli, P., & Oriani, R. (2023). How can organizations leverage big data to innovate their business models? A systematic literature review. *Technovation*, 123, 102713. DOI: 10.1016/j.technovation.2023.102713

Addula, S. R., Meduri, K., Nadella, G. S., & Gonaygunta, H. AI[UNKNOWN ENTITY &!YearPlace;], and Blockchain in Finance: Opportunities and Challenges for the Banking Sector. *International Journal of Advanced Research in Computer and Communication Engineering*, 13(2), 184-190.

Addy, W. A., Ofodile, O. C., Adeoye, O. B., Oyewole, A. T., Okoye, C. C., Odeyemi, O., & Ololade, Y. J. (2024). Data-driven sustainability: How fintech innovations are supporting green finance. *Engineering Science & Technology Journal*, 5(3), 760–773. DOI: 10.51594/estj.v5i3.871

Adebiaye, R., Alshami, M., & Owusu, T. (2023). MACHINE LEARNING MODELS FOR EXTRAPOLATIVE ANALYTICS AS A PANACEA FOR BUSINESS INTELLIGENCE DECISIONS.

Adefarati, T., & Bansal, R. (2019). Application of renewable energy resources in a microgrid power system. *Journal of Engineering*, 5308–5313.

Adula, M., Birbirsa, Z. A., & Kant, S. (2023). The effect of interpersonal, problem solving and technical training skills on performance of Ethiopia textile industry: Continuance, normative and affective commitment as mediators. *Cogent Business & Management*, 10(3), 2286672. DOI: 10.1080/23311975.2023.2286672

Afuah, A. (2003). *Business Models: A Strategic Management Approach*. McGraw-Hill/ Irwin.

Agarwal, S., Iyer, A.P., Panda, A., Madden, S., Mozafari, B., & Stoica, I. (2012). Blink and it's done: interactive queries on very large data.

Aggarwal, K. K., & Yogesh Singh, A. Kaur, O.P.Sangwan (2004) "A Neural Net Based Approach to Test Oracle" ACM SIGSOFT, May 2004, Vol. 29 No. 4.

AgnarAamodt. Enric Plaza; (2019) Foundational Issues, Methodological Variations, System approaches; AlCom -Artificial Intelligence Communications, IOS Press; Vol. 7 issue 1, page. 39-59.

Agrawal, A., Gans, J. S., & Goldfarb, A. (2018). *Prediction machines: the simple economics of artificial intelligence*. Harvard Business Review.

Aha, D. W., Kibler, D., & Albert, M. K. (1991). Instance-based learning algorithms. *Machine Learning*, 6(1), 37–66. DOI: 10.1023/A:1022689900470

Ahmed, D., Hua, H. X., & Bhutta, U. S. (2024). Innovation through Green Finance: A thematic review. *Current Opinion in Environmental Sustainability*, 66, 101402. DOI: 10.1016/j.cosust.2023.101402

Akarsu, B., & Genç, M. S. (2022). Optimization of electricity and hydrogen production with hybrid renewable energy systems. *Fuel*, 324, 324. DOI: 10.1016/j.fuel.2022.124465

Akter, S., Bandara, R. J., & Sajib, S. (2021). How to empower analytics capability to tackle emergency situations? *International Journal of Operations & Production Management*, 41(9), 1469–1494. DOI: 10.1108/IJOPM-11-2020-0805

Al Balawi, S., & Aljohani, N. (2023). Credit Card Fraud Detection System Using Neural Networks. *The International Arab Journal of Information Technology*, 20(2), 234–241. DOI: 10.34028/iajit/20/2/10

Alarfaj, F. K., Malik, I., Khan, H. U., Almusallam, N., Ramzan, M., & Ahmed, M. (2022). Credit card fraud detection using state-of-the-art machine learning and deep learning algorithms. *IEEE Access : Practical Innovations, Open Solutions*, 10, 39700–39715. DOI: 10.1109/ACCESS.2022.3166891

Albuquerque, R., Koskinen, Y., & Zhang, C. (2019). Corporate social responsibility and firm risk: Theory and empirical evidence. *Management Science*, 65(10), 4451–4469. DOI: 10.1287/mnsc.2018.3043

Alfaiz, N.S, Fati, S.M (2022). Enhanced Credit Card Fraud Detection Model Using ML. *MDPI Journal - Electronics*, 11.

Alkhateeb, B. Abu Hijleh, E. Rengasamy and S. Muhammed, Building Refurbishment Strategies and Their Impact on Saving Energy in the United Arab Emirates, *Proceedings of SBE16 Dubai*, 17-19 January 2016, Dubai-UAE

Almazroi, A. A., & Ayub, N. (2023). Online Payment Fraud Detection Model Using ML Techniques. *IEEE Access : Practical Innovations, Open Solutions*, 11, 188–203. DOI: 10.1109/ACCESS.2023.3339226

Almeida, K. C., & Cicconet, F. (2019). Decentralized Hydrothermal Dispatch via Bilevel Optimization. Journal of Control, Automation and Electrical Systems. *Brazilian Society for Automatics–SBA*, 30, 557–567.

Alsayat, A. (2023). Customer decision-making analysis based on big social data using machine learning: A case study of hotels in Mecca. *Neural Computing & Applications*, 35(6), 4701–4722. DOI: 10.1007/s00521-022-07992-x PMID: 36340596

Alshammari, N., & Asumadu, J. 2020. Optimum unit sizing of hybrid renewable energy system utilizing harmony search, Jaya and particle swarm optimization algorithms, Sustainable Cities and Society, Elsevier, 60.

Alshingiti, Z., Rabeah A., Jalal Al-Muhtadi, Qazi Emad Ul Haq, Kashif Saleem and Muhammad H. F (2023). A Deep Learning-based Phishing Detection System Using CNN, LSTM, and LSTM-CNN. *MDPI- Electronics*, 12.

Amit, R., & Zott, C. (2012). Creating value through business model innovation. 2012.

Amit, R., & Zott, C. (2001). Value creation in e-business. *Strategic Management Journal*, 22(6–7), 493–520. DOI: 10.1002/smj.187

Ammari, C., Belatrache, D., Touhami, B., & Makhloufi, S. (2022). Sizing, optimization, control and energy management of hybrid renewable energy system—A review. *Energy and Built Environment, Elsevier*, 3(4), 399–411. DOI: 10.1016/j.enbenv.2021.04.002

Angwin, J., Larson, J., Mattu, S., & Kirchner, L. (2016). Machine Bias. ProPublica. https://www.propublica.org/article/machine-bias-risk-assessments-in-criminal-sentencing

Apreku-Djana, P. K., Ayittah, S. K., Apreku, I. K. O., Ameyaw, F., & Opare, E. A. (2023). The Mediating Effect of Corporate Social Responsibility and Corporate Accountability in the Relationship between Corporate Governance and Value-Based Financial Performance of Banks. *International Journal of Business*, 28(2), 1–36.

Arjun, S., & Moparthi, N. R. (2024). Fraud Detection in Banking Data by Machine Learning Techniques. *Journal of Electrical Systems*, 20(2), 2773–2784. DOI: 10.52783/jes.2056

Arwin, D. W. S., Asmara, R. A., Dimas, R. H. P., & Syamsiana, I. N. (2023, April 28). A perspective on a non-binary knowledge growing system in a pattern recognition use-case. *AIP Conference Proceedings*, 2531(1), 070001. DOI: 10.1063/5.0125810

Asha, R. B., & Suresh Kumar, K. R. (2021). Credit Card Fraud Detection Using Artificial Neural Network. *Global Transitions Proceedings*, 2(1), 35–41. DOI: 10.1016/j.gltp.2021.01.006

Ashfaq, T. Khalid, R, Yahaya, A.S, Aslam, S, Azar, A.T, Alsafari, S. Hameed (2022). A Machine Learning and Blockchain Based Efficient Fraud Detection Mechanism. *MDPI Journal- Sensors*, 22.

Aslam, F., Hunjra, A. I., Ftiti, Z., Louhichi, W., & Shams, T. (2022). Insurance fraud detection: Evidence from artificial intelligence and machine learning. *Research in International Business and Finance*, 62, 101744. DOI: 10.1016/j.ribaf.2022.101744

Asudani, D. S., Nagwani, N. K., & Singh, P. (2023). Impact of word embedding models on text analytics in deep learning environment: A review. *Artificial Intelligence Review*, 56(9), 10345–10425. Advance online publication. DOI: 10.1007/s10462-023-10419-1 PMID: 36844886

Aziz, A. S., Tajuddin, F. N., Hussain, M., Adzman, M., Ghazali, N., Ramli, M., & Zidane, T. 2022. A new optimization strategy for wind/diesel/battery hybrid energy system, Energy, Elsevier, 239

Babar, M., Arif, F., & Irfan, M. (2019). Internet of things-based smart city environments using big data analytics: A survey. In *Recent Trends and Advances in Wireless and IoT-enabled Networks* (pp. 129–138). Springer. DOI: 10.1007/978-3-319-99966-1_12

Badjatiya, P., Gupta, S., Gupta, M., & Varma, V. (2019). Deep learning for hate speech detection in tweets. *International World Wide Web Conference Committee*, 759–760.

Bagchi, D., Mukerjee, A., & Pal, S. (2021). A One Step Further Approach to Fraud Detection. *Journal of Computing Science and Engineering : JCSE*, 2, 112–119.

Bai, C., Zhou, H., & Sarkis, J. (2023). Evaluating Industry 4.0 technology and sustainable development goals–a social perspective. *International Journal of Production Research*, 61(23), 8094–8114. DOI: 10.1080/00207543.2022.2164375

Baiyere, A., Salmela, H., & Tapanainen, T. (2020). Digital transformation and the new logics of business process management. *European Journal of Information Systems*, 29(3), 238–259. DOI: 10.1080/0960085X.2020.1718007

Banerji, D., & Reimer, T. (2019). Startup founders and their LinkedIn connections: Are well-

Ban, G. Y., & Keskin, N. B. (2021). Personalized dynamic pricing with machine learning: High-dimensional features and heterogeneous elasticity. *Management Science*, 67(9), 5549–5568. DOI: 10.1287/mnsc.2020.3680

Beerepoot, I., Di Ciccio, C., Reijers, H. A., Rinderle-Ma, S., Bandara, W., Burattin, A., Calvanese, D., Chen, T., Cohen, I., Depaire, B., Di Federico, G., Dumas, M., van Dun, C., Fehrer, T., Fischer, D. A., Gal, A., Indulska, M., Isahagian, V., Klinkmüller, C., & Zerbato, F. (2023). The biggest business process management problems to solve before we die. *Computers in Industry*, 146, 103837. DOI: 10.1016/j.compind.2022.103837

Beheshti, A., Yakhchi, S., Mousaeirad, S., Ghafari, S. M., Goluguri, S. R., & Edrisi, M. A. (2020). Towards cognitive recommender systems. *Algorithms*, 13(8), 176. DOI: 10.3390/a13080176

Belachew, A. (2024). Impacts of results-based financing improved cookstove intervention on households' livelihood: Evidence from Ethiopia. *Forest Policy and Economics*, 158, 103096. DOI: 10.1016/j.forpol.2023.103096

Belkin, N. J., & Croft, W. B. (1992). Information filtering and information retrieval: Two sides of the same coin? *Communications of the ACM*, 35(12), 29–38. DOI: 10.1145/138859.138861

Benbya, H., Pachidi, S., & Jarvenpaa, S. (2021). Special issue editorial: Artificial intelligence in organizations: Implications for information systems research. *Journal of the Association for Information Systems*, 22(2), 10. DOI: 10.17705/1jais.00662

Berwal, P., Dhatterwal, J. S., Kaswan, K. S., & Kant, S. (2022). *Computer Applications in Engineering and Management*. Chapman and Hall/CRC. DOI: 10.1201/9781003211938

Bjornali, E. S., & Ellingsen, A. (2014). Factors affecting the development of clean-tech

Bocken, N., & Snihur, Y. (2020). Lean Startup and the business model: Experimenting for novelty and impact. *Long Range Planning*, 53(4), 101953. DOI: 10.1016/j.lrp.2019.101953

Boser, B. E., Guyon, I. M., & Vapnik, V. N. (1992). A training algorithm for optimal margin classifiers. Proc. 5th Annu. Workshop Comput. Learn. Theory (COLT), 144–152. https://www.scirp.org/reference/ReferencesPapers?ReferenceID=1409252

Boson, L. T., Elemo, Z., Engida, A., & Kant, S. (2023). Assessment of green supply chain management practices on sustainable business in Ethiopia. [LOMR]. *Logistic and Operation Management Research*, 2(1), 96–104. DOI: 10.31098/lomr.v2i1.1468

Bouchabou, D., Nguyen, S. M., Lohr, C., LeDuc, B., & Kanellos, I. (2021). Using language model to bootstrap human activity recognition ambient sensors based in smart homes. *Electronics (Basel)*, 10(20), 2498. DOI: 10.3390/electronics10202498

Bowman, C., & Ambrosini, V. (2000). Value creation versus value capture: Towards a coherent definition of value in strategy. British journal of management, 11(1), 1-15. Brynjolfsson, E., & Hitt, L. (1996). Paradox lost? Firm-level evidence on the returns to information systems spending. *Management Science*, 42(4).

Bram, J. T., Warwick-Clark, B., Obeysekare, E., & Mehta, K. (2015). Utilization and monetization of healthcare data in developing countries. *Big Data*, 3(2), 59–66. DOI: 10.1089/big.2014.0053 PMID: 26487984

Brandenburger, A. M., & Stuart, H. W.Jr. (1996). Value-based business strategy. *Journal of Economics & Management Strategy*, 5(1), 5–24. DOI: 10.1111/j.1430-9134.1996.00005.x

Bresciani, S., Huarng, K. H., Malhotra, A., & Ferraris, A. (2021). Digital transformation as a springboard for product, process and business model innovation. *Journal of Business Research*, 128, 204–210. DOI: 10.1016/j.jbusres.2021.02.003

Buallay, A., Fadel, S. M., Al-Ajmi, J. Y., & Saudagaran, S. (2020). Sustainability reporting and performance of MENA banks: Is there a trade-off? *Measuring Business Excellence*, 24(2), 197–221. DOI: 10.1108/MBE-09-2018-0078

Business Analytics: Data Analysis & Decision Making" by Christian Albright and Wayne Winston (2019)

Business Analytics: Data Analysis & Decision Making" by S. Christian Albright and Wayne L. Winston.

Business Analytics: The Science of Data-Driven Decision Making" by James R. Evans (2021)

Business Analytics: The Science of Data-Driven Decision Making" by U. Dinesh Kumar (2019)

Business Model Generation: A Handbook for Visionaries, Game Changers, and Challengers" by Alexander Osterwalder and Yves Pigneur (2010)

Butt, S. A., Diaz-Martinez, J. L., Jamal, T., & Ali, A. Emiro De-La-Hoz-Franco, and Muhammad Shoaib. IoT smart health security threats. *In 2019 19th International Conference on Computational Science and Its Applications (ICCSA)*, IEEE, 2019.

Butt, S. A., Diaz-Martinez, J. L., Jamal, T., & Ali, A. Emiro De-La-Hoz-Franco, and Muhammad Shoaib. IoT smart health security threats. *In 2019 19th International Conference on Computational Science and Its Applications (ICCSA)*, pages 26-31. IEEE, 2019.

Butt, A., Imran, F., Helo, P., & Kantola, J. (2024). Strategic design of culture for digital transformation. *Long Range Planning*, 57(2), 102415. Advance online publication. DOI: 10.1016/j.lrp.2024.102415

Calic, G., & Ghasemaghaei, M. (2021). Big data for social benefits: Innovation as a mediator of the relationship between big data and corporate social performance. *Journal of Business Research*, 131, 391–401. DOI: 10.1016/j.jbusres.2020.11.003

California Consumer Privacy Act (CCPA). https://oag.ca.gov/privacy/ccpa/regs

Callon, M., Courtial, J. P., & Laville, F. (1991). Co-word analysis as a tool for describing the network of interactions between basic and technological research: The case of polymer chemsitry. *Scientometrics*, 22(1), 155–205. DOI: 10.1007/BF02019280

Callon, M., Courtial, J. P., Turner, W. A., & Bauin, S. (1983). From translations to problematic networks: An introduction to co-word analysis. *Social Sciences Information. Information Sur les Sciences Sociales*, 22(2), 191–235. DOI: 10.1177/053901883022002003

Cappa, F. (2022). Big data from customers and non-customers through crowdsourcing, citizen science and crowdfunding. *Journal of Knowledge Management*, 26(11), 308–323. DOI: 10.1108/JKM-11-2021-0871

Cappa, F., Oriani, R., Peruffo, E., & McCarthy, I. (2021). Big data for creating and capturing value in the digitalized environment: Unpacking the effects of volume, variety, and veracity on firm performance. *Journal of Product Innovation Management*, 38(1), 49–67. DOI: 10.1111/jpim.12545

Carney, M. (2021). *Value(s): Building a Better World for All*. Public Affairs.

Caserio, C., Trucco, S., Caserio, C., & Trucco, S. (2018). Business intelligence systems. Enterprise Resource Planning and Business Intelligence Systems for Information Quality: An Empirical Analysis in the Italian Setting, 43-73.

Chang, V. (2021). An ethical framework for big data and smart cities. *Technological Forecasting and Social Change*, 165, 1–11. DOI: 10.1016/j.techfore.2020.120559

Charizanos, G., Demirhan, H., & İçen, D. (2024). An Online Fuzzy Fraud Detection Framework for Credit Card Transactions. *Expert Systems with Applications*, 252, 124–127. DOI: 10.1016/j.eswa.2024.124127

Charles, V., Garg, P., Gupta, N., & Agarwal, M. (Eds.). (2023). *Data Analytics and Business Intelligence: Computational Frameworks, Practices, and Applications*. CRC Press. DOI: 10.1201/9781003189640

Chaudhary, R. (2020). Green human resource management and employee green behavior: An empirical analysis. *Corporate Social Responsibility and Environmental Management*, 27(2), 630–641. DOI: 10.1002/csr.1827

Chauhan, N., & Tekta, P. (2020). Fraud Detection and Verification System for Online Transactions: A Brief Overview. *International Journal of Electronic Banking*, 2(4), 267–274. DOI: 10.1504/IJEB-ANK.2020.114762

Chawla, R. N., & Goyal, P. (2022). Emerging trends in digital transformation: A bibliometric analysis. *Benchmarking*, 29(4), 1069–1112. DOI: 10.1108/BIJ-01-2021-0009

Chen, Shangfeng, Hongqing Fang, and Zhijian Liu. "Human activity recognition based on extreme learning machine in a smart home. *Journal of Physics: Conference Series. Vol. 1437. No. 1. IOP Publishing,* 2020.

Chen, T., & Guestrin, C. (2016). XGBoost: A scalable tree boosting system. Proc. 22nd ACM SIGKDD Int. Conf. Knowl. Discovery Data Mining, 785–794. https://arxiv.org/abs/1603.02754 DOI: 10.1145/2939672.2939785

Chenguel, M. B., & Mansour, N. (2024). Green finance: Between commitment and illusion. *Competitiveness Review*, 34(1), 179–192. DOI: 10.1108/CR-10-2022-0162

Chen, J., Wei, W., Guo, C., Tang, L., & Sun, L. (2017). Textual analysis and visualization of research trends in data mining for electronic health records. *Health Policy and Technology*, 6(4), 389–400. DOI: 10.1016/j.hlpt.2017.10.003

Chen, K., Zha, Y., Alwan, L. C., & Zhang, L. (2020). Dynamic pricing in the presence of reference price effect and consumer strategic behaviour. *International Journal of Production Research*, 58(2), 546–561. DOI: 10.1080/00207543.2019.1598592

Chen, X., Zhu, Y., Li, G., & Li, S. (2017). Energy management strategy for grid-connected solar photovoltaic-fuel cell hybrid power system. *Journal of Power Sources*, 363, 420–430.

Chen, Y., Zhou, Y., Zhu, S., & Xu, H. (2012). Detecting ofensive language in social media to protect adolescent online safety. *Proc. - 2012 ASE/IEEE Int. Conf. Privacy, Secur. Risk Trust 2012 ASE/IEEE Int.Conf. Soc. Comput. Soc.*, 71–80.

Cherikbayeva, L., Yerimbetova, A., & Daiyrbayeva, E. "Research of Cluster Analysis Methods for Group Solutions of the Pattern Recognition Problem," 2021 6th International Conference on Computer Science and Engineering (UBMK), Ankara, Turkey, 2021, pp. 1-4, DOI: 10.1109/UBMK52708.2021.9558884

Chesbrough, H. (2006). *Open Business Models: How to Thrive in the New Innovation Landscape.* Harvard Business School Press.

Chong, S., Rahman, A., & Narayan, A. K. (2022). Guest editorial: Accounting in transition: influence of technology, sustainability and diversity. *Pacific Accounting Review*, 34(4), 517–525. DOI: 10.1108/PAR-07-2022-210

Cioffi, D. (2007). The Evolution of Business Analytics." *. Journal of Business Research.*

Clintworth, M., Lyridis, D., & Boulougouris, E. (2023). Financial risk assessment in shipping: A holistic machine learning based methodology. *Maritime Economics & Logistics*, 25(1), 90–121. DOI: 10.1057/s41278-020-00183-2

Competing on Analytics: The New Science of Winning" by Thomas H. Davenport and Jeanne G. Harris (2007)

Cornelis, E., Gorus, E., Van Schelvergem, N., & De Vriendt, P. (2019). The relationship between basic, instrumental, and advanced activities of daily living and executive functioning in geriatric patients with neurocognitive disorders. *International Journal of Geriatric Psychiatry*, 34(6), 889–899. DOI: 10.1002/gps.5087 PMID: 30761619

Dąbrowska, J., Almpanopoulou, A., Brem, A., Chesbrough, H., Cucino, V., Di Minin, A., Giones, F., Hakala, H., Marullo, C., Mention, A.-L., Mortara, L., Nørskov, S., Nylund, P. A., Oddo, C. M., Radziwon, A., & Ritala, P. (2022). Digital transformation, for better or worse: A critical multi-level research agenda. *R & D Management*, 52(5), 930–954. DOI: 10.1111/radm.12531

Das, A., Roy, M., Dutta, S., Ghosh, S., & Das, A. K. (2015). Predicting Trends in the Twitter Social Network: A Machine Learning Approach. https://www.researchgate.net/publication/294482813_Predicting_Trends_in_the_Twitter_Social_Network_A_Machine_Learning_Approach

Das, S., & Chen, M. (2001). Yahoo! for amazon: Extracting market sentiment from stock message boards. International Journal of Engineering Development and Research. http://www.ijedr.org

Datta, A., Tschantz, M. C., & Datta, A. (2015). Automated Experiments on Ad Privacy Settings – A Tale of Opacity, Choice, and Discrimination. *Proceedings on Privacy Enhancing Technologies. Privacy Enhancing Technologies Symposium*, 1(1), 92–112. DOI: 10.1515/popets-2015-0007

de Lima Lemos, R. A., Silva, T. C., & Tabak, B. M. (2022). Propension to customer churn in a financial institution: A machine learning approach. *Neural Computing & Applications*, 34(14), 11751–11768. DOI: 10.1007/s00521-022-07067-x PMID: 35281625

de Lucas Ancillo, A., & Gavrila, S. G. (2023). The impact of research and development on entrepreneurship, innovation, digitization and digital transformation. *Journal of Business Research*, 157, 113566. Advance online publication. DOI: 10.1016/j.jbusres.2022.113566

de Oliveira, S., Felipe, J. V. F., Plácido, J., & Deslandes, A. C. (2020). Spatial navigation and dual-task performance in patients with Dementia that present partial dependence in instrumental activity of daily living. *IBRO Reports*, 9, 52–57. DOI: 10.1016/j.ibror.2020.06.006 PMID: 33336104

Deb, B. C., Rahman, M. M., & Haseeb, M. (2024). Unveiling the impact on corporate social responsibility through green tax and green financing: A PLS-SEM approach. *Environmental Science and Pollution Research International*, 31(1), 1543–1561. DOI: 10.1007/s11356-023-31150-y PMID: 38041735

Del Vecchio, P., Di Minin, A., Petruzzelli, M., Panniello, U., & Pirri, S. (2018). Big data for open innovation in SMEs and large corporations: Trends, opportunities, and challenges. *Creativity and Innovation Management*, 27(1), 6–22. DOI: 10.1111/caim.12224

Dell'Era, C., Di Minin, A., Ferrigno, G., Frattini, F., Landoni, P., & Verganti, R. (2020). Value capture in open innovation processes with radical circles: A qualitative analysis of firms' collaborations with Slow Food, Memphis, and Free Software Foundation. *Technological Forecasting and Social Change*, 158, 120128. DOI: 10.1016/j.techfore.2020.120128

Derbe, T., Melak, D., & Derso, B. (2023). Stakeholders' integration to Social responsibility: Its Implication on Youth Self Employment. *Ethiopian Renaissance Journal of Social Sciences and the Humanities*, 10(1), 41–60. DOI: 10.4314/erjssh.v10i1.3

Dereso, C. W., Kant, S., Muthuraman, M., & Tufa, G. (2023, May). Effect of Point of Service on Health Department Student's Creativity in Comprehensive Universities of Ethiopia: Moderating Role of Public-Private Partnership and Mediating Role of Work Place Learning. In *Proceedings of the International Health Informatics Conference: IHIC 2022* (pp. 135-147). Singapore: Springer Nature Singapore. DOI: 10.1007/978-981-19-9090-8_13

Deslée, A., & Cloarec, J. (2024). Safeguarding Privacy: Ethical Considerations in Data-Driven Marketing. In Matosas-López, L. (Ed.), *The Impact of Digitalization on Current Marketing Strategies* (pp. 147–161). Emerald Publishing Limited., DOI: 10.1108/978-1-83753-686-320241009

Dhanda, U., & Shrotryia, V. K. (2021). Corporate sustainability: The new organizational reality. *Qualitative Research in Organizations and Management*, 16(3/4), 464–487. DOI: 10.1108/QROM-01-2020-1886

Dhruv, A. J., Patel, R., & Doshi, N. Python: the most advanced programming language for computer science applications. *Proceedings of the international conference on cultural heritage, education, sustainable tourism, and innovation technologies -CESIT 2020*, 2021.

Domingos, P., & Pazzani, M. (1997). On the optimality of the simple Bayesian classifier under zero-one loss. *Machine Learning*, 29(2–3), 103–130. https://www.researchgate.net/publication/245220694_On_the_Optimality_of_the_Simple_Bayesian_Classifier_under_Zero-OneLoss

Doni, F., & Fiameni, M. (2024). Can innovation affect the relationship between Environmental, Social, and Governance issues and financial performance? Empirical evidence from the STOXX200 index. *Business Strategy and the Environment*, 33(2), 546–574. DOI: 10.1002/bse.3500

Dr. Bonnie Morris; (1995) Case Based Reasoning AI/ES Update; Fall 1995; West Virginia University; vol. 5 no. 1.

Dreiseitl, S., & Ohno-Machado. (2002). Logistic regression and artificial neural network classification models: A methodology review. *Journal of Biomedical Informatics*, 35(5–6), 352–359. https://www.sciencedirect.com/science/article/pii/S1532046403000340 PMID: 12968784

Duan, Y., Edwards, J. S., & Dwivedi, Y. K. (2019). Artificial Intelligence for Decision Making in the Era of Big Data–Evolution, Challenges, and Research Agenda. *International Journal of Information Management*, 48, 63–71. DOI: 10.1016/j.ijinfomgt.2019.01.021

Dubey, R., Gunasekaran, A., Childe, S. J., Blome, C., & Papadopoulos, T. (2019). Big data and predictive analytics and manufacturing performance: Integrating institutional theory, resource-based view and big data culture. *British Journal of Management*, 30(2), 341–361. DOI: 10.1111/1467-8551.12355

Ebekozien, A., Aigbavboa, C. O., & Ramotshela, M. (2024). A qualitative approach to investigate stakeholders' engagement in construction projects. *Benchmarking*, 31(3), 866–883. DOI: 10.1108/BIJ-11-2021-0663

Ejegwa, P. A., Feng, Y., Tang, S., Agbetayo, J. M., & Dai, X. (2023). New Pythagorean fuzzy-based distance operators and their applications in pattern classification and disease diagnostic analysis. *Neural Computing & Applications*, 35(14), 10083–10095. DOI: 10.1007/s00521-022-07679-3

Ellili, N. O. D. (2022). Impact of ESG disclosure and financial reporting quality on investment efficiency. Corporate Governance: An International Journal of Business in Society.

Enholm, I. M., Papagiannidis, E., Mikalef, P., & Krogstie, J. (2022). Artificial Intelligence and business value: A literature review. *Information Systems Frontiers*, 24(8), 1709–1734. DOI: 10.1007/s10796-021-10186-w

Enkel, E., Bogers, M., & Chesbrough, H. (2020). Exploring open innovation in the digital age: A maturity model and future research directions. *R & D Management*, 50(1), 161–168. DOI: 10.1111/radm.12397

Entezari, A., Aslani, A., Zahedi, R., & Noorollahi, Y. (2023). Artificial intelligence and machine learning in energy systems: A bibliographic perspective. *Energy Strategy Reviews*, 45, 101017. DOI: 10.1016/j.esr.2022.101017

Erevelles, S., Fukawa, N., & Swayne, L. (2016). Big Data consumer analytics and the transformation of marketing. *Journal of Business Research*, 69(2), 897–904. DOI: 10.1016/j.jbusres.2015.07.001

Esenogho, E., Mienye, I. D., Swart, T. G., Aruleba, K., & Obaido, G. (2022). A Neural Network Ensemble with Feature Engineering for Improved Credit Card Fraud Detection. *IEEE Access : Practical Innovations, Open Solutions*, 10, 400–407. DOI: 10.1109/ACCESS.2022.3148298

European Data Market Study 2021-2023. https://digital-strategy.ec.europa.eu/en/library/results-new-european-data-market-study-2021-2023

EY. (2023). Artificial intelligence ESG stakes, Discussion paper. Retrieved from https://assets.ey.com/content/dam/ey-sites/ey-com/en_ca/topics/ai/ey-artificial-intelligence-esg-stakes-discussion-paper.pdf

Fahad, L. G., & Tahir, S. F. (2020). Activity recognition in a smart home using local feature weighting and variants of nearest-neighbors classifiers. *Journal of Ambient Intelligence and Humanized Computing*, 1–10. PMID: 32837595

Falk, S., & van Wynsberghe, A. (2023). Challenging AI for Sustainability: What ought it mean? *AI and Ethics*. Advance online publication. DOI: 10.1007/s43681-023-00323-3

Färber, M., Svetashova, Y., & Harth, A. (2021). *Theories of Meaning for the Internet of Things. Concepts in Action*. Springer.

Faroukhi, A. Z., El Alaoui, I., Gahi, Y., & Amine, A. (2020b). An adaptable big data value chain framework for end-to-end big data monetization. *Big Data and cognitive computing*, 4(4), 34. https://doi.org/ DOI: 10.3390/bdcc4040034

Faroukhi, A. Z., El Alaoui, I., Gahi, Y., & Amine, A. (2020a). Big data monetization throughout Big Data Value Chain: A comprehensive review. *Journal of Big Data*, 7(1), 1–22. DOI: 10.1186/s40537-019-0281-5

Fatima, M., & Pasha, M. (2017). Survey of machine learning algorithms for disease diagnostic. *Journal of Intelligent Learning Systems and Applications*, 9(01), 1–16. DOI: 10.4236/jilsa.2017.91001

Fazilov, F. (2021). *Anti-Corruption Review in global health*. Ilkogretim Online.

Feizizadeh, B., Omarzadeh, D., Kazemi Garajeh, M., Lakes, T., & Blaschke, T. (2023). Machine learning data-driven approaches for land use/cover mapping and trend analysis using Google Earth Engine. *Journal of Environmental Planning and Management*, 66(3), 665–697. DOI: 10.1080/09640568.2021.2001317

Feng, J., Zhang, Y. Q., & Zhang, H. (2017). Improving the co-word analysis method based on semantic distance. *Scientometrics*, 111(3), 1521–1531. DOI: 10.1007/s11192-017-2286-1

Ferrigno, G., Barabuffi, S., Marcazzan, E., & Piccaluga, A. (2024, October). What "V" of the big data influence SMEs' open innovation breadth and depth? An empirical analysis. *R & D Management*, radm.12727. DOI: 10.1111/radm.12727

Ferrigno, G., Crupi, A., Di Minin, A., & Ritala, P. (2023). 50+ years of R&D Management: A retrospective synthesis and new research trajectories. *R & D Management*, 53(5), 900–926. DOI: 10.1111/radm.12592

Ferrigno, G., & Cucino, V. (2021). Innovating and transforming during COVID-19: Insights from Italian firms. *R & D Management*, 51(4), 325–338. DOI: 10.1111/radm.12469

Ferrigno, G., Del Sarto, N., Cucino, V., & Piccaluga, A. (2022). Connecting organizational learning and open innovation research: An integrative framework and insights from case studies of strategic alliances. *The Learning Organization*, 29(6), 615–634. DOI: 10.1108/TLO-03-2021-0030

Ferrigno, G., Del Sarto, N., Piccaluga, A., & Baroncelli, A. (2023). Industry 4.0 base technologies and business models: A bibliometric analysis. *European Journal of Innovation Management*, 26(7), 502–526. DOI: 10.1108/EJIM-02-2023-0107

Ferrigno, G., Martin, X., & Dagnino, G. B. (2024). Explaining the interplay of value creation and value appropriation in strategic alliances: A developmental perspective. *International Journal of Management Reviews*, 26(2), 232–253. DOI: 10.1111/ijmr.12351

Ferrigno, G., Zordan, A., & Di Minin, A. (2022). The emergence of dominant design in the early automotive industry: An historical analysis of Ford's technological experimentation from 1896 to 1906. *Technology Analysis and Strategic Management*, •••, 1–12. DOI: 10.1080/09537325.2022.2074386

Firouzi, F., Farahani, B., Barzegari, M., & Daneshmand, M. (2020). AI-driven data monetization: The other face of data in IoT-based smart and connected health. *IEEE Internet of Things Journal*, 9(8), 5581–5599. DOI: 10.1109/JIOT.2020.3027971

Franco, P., Martinez, J. M., Kim, Y.-C., & Ahmed, M. A. (2021). IoT based approach for load monitoring and activity recognition in smart homes. *IEEE Access : Practical Innovations, Open Solutions*, 9, 45325–45339. DOI: 10.1109/ACCESS.2021.3067029

Frisk, J. E., & Bannister, F. (2017). Improving the use of analytics and big data by changing the decision-making culture: A design approach. *Management Decision*, 55(10), 2074–2088. DOI: 10.1108/MD-07-2016-0460

Fujiyoshi, H., Hirakawa, T., & Yamashita, T. (2019). Deep learning-based image recognition for autonomous driving. *IATSS Research*, 43(4), 244–252. DOI: 10.1016/j.iatssr.2019.11.008

Fu, K. C. (Ed.). (1968). *Sequential methods in pattern recognition and machine learning*. Academic press.

Fu, W., & Irfan, M. (2022). Does green financing develop a cleaner environment for environmental sustainability: Empirical insights from association of southeast Asian nations economies. *Frontiers in Psychology*, 13, 904768. DOI: 10.3389/fpsyg.2022.904768 PMID: 35783812

Fu, Z., He, X., Wang, E., Huo, J., Huang, J., & Wu, D. (2021). Personalized human activity recognition based on integrated wearable sensor and transfer learning. *Sensors (Basel)*, 21(3), 885. DOI: 10.3390/s21030885 PMID: 33525538

Gan, K., Shek, J. K. H., & Mueller, M. A. (2015). Hybrid wind–photovoltaic–diesel–battery system sizing tool development using empirical approach, life-cycle cost and performance analysis: A case study in Scotland. *Energy Conversion and Management*, 106, 479–494. DOI: 10.1016/j.enconman.2015.09.029

Garcia, K. D., Rebelo de Sá, C., Poel, M., Carvalho, T., Mendes-Moreira, J., & João, M. P. (2021). Cardoso, André CPLF de Carvalho, and Joost N. Kok. An ensemble of autonomous auto-encoders for human activity recognition. *Neurocomputing*, 439, 271–280. DOI: 10.1016/j.neucom.2020.01.125

Gaur, D., & Dubey, S. K. Human Activities Analysis Using Machine Learning Approaches. *Proceedings of the International Conference on Paradigms of Communication, Computing, and Data Sciences*. Springer, Singapore, 2022. DOI: 10.1007/978-981-16-5747-4_39

General Data Protection Regulation (GDPR). https://eur-lex.europa.eu/eli/reg/2016/679/oj

Ghaleb, F. A., Saeed, F., Al-Sarem, M., Qasem, S. N., & Al-Hadhrami, T. (2023). Ensemble Synthesized Minority Oversampling Based Generative Adversarial Networks and Random Forest Algorithm for Credit Card Fraud Detection. *IEEE Access : Practical Innovations, Open Solutions*, 11, 694–710. DOI: 10.1109/ACCESS.2023.3306621

Ghasemaghaei, M. (2021). Understanding the impact of big data on firm performance: The necessity of conceptually differentiating among big data characteristics. *International Journal of Information Management*, 57, 102055. DOI: 10.1016/j.ijinfomgt.2019.102055

Ghasemaghaei, M., & Calic, G. (2019a). Does big data enhance firm innovation competency? The mediating role of data-driven insights. *Journal of Business Research*, 104, 69–84. DOI: 10.1016/j.jbusres.2019.07.006

Ghasemaghaei, M., & Calic, G. (2019b). Can big data improve firm decision quality? The role of data quality and data diagnosticity. *Decision Support Systems*, 120, 38–49. DOI: 10.1016/j.dss.2019.03.008

Ghasemaghaei, M., & Calic, G. (2020). Assessing the impact of big data on firm innovation performance: Big data is not always better data. *Journal of Business Research*, 108, 147–162. DOI: 10.1016/j.jbusres.2019.09.062

Ghenai, C., & Janajreh, I. (2016). Ghenai, and I. Janajreh, "Design of Solar-Biomass Hybrid Microgrid System in Sharjah". *Energy Procedia*, 103, 357–362. DOI: 10.1016/j.egypro.2016.11.299

Ghenai, C., Salameh, T., & Merabet, A. (2020, April). Technico-economic analysis of off grid solar PV/Fuel cell energy system for residential community in desert region. *International Journal of Hydrogen Energy*, 45(20), 11460–11470. DOI: 10.1016/j.ijhydene.2018.05.110

Giorgi, S., Lavagna, M., Wang, K., Osmani, M., Liu, G., & Campioli, A. (2022). Drivers and barriers towards circular economy in the building sector: Stakeholder interviews and analysis of five European countries policies and practices. *Journal of Cleaner Production*, 336, 130395. DOI: 10.1016/j.jclepro.2022.130395

Gitari, N.D., Zuping, Z., Damien, H., & Long, J. (2015). A lexicon-based approach for hate speech detection. Int. J. Multimed. Ubiquitous Eng., 10, 215–230. https://doi.org/.10.4.21DOI: 10.14257/ijmue.2015

Gonzales, R. M. D., & Hargreaves, C. A. (2022). How can we use artificial intelligence for stock recommendation and risk management? A proposed decision support system. *International Journal of Information Management Data Insights*, 2(2), 100130. DOI: 10.1016/j.jjimei.2022.100130

Grigorios, L., Magrizos, S., Kostopoulos, I., Drossos, D., & Santos, D. (2022). Overt and covert customer data collection in online personalized advertising: The role of user emotions. *Journal of Business Research*, 141, 308–320. DOI: 10.1016/j.jbusres.2021.12.025

Guo, Lingfeng, Runze Song, Jiang Wu, Zeqiu Xu, and Fanyi Zhao (2024). Integrating a Machine Learning-Driven Fraud Detection System Based on a Risk Management Framework, 1.

Guo, Y., Zhou, J., Qin, Q., Wei, Y., & Zhang, W. (2023, March 1). An Improved Algorithm and Implementation of Data Mining for Intelligent Manufacturing Association Rules Based on Pattern Recognition. *IEEE Consumer Electronics Magazine*, 12(2), 94–99. DOI: 10.1109/MCE.2022.3149210

Gupta, A., Lohani, M. C., & Manchanda, M. (2021). Financial Fraud Detection Using Naive Bayes Algorithm in Highly Imbalance Data Set. *Journal of Discrete Mathematical Sciences and Cryptography*, 24(5), 1559–1572. DOI: 10.1080/09720529.2021.1969733

Gyamfi, B. A., Agozie, D. Q., & Bekun, F. V. (2022). Can technological innovation, foreign direct investment and natural resources ease some burden for the BRICS economies within current industrial era? *Technology in Society*, 70, 102037. Advance online publication. DOI: 10.1016/j.techsoc.2022.102037

Habil, S., El-Deeb, S., & El-Bassiouny, N. (2023). AI-based recommendation systems: the ultimate solution for market prediction and targeting. In *The Palgrave Handbook of Interactive Marketing* (pp. 683–704). Springer International Publishing. DOI: 10.1007/978-3-031-14961-0_30

Hanafizadeh, P., Barkhordari Firouzabadi, M., & Vu, K. M. (2021). Insight monetization intermediary platform using recommender systems. *Electronic Markets*, 31(2), 269–293. DOI: 10.1007/s12525-020-00449-w

Hao, X., & Demir, E. (2023). Artificial intelligence in supply chain decision-making: an environmental, social, and governance triggering and technological inhibiting protocol. Journal of Modelling in Management, ahead-of-print. DOI: 10.1108/JM2-01-2023-0009

Hasan, Iqbal, and S. A. Rizvi (2022). AI-driven fraud detection and mitigation in e-commerce transactions. *Proceedings of Data Analytics and Management: ICDAM*, 1.

Hashemi, S. K., Mirtaheri, S. L., & Greco, S. (2023). Fraud Detection in Banking Data by Machine Learning Techniques. *IEEE Access : Practical Innovations, Open Solutions*, 11, 3034–3043. DOI: 10.1109/ACCESS.2022.3232287

Hassenzahl, M., & Tractinsky, N. (2006). User experience-a research agenda. *Behaviour & Information Technology*, 25(2), 91–97. DOI: 10.1080/01449290500330331

Hernández, E., Sittón, I., Rodríguez, S., Gil, A. B., & García, R. J. (2019). An investment recommender multi-agent system in financial technology. In *International Joint Conference SOCO'18-CISIS'18-ICEUTE'18: San Sebastián, Spain,June 6-8, 2018Proceedings 13* (pp. 3-10). Springer International Publishing. DOI: 10.1007/978-3-319-94120-2_1

Herschel, R., & Miori, V. M. (2017). Ethics & Big Data. *Technology in Society*, 49, 31–36. DOI: 10.1016/j.techsoc.2017.03.003

Heydari, A., & Askarzadeh, A. (2016). Optimization of a biomass-based photovoltaic power plant for an off-grid application subject to loss of power supply probability concept. *Applied Energy*, 165, 601–611. DOI: 10.1016/j.apenergy.2015.12.095

Hilal, W., Gadsden, S. A., & Yawney, J. (2022). Financial Fraud: A Review of Anomaly Detection Techniques and Recent Advances. *Expert Systems with Applications*, 193, 193. DOI: 10.1016/j.eswa.2021.116429

Hirsch, P. B. (2021). Footprints in the cloud: The hidden cost of IT infrastructure. *The Journal of Business Strategy*, 43(1), 65–68. DOI: 10.1108/JBS-11-2021-0175

Hong, L. (2011). Predicting Popular Messages in Twitter. https://citeseerx.ist.psu.edu/document?repid=rep1&type=pdf&doi=a772b2d623e90159021d093333c55dbeeac7bd2c

Howe, J. (2006). The rise of crowdsourcing. *Wired magazine, 14*(6), 176-183.

Hu, Tang, Tang, & Liu. (2013). Exploiting social relations for sentiment analysis in microblogging. Proceedings of the Sixth ACM International Conference on Web Search and Data Mining, WSDM '13, 537–546. https://dl.acm.org/doi/10.1145/2488388.2488442

Huang, S. Y., & Lee, C. J. (2022). Predicting continuance intention to fintech chatbot. *Computers in Human Behavior*, 129, 107027. DOI: 10.1016/j.chb.2021.107027

Hunger, D. L., & Wheelen, T. L. (2008). *Concepts: Strategic Management and Business Policy*. Prentice Hall.

Husnah, H., & Fahlevi, M. (2023). How do corporate social responsibility and sustainable development goals shape financial performance in Indonesia's mining industry? *Uncertain Supply Chain Management*, 11(3), 1383–1394. DOI: 10.5267/j.uscm.2023.5.099

Hussein, Ameer S., Rihab S. K., Shaima M. Mohamed N., and Haider Salim A. (2021). Credit Card Fraud Detection Using Fuzzy Rough Nearest Neighbor and Sequential Minimal Optimization with Logistic Regression. *International Journal of Interactive Mobile Technologies*, 15.

Hu, W., Shang, Q., Bian, X., & Zhu, R. (2021, December 29). Energy management strategy of hybrid energy storage system based on fuzzy control for ships. *The International Journal of Low Carbon Technologies*, 17, 169–175. DOI: 10.1093/ijlct/ctab094

Ibe-enwo, G., Igbudu, N., Garanti, Z., & Popoola, T. (2019). Assessing the relevance of green banking practice on bank loyalty: The mediating effect of green image and bank trust. *Sustainability (Basel)*, 11(17), 4651. DOI: 10.3390/su11174651

Ibrahim, R. L., Al-mulali, U., Ozturk, I., Bello, A. K., & Raimi, L. (2022). On the criticality of renewable energy to sustainable development: Do green financial development, technological innovation, and economic complexity matter for China? *Renewable Energy*, 199, 262–277. DOI: 10.1016/j.renene.2022.08.101

Ileberi, E., Sun, Y., & Wang, Z. (2021). Performance Evaluation of ML Methods for CC Fraud Detection Using SMOTE and AdaBoost. *IEEE Access : Practical Innovations, Open Solutions*, 9, 86–94. DOI: 10.1109/ACCESS.2021.3134330

Ileberi, E., Sun, Y., & Wang, Z. (2022). A Machine Learning based Credit Card Fraud Detection using the GA algorithm for feature selection. *Journal of Big Data*, 9(1), 24. DOI: 10.1186/s40537-022-00573-8

Ingi Sigurbergsson, G., & Derczynski, L. (2019). Offensive Language and Hate Speech Detection for Danish. arXiv e-prints. arXiv:1908.04531.

Inmon, W. H. (1996). *Building the Data Warehouse*. John Wiley & Sons.

Innan, N., Sawaika, A., Dhor, A., Dutta, S., Thota, S., Gokal, H., Patel, N., Khan, M. A.-Z., Theodonis, I., & Bennai, M. (2024). Financial Fraud Detection Using Quantum Graph Neural Networks. *Quantum Machine Intelligence*, 6(1), 7. DOI: 10.1007/s42484-024-00143-6

International Energy Agency (IEA) Reports. https://www.iea.org/reports

International Renewable Energy Agency (IRENA) Reports. https://www.irena.org/reports

IPCC Special Report on Global Warming of 1.5°C: https://www.ipcc.ch/sr15/

Iscan, C., Kumas, O., Akbulut, F. P., & Akbulut, A. (2023). Wallet-Based Transaction Fraud Prevention through LightGBM with the Focus on Minimizing False Alarms. *IEEE Access : Practical Innovations, Open Solutions*, 11, 65–74. DOI: 10.1109/ACCESS.2023.3321666

Isinkaye, F. O., Folajimi, Y. O., & Ojokoh, B. A. (2015). Recommendation systems: Principles, methods and evaluation. *Egyptian informatics journal, 16*(3), 261-273.

Jaber, T. A. (2022). Artificial intelligence in computer networks. *Periodicals of Engineering and Natural Sciences*, 10(1), 309–322. DOI: 10.21533/pen.v10i1.2616

Jedynak, M., Czakon, W., Kuźniarska, A., & Mania, K. (2021). Digital transformation of organizations: What do we know and where to go next? [DOI]. *Journal of Organizational Change Management*, 34(3), 629–652. DOI: 10.1108/JOCM-10-2020-0336

Jöhnk, J., Weißert, M., & Wyrtki, K. (2021). Ready or not, AI comes—An interview study of organizational AI readiness factors. *Business & Information Systems Engineering*, 63(1), 5–20. DOI: 10.1007/s12599-020-00676-7

Johnson, C. E.Jr, Stout, J. H., & Walter, A. C. (2020). Profound Change: The Evolution of ESG. *Business Lawyer*, 75, 2567–2608.

Johnson, J. S., Friend, S. B., & Lee, H. S. (2017). Big Data Facilitation, Utilization, and Monetization: Exploring the 3Vs in a New Product Development Process. *Journal of Product Innovation Management*, 34(5), 640–658. DOI: 10.1111/jpim.12397

Johnson, W. M., Christensen, C. M., & Kagerman, H. (2008). Reinventing Your Business Model. *Harvard Business Review*, 86(12), 57–68.

Jovanovic, S. Milos, Zivkovic, M, Tanaskovic, Bacanin (2022). Tuning ML Models Using a Group Search Firefly Algorithm for Credit Card Fraud Detection. *MDPI Journal- Mathematics*, 10.

Kar, A. K., Choudhary, S. K., & Singh, V. K. (2022). How can artificial intelligence impact sustainability: A systematic literature review. *Journal of Cleaner Production*, 376, 134120. Advance online publication. DOI: 10.1016/j.jclepro.2022.134120

Karthika, Jegadeesan, Senthilselvi, Ayothi (2023). Smart Credit Card Fraud Detection System based on Dilated Convolutional Neural Network with Sampling Technique. *Multimedia Tools Applications*, 82, 01-18.

Khaleel, M., Ahmed, A. A., & Alsharif, A. (2023). Artificial Intelligence in Engineering. *Brilliance: Research of Artificial Intelligence*, 3(1), 32–42. DOI: 10.47709/brilliance.v3i1.2170

Khalid, A. Rehman, N. Owoh, Omair U., Moses A., Jude O., John A. (2024). Enhancing Credit Card Fraud Detection: An Ensemble Machine Learning Approach. *Big Data and Cognitive Computing*, 8.

Khan, H. U., Alomari, M. K., Khan, S., Nazir, S., Gill, A. Q., Al-Maadid, A. A., Abu-Shawish, Z. K., & Hassan, M. K. (2021). *Systematic analysis of safety and security risks in smart homes*. CMC- Computers Materials & Continua.

Khan, M. A., Saqib, S., Alyas, T., Rehman, A. U., Saeed, Y., Zeb, A., & Mohamed, E. M. (2020). Effective demand forecasting model using business intelligence empowered with machine learning. *IEEE Access : Practical Innovations, Open Solutions*, 8, 116013–116023. DOI: 10.1109/ACCESS.2020.3003790

Khan, N. U., Anwar, M., Li, S., & Khattak, M. S. (2021). Intellectual capital, financial resources, and green supply chain management as predictors of financial and environmental performance. *Environmental Science and Pollution Research International*, 28(16), 19755–19767. DOI: 10.1007/s11356-020-12243-4 PMID: 33405102

Khedmati, Mohamad, Masoud Erfani, Mohammad GhasemiGol (2020). Applying Support Vector Data Description for Fraud Detection. *ArXiv Journal*, 618.

Kim, H., Choi, H., Kang, H., An, J., Yeom, S., & Hong, T. (2021). A systematic review of the smart energy conservation system: From smart homes to sustainable smart cities. *Renewable & Sustainable Energy Reviews*, 140, 110755. DOI: 10.1016/j.rser.2021.110755

Kitchin, R. (2014). Big Data, New Epistemologies and Paradigm Shifts." *. *Big Data & Society*, 1(1), 2053951714528481. DOI: 10.1177/2053951714528481

Kitsios, F., & Kamariotou, M. (2021). Artificial Intelligence and Business Strategy towards Digital Transformation: A Research Agenda. *Sustainability (Basel)*, 13(4), 2025. DOI: 10.3390/su13042025

Kleinberg, J. (2003). Bursty and hierarchical structure in streams. *Data Mining and Knowledge Discovery*, 7(4), 373–397. DOI: 10.1023/A:1024940629314

Konopik, J., Jahn, C., Schuster, T., Hoßbach, N., & Pflaum, A. (2022). *Mastering the digital transformation through organizational capabilities: A conceptual framework*. Digital Business., DOI: 10.1016/j.digbus.2021.100019

Kopalle, P. K., Pauwels, K., Akella, L. Y., & Gangwar, M. (2023). Dynamic pricing: Definition, implications for managers, and future research directions. *Journal of Retailing*, 99(4), 580–593. DOI: 10.1016/j.jretai.2023.11.003

Kouadria, A., Nouali, O., & Al-Shamri, M. Y. H. (2020). A multi-criteria collaborative filtering recommender system using learning-to-rank and rank aggregation. *Arabian Journal for Science and Engineering*, 45(4), 2835–2845. DOI: 10.1007/s13369-019-04180-3

Kraus, S., Jones, P., Kailer, N., Weinmann, A., Chaparro-Banegas, N., & Roig-Tierno, N. (2021). Digital transformation: An overview of the current state of the art of research. *SAGE Open*, 11(3), 21582440211047576. DOI: 10.1177/21582440211047576

Krishna. Prasad, K. (2020). A Literature Review on Application of Sentiment Analysis Using Machine Learning Techniques. *International Journal of Applied Engineering and Management Letters*, 4(2), 41–77. https://papers.ssrn.com/sol3/papers.cfm?abstract_id=3674982

Krishnamoorthy, R. (2021). Environmental, Social, and Governance (ESG) Investing: Doing Good to Do Well. *Open Journal of Social Sciences*, 9(7), 189–197. DOI: 10.4236/jss.2021.97013

La Torre, M., Sabelfeld, S., Blomkvist, M., Tarquinio, L., & Dumay, J. (2018). Harmonising non-financial reporting regulation in Europe: Practical forces and projections for future research. Meditari Accountancy Research, 26(4), 598-621.

Lai, W., Zhang, N., & Yu, J. (2019). Artificial intelligence-based dynamic power dispatch for grid-connected solar PV-fuel cell hybrid power system. *Energies*, 12(24), 4716.

Lambert, P. Gilman, and P. Lilienthal, "Micropower system modeling with HOMER," Chap. 15 in Integration of Alternative Sources of Energy, by F. A. Farret and M. G. Simoes, John Wiley & Sons, 2006.

Lambert, E., & Deyganto, K. O. (2024). The Impact of Green Legacy on Climate Change in Ethiopia. *Green and Low-Carbon Economy*, 2(2), 97–105. DOI: 10.47852/bonviewGLCE32021372

Laney, D. (2001). *3D Data Management: Controlling Data Volume*. Velocity, and Variety.

Lan, S., Wen, S., Hong, Y.-Y., Yu, D. C., & Zhang, L. (2015). Wena,Y-Y. Hong, D. C. Yu, and L. Zhang, "Optimal sizing of hybrid PV/diesel/battery in ship power system". *Applied Energy*, 158, 26–34. DOI: 10.1016/j.apenergy.2015.08.031

Larsson, S. (2019). Artificial Intelligence as a Normative Societal Challenge: Bias, Responsibility, and Transparency. In Festschrift for Håkan Hydén. Lund: Juristförlaget.

Latifah, I. N., Suhendra, A. A., & Mufidah, I. (2024). Factors affecting job satisfaction and employee performance: A case study in an Indonesian sharia property companies. *International Journal of Productivity and Performance Management*, 73(3), 719–748. DOI: 10.1108/IJPPM-03-2021-0132

Laux, J., Wachter, S., & Mittelstadt, B. (2024). Three pathways for standardisation and ethical disclosure by default under the European Union Artificial Intelligence Act. *Computer Law & Security Report*, 53, 105957. Advance online publication. DOI: 10.1016/j.clsr.2024.105957

Lawrence, J., Rasche, A., & Kenny, K. (2018). Sustainability as Opportunity: Unilever's Sustainable Living Plan. In Lenssen, G., & Smith, N. (Eds.), *Managing Sustainable Business* (pp. 435–455). Springer. DOI: 10.1007/978-94-024-1144-7_21

Lee, Y., Yoon, S., & Jung, K. (2018). Comparative Studies of Detecting Abusive Language on Twitter. CoRR. abs/1808.1.

Lee, Y.-J., & Zhang, X. T. (2019). AI-Generated Corporate Environmental Data: An Event Study with Predictive Power. In J. J. Choi & B. Ozkan (Eds.), Disruptive Innovation in Business and Finance in the Digital World (Vol. 20, pp. 65-83). Emerald Publishing Limited. DOI: 10.1108/S1569-376720190000020009

Lee, S., Khan, M. Q., & Husen, M. N. (2021, February). Continuous Car Driving Intent Detection Using Structural Pattern Recognition. *IEEE Transactions on Intelligent Transportation Systems*, 22(2), 1001–1013. DOI: 10.1109/TITS.2019.2961928

Li, Shasha, Tiejun Cui, and Muhammad Alam. "Reliability analysis of the internet of things using Space Fault Network. *Alexandria Engineering Journal*, pages, 1259-1270, 2021.

LINKS:

Li, Q., Gravina, R., Li, Y., Alsamhi, S. H., Sun, F., & Fortino, G. (2020). Multi-user activity recognition: Challenges and opportunities. *Information Fusion*, 63, 121–135. DOI: 10.1016/j.inffus.2020.06.004

Liu, Aiming, Kun Chen, Quan Liu, Qingsong Ai, Yi Xie, Anqi Chen (2017). Feature Selection for Motor Imagery EEG Classification based on Firefly Algorithm and Learning Automata. *MDPI Journal: Sensors*, 17.

Liu, J., Zhang, Y., Wang, X., Deng, Y., & Wu, X. (2019). Dynamic pricing on e-commerce platform with deep reinforcement learning: A field experiment. *arXiv preprint arXiv:1912.02572*.

Li, X., Wang, Z., Chen, C. H., & Zheng, P. (2021). A data-driven reversible framework for achieving Sustainable Smart product-service systems. *Journal of Cleaner Production*, 279, 123618. Advance online publication. DOI: 10.1016/j.jclepro.2020.123618

Li, Z. (2018). Development of machine learning and several learning methods [J]. *Industry and Science Forum*, 15(10), 198–199.

Lokanan, M. E. (2024). Predicting Money Laundering Using Machine Learning and Artificial Neural Networks Algorithms in Banks. *Journal of Applied Security Research*, 19(1), 20–44. DOI: 10.1080/19361610.2022.2114744

Lourenço, I., Branco, M., Curto, J., & Eugénio, T. (2012). How does the market value corporate sustainability performance? *Journal of Business Ethics*, 108(4), 417–428. DOI: 10.1007/s10551-011-1102-8

Lu, J., Wu, D., Mao, M., Wang, W., & Zhang, G. (2015). Recommender system application developments: A survey. *Decision Support Systems*, 74, 12–32. DOI: 10.1016/j.dss.2015.03.008

M. N. Ashtiani and B. Raahemi (2022). Intelligent Fraud Detection in Financial Statements Using ML and Data Mining: A Systematic Literature Review. *IEEE Access,* 10, 04-25.

Macpherson, M., Gasperini, A., & Bosco, M. (2021). Artificial Intelligence and FinTech Technologies for ESG Data and Analysis. DOI: 10.2139/ssrn.3790774

Mahmood, S., Chadhar, M., & Firmin, S. (2024). Digital resilience framework for managing crisis: A qualitative study in the higher education and research sector. *Journal of Contingencies and Crisis Management*, 32(1), e12549. DOI: 10.1111/1468-5973.12549

Makridakis, S. (2017). The forthcoming Artificial Intelligence (AI) revolution: Its impact on society and firms. *Futures*, 90, 46–60. DOI: 10.1016/j.futures.2017.03.006

Malik, A., Parihar, V., Srivastava, J., Kaur, H., & Abidin, S. "Prognosis of Diabetes Mellitus Based on Machine Learning Algorithms," 2023 10th International Conference on Computing for Sustainable Global Development (INDIACom), New Delhi, India, 2023, pp. 1466-1472.

Malik, A., Parihar, V., Bhushan, B., Srivastava, J., & Karim, L. (2023). Artificial Intelligence-Based React Application (Powered by Conversational ALAN-AI Voice Assistance). In Sharma, D. K., Peng, S. L., Sharma, R., & Jeon, G. (Eds.), *Micro-Electronics and Telecommunication Engineering. Lecture Notes in Networks and Systems* (Vol. 617). Springer., DOI: 10.1007/978-981-19-9512-5_47

Manaf, A., & Singh, S. Computer Vision-based Survey on Human Activity Recognition System, Challenges and Applications. *2021 3rd International Conference on Signal Processing and Communication (ICPSC)*. IEEE, 2021.

Manjeevan, S., & Chee Peng, C. P. (2024). An intelligent payment card fraud detection system. *Annals of Operations Research*, 334(1-3), 445–467. DOI: 10.1007/s10479-021-04149-2

Marion, T. J., & Fixson, S. K. (2021). The transformation of the innovation process: How digital tools are changing work, collaboration, and organizations in new product development. *Journal of Product Innovation Management*, 38(1), 192–215. DOI: 10.1111/jpim.12547

Massa, L., Tucci, C. L., & Afuah, A. (2017). A critical assessment of business model research. *The Academy of Management Annals*, 11(1), 73–104. DOI: 10.5465/annals.2014.0072

Ma, Y., Arshad, S., Muniraju, S., Torkildson, E., Rantala, E., Doppler, K., & Zhou, G. (2021). *Location- and person-independent activity recognition with WiFi, deep neural networks, and reinforcement learning*. ACM Transactions on Internet of Things. DOI: 10.1145/3424739

McAfee, A., Brynjolfsson, E., Davenport, T. H., Patil, D. J., & Barton, D. (2012). Big data: The management revolution. *Harvard Business Review*, 90(10), 60–68. https://hbr.org/2012/10/big-data-the-management-revolution PMID: 23074865

McDonnell, M.-H., & Cobb, J. (2020). Take a Stand or Keep Your Seat: Board Turnover after Social Movement Boycotts. *Academy of Management Journal*, 63(4), 1028–1053. DOI: 10.5465/amj.2017.0890

Megdad, Mosa MM, Samy S. Abu-Naser and Bassem S. Abu-Nasser (2022). Fraudulent Financial Transactions Detection Using ML. *International Journal of Academic Information Systems Research*, 6.

Mehbodniya, A., Alam, I., Pande, S., Neware, R., Rane, K. P., Shabaz, M., & Madhavan, M. V. (2021). Financial fraud detection in healthcare using ML and deep learning techniques. *Security and Communication Networks*, 2021, 1–8. DOI: 10.1155/2021/9293877

Merabet, K., Tawfique Ahmed, K., Ibrahim, H., Beguenane, R., & Ghias, A. M. Y. M. (2017). Ahmed, H. Ibrahim, R. Beguenane, and A. Ghias, "Energy management and control system for laboratory scale microgrid based wind-PV-battery,". *IEEE Transactions on Sustainable Energy*, 8(1), 145–154. DOI: 10.1109/TSTE.2016.2587828

Messeni Petruzzelli, A., Murgia, G., & Parmentola, A. (2022). How can open innovation support SMEs in the adoption of I4. 0 technologies? An empirical analysis. *R & D Management*, 52(4), 615–632. DOI: 10.1111/radm.12507

Meyer, G., Adomavicius, G., Johnson, P. E., Elidrisi, M., Rush, W. A., Sperl-Hillen, J. M., & O'Connor, P. J. (2014). A machine learning approach to improving dynamic decision making. *Information Systems Research*, 25(2), 239–263. DOI: 10.1287/isre.2014.0513

Mikalef, P., Boura, M., Lekakos, G., & Krogstie, J. (2019). Big data analytics capabilities and innovation: The mediating role of dynamic capabilities and moderating effect of the environment. *British Journal of Management*, 30(2), 272–298. DOI: 10.1111/1467-8551.12343

Miller, T. (2019). Explanation in artificial intelligence: Insights from the social sciences. *Artificial Intelligence*, 267, 1–38. DOI: 10.1016/j.artint.2018.07.007

Mitra, S., & Pal, S. K. (2005). Fuzzy sets in pattern recognition and machine intelligence. *Fuzzy Sets and Systems*, 156(3), 381–386. DOI: 10.1016/j.fss.2005.05.035

Mohamed, N., Al-Jaroodi, J., & Jawhar, I. Towards fault-tolerant fog computing for IoT-based smart city applications. *In 2019 IEEE 9th Annual Computing and Communication Workshop and Conference (CCWC)*, pages 0752- 0757. IEEE, 2019.

Morinaga, S. (2012). Survey on mining subjective data on the web. *Data Mining and Knowledge Discovery*, 24(3), 478–514. DOI: 10.1007/s10618-011-0238-6

Moro-Visconti, R. (2022). *Augmented Corporate Valuation: From Digital Networking to ESG Compliance*. Palgrave Macmillan. DOI: 10.1007/978-3-030-97117-5

Morris, M. X., Rajesh, A., Asaad, M., Hassan, A., Saadoun, R., & Butler, C. E. (2023). Deep learning applications in surgery: Current uses and future directions. *The American Surgeon*, 89(1), 36–42. DOI: 10.1177/00031348221101490 PMID: 35567312

Morris, S. A., Yen, G., Wu, Z., & Asnake, B. (2003). Time line visualization of research fronts. *Journal of the American Society for Information Science and Technology*, 54(5), 413–422. DOI: 10.1002/asi.10227

Mosa, D. T., Sorour, S. E., Abohany, A. A., & Maghraby, F. A. (2024). CCFD: Efficient Credit Card Fraud Detection Using Meta-Heuristic Techniques and Machine Learning Algorithms. *Mathematics*, 12(14), 2250. DOI: 10.3390/math12142250

Mukhuty, S., Upadhyay, A., & Rothwell, H. (2022). Strategic sustainable development of Industry 4.0 through the lens of social responsibility: The role of human resource practices. *Business Strategy and the Environment*, 31(5), 2068–2081. DOI: 10.1002/bse.3008

Murugan, M. S., & Kala, T. (2023). Large-scale data-driven financial risk management & analysis using machine learning strategies. *Measurement. Sensors*, 27, 100756. DOI: 10.1016/j.measen.2023.100756

Musleh Al-Sartawi, A. M., Hussainey, K., & Razzaque, A. (2022). The role of artificial intelligence in sustainable finance. *Journal of Sustainable Finance & Investment*, 1–6. DOI: 10.1080/20430795.2022.2057405

Musleh Al-Sartawi, A. M., Razzaque, A., & Kamal, M. M. (Eds.). (2021). *Artificial Intelligence Systems and the Internet of Things in the Digital Era. EAMMIS 2021. Lecture Notes in Networks and Systems* (Vol. 239). Springer.

Nabrawi, E., & Alanazi, A. (2023). Fraud detection in healthcare insurance claims using machine learning. *Risks*, 11(9), 160. DOI: 10.3390/risks11090160

Nadkarni, S., & Prügl, R. (2021). *Digital transformation: a review, synthesis and opportunities for future research*. Management Review Quarterly., DOI: 10.1007/s11301-020-00185-7

Na, J., Yang, H., Gu, Q., & Huang, J. (2019). Machine learning and its algorithm and development analysis [J] [Theoretical Edition]. *Information and Computer Science*, 87(1), 83–84.

Najjar, M. S., & Kettinger, W. J. (2013). Data Monetization: Lessons from a Retailer's Journey. *MIS Quarterly Executive*, 12(4). https://digitalcommons.memphis.edu/facpubs/11054

Najmi, A., Rashidi, T. H., Abbasi, A., & Waller, S. T. (2017). Reviewing the transport domain: An evolutionary bibliometrics and network analysis. *Scientometrics*, 110(2), 843–865. DOI: 10.1007/s11192-016-2171-3

Nakra, V., Pandi, K. G. P., Paripati, L., Choppadandi, A., & Chanchela, P. (2024). Leveraging Machine Learning Algorithms for Real-Time Fraud Detection in Digital Payment Systems. *International Journal of Multidisciplinary Innovation and Research Methodology*, 3, 165–175.

Nama, F. A., & Obaid, A. J. (2024). Financial Fraud Identification Using Deep Learning Techniques. *Al-Salam Journal for Engineering and Technology*, 3(1), 141–147. DOI: 10.55145/ajest.2024.03.01.012

Naqvi, A. (Ed.). (2021). *Artificial intelligence for asset management and investment: a strategic perspective*. Wiley. DOI: 10.1002/9781119601838

Nieminen, J. H. (2024). Assessment for Inclusion: Rethinking inclusive assessment in higher education. *Teaching in Higher Education*, 29(4), 841–859. Advance online publication. DOI: 10.1080/13562517.2021.2021395

Nirino, N., Ferraris, A., Miglietta, N., & Invernizzi, A. C. (2022). Intellectual capital: The missing link in the corporate social responsibility–financial performance relationship. *Journal of Intellectual Capital*, 23(2), 420–438. DOI: 10.1108/JIC-02-2020-0038

Nishant, R., Kennedy, M., & Corbett, J. (2020). Artificial Intelligence for Sustainability: Challenges, Opportunities, and a Research Agenda. *International Journal of Information Management*, 53, 102104. DOI: 10.1016/j.ijinfomgt.2020.102104

Niu, T., & Zhang, Q. "Research on Small Object Pattern Recognition Technology based on Computer Deep Learning: Improved YOLOX Model as an example," 2022 2nd International Conference on Social Sciences and Intelligence Management (SSIM), Taichung, Taiwan, 2022, pp. 93-98, DOI: 10.1109/SSIM55504.2022.10047938

Obayya, M., Maashi, M. S., Nemri, N., Mohsen, H., Motwakel, A., Osman, A. E., Alneil, A. A., & Alsaid, M. I. (2023). Hyperparameter optimizer with deep learning-based decision-support systems for histopathological breast cancer diagnosis. *Cancers (Basel)*, 15(3), 885. DOI: 10.3390/cancers15030885 PMID: 36765839

Ofulue, J., & Benyoucef, M. (2022). Data monetization: insights from a technology-enabled literature review and research agenda. *Management Review Quarterly*, 1-45. https://doi.org/DOI: 10.1007/s11301-022-00309-1

Olushola, A., & Mart, J. (2024). Fraud Detection Using Machine Learning. *ScienceOpenPreprints*.

Osegi, E. N, E. F. Jumbo (2021). Comparative Analysis of Credit Card Fraud Detection in Simulated Annealing Trained Artificial Neural Network and Hierarchical Temporal Memory. *ML with Applications*, 6.

Osterwalder, A., & Pigneur, Y. (2010). *Business Model Generation*. John Wiley and Sons.

Oyebode, O., & Orji, R. (2020). A hybrid recommender system for product sales in a banking environment. *Journal of Banking and Financial Technology*, 4(1), 15–25. DOI: 10.1007/s42786-019-00014-w

Pang, B., Lee, L., & Vaithyanathan, S. (2002). Thumbs up? Sentiment classification using machine learning techniques. Proceedings of the ACL-02 Conference on Empirical Methods in Natural Language Processing, 10, 79–86. https://aclanthology.org/W02-1011

Pang, X., Yang, H., Shen, W., & Blaabjerg, F. (2019). Techno-economic analysis and optimization of grid-connected solar photovoltaic-fuel cell hybrid systems. *IEEE Transactions on Sustainable Energy*, 10(4), 1827–1837.

Panigrahi, A., Nayak, A. K., Paul, R., Sahu, B., & Kant, S. (2022). CTB-PKI: Clustering and trust enabled blockchain based PKI system for efficient communication in P2P network. *IEEE Access : Practical Innovations, Open Solutions*, 10, 124277–124290. DOI: 10.1109/ACCESS.2022.3222807

Panigrahi, A., Pati, A., Sahu, B., Das, M. N., Nayak, D. S. K., Sahoo, G., & Kant, S. (2023). En-MinWhale: An ensemble approach based on MRMR and Whale optimization for Cancer diagnosis. *IEEE Access : Practical Innovations, Open Solutions*, 11, 113526–113542. DOI: 10.1109/ACCESS.2023.3318261

Paradza, D., & Daramola, O. (2021). Business intelligence and business value in organisations: A systematic literature review. *Sustainability (Basel)*, 13(20), 11382. DOI: 10.3390/su132011382

Paranjape-Voditel, P., & Deshpande, U. (2013). A stock market portfolio recommender system based on association rule mining. *Applied Soft Computing*, 13(2), 1055–1063. DOI: 10.1016/j.asoc.2012.09.012

Parihar, V., & Yadav, S. (2022). Comparative analysis of different machine learning algorithms to predict online shoppers' behaviour. *International Journal of Advanced Networking and Applications*, 13(06), 5169–5182. DOI: 10.35444/IJANA.2022.13603

Park, J. H., & Fung, P. (2017). One-step and Two-step Classification for Abusive Language Detection on Twitter. DOI: 10.18653/v1/W17-3006

Pasquale, F. (2015). *The Black Box Society. The Secret Algorithms That Control Money and Information.* Harvard University Press. DOI: 10.4159/harvard.9780674736061

Patel, N., Lu, Y., & Verma, R. (2018). Hydrogen production, storage, and management in solar photovoltaic-fuel cell hybrid systems. *International Journal of Hydrogen Energy*, 43(29), 13209–13225.

Patnaikuni, S., & Gengaje, S. (2021). A Theoretical Foundation for Syntactico-Semantic Pattern Recognition. *IEEE Access : Practical Innovations, Open Solutions*, 9, 135879–135889. DOI: 10.1109/ACCESS.2021.3115445

Pattern Recognition and Machine Learning" by Christopher M. Bishop

Paul, C. J., & Weinthal, E. (2019). The development of Ethiopia's Climate Resilient Green Economy 2011–2014: Implications for rural adaptation. *Climate and Development*, 11(3), 193–202. DOI: 10.1080/17565529.2018.1442802

Pelle, R., Alcântara, C., & Moreira, V. P. (2018). A classifier ensemble for offensive text detection. https://www.researchgate.net/publication/330300271_A_Classifier_Ensemble_for_Offensive_Text _DetectionDOI: 10.5753/webmedia.2018.4582

Peng, Y. & Tao, C. (2022). Can digital transformation promote enterprise performance?—From the perspective of public policy and innovation. Journal of Innovation & Knowledge. https://doi.org/DOI: 10.1016/j.jik.2022.100198

Peng, C. Y. J., Lee, K. L., & Ingersoll, G. M. (2002). An introduction to logistic regression analysis and reporting. *The Journal of Educational Research*, 96(1), 3–14. DOI: 10.1080/00220670209598786

Pennacchiotti, M., & Popescu, A.-M. (2021). A Machine Learning Approach to Twitter User Classification. *Proceedings of the International AAAI Conference on Web and Social Media, 5*(1), 281-288. DOI: 10.1609/icwsm.v5i1.14139

Pirone, D., Cimorelli, L., Del Giudice, G., & Pianese, D. (2023). Short-term rainfall forecasting using cumulative precipitation fields from station data: A probabilistic machine learning approach. *Journal of Hydrology (Amsterdam)*, 617, 128949. DOI: 10.1016/j.jhydrol.2022.128949

Poongodi, K., & Kumar, D. (2021). Support Vector Machine with Information Gain Based Classification for Credit Card Fraud Detection System. *The International Arab Journal of Information Technology*, 18, 199–207.

Prabhu, N., & Aithal, P. S. (2023). Inbound Corporate Social Responsibility Model for Selected Indian Banks and Their Proposed Impact on Attracting and Retaining Customers–A Case Study. [IJAEML]. *International Journal of Applied Engineering and Management Letters*, 7(3), 55–74. DOI: 10.47992/IJAEML.2581.7000.0188

Ptaszynski, M., Lempa, P., Masui, F., Kimura, Y., Rzepka, R., Araki, K., Wroczynski, M., & Leliwa, G. (2019). Brute-Force Sentence Pattern Extortion from Harmful Messages for Cyberbullying Detection. *Journal of the Association for Information Systems*, 20(8), 1075–1128. DOI: 10.17705/1jais.00562

PwC. (2019). *Putting value on data.* https://www.pwc.co.uk/data-analytics/documents/putting-value -on-data.pdf

Quach, S., Thaichon, P., Martin, K. D., Weaven, S., & Palmatier, R. W. (2022). Digital technologies: Tensions in privacy and data. *Journal of the Academy of Marketing Science*, 50(6), 1299–1323. DOI: 10.1007/s11747-022-00845-y PMID: 35281634

Qu, B., Qiao, B., Zhu, Y., Liang, J., & Wang, L. (2017, December 1). Dynamic Power Dispatch Considering Electric Vehicles and Wind Power Using Decomposition Based Multi-Objective Evolutionary Algorithm. *Energies*, 10(12), 1991. DOI: 10.3390/en10121991

Quinting, J. F., & Grams, C. M. (2021). Toward a systematic evaluation of warm conveyor belts in numerical weather prediction and climate models. Predictor selection and logistic regression model. *Journal of the Atmospheric Sciences*, 78(5), 1465–1485. DOI: 10.1175/JAS-D-20-0139.1

Ragab, M., Ashary, E. B., Aljedaibi, W. H., Alzahrani, I. R., Kumar, A., Gupta, D., & Mansour, R. F. (2023). A novel metaheuristics with adaptive neuro-fuzzy inference system for decision making on autonomous unmanned aerial vehicle systems. *ISA Transactions*, 132, 16–23. DOI: 10.1016/j.isatra.2022.04.006 PMID: 35523604

Raja, R. V., Kumar, G., & Selvakumar, A. (2022). PERCEIVED RISK & PRICE IN E-SOURCES: ANALYSING PURCHASE DECISIONS IN BUYING MOBILE PHONES. *Annals of Forest Research*, 65(1), 3438–3448.

Ramasubramanian, A. K., Aiman, S. M., & Papakostas, N. (2021). On using human activity recognition sensors to improve the performance of collaborative mobile manipulators: Review and outlook. *Procedia CIRP*, 97, 211–216. DOI: 10.1016/j.procir.2020.05.227

Rauf, F., Wang, W., & Voinea, C. L. (2024). Interaction of Corporate Social Responsibility Reporting at the Crossroads of Green Innovation Performance and Firm Performance: The Moderating Role of the Enterprise Life Stage. *Sustainability (Basel)*, 16(5), 1821. DOI: 10.3390/su16051821

Reddy, Dhoma H, and N. Sirisha (2022). An Analysis of the Supervised Learning Approach for Online Fraud Detection. *Computational Intelligence and Machine Learning*, 3.

Resnick, P., & Varian, H. R. (1997). Recommender systems. *Communications of the ACM*, 40(3), 56–59. DOI: 10.1145/245108.245121

Riandy, C. N., Hapsari, I., Hariyanto, E., & Pratama, B. C. (2023). Intellectual Capital: The Role of Green Accounting on Corporate Social Responsibility. *South Asian Journal of Social Studies and Economics*, 20(4), 140–155. DOI: 10.9734/sajsse/2023/v20i4749

Riany, M., Sukmadilaga, C., & Yunita, D. (2021). Detecting Fraudulent Financial Reporting Using Artificial Neural Network. *Journal of Accounting Auditing and Business*, 4(2), 60–69. DOI: 10.24198/jaab.v4i2.34914

Ritala, P., Keränen, J., Fishburn, J., & Ruokonen, M. (2024). Selling and monetizing data in B2B markets: Four data-driven value propositions. *Technovation*, 130, 102935. DOI: 10.1016/j.technovation.2023.102935

Ritchie, Hannah, and Max Roser. Urbanization. *Our world in data*, 2018.

Ritter, T., & Pedersen, C. L. (2020). Digitization capability and the digitalization of business models in business-to-business firms: Past, present, and future. *Industrial Marketing Management*, 86, 180–190. Advance online publication. DOI: 10.1016/j.indmarman.2019.11.019

Ronald, M., Poulose, A., & Han, D. S. (2021). iSPLInception: An inception-ResNet deep learning architecture for human activity recognition. *IEEE Access : Practical Innovations, Open Solutions*, 9, 68985–69001. DOI: 10.1109/ACCESS.2021.3078184

Rout and Minakhi (2021). Analysis and Comparison of Credit Card Fraud Detection Using ML. *Artificial Intelligence and ML in Business Management*, 81-93.

Run, Z., & Wang, Y. (2018). Research on machine learning and its algorithm and development [J] [Natural Science Edition]. *Journal of Communication University of China*, 23(02), 10–18.

Ryngksai, I., & Chameikho, L. (2014). Recommender systems: types of filtering techniques. *International Journal of Engineering Researck & Technology, Gujarat*, 3(2278-0181), 251-254.

S. Alghamdi, T. Daim, S. Alzahrani (2024). Technology Assessment for Cybersecurity Organizational Readiness: Case of Airlines Sector and Electronic PaymenT. *IEEE Transactions on Engineering Management*, 71, 01-18.

Sadowski, Jathan, Yolande Strengers, and Jenny Kennedy. More work for Big Mother: Revaluing care and control in smart homes. *Environment and Planning A: Economy and Space*, 2021.

Sætra, H. S. (2021). A Framework for Evaluating and Disclosing the ESG Related Impacts of AI with the SDGs. *Sustainability (Basel)*, 13(15), 8503. DOI: 10.3390/su13158503

Safari, E., & Peykari, M. (2022). Improving the Multilayer Perceptron Neural Network using Teaching-Learning Optimization Algorithm in Detecting Credit Card Fraud. *Journal of Industrial and Systems Engineering*, 2, 159–171.

Safavian, S. R., & Landgrebe, D. (1991, May/June). A survey of decision tree classifier methodology. *IEEE Transactions on Systems, Man, and Cybernetics*, 21(3), 660–674. DOI: 10.1109/21.97458

Saggi, M. K., & Jain, S. (2018). A survey towards an integration of big data analytics to big insights for value-creation. *Information Processing & Management*, 54(5), 758–790. DOI: 10.1016/j.ipm.2018.01.010

Santosh, K. C., Antani, S., Guru, D. S., & Dey, N. (Eds.). (2019). *Medical imaging: artificial intelligence, image recognition, and machine learning techniques.* CRC Press. DOI: 10.1201/9780429029417

Sarkar, M., Ayon, E. H., Mia, M. T., Ray, R. K., Chowdhury, M. S., Ghosh, B. P., & Puja, A. R. (2023). Optimizing E-Commerce Profits: A Comprehensive Machine Learning Framework for Dynamic Pricing and Predicting Online Purchases. *Journal of Computer Science and Technology Studies*, 5(4), 186–193. DOI: 10.32996/jcsts.2023.5.4.19

Sarker, I. H. (2021). Machine Learning: Algorithms, Real-World Applications and Research Directions. *SN Computer Science*, 2(3), 160–181. DOI: 10.1007/s42979-021-00592-x PMID: 33778771

Sathishkumar, V. E., Cho, J., Subramanian, M., & Naren, O. S. (2023). Forest fire and smoke detection using deep learning-based learning without forgetting. *Fire Ecology*, 19(1), 1–17. DOI: 10.1186/s42408-022-00165-0

Sawant, N., Li, J., & Wang, J. Z. (2011). Automatic image semantic interpretation using social action and tagging data. *Multimedia Tools and Applications*, 51(1), 213–246. DOI: 10.1007/s11042-010-0650-8

Scholz, T. (2016). *Platform cooperativism. Challenging the corporate sharing economy.* New York, NY: Rosa Luxemburg Foundation, 436. https://rosalux.nyc/wp-content/uploads/2020/11/RLS-NYC_platformcoop.pdf

Sendari, S., Ilham, A. E. Z., Lestari, D. C., & Hariyadi, H. P. (2020). Opinion Analysis for Emotional Classification on Emoji Tweets using the Naïve Bayes Algorithm. Knowledge Engineering and Data Science, 3(1), 50–59. https://core.ac.uk/download/pdf/354311294.pdf

Sen, R., & Bhattacharyya, S. C. (2014). Off-grid electricity generation with renewable energy technologies in India: An application of HOMER. *Renewable Energy*, 62, 388–398. DOI: 10.1016/j.renene.2013.07.028

Serey, J., Alfaro, M., Fuertes, G., Vargas, M., Durán, C., Ternero, R., Rivera, R., & Sabattin, J. (2023). Pattern recognition and deep learning technologies, enablers of industry 4.0, and their role in engineering research. *Symmetry*, 15(2), 535. DOI: 10.3390/sym15020535

Sestino, A., & De Mauro, A. (2022). Leveraging artificial intelligence in business: Implications, applications, and methods. *Technology Analysis and Strategic Management*, 34(1), 16–29. DOI: 10.1080/09537325.2021.1883583

Sharifani, K., & Amini, M. (2023). Machine Learning and Deep Learning: A Review of Methods and Applications. *World Information Technology and Engineering Journal*, 10(07), 3897–3904.

Shaukat, M. B., Latif, K. F., Sajjad, A., & Eweje, G. (2022). Revisiting the relationship between sustainable project management and project success: The moderating role of stakeholder engagement and team building. *Sustainable Development (Bradford)*, 30(1), 58–75. DOI: 10.1002/sd.2228

Sherly, K. K., & Nedunchezhian, R. (2015). A Improved Incremental and Interactive Frequent Pattern Mining Techniques for Market Based Analysis And Fraud Detection in Distributed And Parallel Systems. *Indian Journal of Science and Technology*, ●●●, 8.

Shin, D., Vaccari, S., & Zeevi, A. (2023). Dynamic pricing with online reviews. *Management Science*, 69(2), 824–845. DOI: 10.1287/mnsc.2022.4387

Shi, Y., Larson, M., & Hanjalic, A. (2014). Collaborative filtering beyond the user-item matrix: A survey of the state of the art and future challenges. *ACM Computing Surveys*, 47(1), 1–45. DOI: 10.1145/2556270

Shmueli, G., & Koppius, O. R. (2011). Predictive Analytics in Information Systems Research." *. *Management Information Systems Quarterly*, 35(3), 553. DOI: 10.2307/23042796

Shrestha, Y. R., Krishna, V., & von Krogh, G. (2021). Augmenting organizational decision-making with deep learning algorithms: Principles, promises, and challenges. *Journal of Business Research*, 123, 588–603. DOI: 10.1016/j.jbusres.2020.09.068

Siami, M., Naderpour, M., & Lu, J. (2021, March). A Mobile Telematics Pattern Recognition Framework for Driving Behavior Extraction. *IEEE Transactions on Intelligent Transportation Systems*, 22(3), 1459–1472. DOI: 10.1109/TITS.2020.2971214

Singh, A., Anurag, J., & Biable, S. E. (2022). Financial Fraud Detection Approach based on Firefly Optimization Algorithm and Support Vector Machine. *Applied Computational Intelligence and Soft Computing*, 2022, 1–10. DOI: 10.1155/2022/1468015

Singh, A., & Chouhan, T. (2023). Artificial Intelligence in HRM: Role of Emotional–Social Intelligence and Future Work Skill. In Tyagi, P., Chilamkurti, N., Grima, S., Sood, K., & Balusamy, B. (Eds.), *The Adoption and Effect of Artificial Intelligence on Human Resources Management, Part A* (pp. 175–196). Emerald Studies in Finance, Insurance, and Risk Management. DOI: 10.1108/978-1-80382-027-920231009

Singh, P. P., Anik, F. I., Senapati, R., Sinha, A., Sakib, N., & Hossain, E. (2024). Investigating customer churn in banking: A machine learning approach and visualization app for data science and management. *Data Science and Management*, 7(1), 7–16. DOI: 10.1016/j.dsm.2023.09.002

Sinha, A., Ghosh, V., Hussain, N., Nguyen, D. K., & Das, N. (2023). Green financing of renewable energy generation: Capturing the role of exogenous moderation for ensuring sustainable development. *Energy Economics*, 126, 107021. DOI: 10.1016/j.eneco.2023.107021

Sjödin, D., Parida, V., Jovanovic, M., & Visnjic, I. (2020). Value creation and value capture alignment in business model innovation: A process view on outcome-based business models. *Journal of Product Innovation Management*, 37(2), 158–183. DOI: 10.1111/jpim.12516

Sollberger, V. D., Korthaus, A., Barg, A., & Pagenstert, G. (2023). Long-term results after anterior cruciate ligament reconstruction using patellar tendon versus hamstring tendon autograft with a minimum follow-up of 10 years—A systematic review. *Archives of Orthopaedic and Trauma Surgery*, 143(7), 4277–4289. DOI: 10.1007/s00402-022-04687-9 PMID: 36441213

Sood, K., Pathak, P., Jain, J., & Gupta, S. (2023). How does an investor prioritize ESG factors in India? An assessment based on fuzzy AHP. *Managerial Finance*, 49(1), 66–87. DOI: 10.1108/MF-04-2022-0162

Soori, M., Arezoo, B., & Dastres, R. (2023). Artificial intelligence, machine learning and deep learning in advanced robotics, A review. *Cognitive Robotics*.

Sorour, S. E., AlBarrak, K. M., Abohany, A. A., & Amr, A. (2024). Abd El-Mageed. Credit Card Fraud Detection Using the Brown Bear Optimization Algorithm. *Alexandria Engineering Journal*, 104, 171–192. DOI: 10.1016/j.aej.2024.06.040

Sovacool, B. K., & Dylan, D. (2020). Furszyfer Del Rio. Smart home technologies in Europe: A critical review of concepts, benefits, risks, and policies. *Renewable & Sustainable Energy Reviews*, 120, 109663. DOI: 10.1016/j.rser.2019.109663

Srinivasan, S. M., Shah, P., & Surendra, S. S. (2021). An Approach to Enhance Business Intelligence and Operations by Sentimental Analysis. Journal of System and Management Sciences, 11(3), 27-40. https://www.researchgate.net/publication/355859167DOI: 10.33168/JSMS.2021.0302

Srivastava, S. (2023). Harnessing the Power of AI Sentiment Analysis-10 Benefits and Use Cases for Business. https://appinventiv.com/blog/ai-sentiment-analysis-in-business

start-ups: A literature review. Energy Procedia, 58, 43-50. Blocker, C. P., Cannon, J. P., Panagopoulos, N. G., & Sager, J. K. (2012). The role of the sales force in value creation and appropriation: new directions for research. Journal of Personal Selling & Sales Management, 32(1), 15-27.

Storytelling with Data" by Cole Nussbaumer Knaflic

Stuck, M., & Grunes, A. (2016). *Big data and competition policy*. Oxford University Press. DOI: 10.1093/law:ocl/9780198788133.001.0001

Sulaiman, S. S., Nadher, I., & Hameed, S. M. (2024). Credit Card Fraud Detection Using Improved Deep Learning Models. *Computers, Materials & Continua*, 78(1), 1049–1069. DOI: 10.32604/cmc.2023.046051

Sumayh, S. (2021). A Sentiment Analysis Approach to Predict an Individual's Awareness of the Precautionary Procedures to Prevent COVID-19 Outbreaks in Saudi Arabia. *International Journal of Environmental Research and Public Health*, 18(1), 218. DOI: 10.3390/ijerph18010218 PMID: 35010479

Taha, A. A., & Malebary, S. J. (2020). An Intelligent Approach to CC Fraud Detection Using an Optimized Light Gradient Boosting Machine. *IEEE Access : Practical Innovations, Open Solutions*, 8, 25579–25587. DOI: 10.1109/ACCESS.2020.2971354

Tang, C. I., Perez-Pozuelo, I., Spathis, D., Brage, S., Wareham, N., & Mascolo, C. Selfhar: Improving human activity recognition through self-training with unlabeled data. *arXiv preprint arXiv:2102.06073*, 2021.

Tang, S., Jin, L., & Cheng, F. (2021). Fraud Detection in Online Product Review Systems via Heterogeneous Graph Transformer. *IEEE Access : Practical Innovations, Open Solutions*, 9, 64–73. DOI: 10.1109/ACCESS.2021.3084924

Tarmuji, I., Maelah, R., & Tarmuji, N. H. (2016). The impact of environmental, social and governance practices (ESG) on economic performance: Evidence from ESG score. International Journal of Trade. *Economics and Finance*, 7(3), 67–74.

Teece, D. J., & Linden, G. (2017). Business models, value capture, and the digital enterprise. *Journal of organization design*, 6, 1-14. https://doi.org/DOI: 10.1186/s41469-017-0018-x

Teece, J. D. (2010). Business Models, Business Strategy and Innovation. *Long Range Planning*, 43(2), 172–194. DOI: 10.1016/j.lrp.2009.07.003

Thukral, V., Latvala, L., Swenson, M., & Horn, J. (2023). Customer journey optimisation using large language models: Best practices and pitfalls in generative AI. *Applied Marketing Analytics*, 9(3), 281–292. DOI: 10.69554/DMIV5161

Tokgöz, E., & Carro, M. A. (2023). Applications of artificial intelligence, machine learning, and deep learning on facial plastic surgeries. In *Cosmetic and reconstructive facial plastic surgery: A review of medical and biomedical engineering and science concepts* (pp. 281–306). Springer Nature Switzerland. DOI: 10.1007/978-3-031-31168-0_9

Tong, R. (2001). *An operational system for detecting and tracking opinions in on-line discussions. In Working Notes of the SIGIR Workshop on Operational Text Classification.* https://dl.acm.org/doi/10.1007/s10579-020-09515-3

Tosun, C., Parvez, M. O., Bilim, Y., & Yu, L. (2022). Effects of green transformational leadership on green performance of employees via the mediating role of corporate social responsibility: Reflection from North Cyprus. *International Journal of Hospitality Management*, 103, 103218. DOI: 10.1016/j.ijhm.2022.103218

Trabucchi, D., & Buganza, T. (2019). Data-driven innovation: Switching the perspective on Big Data. *European Journal of Innovation Management*, 22(1), 23–40. DOI: 10.1108/EJIM-01-2018-0017

Tran, M. Q., Amer, M., Abdelaziz, A. Y., Dai, H. J., Liu, M. K., & Elsisi, M. (2023). Robust fault recognition and correction scheme for induction motors using an effective IoT with deep learning approach. *Measurement*, 207, 112398. DOI: 10.1016/j.measurement.2022.112398

Tripathi, A., Mathure, J., Deotarse, S., Rai, D., & Gadhikar, L. "Linear Regression Approach For Stock Chart Pattern Recognition," 2023 5th Biennial International Conference on Nascent Technologies in Engineering (ICNTE), Navi Mumbai, India, 2023, pp. 1-6, DOI: 10.1109/ICNTE56631.2023.10146731

Trivedi, N. K., Simaiya, S., Lilhore, U. K., & Sharma, S. K. (2020). An efficient credit card fraud detection model based on machine learning methods. *International Journal of Advanced Science and Technology*, 29, 14–24.

Trujillo, J. (2021). The Intelligence of Machines. Filosofija. Sociologija. 2021, 32(1), 84–92. DOI: 10.6001/fil-soc.v32i1.4383

Tsegay, B. (2023). *Green Economy for Climate Change Mitigation and Poverty Reduction in Sub-Saharan Africa: A Critical Analysis of Carbon Finance in Ethiopia* (Doctoral dissertation, SOAS University of London).

Turney, P. D. (2002). Thumbs up or thumbs down? Semantic orientation applied to unsupervised classification of reviews. Proceedings of the 40th Annual Meeting on Association for Computational Linguistics, ACL '02, 417–424. https://aclanthology.org/P02-1053.pdf

Udayakumar, R., Joshi, A., Boomiga, S. S., & Sugumar, R. (2023). Deep Fraud Net: A Deep Learning Approach for Cyber Security and Financial Fraud Detection and Classification. *Journal of Internet Services and Information Security*, 13, 138–157. DOI: 10.58346/JISIS.2023.I4.010

United Nations Sustainable Development Goals (SDGs) - Goal 7: Affordable and Clean Energy: https://sdgs.un.org/goals/goal7

United Nations. (1987). *Report of the World Commission on Environment and Development: Our Common Future ('Brundtland Report')*. Oxford University Press.

Urbinati, A., Bogers, M., Chiesa, V., & Frattini, F. (2019). Creating and capturing value from Big Data: A multiple-case study analysis of provider companies. *Technovation*, 84, 21–36. DOI: 10.1016/j.technovation.2018.07.004

Van Eck, N. J., & Waltman, L. (2014). Visualizing bibliometric networks. In Ding, Y., Rousseau, R., & Wolfram, D. (Eds.), *Measuring Scholarly Impact: Methods and Practice* (pp. 285–320). Springer. DOI: 10.1007/978-3-319-10377-8_13

Van Eck, N. J., Waltman, L., Dekker, R., & van den Berg, J. (2010). A comparison of two techniques for bibliometric mapping: Multidimensional scaling and VOS. *Journal of the American Society for Information Science and Technology*, 61(12), 2405–2416. DOI: 10.1002/asi.21421

Van Veldhoven, Z., & Vanthienen, J. (2022). Digital transformation as an interaction-driven perspective between business, society, and technology. *Electronic Markets*, 32(2), 629–644. Advance online publication. DOI: 10.1007/s12525-021-00464-5 PMID: 35602117

Vanini, P., & Sebastiano, R. (2023). Online Payment Fraud: From Anomaly Detection to Risk Management. *Financial Innovation*, 9(1), 9. DOI: 10.1186/s40854-023-00470-w

Vengatesan, K., Kumar, A., Yuvraj, S., Kumar, V., & Sabnis, S. (2020). Credit Card Fraud Detection Using Data Analytic Techniques. *Advances in Mathematics: Scientific Journal*, 9, 1185–1196.

Verbin, I. (2020). *Corporate Responsibility in the Digital Age: A Practitioner's Roadmap for Corporate Responsibility in the Digital Age*. Routledge. DOI: 10.4324/9781003054795

Vinuesa, R., Azizpour, H., Leite, I., Balaam, M., Dignum, V., Domisch, S., Felländer, A., Daniela Langhans, S., Tegmark, M., & Fuso Nerini, F. (2020). The role of artificial intelligence in achieving the Sustainable Development Goals. *Nature Communications*, 11(1), 1–10. DOI: 10.1038/s41467-019-14108-y PMID: 31932590

Vipin Kumar Choudhary, Divya. (2017). Credit Card Fraud detection using Frequent pattern mining using FP-Modified Tree and Apriori Growth. *International Journal of Advanced Technology and Innovative Research*, 9, 2370–2373.

Vismayaa, V., Pooja, K. R., Alekhya, A., Malavika, C. N., Nair, B. B., & Kumar, P. N. (2020). Classifier based stock trading recommender systems for Indian stocks: An empirical evaluation. *computational Economics, 55*, 901-923.

Wahid, A., Msahli, M., Bifet, A., & Memmi, G.Wahid & Abdul. (2024). NFA: A Neural Factorization Autoencoder based Online Telephony Fraud Detection. *Digital Communications and Networks*, 10(1), 158–167. DOI: 10.1016/j.dcan.2023.03.002

Walker, J., Pekmezovic, A., & Walker, G. (2019). *Sustainable Development Goals: Harnessing Business to Achieve the SDGs through Finance, Technology and Law Reform.* John Wiley & Sons. DOI: 10.1002/9781119541851

Wamba, S. F., Akter, S., Edwards, A., Chopin, G., & Gnanzou, D. (2015). How 'big data' can make big impact: Findings from a systematic review and a longitudinal case study. *International Journal of Production Economics*, 165, 234–246. DOI: 10.1016/j.ijpe.2014.12.031

Wang, Y., & Witten, I. (1997). Inducing model trees for continuous classes. Proc. 9th Eur. Conf. Mach. Learn._https://www.researchgate.net/publication/33051395_Induction_of_model_trees_for_predicting _continuous_classes

Wang, A., Chen, H., Zheng, C., Zhao, L., Liu, J., & Wang, L. Evaluation of random forest for complex human activity recognition using wearable sensors. *In2020 International Conference on Networking and Network Applications (NaNA),* pp. 310-315. IEEE, 2020. DOI: 10.1109/NaNA51271.2020.00060

Wang, C., & Changqi, W. (2020). LAW: Learning Automatic Windows for Online Payment Fraud Detection. *IEEE Transactions on Dependable and Secure Computing*, 18, 22–35. DOI: 10.1109/TDSC.2020.3037784

Wang, D., & Zhu, H. (2022). Representing Fine-Grained Co-Occurrences for Behavior-Based Fraud Detection in Online Payment Services. *IEEE Transactions on Dependable and Secure Computing*, 19(1), 301–315. DOI: 10.1109/TDSC.2020.2991872

Wang, J., Xu, C., Zhang, J., & Zhong, R. (2022). Big data analytics for intelligent manufacturing systems: A review. *Journal of Manufacturing Systems*, 62, 738–752. Advance online publication. DOI: 10.1016/j.jmsy.2021.03.005

Wang, S., Ding, W., Li, J., Yuan, Y., Ouyang, L., & Wang, F. Y. (2019). Decentralized autonomous organizations: Concept, model, and applications. *IEEE Transactions on Computational Social Systems*, 6(5), 870–878. DOI: 10.1109/TCSS.2019.2938190

Wang, Y., Li, W., Liu, Z., & Li, L. (2023, February 24). An Energy Management Strategy for Hybrid Energy Storage System Based on Reinforcement Learning. *World Electric Vehicle Journal*, 14(3), 57. DOI: 10.3390/wevj14030057

Wang, Z., Zhao, H., & Wang, Y. (2015). Social networks in marketing research 2001-2014: A co-word analysis. *Scientometrics*, 105(1), 65–82. DOI: 10.1007/s11192-015-1672-9

Warghade, S., Desai, S., & Patil, V. (2020). Credit card fraud detection from imbalanced dataset using machine learning algorithm. *International Journal of Computer Trends and Technology*, 68(3), 22–28. DOI: 10.14445/22312803/IJCTT-V68I3P105

Watson, D. (2005). Business Models. Petersfield: Harriman House Ltd.

Watson, I., & Gardingen, D. (1999) A Distributed Case-Based Reasoning Application for Engineering Sales Support; *Proc. 16th Int. Joint Conf. on Artificial Intelligence (IJCAI-99)*; 1999; Vol. 1, page 600-605.

Wei, P., Li, Y., Zhang, Z., Tao, H., Li, Z., & Liu, D. (2019) An optimization method for intrusion detection classification model based on deep belief network; IEEE. 2019; vol.7 issue 87; page 593–605.

Weiss, S. M., & Kapouleas, I. (1989, August). An empirical comparison of pattern recognition, neural nets, and machine learning classification methods. *IJCAI (United States)*, 89, 781–787.

Wiebe, J. (2000). *Learning subjective adjectives from corpora. In Proceedings of the Seventeenth National Conference on Artificial Intelligence and Twelfth Conference on Innovative Applications of Artificial Intelligence.* AAAI Press. https://cdn.aaai.org/AAAI/2000/AAAI00-113.pdf

Wiecek, Elyssa, Fernanda S. Tonin, Andrea Torres-Robles, Shalom I. Benrimoj, Fernando Fernandez-Llimos, and Victoria Garcia-Cardenas. Temporal effectiveness of interventions to improve medication adherence: *A network meta-analysis,* 2019.

Winter, S., Maslowska, E., & Vos, A. L. (2021). The effects of trait-based personalization in social media advertising. *Computers in Human Behavior*, 114, 106525. DOI: 10.1016/j.chb.2020.106525

Wixom, B. H., & Ross, J. W. (2017). How to monetize your data. *MIT Sloan Management Review*, 58(3), 9–13. DOI: 10.7551/mitpress/11633.003.0009

World Energy Outlook 2020 by the IEA: https://www.iea.org/reports/world-energy-outlook-2020

Woroch, R., & Strobel, G. (2022). Show me the Money: How to monetize data in data-driven business models? *Wirtschaftsinformatik, Proceedings*, 13. https://aisel.aisnet.org/wi2022/digital_business_models/digital_business_models/13

Wu, J., Xu, C., Han, X., Zhou, D., Zhang, M., Li, H., & Tan, K. C. (2022, November 1). Progressive Tandem Learning for Pattern Recognition With Deep Spiking Neural Networks. *IEEE Transactions on Pattern Analysis and Machine Intelligence*, 44(11), 7824–7840. DOI: 10.1109/TPAMI.2021.3114196 PMID: 34546918

Xie, J., Nozawa, W., Yagi, M., Fujii, H., & Managi, S. (2019). Do environmental, social, and governance activities improve corporate financial performance? *Business Strategy and the Environment*, 28(2), 286–300. DOI: 10.1002/bse.2224

Xu, D., & Yingjie, T. (2015). A comprehensive survey of clustering algorithms. *Annals of Data Science*, 2(2), 165–193. DOI: 10.1007/s40745-015-0040-1

Xu, N., Lovreglio, R., Kuligowski, E. D., Cova, T. J., Nilsson, D., & Zhao, X. (2023). Predicting and Assessing Wildfire Evacuation Decision-Making Using Machine Learning: Findings from the 2019 Kincade Fire. *Fire Technology*, 59(2), 793–825. DOI: 10.1007/s10694-023-01363-1

Xu, T. (2024). Fraud Detection in Credit Risk Assessment Using Supervised Learning Algorithms. *Computer Life*, 12(2), 30–36. DOI: 10.54097/qw9j1892

Yadav, S. K., Tiwari, K., Pandey, H. M., & Akbar, S. A. (2021). A review of multimodal human activity recognition with special emphasis on classification, applications, challenges and future directions. *Knowledge-Based Systems*, 223, 106970. DOI: 10.1016/j.knosys.2021.106970

Yan, B. N., Lee, T. S., & Lee, T. P. (2015). Analysis of research papers on E-commerce (2000-2013): Based on a text mining approach. *Scientometrics*, 105(1), 403–417. DOI: 10.1007/s11192-015-1675-6

Yan, C., Li, M., & Liu, W. (2020). Prediction of bank telephone marketing results based on improved whale algorithms optimizing S_Kohonen network. *Applied Soft Computing*, 92, 106259. DOI: 10.1016/j.asoc.2020.106259

Yang, J., Xiu, P., Sun, L., Ying, L., & Muthu, B. (2022). Social media data analytics for business decision making system to competitive analysis. *Information Processing & Management*, 59(1), 102751. DOI: 10.1016/j.ipm.2021.102751

Yang, X. L., Chu, X., & Zhou, M.-T. (2020). Fog-Enabled Smart Home and User Behavior Recognition. In *Fog-Enabled Intelligent IoT Systems*. Springer. DOI: 10.1007/978-3-030-23185-9_7

Yang, Y., Shi, S., & Wu, J. (2022). Digital financial inclusion to corporation value: The mediating effect of ambidextrous innovation. *Sustainability (Basel)*, 14(24), 16621. DOI: 10.3390/su142416621

Yilmaz, H. R., Ozcalik, H. R., Aksu, M., & Karapınar, C. (2015). Ozcalikb, M. Aksua, and C. Karapınara, "Dynamic simulation of a PV-diesel-battery hybrid plant for off grid electricity supply,". *Energy Procedia*, 75, 381–387. DOI: 10.1016/j.egypro.2015.07.396

Yimer, G. A.Gebreysus Abegaz Yimer. (2024). Sustainable Finance in Africa: A Comparative Overview. *Mizan Law Review*, 18(1), 123–160. DOI: 10.4314/mlr.v18i1.5

Yoon, B., Lee, J. H., & Byun, R. (2018). Does ESG performance enhance firm value? Evidence from Korea. *Sustainability (Basel)*, 10(10), 3635. DOI: 10.3390/su10103635

Zaid, A. A., & Sleimi, M. (2023). Effect of total quality management on business sustainability: The mediating role of green supply chain management practices. *Journal of Environmental Planning and Management*, 66(3), 524–548. DOI: 10.1080/09640568.2021.1997730

Zaidan, A. A., & Zaidan, B. B. (2020). A review on an intelligent process for smart home applications based on IoT: Coherent taxonomy, motivation, open challenges, and recommendations. *Artificial Intelligence Review*, 53(1), 141–165. DOI: 10.1007/s10462-018-9648-9

Zaki, A. M., Khodadadi, N., Lim, W. H., & Towfek, S. K. (2024). Predictive analytics and machine learning in direct marketing for anticipating bank term deposit subscriptions. *American Journal of Business and Operations Research*, 11(1), 79–88. DOI: 10.54216/AJBOR.110110

Zaki, M. J. (2000). Scalable algorithms for association mining. *IEEE Transactions on Knowledge and Data Engineering*, 12(3), 372–390. DOI: 10.1109/69.846291

Zamani, E. D., Griva, A., Spanaki, K., O'Raghallaigh, P., & Sammon, D. (2024). Making sense of business analytics in project selection and prioritisation: Insights from the start-up trenches. *Information Technology & People*, 37(2), 895–918. DOI: 10.1108/ITP-09-2020-0633

Zhang, C. (2018). Research on the development of machine learning and data mining [C]. 2010-2011 Development Report of Control Science and Engineering Discipline. *Chinese Society of Automation*, 223, 82–89.

Zhang, D., Bhandari, B., & Black, D. (2020). Credit Card Fraud Detection Using Weighted Support Vector Machine. *Applied Mathematics*, 11(12), 1275–1291. DOI: 10.4236/am.2020.1112087

Zhang, J., Yu, Q., Zheng, F., Long, C., Lu, Z., & Duan, Z. (2016). Comparing keywords plus of WOS and author keywords: A case study of patient adherence research. *Journal of the Association for Information Science and Technology*, 67(4), 967–972. DOI: 10.1002/asi.23437

Zhang, T., Yang, H., Li, Z., & Meng, Y. (2018). Life cycle assessment of grid-connected solar photovoltaic-fuel cell hybrid systems. *Energy*, 150, 393–403.

Zhang, W., Deng, Y., & Qu, J. (2020). Techno-economic optimization of solar photovoltaic-fuel cell hybrid power systems for carbon reduction and energy efficiency improvement. *Energy Conversion and Management*, 213, 112831. DOI: 10.1016/j.enconman.2020.112831

Zhang, Z., Chen, L., Liu, Q., & Wang, P. (2020). A Fraud Detection Method for Low-Frequency Transaction. *IEEE Access : Practical Innovations, Open Solutions*, 8, 210–220. DOI: 10.1109/ACCESS.2020.2970614

Zhao, J., & Fariñas, B. G. (2023). Artificial Intelligence and Sustainable Decisions. *European Business Organization Law Review*, 24(1), 1–39. DOI: 10.1007/s40804-022-00262-2

Zhou, H., Sun, G., Fu, S., Wang, L., Hu, J., & Gao, Y. (2021). Internet Financial Fraud Detection Based on a Distributed Big Data Approach With Node2ve. *IEEE Access : Practical Innovations, Open Solutions*, 9, 78–86.

Zillner, S. (2021a). Business models and ecosystem for big data. In Curry, E., Metzger, A., Zillner, S., Pazzaglia, J. C., & García Robles, A. (Eds.), *The Elements of Big Data Value: Foundations of the Research and Innovation Ecosystem* (pp. 269–288). Springer International Publishing., DOI: 10.1007/978-3-030-68176-0_11

Zoltners, A. A., Sinha, P., Sahay, D., Shastri, A., & Lorimer, S. E. (2021). Practical insights for sales force digitalization success. *Journal of Personal Selling & Sales Management*, 41(2), 87–102. DOI: 10.1080/08853134.2021.1908144

About the Contributors

Ambika N. is an MCA, MPhil, and Ph.D. in computer science. She completed her Ph.D. from Bharathiar university in the year 2015. She has 18 years of teaching experience and works for St.Francis College, Bangalore. She has guided BCA, MCA, and M.Tech students in their projects. Her expertise includes wireless sensor networks, the Internet of things, and cybersecurity. She gives guest lectures on her expertise. She reviews books, conferences (national/international), encyclopedias, and journals. She is advisory committee member of some conferences. She has many publications in National & international conferences, international books, national and international journals, and encyclopedias. She has some patent publications (National) and has received 5 copyrights in the computer science division.

Vishal Jain is presently working as Professor (CSE) at the Department of Computer Science and Engineering, School of Engineering and Technology, Sharda University, Greater Noida, India. Before that, he worked for several years as an Associate Professor at Bharati Vidyapeeth's Institute of Computer Applications and Management (BVICAM), New Delhi. He has more than 18 years of experience in the academics. He has earned degrees: Ph.D (CSE), M.Tech (CSE), MBA (HR), MCA, MCP, and CCNA. He has more than 1900 research citations with Google Scholar (h-index score 21 and i-10 index 49) and has authored more than 150 research papers in professional journals and conferences. He has authored and edited more than 60 books (most of them are indexed at the Scopus) with various reputed publishers, including Elsevier, Springer, IET, Apple Academic Press, CRC, Taylor and Francis Group, Scrivener, Wiley, Emerald, NOVA Science, River Publishers, IGI-Global and Bentham Science. He has more than 160 Scopus publications. He is the book series editor of 10 book series with the reputed international publishers. His research areas include machine learning, information retrieval, semantic web, ontology engineering, data mining, ad hoc networks, sensor networks and network security. He received a Young Active Member Award for the year 2012–13 from the Computer Society of India, and Best Faculty Award for the year 2017 and Best Researcher Award for the year 2019 from BVICAM, New Delhi.

Cristian González García is an Associate Professor in the Department of Computer Science, University of Oviedo (Spain). He is a Technical Engineer in Computer Systems, MSc in Web Engineering, and PhD in Computers Science. He has been a visiting PhD candidate at the University of Manchester. Besides, he has been at the University of South Florida and in the INESC-ID in Lisbon as visiting professor. He has also been working on different national and regional projects, as well as in projects with private companies. He has published 19 journal articles, 13 conference articles, 3 book chapters, and has been the editor of 2 books. Furthermore, he has been on the advisory board of 1 journal, 2 books, and 1 international conference. He has managed 4 teaching innovation projects and participated in other 4. He has managed more than 40 Degree Final Projects, and 1 Erasmus agreement. His research interests include the Internet of Things, Web Engineering, Mobile Devices, Artificial Intelligence, Big Data, Modelling Software with DSL and MDE, and Teaching Innovation.

Dac-Nhuong Le (Lê Đ c Như ng) has an MSc and PhD in computer science from Vietnam National University, Vietnam in 2009 and 2015, respectively. He is an Associate Professor of Computer Science and Dean of the Faculty of Information Technology at Haiphong University, Vietnam. He has 20+ years of academic teaching experience in computer science. He has many publications in reputed international conferences, journals, and book chapters (Indexed by SCIE, SSCI, ESCI, Scopus). His research areas include intelligence computing, multi-objective optimization, network security, cloud computing, virtual reality/augmented reality, and IoT. Recently, he has served on the technical program committee, conducted technical reviews, and acted as a track chair for international conferences under the Springer-ASIC/LNAI/CISC Series. He also serves on the editorial board of international journals and has edited/authored 30+ computer science books published by Springer, Wiley, CRC Press, IET, IGI Global, and Bentham Publishers.

***

Saverio Barabuffi is a postdoctoral researcher in Management at Institute of Management and L'EMbeDS Department at Sant'Anna School of Advanced Studies (Pisa, Italy). He obtained a PhD in Economics at Università degli Studi di Roma 3. He has held visiting positions at University of Sussex. Before starting the PhD program, he studied economics at University of Pisa (master degree). His research fields include econometrics, big data, and artificial intelligence, with a special focus on China.

Vikramaditya Dave is an Associate Professor at the Department of Electrical Engineering, College of Technology and Engineering. He did his BE (Hons.) and ME (Hons.) from MBM Engineering College. He did his PhD from IIT Roorkee. He has experience of 16 years teaching and four years of field experience. He has published near about 50 research papers in different national and international journals and conference proceedings. He is an author of six books. He holds membership of different professional bodies like Institution of Engineers, American Vacuum Society, etc. He has recently awarded by the Government of Rajasthan for his excellent services in technical education. His area of research includes renewable energy sources, artificial intelligence, solar photovoltaics, nanotechnology, data science, etc.

Giulio Ferrigno is a Senior Assistant Professor at Sant'Anna School of Advanced Studies of Pisa. He has held visiting positions at the University of Cambridge, Tilburg University, and the University of Umea. His main research themes include strategic alliances, big data, and Industry 4.0. His works have been published in Small Business Economics, Technological Forecasting and Social Change, International Journal of Management Reviews, R&D Management, Technology Analysis & Strategic Management, Review of Managerial Science, European Journal of Innovation Management, International Journal of Entrepreneurial Behavior & Research, Journal of Small Business and Enterprise development. He is an Associate Editor of Technology Analysis & Strategic Management.

Vishal Jain is presently working as an Associate Professor at Department of Computer Science and Engineering, School of Engineering and Technology, Sharda University, Greater Noida, U. P. India. Before that, he has worked for several years as an Associate Professor at Bharati Vidyapeeth's Institute of Computer Applications and Management (BVICAM), New Delhi. He has more than 14 years of experience in the academics. He obtained Ph.D (CSE), M.Tech (CSE), MBA (HR), MCA, MCP and CCNA. He has authored more than 90 research papers in reputed conferences and journals, including Web of Science and Scopus. He has authored and edited more than 30 books with various reputed publishers, including Elsevier, Springer, Apple Academic Press, CRC, Taylor and Francis Group, Scrivener, Wiley, Emerald, NOVA Science and IGI-Global. His research areas include information retrieval, semantic web, ontology engineering, data mining, ad hoc networks, and sensor networks. He received a Young Active Member Award for the year 2012–13 from the Computer Society of India, Best Faculty Award for the year 2017 and Best Researcher Award for the year 2019 from BVICAM, New Delhi.

C Manjunath is currently working as assistant professor in APS College of arts and science and faculty in Prof.N. Ananthachar Memorial Center.He has also worked as data scientist, project team lead and trainer in IT Company.I envision himself nurturing his technical competencies in various domains such as data analytics, machine learning, statistics, big-data engineering.I have also trained many students for different subjects like- Problem solving Techinque using C, Computer Network, Data analytics,OOPs using java, Machine learning,Mobile application development.He also presented a paper in national conference. At APS College of Arts and Science, Manjunath is dedicated to fostering a dynamic learning environment, blending theoretical concepts with real-world applications. They are committed to nurturing the next generation of tech-savvy professionals, instilling in them a passion for innovation and problem-solving. With a keen eye for emerging trends in technology and a dedication to scholarly research, Manjunath aims to empower students with the knowledge and skills needed to thrive in an increasingly data-driven world.

Enrico Marcazzan is post-doc research fellow at Sant'Anna School of Advanced Studies of Pisa. He gained a PhD in Management at the University of Padova, Italy. Before starting the PhD program, he studied in the field of economics at University of Verona (bachelor degree) and in management for social economy at University of Bologna (master degree), Italy. His research fields include resilience and crisis management, with a special focus on the pre-crisis stage and the small and mediumsized enterprises, and topics at the intersection between Civil Economy and Management. His works have been published in Journal of Small Business and Enterprise development.

Dhrupad Mathur has been an Associate Professor in IT Management Area with S P Jain School of Global Management, Dubai, UAE since 2008. Within this tenure, he has served in various administrative positions, including Director of Industry Projects from 2008 to 2016 and Assistant Dean of the Executive MBA program in 2016–2017. He is currently the Deputy Director – Faculty Management. With approximately 18 years of professional experience in ICT education, policy, and consulting, Dr. Mathur is a Science graduate with an MBA and a master's degree in Public Administration. His doctoral degree from JNVU India (PhD, 2004) is in the area of e-Business Transformations.

Sabyasachi Pramanik is a professional IEEE member. He obtained a PhD in Computer Science and Engineering from Sri Satya Sai University of Technology and Medical Sciences, Bhopal, India. Presently, he is an Associate Professor, Department of Computer Science and Engineering, Haldia Institute of Technology, India. He has many publications in various reputed international conferences, journals, and book chapters (Indexed by SCIE, Scopus, ESCI, etc). He is doing research in the fields of Artificial Intelligence, Data Privacy, Cybersecurity, Network Security, and Machine Learning. He also serves on the editorial boards of several international journals. He is a reviewer of journal articles from IEEE, Springer, Elsevier, Inderscience, IET and IGI Global. He has reviewed many conference papers, has been a keynote speaker, session chair, and technical program committee member at many international conferences. He has authored a book on Wireless Sensor Network. He has edited 8 books from IGI Global, CRC Press, Springer and Wiley Publications.

Giulia Rita Sala is an MSc student at Esade Business School (Barcelona, Spain). Previously, she obtained a bachelor's degree at the Catholic University of the Sacred Heart (Milan, Italy). Her academic journey is further enhanced by exchanges at Georgetown University (Washington, D.C., USA) and Universidad Carlos III de Madrid (Spain). Her expertise dives into strategy, M&A, and public policy, enriched by hands-on experience in international consulting environments.

Satya Shree is a respected academic and educator, currently serving as the Head of the Department of Computer Science at A.P.S. College of Arts & Science in Bangalore, India. With over 24 years of teaching experience and an additional 3 years in the technical field, she has established herself as a leading figure in computer science education. Education and Academic Background: Satyashree holds a Master of Science in Information Technology from Kuvempu University, Shimogga, and a Bachelor of Engineering from Gulbarga University. Her early education was completed at Govt PU Science College in Lingusgur and Amareshwar Girls High School in Raichur District. Professional Achievements and Awards: Throughout her career, Satyashree has received several prestigious awards, recognizing her contributions to education. Notably, she was awarded the "Bharat Vidya Rattan Award" in 2018 and the "Dr. A.P.J. Abdul Kalam Educational Excellence Award" in 2019. Additionally, she received the "Best Lecturer – Computer Science" award at the Karnataka Educational Awards in 2019 and the "Best Professor for Computer Science" award in 2021 at the Karnataka Excellence Awards by VCCM Trust. Furthermore, she has consistently been honored with the "Best Teacher Award" from her institution. Publications and Conferences: Satyashree has presented research papers at various national conferences, covering topics such as cloud computing, software testing, mobile computing, and biomedical signal processing. Her work has been presented at renowned institutions like the Presidency College and Bangalore City College, among others. Workshops, Seminars, and Other Contributions: Beyond her academic work, Satyashree has actively participated in and organized workshops and seminars on topics like cloud computing and image processing. She has served as a judge for technical speeches and has been an organizing secretary for national conferences. Additionally, she has taken on roles such as Project Guide for undergraduate and postgraduate programs at various universities, External Examiner for practical examinations, and Board of Examiner for National College Basavana Gudi. Work Experience: In addition to her current role at A.P.S. College of Arts & Science, Satyashree has served as an Assistant Professor and Head of the Department of Computer Science at A.P.S. College of Commerce. She has also held positions as a Course Coordinator at Alpha Computers and Joseph's Computer Institute in Raichur and Bellary, respectively. Professional Objective: Satyashree's professional objective is to continue expanding her knowledge and contributing creative solutions to advance the field of computer science and education. Her commitment to excellence and her numerous accolades underscore her dedication to these goals.

Pooja Soni is a Research Scholar at the Department of Electrical Engineering, College of Technology and Engineering. She completed her BTech in 2014 from Oriental Institute of Science & Technology,

Bhopal, RGPV University (M.P.) and M.Tech (Hons.) from Mandsaur University in 2018. Currently, she is pursuing her PhD at Maharana Pratap University of Agriculture and Technology. Pooja has a teaching experience of four years. Her research is focused on the field of artificial intelligence, where she has worked on optimisation of hybrid renewable energy sources, tech-economically and energy management. Her work has the potential to revolutionize the energy sector, and she has received accolades for her contributions to this field. Pooja's dedication and hard work have made her an inspiration to many in the academic community, and her future looks bright as she continues to pursue her passion for research in electrical engineering.

Siji A. Thomas, is an Industry professional, currently accomplishing her career with practical & solid understanding of Industrial Management Systems. Her great vocation and passion in technical publications has led to develop herself as a professional Independent Researcher and has now specialized in Robotics, Machine Learning, Medical Image Analysis and Internet of Things, where she has made her major contributions. Her milestones in research career proven her expertise in peer reviewing technical articles and book chapters. She is the recipient of National Special Jury Award for designing and developing a Smart Biomedical Device, which showcases her unwavering commitment to innovations and she has been honoured with several academic excellence awards. She has proven her strong professional dedication in various roles including Assistant Professor, US Online Tutor, Jr. Calibration and Maintenance Engineer, Faculty Development Program Coordinator, Skill Development in Charge and Placement Coordinator. She is proficient in Circuit Design & Raspberry Pi and her functional competencies include MATLAB and Lab VIEW, thereby leveraging her focus in driving technological innovations. Ms. Thomas earned her Master's degree in Communication Engineering from APJ Abdul Kalam Technological University, India, and her Bachelor's degree in Electronics and Instrumentation Engineering from Mahatma Gandhi University, India.

Sini Kurien Thomas, based in Chicago, USA, is an accomplished Independent Researcher specializing in Project Management Systems, Machine Learning, Battery Management Systems, Power Electronics, and Communication Engineering. With a diverse professional background spanning over five years, she has held pivotal roles including Software Engineer, Jr. Biomedical Instrumentation Lab Engineer, Electronics Circuits Lab-in-charge and Lecturer. Ms. Thomas earned her Master's degree in Communication Engineering from APJ Abdul Kalam Technological University, India, and her Bachelor's degree in Electronics and Communication Engineering from Mahatma Gandhi University, India. Her research interests primarily focus on the intersection of Battery Management Systems, Power Electronics, and Advanced Communication Systems, where she has made significant contributions, showcasing her commitment to technological advancement and addressing contemporary challenges. Proficient in Circuit Design tools such as LT Spice, Altium Designer, and MATLAB, Ms. Thomas also demonstrates excellence in PCB Design, encompassing footprint and 3D model design, as well as electronic design using Arduino Uno R3, thereby highlighting her pivotal role in driving innovation in technology.

Minh Tung Tran gains (his 1st Doctoral Degree) a Doctor of Business Administration (DBA Degree) in Marketing Management from University of Technology and Management (UITM), Poland and a Master of Science in Business Information Systems from Heilbronn University, German. He is currently Director of FSB Danang - FPT School of Business and Technology (FSB) - FPT University, Vietnam cum Business Lecturer of MBA Program at FSB. He has over 18 years of work experience and over 12 years in teaching and sharing at both over 40 Enterprises and over 22 Higher Educational Institutions in Vietnam. His research interests are in Social Media, PR, Marketing, Marketing in Higher Education, Innovation Teaching Methodology, Data Driven Marketing, Information Systems, Standards Based Curriculum, Experience Learning and Gamification in Education. Recently, he has completed and obtained (his 2nd and 3rd Doctoral Degree) EdD - Professional Doctorate in Educational Administration & Leadership and Doctor of Philosophy (Ph.D.) in Media and Communication from European International University, EIU-Paris, France, in 2023 which can assist him in his personal development plan (PDP) and professional career in current role in leading and administrating.

Index

A

Accuracy 2, 3, 4, 5, 8, 9, 10, 11, 12, 13, 14, 15, 19, 20, 21, 22, 23, 24, 25, 42, 46, 60, 72, 73, 90, 132, 144, 180, 183, 184, 193, 194, 197, 198, 199, 200, 210, 236, 241, 242

AI 27, 28, 32, 33, 35, 36, 43, 52, 55, 56, 57, 58, 59, 60, 61, 62, 63, 64, 65, 66, 67, 68, 69, 70, 71, 72, 73, 84, 106, 117, 119, 124, 125, 131, 132, 133, 137, 143, 144, 145, 147, 148, 176, 177, 182, 187, 188, 208, 223, 226, 227, 228, 229, 230, 231, 233, 234, 235, 237, 238, 239, 240, 241, 242, 244, 245, 246, 247, 248

Artificial Intelligence 29, 32, 35, 43, 53, 55, 56, 57, 58, 59, 60, 61, 62, 63, 64, 65, 66, 67, 68, 69, 70, 71, 72, 73, 83, 84, 85, 116, 117, 119, 124, 125, 126, 127, 131, 132, 137, 142, 143, 156, 176, 187, 188, 189, 190, 203, 229, 231, 237, 238, 239, 240, 241, 242, 244, 245, 247

B

Big Data 21, 27, 28, 30, 68, 70, 85, 96, 97, 106, 126, 128, 179, 201, 205, 206, 207, 209, 210, 211, 212, 216, 217, 218, 219, 220, 221, 222, 223, 224, 225, 226, 240

Business Analysis 75, 76, 77, 82, 87, 93, 94, 95

Business Analyst 76

Business Data Analytics 87, 92, 93, 94, 95, 96, 97, 98, 99, 100, 101, 106

Business Model 82, 83, 87, 88, 89, 90, 91, 98, 100, 105, 107, 108, 119, 120, 126, 127, 128, 205, 206, 211, 212, 218, 224, 225, 226

Business Models 65, 77, 82, 84, 87, 88, 90, 102, 105, 106, 107, 116, 118, 119, 127, 128, 162, 205, 209, 211, 217, 218, 220, 221, 222, 223, 225, 226

Business Model Transformation 108

C

Change Management 69, 80

Classification 3, 5, 14, 21, 22, 28, 29, 32, 34, 37, 38, 39, 40, 41, 42, 43, 44, 50, 51, 52, 53, 96, 110, 112, 178, 179, 180, 181, 182, 184, 187, 190, 193, 194, 196, 197, 198, 199, 200, 203

Companies 43, 55, 57, 58, 59, 63, 65, 66, 71, 72, 84, 87, 96, 106, 113, 116, 117, 118, 119, 120, 126, 161, 162, 163, 164, 165, 168, 169, 176, 206, 207, 208, 209, 210, 211, 213, 214, 215, 216, 217, 218, 219, 220, 225, 226, 229, 230, 232, 237, 239, 246

Corporate Social Responsibility 56, 57, 60, 68, 159, 160, 161, 162, 163, 164, 165, 166, 167, 168, 169, 170, 171, 172, 173, 174

Customer Segmentation 109, 120, 184

D

Data 1, 2, 3, 4, 8, 9, 10, 11, 12, 13, 14, 15, 17, 18, 19, 20, 21, 22, 24, 25, 26, 27, 28, 29, 30, 31, 32, 33, 34, 36, 37, 39, 40, 41, 42, 43, 44, 45, 46, 47, 48, 51, 52, 56, 57, 58, 59, 60, 63, 64, 65, 66, 67, 68, 69, 70, 71, 72, 73, 76, 79, 81, 84, 85, 87, 90, 91, 92, 93, 94, 95, 96, 97, 98, 99, 100, 101, 102, 103, 105, 106, 108, 109, 110, 111, 112, 113, 114, 115, 116, 117, 118, 119, 120, 122, 123, 124, 126, 127, 128, 130, 131, 132, 133, 134, 135, 143, 144, 145, 148, 154, 160, 172, 175, 176, 178, 179, 180, 181, 182, 183, 184, 185, 186, 187, 188, 189, 191, 193, 195, 196, 197, 198, 199, 200, 201, 202, 203, 205, 206, 207, 208, 209, 210, 211, 212, 213, 214, 215, 216, 217, 218, 219, 220, 221, 222, 223, 224, 225, 226, 228, 229, 230, 231, 233, 234, 235, 236, 237, 238, 239, 240, 241, 242, 243, 244, 245, 246, 247, 248

Data-Driven Innovation Canvas 226

Data-Driven Innovation Framework 205, 226

Data-Driven Insights 105, 209, 224

Data Monetization 205, 206, 207, 208, 209, 210, 211, 213, 216, 217, 218, 220, 221, 223, 224, 225, 226

Data Monetization Issues 226

Decision Making 13, 19, 64, 68, 85, 108, 114, 116, 127, 133, 145, 188, 189

Digital Transformation 56, 60, 68, 69, 75, 76, 77, 78, 80, 81, 82, 83, 84, 85, 108, 205, 206

Dynamic Pricing 111, 129, 133, 136, 185

E

E-Commerce 1, 2, 4, 27, 97, 102, 103, 112, 118, 120, 129, 132, 136, 231, 246

F

Filtering 46, 195, 196, 231, 232, 236, 239, 242, 243, 247, 248

Fintech 60, 69, 172, 227, 237, 248

Framework 2, 12, 13, 26, 27, 40, 44, 45, 57, 58, 60, 61, 64, 65, 66, 70, 72, 75, 76, 82, 84, 87, 98, 99,

Printed in the United States
by Baker & Taylor Publisher Services